Economics, Culture and Development

This book examines the treatment of culture and development in the discipline of economics, thereby filling a conspicuous gap in current literature. Economics has come a long way to join the 'cultural turn' that has swept the humanities and social sciences in the last half century. This volume identifies some of the issues that major philosophies of economics must address to better grasp the cultural complexity of contemporary economies.

Economics, Culture and Development is an extensive survey of the place of culture and development in four theoretical economic perspectives—Neoclassical, Marxian, Institutionalist, and Feminist. Organized into nine chapters with three appendices and a compendium of over 50 interpretations of culture by economists, this book covers vast grounds from classical political economy to contemporary economic thought. The literatures reviewed include original and new institutionalism, cultural economics, postmodern Marxism, economic feminism, and the current culture and development discourse on subjects such as economic growth in East Asia, businesswomen entrepreneurs in West Africa, and comparative development in different parts of Europe.

Zein-Elabdin carries the project further by borrowing some of the insights from postcolonial theory to call for a more profound rethinking of the place of culture and of currently devalued cultures in economic theory. This book is of great interest to those who study Economics, Economic Development, International Relations, Feminist Economics, and Cultural Studies.

Eiman O. Zein-Elabdin is Professor of Economics at Franklin & Marshall College, in Lancaster, Pennsylvania, USA.

Routledge Frontiers of Political Economy

For a complete list of titles in this series, please visit www.routledge.com/books/series/SE0345

Economics, Culture and Development

Eiman O. Zein-Elabdin

Routledge
Taylor & Francis Group

LONDON AND NEW YORK

First published 2016
by Routledge
2 Park Square, Milton Park, Abingdon, Oxon OX14 4RN

by Routledge
711 Third Avenue, New York, NY 10017

First issued in paperback 2017

Routledge is an imprint of the Taylor & Francis Group, an informa business

British Library Cataloguing in Publication Data
A catalogue record for this book is available from the British Library

Library of Congress Cataloging in Publication Data
Zein-Elabdin, Eiman O., 1957–
Economics, culture and development/Eiman Zein-Elabdin.
pages cm
Includes index.
1. Economics—History—21st century. 2. Economic development. 3. Feminist
economics. 4. Culture—Economic aspects. I. Title.
HB75.Z45 2015
330—dc23
2015013422

ISBN 13: 978-1-138-49874-7 (pbk)
ISBN 13: 978-0-415-55192-2 (hbk)

Typeset in Times New Roman
by Book Now Ltd, London

Contents

Preface

This book represents the result of a long-standing interest in, and often puzzlement at, discussions of the concept-phenomenon of 'culture,' especially as it relates to the vexing question of 'development,' in major economic orthodoxies—Neoclassical, Marxian, and Institutionalist. These three, in their different varieties, intensities, and deep divisions, constitute a powerful narrative in contemporary social science discourse. The primary aim of this book is to contribute a source for discussions of culture, and culture and development that helps reveal some deep connections between bodies of thought that appear disparate, largely autonomous, or even conflicting, without which, a profound contemplation of 'culture' or 'development' would not be worthwhile.

In this volume, I do not offer a theory of culture or development, or a comprehensive analysis of economic treatments of these two concerns. Deeper reflection will take another text. My only intention in this volume is to present a tentative account of the presence and absence of culture in Economics, and the ways in which it inhabits the discipline, and to offer some preliminary observations and questions regarding culture and economic development. This volume is intended as a necessary beginning toward a greater understanding of an extremely complex terrain.

Even with this more limited task, the scope of the book is daunting; some might say absurd. For my purpose, this is unavoidable. In Economics, there are books about Development, and books about Economics 'proper,' with the two subjects carefully bracketed away from one another. Similarly, there are books about Women or Gender, and other books about Economics 'proper.' Here, I cut across all these areas, working against the entrenched division of labor, in order to trace the commonalities that make the specialist discussion of these subjects so inadequate. As in past work, I call this approach *panoramic*.

On previous occasions, I argued against strong disciplinarity—as manifested in strict specialization in the production of academic knowledge—and suggested a 'counter-disciplinary' strategy. I remain convinced this is necessary. Nonetheless, in this book, I devote most attention to the discipline of economics, with an eye toward its rootedness in the philosophical (cultural) grounds of European modernity in order to show the implications of the division of labor within Economics itself. A singular focus on this discipline sheds a unique light on and puts certain vital issues in sharp relief. This, I believe, is a necessary step for a counter-disciplinary approach.

Acknowledgments

I am deeply grateful to three anonymous reviewers, who thoughtfully commented on the book proposal, and greatly thankful for the patience of Routledge editors, as the publication of this book has been delayed several times due to a medley of circumstances. It is also my fortune to have insightful, learned, and kind friends and colleagues who have contributed immensely to my thinking generally and gave much needed critical feedback on different parts of this manuscript: Michael Billig, Antonio Callari, S. Charusheela, Colin Danby, Sean Flaherty, Gillian Hewitson, Janet Knoedler, Kirsten Madden, Neil Perry, and Mwangi wa Gĩthĩnji. All omissions, errors, and gaps in understanding are mine. At Franklin & Marshall, I especially would like to acknowledge the great help I received from Tami Lantz, the Economics Department Coordinator, the Library staff, and student workers as well as those who have attended my classes over the years.

My greatest gratitude goes to my dearest companion Tony Maynard for sharing his wealth of intellect, wit, and knowledge, for reading and commenting on my work, and for lovingly supporting all my adventures—wise and unwise. As always, I remain permanently indebted to my beloved parents, sisters, and brothers everywhere.

Eiman Osman Zein-Elabdin
Lancaster, Pennsylvania
March 2015

1 Economics, culture, and development

Culture – Like 'democracy,' this is a term which needs to be, not only defined, but illustrated, almost every time we use it.

(T.S. Eliot 1949 [1940]: 197)

Introduction

'Culture' is currently enjoying tremendous vogue in Economics across different schools of thought. Many books examine the intersection of culture and economics, particularly in 'the arts,' as demonstrated by the publication of the *Handbook of the Economics of Art and Culture* (Ginsburgh and Throsby 2006). Many others are preoccupied with the relationship between culture and 'development.' A symposium on "cultural economics" (*Journal of Economic Perspectives*, Spring 2006) and an entry on "Culture and Economics" in the *New Palgrave Dictionary* (Fernández 2008) mark the arrival of culture in the general discourse of Economics. Today it is fashionable for economists to invoke Anthropology and to cite Gramsci, Weber, and Durkheim.[1]

The factors behind the heightened profile of culture in Economics are many, but all form part of the general current that produced 'the cultural turn' in the humanities and social sciences in the second half of the twentieth century. In broad terms, this includes the rise of multiculturalism in European-majority countries, increasing globalization, the disintegration of socialist regimes in Eastern Europe and Central Asia, and corresponding debates over the role of the state. Alan Peacock and Ilde Rizzo (1994) suggest that, at least in part, economic concern with 'the culture industry'—arts and other works of creativity—was motivated by the need to maintain state support for the arts in the face of budgetary cuts in the USA and Europe since the 1980s. These various influences have joined with theoretical and methodological exigencies within the discipline of Economics to produce the current interest in culture.[2]

In this book, I trace the presence and absence of culture in economic literature, particularly in relation to the process of development. What I am trying to identify is culture in its meaning as the broad, but contested, shared everyday sensibilities and practices—including economic ones—of a society or a group, which sanction and censor its participants in multiple ways that may not always be fully coherent. Though a shaper of action and knowledge, culture—the concept-phenomenon—is shaped by and changes in accord with individual idiosyncrasies, social gaps, and fissures, and encounters with 'other' cultural horizons; I do not see it as a single force that predates and explains all (see Appendix II for a sample of economists' ideas of culture). As the coming chapters show, many different things are associated with culture—some include practice, others confine it to the generation of meaning. Often, the word merely signifies a difference of some sort. In many discussions of economic development, culture is synonymous with backwardness, and sometimes may appear to be a metaphor for 'race.' My interpretation is more encompassing than most (i.e., it includes both the capacity to generate meaning and produce practices that differentiate some groups from others), but does not imply completeness, permanence, or full coherence.

My aim in this project is to outline the extent to which economists have noted the ways in which culture shapes economic action and knowledge, and how they have approached the cultures of those countries discursively marked as 'under' or 'less' developed. Homi Bhabha (1994) suggests that culture is (more consciously) invoked—as it were—only at the point of confrontation with difference, the moment of encounter with an Other. With this in mind, I look at how economists have experienced, negotiated, and/or endured such encounters. My intent is not to aggregate all economic thought into a 'Western worldview' devoid of heterogeneity and muted subjectivities.[3] However, the major philosophies of Economics share a specific apprehension of being, knowledge, and history that takes European modernity as intrinsically superior, all knowing, and uniquely historical (Zein-Elabdin 2004).[4] The twentieth-century discourse of international development has served to universalize this apprehension.

Taking a broad look at the treatment of culture in Economics reveals that the majority of economic thought is rooted in a *dualistic ontology*, that is, an apprehension of 'reality' in a binary framework that leaves no conceptual space for in-betweenness and alterity. This is most foundationally manifested in the theoretical separation of 'culture' from 'economy' as two fundamentally different realms, which ultimately rests on the archaic dualism of ideal/material. In this conception, culture has to do with the mental and symbolic, while economy signifies tangible subsistence, provisioning, resource management, and accumulation. This pervasive dichotomy—and dualistic modes of thought in general—have been the subject of extensive debates, and the basis for much of the philosophical revolt against modernism.[5] In Economics, this revolt appears most commonly among heterodox thinkers, who have long rejected dichotomies such as object/subject, positive/normative, and fact/value (Dow 1990; Nelson 1992; Waller 1994; Jackson 1999). Feminists, in addition, have challenged the cultural dualisms of public/private, market/household, and market/non-market (Waller and Jennings 1990; Jennings 1993, 1999). Indeed, many colleagues have questioned the separation of culture from economy (Ruttan 1988; Nelson 1993; Kabeer 1991, 1994; Harcourt 1995; Jackson 1996, 2009; Fine 2002). These interventions have been sporadic and, for the most part, have targeted methodological concerns, often detached from substantive content.

In this book, I take all these contributions on board, and go further to argue that, *in general, dualistic ontology forms a common thread in the treatment of culture among major economic philosophies, albeit differently and to various degrees. This pattern is amplified in the field of development with the addition of more dichotomies, and an overwhelming tendency to reductively theorize culture as either an obstacle to or a driving force behind economic growth.* Dualism is often defined by the assumption that "phenomena are separable into two mutually exclusive categories or principles" (Jennings 1999: 142). Here, I do not necessarily associate it with antagonistic pairs, but with all binary, all-or-nothing, analytical perspectives that in effect preclude adequate understanding of *economic hybridity*—economies and socialities that do not comply with and exceed the dualisms. To be sure, some binary distinctions are necessary for analytical purposes. The problem arises when these exist at a deep axiomatic level that obscures their epistemological consequences. To the extent that dualistic philosophy has been critiqued in social science and humanities discourses since the late twentieth century, this book adds little.[6] My primary concern in this volume is to reveal its pervasiveness and depth in Economics, and its manifestations in approaches to culture.

The aim of this volume is to draw a map of culture in Economics that will hopefully facilitate more systematic, in-depth study of individual contributions. There are many questions and problematics in and about the idea-phenomenon of culture to wrestle with. In this book I only highlight the problem of dualism in economic treatments of it. This first chapter begins with a schematic review of culture's discursive journey from Anthropology to the field of Cultural Studies, with an eye toward their relationship to Economics. This is a mere sketch that has to gloss over the richness of both fields.[7] The next section outlines the landscape of culture in the three most established economic traditions—Neoclassical, Marxian, and Veblenian Institutionalist—and the more recent field of Feminist Economics since culture is at the heart of its case against the economics profession. In the fourth section I turn to the treatment of culture in the field of development. The chapter ends with an overview of the book and a note on method.

Although general social science and humanities discourse is vital to any survey of culture, for practicality my survey is limited to economics publications and only the most pertinent literature in other fields. Because of these limitations at least three relevant subjects are not pursued except tangentially: 'race,' globalization, and ecological sustainability.[8] Similarly, I have not included any discussion of development policy and record (growth trends, structural adjustment, inequality, and so on) since my immediate interest is directed at theoretical explorations of culture in development thought rather than the development process itself.

From Anthropology to Cultural Studies

The word 'culture' has meant many things, from cultivation of a plant or organism, growth of human intellect and spiritual faculties (distance from 'nature'), art and other products and occupations of creativity (the 'culture industry'), to honoring with worship (cult), and inhabiting a foreign place (colonizing). All these meanings may be encompassed within the familiar phrase "a whole way of life." It is this versatility, which prompted Raymond Williams to offer his often-cited remark that culture "is one of the two or three most complicated words in the English language" (1983 [1976]: 87). T.S. Eliot (1949 [1940]) had earlier suggested that the word must be defined every time it is uttered, and, long before him, J.G. Herder warned, "nothing is more indeterminate than this word" (Williams 1983 [1976]: 89). This elusiveness of meaning has long shielded culture from the modeling, quantifying impulse that dominates Economics—until recently. In the following paragraphs I take a quick look at the fields of Anthropology and Cultural Studies as they have influenced thinking about culture in Economics.

Anthropology has undergone a seismic transformation from ideas of primitivism, to questioning its own complicity in Europe's imperial projects.[9] Still, E. B. Tylor's founding concept of culture—the "complex whole which includes knowledge, belief, art, morals, law, custom, and any other capabilities and habits acquired by man as a member of society" (1883 [1871]: 1)—remains a relevant point of departure for current discussions. The scope and crux of meaning he provided have been less of an issue than the theoretical framework within which the concept of culture was to be placed, and the weight assigned to different aspects of it (material, symbolic, regulative, and so on). Tylor's evolutionist concept was problematized and revised by scores of anthropologists and sociologists—Weber, Boas, Malinowski, Parsons, among many others—with the evolutionary interpretation giving way to a more relativist orientation (see Stocking 1968; Geertz 1973; Friedman 1994; Wilk 1996).[10]

By the mid-twentieth century the project of international development had given rise to debates about the content and political implications of anthropological research. As Arturo Escobar (1995) has shown, the debate over Karl Polanyi's (1957) classification of economies into formal and substantive revealed that Economic Anthropology was either "inside" this project, with formalists advocating for development, or "outside," with substantivists highlighting its threat to native cultures. The formalist/substantivist debate was never resolved, but many took Clifford Geertz's (1963: 144) conclusion that "a modern economic system may be compatible with a wider range of non-economic cultural patterns and social structures than has often been thought," and moved on. Since then, Economic Anthropology has grown into new ethnographic horizons and theoretical perspectives. The most pertinent of these is the "neo-Weberian" direction, which "self-consciously" sees all cultural forms as "ideal types" (Billig 2000: 783) and realizes that the substantive nature of an economy is not unique to 'primitive' or 'non-market' societies; even "the most urban, complex, capitalist setting" is embedded in culture (ibid.: 772).

Throughout this long journey, the relationship between Anthropology and Economics has fluctuated, but most anthropologists took economic theory, Neoclassical or Marxian, at face value. In the opposite direction, Anthropology had a long established presence in the Institutionalist School (Veblen 1898), and in scattered discussions of regional economies, especially in Africa (see Zein-Elabdin 1998).[11] In general, the most profound and lasting influence of anthropological discourse has been in development economics, where the modernity/tradition dualism served as an explicit basis for the appropriately named "dualistic models" of W.A. Lewis (1954), W.W. Rostow (1971 [1960]), among others, and continues to ground the theoretical divide between 'developed' and 'under(less)developed' countries.

The interest in culture has brought Anthropology into Economics in an unprecedented manner, as seen in several high profile publications (Geertz 1978; North 1990). In development economics, this trend began with Vernon Ruttan's article "Cultural Endowments and Economic Development: What Can We Learn from Anthropology?" (1988), in which he argues that this discipline's focus on culture and "insistence on descriptive realism" (ibid.: 257) provide a rich body of material for economic interpretation. He favors the interpretive approach (Geertz 1973) over cultural materialism (Harris 1979) because, for him, the latter is too full of determinism to shed light on how culture impacts economic change. Ruttan's article seems to have opened the door for more conversation between the two disciplines. Today there is a higher level of freedom among economists to draw on anthropological insights and even adopt the ethnographic method (e.g., Chamlee-Wright 1997; Wyss 1999).

The almost exclusive identification of culture with Anthropology was broken with the emergence of Cultural Studies in 1950s Britain. In *Culture and Society* (1961), generally considered the field's fountain of inspiration, Williams argued that the evolution of the idea of culture from several diverse meanings to become mostly associated with the notion of a "whole way of life" had signaled a response to broad economic, political, and aesthetic changes in British life since the eighteenth century. He examined this twofold process of change—in the meaning of culture and in social institutions and practices—as reflected in the work of English Romantics and such major intellectual figures as J.S. Mill and T.S. Eliot. Williams concluded that the time was ripe for a "new general theory of culture" (1961: 12), one that illuminated relationships among disparate elements of society (see also Mulhern 2009).

Cultural Studies, often identified with postcolonial critique (e.g., Said 1979), has since expanded in scope, at times appearing to absorb all contemporary work on culture outside conventional Anthropology. Unlike Anthropology, however, Cultural Studies has no well-defined method or parameters, except that from the beginning it emphasized subjectivity and political consciousness (Hall 1980; During 1993). A recent development has been the emergence of "cultural policy studies," which converges with the field of Cultural Economics in its interest in the media and arts. Economists who draw upon Cultural Studies are quite diverse, including those preoccupied with the culture industry from a Neoclassical point of view (Ginsburgh and Throsby 2006), those committed to methodological individualism in an Austrian sense (Lavoie and Chamlee-Wright 2000), postmodern Marxists who value subjectivity (Amariglio *et al.* 1988), and those concerned with issues of postcoloniality and cultural hegemony (Charusheela and Zein-Elabdin 2003).

Beside Anthropology and Cultural Studies, explorations of culture in
Economics have also been informed by work in several other fields, including
Sociology (Granovetter 1985; Schoenberger 1997; Hofstede 2001; Harrison
and Berger 2006), Geography (Bell 1976; Harvey 1989), and Political Science
(Granato *et al.* 1996), among other examples.[12] Any survey, such as the present
one, must pay attention to this diversity of influences and inspiration, which
produces different meanings, methods, and perspectives on the ideas of culture
adopted in Economics.[13] This is especially important since in much of the literature, explicit definitions of culture are seldom given, and, even when they are,
there is typically very little substantive elaboration on them to illuminate just what
authors have in mind.

Culture in Economics

Theoretical explorations of culture (as a concept-phenomenon) and economic
action and knowledge have been undertaken at various, overlapping levels,
including: (1) the role of culture in the operation—and, therefore, explanation—
of economic phenomena; (2) its role in the construction of economic knowledge;
(3) the cultural influence of the discipline of economics on society at large; and
(4) the internal culture of the economics profession.[14] In this book, I concentrate
on the first level, with an eye toward the second; that is, on economic analyses
of the ways in which culture enters into the formation of economic phenomena,
and on economists' dispositions toward different cultures, which mostly surface
in explanations of comparative growth and development. In other words, I am
concerned with culture as both the subject of and operator on economic inquiry.

Though an extensive, tangled body of thought, Economics is amenable to
grouping into three major paradigmatic spheres: Neoclassical, Marxian, and
Veblenian (original) Institutionalist.[15] Determining boundaries can be a matter
of debate since each contains several strands and debates, the three schools of
thought share philosophical roots and methods, and thought often crosses conventional borders. Nevertheless, the basic three-spheres taxonomy is justified in that
each coheres in a distinct theory of value and vision of society. For Neoclassical
economics ('the mainstream'), the economic problem consists of a boundless
series of individual-induced and centered optimizing choices; Marxian theory
prioritizes class relations and processes and material dynamics of power; while
Veblenian Institutionalism rejects universalist conceptions in favor of a culturally embedded, evolutionary view of economic processes.[16] All three traditions
have drawn some criticism from Feminist economists for different expressions of
androcentrism. The details and finer points of each scholarly sphere will unfold in
the coming chapters. Below, I outline the landscape of culture in each.

For most of the twentieth century, the concept of culture was largely absent
from Neoclassical scholarship. Apart from a few contributions on 'the arts'
(Baumol and Bowen 1966), the word culture surfaced mainly within special
forums such as the 1970 American Economic Association symposium on "the
supply of black American economists." In one panel, Vernon Dixon suggested

that, since economic behavior is learned, the supply of 'black' economists partly depends on the willingness of the profession to admit the possibility of a 'black economics,' that is, "a body of theory that is consistent with or based on the cultural uniqueness of Afro-Americans" (1970: 424), as a complement, rather than a rival, to Neoclassical theory. In opposition, Kenneth Boulding (1970) argued economic thought could not be "culture-bound" because it studies the ancient and pervasive phenomenon of exchange. Yet, he acknowledged a disciplinary bias against group-oriented modes of social organization, which he attributed to the historical and geographical origins of Economics and modern economic growth. Although this observation renders all economic thought culture-bound, Boulding insisted this was only true in the field of development. This type of conversation took place only once in a long while.[17]

Today, Neoclassical discussions of culture span three overlapping research programs. The first is the Preferences Approach (PA), reflecting the influence of Gary Becker's work (1976, 1996). In this approach, culture is conceptualized as "differences in beliefs and preferences that vary systematically across groups of individuals separated by space (either geographic or social) or time" (Fernández 2008: 2). Here, culture enters as an argument in individuals' decision functions. The second program is Cultural Economics (CE), which examines the culture industry, relying on standard tools of microeconomic theory (Blaug 2001; Ginsburgh and Throsby 2006), with some authors exploring the more philosophical question of cultural vis-à-vis economic value (McCain 2006).[18] The third research program is contained in the New Institutional Economics (NIE), in which culture is represented as a constraint on individual optimizing agency (North 1990; Drobak and Nye 1997). Many studies across the three research programs aim to model and quantify the economic 'effect' of culture as approximated by variables such as language, religion, or 'trust' (Lazear 1999; Guiso *et al* 2006). Of the three, NIE deals most directly with the question of development (e.g., Tabellini 2005). Yet, despite the impressive volume of research, authors begin and end with the rational choice model intact, and culture suspended within the dualism of preferences/constraints.

In the Marxian school, the place of culture has been subjected to a great deal of scrutiny in the past few decades. Williams (1961: 260) concluded that the 'formula' of base and superstructure, even if taken as mere analogy, has had the effect of diminishing the import of culture in Marxian theory. In the texts of influential twentieth-century interpreters of Marx's economic philosophy (Sweezy 1970 [1942]; Baran 1973 [1957]; Mandel 1975), all cultures outside of modern Europe were analytically treated as an inert mass in the historical path of capitalism. But, eventually, the general current that brought cultural problematics to the forefront of academic discourse, building on the contributions of Gramsci (1985) and Althusser (1970), also led to considerable revisions of Marxian political economy. These are most sharply articulated in the postmodernist project of Rethinking Marxism (Resnick and Wolff 1985, 1987; Amariglio *et al.* 1996; Callari and Ruccio 1996). The hallmark of this intervention is the reinterpretation of class as a process, rather than a group, and accordingly theorizing culture as "processes of the production and circulation of meaning" (Amariglio *et al.* 1988: 487). As a result, more attention has been directed to previously neglected themes such as subjectivity and consumption (Pietrykowski 1994). All the same, class remains the "guiding thread" of this approach, which has in effect produced a new dichotomy of class/nonclass. It is worthwhile, therefore, to examine the extent to which postmodernist revisions have transcended the dualistic framework of classical Marxism.

In contrast to Marxian and Neoclassical philosophies, commitment to the idea of culture forms the philosophical backbone of the original Institutionalist tradition; it is a "core concept" (Mayhew 1987; Jennings and Waller 1995).[19] The understanding of culture here goes farthest in the direction of Anthropology. This is in full display in W.C. Neale's description of it as "a primary and therefore undefined rubric for all the rules and folkviews to which its members subscribe" (1990: 335). At the same time, Institutionalists emphasize the idea of instrumental valuation, a tool-oriented, problem-solving tendency thought to be constituent of the human make-up. These two ideas are expressed in the distinction between ceremonial (institutional) and instrumental (technological) aspects of culture—aka the "Veblenian dichotomy" (Waller 1982, 1999). The discourse of international development has exposed the dualism of this conception. Following the work of Clarence Ayres (1962 [1944]), culture lost some of its theoretical significance to instrumental valuation, and a universalist vision driven by emphasis on technological advance took over. The result has been what I call an Institutionalist estrangement from culture (Zein-Elabdin 2009).

The upshot of all this is that each of the three schools of economic thought conceives culture within a very distinct, but dualistic theoretical framework. This could be summed up in four *paradigmatic dualisms*:

Neoclassicism	Preferences/Constraints
Modernist Marxism	Base structure/Superstructure
Postmodern Marxism	Class/Nonclass
Veblenian Institutionalism	Instrumental/Ceremonial

These binary distinctions frame each paradigm within two poles that define and structure a certain way of apprehending social 'reality.' To be sure, the scene in each tradition is more complex than it is depicted here. Nevertheless, two tentative observations may be offered. First, these dualisms should not be seen as mere analytical distinctions. Analytical strategies generally tend to follow ontological convictions, and they engender epistemological consequences. In this case, the consequence is a limited, binary conception of culture, and an inability to grasp economic hybridity; that is, relations and processes found at the intersection and deep fusion of a multiplicity of cultural currents—a salient feature of contemporary societies (Zein-Elabdin 2009). I return to this point in Chapter 9. The need for analytical schema is understandable. The problem arises when these become embedded on a deep, axiomatic level in the discourse that obscures their theoretical and political ramifications.

Second, the ontological roots of these paradigmatic dualisms seem to lie in a more general existential dichotomy of desire/limits: that is, conflict between desire, freedom, and possibilities, on one hand; and limits, boundaries, and finality, on the other. The sharpest illustration of this is the preferences/constraints dichotomy of Neoclassicism, but it can also be located in the Institutionalist and Marxian traditions though the parallel is not so quickly demonstrable. Thus, throughout economic literature, culture has been conceptualized as a force that either liberates or limits some individual agency or social process, a catalyst for or an obstacle to economic growth and development. In this book, I will not delve deeply into the existential dimension, and instead concentrate on the more immediate manifestations of dualism in economic analyses of culture.

In Feminist Economics the issues are somewhat different. Feminists have contributed tremendously to raising the profile of culture in Economics by pointing out that the dominant models, which offer a narrow interpretation of economy, are grounded in gendered cultural values (Ferber and Nelson 1993; Barker and Kuiper 2003). Most importantly for the issue at hand, Feminists reject the Cartesian dualism of mind/body and all that flows from it (Nelson 1992; Jennings 1993; Barker 1998). Accordingly, several have criticized the theoretical separation between culture and economy (Kabeer 1994; Harcourt 1995). Unfortunately, the emphasis on gender as the central category of analysis has invited a partial treatment of culture reflected most clearly in the approach to development and the question of 'third world women' (Zein-Elabdin 2003; Charusheela and Zein-Elabdin 2003). So far, most of the Feminist Economic critique of dualisms has been confined to those with a transparent gender association (e.g., market/household), overlooking such powerful cultural dualisms as developed/under(less)developed that do have considerable policy implications for many women worldwide (see Chapter 8). It is plausible then to wonder whether the partial treatment of culture has hindered Feminist Economics from having an even bigger impact on the status of culture in the discipline.

In sum, there is now a substantial effort by economists to investigate and account for the role of cultural values, habits, and expression in economic action and knowledge. There are *shallow* as well as *deep* and sophisticated contributions. In this book, I merely broach the outlines of this landscape as an entry point to more critical systematic study.

Culture and development

If "culture is one of the two or three most complicated words in the English language" (Williams 1983 [1976]: 87), development must be one of the other two.[20] The general meaning attached to it in the last century is captured in Benjamin Higgins' description: "wide and deep improvements in welfare for the masses of the population" (1977: 100), with welfare being measured against the level of income historically reached in the North Atlantic region, and accompanying social cultural constituents—large-scale mechanization, a market system, urban agglomeration, and a rapid pace of life. Although this is an increasingly contested prototype, it remains the global *desideratum* of most economic discourse and policy. Development economists were tasked with determining how this prototype could be replicated on a global scale, across different societies and cultures. In other words, development economics is inherently mounted on the theoretical erasure of cultures that might be or seem incompatible with this 'way of life.'[21] In this section, I sketch the evolution of this field's treatment of culture, focusing primarily on Neoclassical discourse, and briefly highlight its rootedness in dualistic ontology.

Since its emergence in post-WWII geopolitics, development economics has presented three stances on culture, which may be described as: *hospitality*, *retreat*, and *return*. The first stance, dominating in the field's formative years, embodied a conviction that cultural beliefs and habits had significant implications for economic growth (Lewis 1955). Emblematic of this position is B.F. Hoselitz' (1952) role in launching the Research Center in Economic Development and Cultural Change, and the journal bearing the same name at the University of Chicago. Overall, different camps of economists quarreled over policy details—e.g., balanced growth or big push—but never doubted the desirability of 'modernization.' Marxian and Institutionalist authors, though critical of Neoclassical models (e.g., Frank 1966; Myrdal 1968), were equally committed to the agenda of 'third world development.' And, although many thought cultural beliefs in low-income countries represented an obstacle to economic growth, most showed great openness to the concept of culture itself as an explanatory variable. The dualism of culture/economy was crystalized in the common reference to 'non-economic barriers'—attitudes, beliefs, and customs—to development.

By the 1970s, development economics had become more disputed and diverse. Ester Boserup's book *Woman's Role in Economic Development* (1989 [1970]), which inspired the now defunct field of women in development (WID), revealed that, across less industrialized world regions, economic growth was accompanied by a widening gap between men and women in income, formal education, land ownership, and use of new technologies. Yet, the cultural dimensions of this finding did not register in the discipline's mind. As a result, the WID revolution did little to elevate the status of culture in Economics broadly. Instead, by the 1980s, "counter-revolution" authors (most vocally, Lal 1985) were asserting the universal validity of optimizing behavior, thereby foreclosing any potential for consideration of cultural difference. A period of skepticism and critical reflection (Hirschman 1981; Sen 1983; Lewis 1984) ended with the announcement of a New Development Economics (NDE) (Stiglitz 1986).[22] Proponents of this view maintain that superior modeling could capture the 'mechanics of development' without having to account for cultural variability (Lucas 1988; Krugman 1995). This position represents a *retreat* from culture.

The third stance, surfacing almost simultaneously with NDE, was driven by the search for explanations of rapid economic growth in East Asia, and greater awareness of the global diversity of cultures (Berger and Hsiao 1988; Ruttan 1988). One strand of this culture and development (CAD) literature is policy-driven, generally concerned with "mainstreaming culture in development work" (Wolfensohn *et al.* 2000: 11), and mostly contained in World Bank, UN, and other multidisciplinary discussions such as the human development and capabilities perspective (e.g., Fukuda-Par and Kumar 2003; Sen 1998, 2004). So far, the most concrete outcome of this effort has been the construction of more than 70 "cultural indicators of development" (McKinley 1998; Fukuda-Parr 2000).[23] A more analytical strand of CAD writings seeks to model and, if possible, quantitatively measure the impact of "cultural determinants" of economic growth, be they 'individualism' or 'Confucian dynamism' (e.g., Gray 1996). This embrace of culture as a subject of development analyses marks a clear 'return' to the hospitality stance, except that most authors no longer see cultural traditions as a mammoth obstacle to economic growth. In the case of East Asia, they are considered a source of superior economic performance (Park 1997; Hayami 1998).

Despite this shift in perspective, the theoretical break between culture and economy, rooted in the ideal/material dualism, remains the basis of most analyses. Today, instead of cultural barriers (Hoselitz 1952), we find discussions of cultural determinants (Dieckmann 1996) of economic development that operate on economic factors from an external perch. Dualism is also transparent in that in all debates over culture and development, the underlying question has been which factor precedes the other: do cultural beliefs 'determine' or 'affect' the rate of economic growth? Or does growth necessarily alter cultural norms? In the literature this debate has been framed as an opposition between a materialist Marxian interpretation (economy → culture) and an idealist one (culture → economy), typically associated with Max Weber.[24] Weber's thesis (1958 [1930]) on the role of Protestant teachings in the rise of capitalism has gained immense popularity in CAD discourse, serving as an essential source for those seeking to establish causality from cultural variables to economic outcomes (e.g., Chamlee-Wright 1997; Temin 1997; Tabellini 2005). Whether Weber was an idealist or not is beside the point, both current interpretations are predicated on a perceived ontological rift between 'the material/economic' and 'the ideal/cultural' as two fundamentally different realms.[25]

Beyond this dualistic conception of the relationship between culture and development, the development discourse relies on a series of other well-worn dichotomies borrowed directly or indirectly from mid-twentieth-century Anthropology. The modernity/tradition divide was used early on to theorize both economic sectors and entire societies (Lewis 1954; Rostow 1971 [1960]); it persists today in CAD scholarship (Marini 2004). The perceived distinction between 'individualist' and 'collectivist' attitudes and societies, found in early development economics, has also returned (Greif 1994; Gray 1996). Underlying these dichotomies is the broader opposition between the 'universal' and the 'particular' (or 'relative').[26] When all these are grouped together, they form a set of *development dualisms*:

Modern	Traditional
Individualist	Collective(Collectivist)
Developed	Under(less)developed
Universal	Particular

There is a great deal to unpack here, but I will only stress three points.

First, unlike the paradigmatic dualisms discussed in the previous section, which are self-contained within each school of economic thought, the development dualisms are mutually reinforcing. Traditional societies are thought to hold collectivist sensibilities, and this constitutes a major cause of their underdevelopment (see Greif, 1994, for this type of argument). Second, the development dualisms are hierarchical, i.e., one of the two terms in each pair is accorded a superior status (*à la* male/female in the context of gender). The left side of each pair represents the realm of economy, with its putative universal logic, which also signifies modernity and development. The right-hand—subaltern—side constitutes the repository of the 'non-economic,' the traditional and, hence, underdeveloped. The primary goal of public policy is to effect movement from the inferior to the superior side. Third, the main similarity between the two sets of dualisms (paradigmatic and development) lies in that both are ultimately rooted in the existential problem of desire/limits. In each dualism, the left-hand term stands for the desired (e.g., preferences, modernity), while the right-hand side represents the limiting—or at least complicating—factors (constraints, tradition). Thus, economic development represents the universally desired goal, whereas cultural habits and beliefs form the particulars that must be altered (when they are obstacles) or harnessed (where they are catalysts) for countries to develop. The development dualisms constitute a thoroughly binary conception that precludes adequate understanding of *hybrid spaces* in either 'developed' or 'underdeveloped' economies, and all the in-between, that never gets articulated as a positivity but only a negative of 'the economic' (Zein-Elabdin 2011).

To summarize, from its very beginning, development economics has struggled with the concept-phenomenon of culture, sometimes more explicitly than other times, but always near the surface, generally governed by the dualistic ontology of economic discourse at large. The hermeneutic tale I have offered here requires more reflection. Yet, it is worth telling. The observations presented in the coming chapters report the results of my reading of the complex terrain of culture and development in Economics, perhaps not cautiously enough, and certainly without claims of rigor or finality.

Overview of the book

The aim of this book is a broad—though not comprehensive—survey. It should be read as a tentative account of the presence as well as absence of culture in Economics, with some preliminary observations regarding culture and development. Chapter 2 examines the place of culture in Classical Political Economy and the beginnings of Neoclassicism. Chapters 3–6 review approaches to cultural problematics in Neoclassical, Institutionalist, and Marxian economics, from classical to contemporary formulations. Chapter 7 is devoted to Neoclassical development economics. Writings on development in Marxian and Institutionalist literatures are examined in their respective chapters. Feminist economic thought, with particular emphasis on women/gender and development, is discussed in Chapter 8. The final chapter, Chapter 9, concludes with a few synthesizing thoughts on the current landscape of culture and development in Economics, and propositions for future research.

In terms of method, the only 'tool' I rely on in this book is close reading of texts, using the *panoramic* approach I introduced elsewhere, which targets the common premises of different philosophies of economics to get at their unifying metaphysics (Zein-Elabdin 2001, 2004).[27] This is a *meta*-analytic survey. In consequence, I did not delve deeply into specific theories, technical details, or ancillary debates. Although many themes and issues in the texts reviewed could be engaged in more critical depth, I have kept the discussion at the level of a general overview. In the main chapters I identify literal references for illustration more often than present a holistic analysis of certain ideas and arguments. The panoramic strategy runs the risk of being too general for meaningful assessment of particular theories and contributions. Nonetheless, it is sufficient for an outline of a landscape.

Two method-related concerns require clarification. The first is determining which specific cultural aspects to include—religion, gender relations, aesthetics, language, or politics, among many others. In Economics it is common to discuss particular themes without drawing connections between the different parts, or referring to a whole. This is not necessarily objectionable. Analytically, it avoids projecting culture as an all-encompassing entity. At the same time, however, this partial approach may signal a want of understanding of culture at the level of holistic relationship to economic phenomena. In this book I do not single out one cultural aspect except development. The second method-related concern has to do with the terms: culture, society, institutions, and tradition, which are exceedingly common throughout the literature, often used interchangeably and ambiguously. In general, I take society to be the group, and culture as that which the group shares and experiences unevenly, which includes institutions and traditions.

In the end, I do not believe I have revealed any unknowns, but merely drawn connections that may not have been seen clearly or emphasized so far. I offer this broad survey, realizing that 'culture' cannot admit a universal definition of itself, and bearing in mind that the idea of culture may be forever mired in archaic humanism, and might have to be discarded, together with the twentieth-century trope of 'development.' What to do about Economics is a question for later thought.

Notes

1 General books on culture include Stanfield (1995), Casson (1997), Throsby (2001), Fine (2002), Cullenberg and Pattanaik (2004), Jones (2006), and Jackson (2009). For the arts, see Towse and Abdul Khakee (1992), Peacock and Rizzo (1994), Klamer (1996), Hutter and Rizzo (1997), Towse (1997), Hutter and Throsby (2008), and de Jong (2009). For examples of work on culture and development, see Dieckmann (1996), Chamlee-Wright (1997), Lian and Oneal (1997), Wolfensohn *et al.* (2000), Marini (2004), and Tabellini (2005). These citations represent merely a sample of work in which the words culture or cultural appear in the title. Appendix I gives a more extended chronological record of such work. Of course, some texts contain significant discussions of culture without including the word in the title, e.g., Scitovsky's *The Joyless Economy* (1976). As the coming chapters will show, frequently, the word culture itself is never mentioned, but surrogates of it such as custom, norms, values, or tradition are used instead.

2 To these factors one must add the philosophical challenges to Modernity by feminist, postmodernist, and postcolonial critics. For examples of these critiques in Economics, see McCloskey (1985), Ferber and Nelson (1993, 2003), Callari and Ruccio (1996), and Zein-Elabdin and Charusheela (2004).

3 Like all big categories, the term Western is problematic of course (see Zein-Elabdin 2001). In this book, my references to 'the West' are made strictly as they appear in the literature. See Young (1995) for a critical history of cultural difference in Europe. On the exclusion of women, the working classes, certain ethnic groups, and colonial subjects from classical and contemporary economic thought, see Albelda (1997), Dimand (2004), and Zein-Elabdin and Charusheela (2004).

4 For T.S. Eliot, the "cultural unity of Europe" (1949 [1940]: 195) was inherent "in the ancient civilisations of Greece, Rome and Israel" and "two thousand years of Christianity" (ibid.: 201). Whether one agrees with Eliot's view or not, the notion of a distinct European or Western culture is maintained even in the writings of such contemporary critics as Foucault (1970). See Hay (1968 [1957]) for a historical account of the "idea of Europe," and Said (1979) on the political ramifications of this idea. For the emergent literature on culture and development in Europe, see the European Task Force on Culture and Development (1997) and Kovács (2006).

5 A full discussion of this subject is beyond the scope of this book. For more on dualisms in Economics, see Mini (1974), Dow (1990), Jackson (1999), and Jennings (1999). Also see Althusser and Balibar (1970) on other binaries such as essence/phenomena or necessity/contingency, Althusser calls them "fallacies."

6 Many authors in other disciplines have challenged the ideal/material dualism, with Sahlins describing it as an "antique" dualism (1976: ix) that has been transcended by the very concept of culture. Current research in neuroscience and bio-anthropology further throws such dichotomies into question (e.g., see Boyd and Richerson 2000).

7 For example, I have not made any reference to Romanticism, or distinguished between British and German currents of culture discourses. For more on culture, including key contributors not mentioned in this book, see Williams (1983 [1976]), During (1993), and Young (1995).

8 For culture and race, see Stocking (1968), Darity and Williams (1985), Reimers (1985), Jennings and Champlin (1994), and Mason (1996). For globalization, see Rao (1998) and Cullenberg and Pattanaik (2004). See Throsby (1995), World Bank (1999), Streeten (2000), and Wolfensohn *et al.* (2000) for discussions of sustainability as it relates to culture. Meier and Stiglitz (2000), World Bank (2000), and Chang (2003) offer a sample of development policy issues and literature.

9 Fabian (1983) suggests that the concept of time in Anthropology has played a pivotal role in preserving and widening the theoretical distance between Europe and its Others by denying them co-evalness. See Halperin (1988) and Escobar (1995) for other contributions to Anthropology's self-critique.

10 For classic elaborations of concepts of culture in Anthropology, see Malinowski (1930–31) and Kroeber and Kluckhohn (1952). For more contemporary discussions of the culture concept, see Geertz (1973), Schneider and Bonjean (1973), Bhabha (1994), Friedman (1994), and Eagleton (2000).

11 Hart's (1973) idea of the informal sector has passed into common usage in Economics. Other work that gained currency in the discipline includes Meillassoux's (1972) critique of Marxian anthropology, and Gudeman's (1986) concept of local models. For more on Economic Anthropology, see Strassmann (1974), Ruttan (1988), and Wilk (1996). See Mayhew (1980), Geertz (1984), Alverson (1986), Goldschmidt and Remmele (2005), and Maseland (2008) on the relationship between Anthropology and Economics.

12 In addition, quantitative sociological sources such as the *World Values Survey* and Hofstede's 'cultural dimensions' index (see Chapters 3, 5, and 7 in this book) have become popular among those attempting to mathematically represent culture. Adkisson

(2014) gives a helpful review of the quantitative literature in Economics. See DiMaggio (1994) for a review of the treatment of culture in Sociology and Economics, and Fukuyama (2001) for the Sociology literatures on culture and development.

13 In the other direction, economists have also contributed to recent work in Sociology (Harrison and Berger 2006). The term "economy" has been appropriated in other disciplines, with different connotations that are not readily accessible to many economists; see Amariglio and Ruccio (1999) for a helpful elucidation of this trend.

14 For examples of these explorations, see Benton (1982), Ridley (1983), Strassmann (1993), Rao (1998), Reder (1999), Austen (2000), Throsby (2001), Streeten (2006), and Jackson (2009).

15 There is no space here to bring attention to other perspectives such as Keynes's (see Boulding 1973; Goodwin 2006; Katzner 2008), Austrian economics, and economic criticism (see Lavoie and Chamlee-Wright 2000; Garnett 1999; Woodmansee and Osteen 1999). For contributions that disrupt the three-sphere grouping see Klamer (1991, 1996), Casson (1993), Bowles (1998), and Rosenbaum (1999).

16 The mainstream is mostly identified with a mathematical "non-discursive" method (Romer 1993; Krugman 1995). For Dow (1995), it includes general equilibrium, Neoclassical, new classical, and game theory, since they all entail mathematical formalism and determinism. I subsume all of the above under the banner of Neoclassicism. See Foldvary (1996), Colander (2000), Rima (2001), and Hodgson (2007) for more on the topography of the discipline.

17 The American Economic Association held another forum in 1985 on the role of culture and race in labor market disparities as indicated by differences in wage rates and labor force participation. See the contributions by Darity and Williams (1985) and Reimers (1985). A decade later, another conference debated the question of whether a distinctly European economics could be identified. See Buchanan's (1995) ambivalent answer to this question.

18 Institutionalists have used the term "cultural economics" to describe their own approach (Boulding 1973; Mayhew 1994). In Anthropology, the term refers to the idea that humans make rational—goal-driven—choices within the bounds of certain shared norms (Wilk 1996). In this book, for the sake of clarity, I reserve the term Cultural Economics for the Neoclassical subfield (see Chapter 3).

19 The word institutional is also deployed in a more generic sense to denote general analyses of organizations and social settings. Here, I apply the term Institutional Economics exclusively to scholarship grounded in a specific theory of institutions of the original (Veblenian) or the new (Neoclassical) brand.

20 Williams' original edition of *Keywords* in 1976 did not include an entry on development. It was added in the second edition. For surveys of the vast literature in development economics, see Meier (1984), Rostow (1990), Bardhan (1993), Meier and Stiglitz (2000), and Benería and Bisnath (2001). For critical interventions, see Marglin and Marglin (1990), Harcourt (1994), and Nudler and Lutz (1996). The philosophical roots and historical origins of the concept of development have been covered widely. See Bury (1932), Nisbet (1969), and Arndt (1987). I have discussed the philosophical and cultural premises of the economic development discourse elsewhere, see Zein-Elabdin (1998, 2001). Appendix III gives a chronological bibliography of development literature in Economics.

21 As I argue elsewhere, Economics contains a process of *double erasure*, namely, "erasure of certain cultures by theorizing them as inferior (less developed), and erasure of the work of cultural hegemony" (Zein-Elabdin 2004: 28). The first delegitimizes those cultures as agents of economic knowledge, in effect, barring them from participating in the discursive construction of economic meaning; while the second erasure masks hegemony under the claim or perception that Economics is a value-free 'science.' Also see Chapter 2 in this book.

22 The reflections revealed a sense that development was a hybrid field, "more like the manufacture of a car, buying windshields here, tires there, carburetors some other place"

(Lewis 1984: 8). This period also witnessed the rise of the post-development critique—a multi-disciplinary effort prompted in part by disenchantment with the record of development projects worldwide. See Sachs (1992), Latouche (1993), and Rahnema (1997).

23 The United Nations designated 1988–1997 as the "World Decade for Cultural Development." Indicators are categorized into three dimensions: creativity, freedom, and dialogue as measured by such variables as tourism and trade in 'cultural goods.' The World Commission on Culture and Development was established in 1994, and published its first report the following year (1995). The World Bank launched its own initiative on culture and development (Serageldin and Taboroff 1994). Also see UNESCO (1998, 2000).

24 See the exchange between O'Neil (1995) and Armour (1995). Jackson (2009) discusses idealism and materialism in economic thought, including comments on Keynes, Polanyi, and Schumpeter.

25 Billig (2000: 780) suggests that Weber was neither a materialist, nor an idealist; he did not see culture as an external "corporeal entity." This might explain why Weber (2012 [1947]) did not name culture in his seven categories of "economic action" (*Wirtschaften*): social action, meaning and subjectivity, the modern market economy, consciousness, technology, power of control and disposal, and the concept of goods.

26 Other common dualisms in development analyses and in Economics generally include formal/informal, market/state, market/household, and consumption/production, among others. For more on debates about universalism and particularism or relativism, see Friedman (1994), Nussbaum (1995), Young (1995), Wilk (1996), and Adkisson (2014). Maseland (2008) has argued that the banishment of culture from Economics to Anthropology and Sociology reflected a division of labor in which economists study the universal, while anthropologists specialize in the particular.

27 For some thoughts on reading texts, see Althusser and Balibar (1970). Their remarks are made with specific reference to Marxian epistemology, but they have wider applicability. Additional methodological principles are laid out in Zein-Elabdin (2004) and Zein-Elabdin and Charusheela (2004: Introduction).

References

Adkisson, Richard (2014) "Quantifying Culture: Problems and Promises," *Journal of Economic Issues*, 48 (1): 89–107.

Albelda, Randy (1997) *Economics and Feminism: Disturbances in the Field*, New York: Twayne Publishers.

Althusser, Louis (1970) "Contradiction and Overdetermination," in *For Marx*, trans. Ben Brewster, New York: Vintage Books.

—— and Etienne Balibar (1970) *Reading Capital*, London: Verso.

Alverson, Hoyt (1986) "Culture and Economy: Games That 'Play People,'" *Journal of Economic Issues* 20 (3): 661–679.

Amariglio, Jack L., Antonio Callari, Stephen Resnick, David Ruccio, and Richard Wolff (1996) "Nondeterminist Marxism: The Birth of a Postmodern Tradition in Economics," in Fred Foldvary (ed.) *Beyond Neoclassical Economics: Heterodox Approaches to Economic Theory*, Cheltenham: Edward Elgar, 134–147.

Amariglio, Jack L., Stephen A. Resnick, and Richard D. Wolff (1988) "Class, Power, and Culture," in Cary Nelson and Lawrence Grossberg (eds.) *Marxism and the Interpretation of Culture*, Urbana-Champaign, IL: University of Illinois Press, 487–501.

Amariglio, Jack L. and David F. Ruccio (1999) "Literary/Cultural 'Economies,' Economic Discourse, and the Question of Marxism," in Martha Woodmansee and Mark Osteen (eds.) *The New Economic Criticism: Studies at the Intersection of Literature and Economics*, London: Routledge, 381–400.

Armour, Leslie (1995) "Economics and Social Reality: Professor O'Neil and the Problem of Culture," *International Journal of Social Economics*, 22 (9/10/11): 79–87.

Arndt, H.W. (1987) *Economic Development: The History of an Idea*, Chicago: University of Chicago Press.

Austen, Siobahn (2000) "Culture and the Labor Market," *Review of Social Economy*, 58 (4): 505–521.

Ayres, Clarence E. (1962 [1944]) *The Theory of Economic Progress: A Study of the Fundamentals of Economic Development and Cultural Change*, New York: Schocken Books.

Baran, Paul A. (1973 [1957]) *The Political Economy of Growth*, Harmondsworth: Penguin Books.

Bardhan, Pranab (1993) "Economics of Development and the Development of Economics," *Journal of Economic Perspectives*, 7 (2): 129–142.

Barker, Drucilla K. (1998) "Dualisms, Discourse, and Development," *Hypatia*, 13 (3): 83–94.

——and Edith Kuiper (eds.) (2003) *Toward a Feminist Philosophy of Economics*, London: Routledge.

Baumol, William J. and William G. Bowen (1966) *Performing Arts: The Economic Dilemma*, New York: Twentieth Century Fund.

Becker, Gary S. (1976) *The Economic Approach to Human Behavior*, Chicago: University of Chicago Press.

—— (1996) *Accounting for Tastes*, Cambridge, MA: Harvard University Press.

Bell, Daniel (1976) *The Cultural Contradictions of Capitalism*, New York: Basic Books.

Benería, Lourdes and Savitri Bisnath (eds.) (2001) *Gender and Development: Theoretical, Empirical, and Practical Approaches*, vols. I, II, Cheltenham: Edward Elgar Publishing.

Benton, Raymond Jr. (1982) "Economics as a Cultural System," *Journal of Economic Issues*, 26 (2): 461–469.

Berger, Peter L. and Hsin-Huang Michael Hsiao (eds.) (1988) *In Search of an East Asian Development Model*, Oxford: Transaction Books.

Bhabha, Homi K. (1994) *The Location of Culture*, London: Routledge.

Billig, Michael S. (2000) "Institutions and Culture: Neo-Weberian Economic Anthropology," *Journal of Economic Issues*, 34 (4): 771–788.

Blaug, Mark (2001) "Where Are We Now on Cultural Economics?" *Journal of Economic Surveys*, 15 (2): 123–143.

Boserup, Ester (1989 [1970]) *Woman's Role in Economic Development*, London: Earthscan Publications.

Boulding, Kenneth E. (1970) "Increasing the supply Of Black Economists: Is Economics Culture-Bound?" *American Economic Review Supplement*, 60 (2): S406–S411.

—— (1973) "Toward the Development of a Cultural Economics," in Louis Schneider and Charles Bonjean (eds.) *The Idea of Culture in the Social Sciences*, Cambridge: Cambridge University Press, 47–64.

Bowles, Samuel (1998) "Endogenous Preferences: The Cultural Consequences of Markets and Other Economic Institutions," *Journal of Economic Literature*, 36 (1): 75–111.

Boyd, Robert and Peter J. Richerson (2000) "Climate, Culture, and the Evolution of Cognition," in Cecilia M. Heyes and Ludwig Huber (eds.) *The Evolution of Cognition*, Cambridge, MA: MIT Press, 66–82.

Buchanan, James M. (1995) "Economic Science and Cultural Diversity," *Kyklos*, 48 (2): 193–200.

Bury, J.B. (1932) *The Idea of Progress: An Inquiry into Its Origin and Growth*, New York: The Macmillan Company.

Callari, Antonio and David F. Ruccio (eds.) (1996) *Postmodern Materialism and the Future of Marxist Theory: Essays in the Althusserian Tradition*, Hanover, NH: Wesleyan University Press.

Casson, Mark (1993) "Cultural Determinants of Economic Performance," *Journal of Comparative Economics*, 17: 418–442.

—— (ed.) (1997) *Culture, Social Norms, and Economics*, vols I, II, Cheltenham: Edward Elgar.

Chamlee-Wright, Emily (1997) *The Cultural Foundations of Economic Development: Urban Female Entrepreneurship in Ghana*, London: Routledge.

Chang, Ha-Joon (ed.) (2003) *Rethinking Development Economics*, London: Anthem Press.

Charusheela, S. and Eiman Zein-Elabdin (2003) "Feminism, Postcolonial Thought, and Economics," in Marianne A. Ferber and Julie A. Nelson (eds.) *Feminist Economics Today: Beyond Economic Man*, Chicago: University of Chicago Press, 175–192.

Colander, David (2000) "The Death of Neoclassical Economics," *Journal of the History of Economic Thought*, 22 (2): 127–143.

Cullenberg, Stephen and Prasanta K. Pattanaik (eds.) (2004) *Globalization, Culture, and the Limits of the Market: Essays in Economics and Philosophy*, New York: Oxford University Press.

Darity, William Jr. and Rhonda M. Williams (1985) "Peddlers Forever? Culture, Competition, and Discrimination," *American Economic Review*, 75 (2): 256–261.

De Jong, Eelke (2009) *Culture and Economics: On Values, Economics and International Business*, London: Routledge.

Dieckmann, Oliver (1996) "Cultural Determinants of Economic Growth: Theory and Evidence," *Journal of Cultural Economics*, 20 (4): 297–320.

DiMaggio, Paul (1994) "Culture and Economy," in Neil J. Smelser and Richard Swedberg (eds.) *The Handbook of Economic Sociology*, Princeton, NJ: Princeton University Press, 27–57.

Dimand, Robert W. (2004) "Classical Political Economy and Orientalism: Nassau Senior's Eastern Tours," in E. Zein-Elabdin and S. Charusheela (eds.) *Postcolonialism Meets Economics*, London: Routledge, 73–90.

Dixon, Vernon, J. (1970) "The Di-Unital Approach to 'Black Economics'," *American Economic Review, Papers and Proceedings*, 60 (2): 424–429.

Dow, Sheila C. (1990) "Beyond Dualism," *Cambridge Journal of Economics*, 14 (2): 143–157.

—— (1995) "The Appeal of Neoclassical Economics: Some Insights from Keynes's Epistemology," *Cambridge Journal of Economics*, 19 (6): 715–733.

Drobak, John N. and John V.C. Nye (eds.) (1997) *The Frontiers of the New Institutional Economics*, San Diego, CA: Academic Press.

During, Simon (ed.) (1993) *The Cultural Studies Reader*, London: Routledge.

Eagleton, Terry (2000) *The Idea of Culture*, Oxford: Blackwell.

Eliot, T.S. (1949 [1940]) *Christianity and Culture: The Idea of a Christian Society and Notes Towards the Definition of Culture*, New York: Harcourt, Brace & World.

Escobar, Arturo (1995) *Encountering Development: The Making and Unmaking of the Third World*, Princeton, NJ: Princeton University Press.

European Task Force on Culture and Development (1997) *In from the Margins: A Contribution to the Debate on Culture and Development in Europe*, Strasbourg: Council of Europe Publishing.

Fabian, Johannes (1983) *Time and the Other: How Anthropology Makes its Object*, New York: Columbia University Press.

Ferber, Marianne A. and Julie A. Nelson (eds.) (1993) *Beyond Economic Man: Feminist Theory and Economics*, Chicago: University of Chicago Press.

—— (eds.) (2003) *Feminist Economics Today: Beyond Economic Man*, Chicago: University of Chicago Press.

Fernández, Raquel (2008) "Culture and Economics," in Steven N. Durlauf and Lawrence E. Blume (eds.) *The New Palgrave Dictionary of Economics Online*, 2nd edn, Basingstoke: Palgrave Macmillan. Available at: www.dictionaryofeconomics.com/article?id=pde2008_E000282 doi:10.1057/9780230226203.0346.

Fine, Ben (2002) *The World of Consumption: The Material and Cultural Revisited*, London: Routledge.

Foldvary, Fred E. (ed.) (1996) *Beyond Neoclassical Economics: Heterodox Approaches to Economic Theory*, Cheltenham: Edward Elgar.

Foucault, Michel (1970) *The Order of Things: An Archeology of the Human Sciences*, New York: Pantheon Books.

Frank, André Gunder (1966) "The Development of Underdevelopment," *Monthly Review*, 18 (4): 17–31.

Friedman, Jonathan (1994) *Cultural Identity and Global Process*, London: Sage.

Fukuda-Parr, Sakiko (2000) "In Search of Indicators of Culture and Development: Progress and Proposals," in *The World Culture Report 2000*, Paris: UNESCO Publishing, 278–283.

—— and A.K. Shiva Kumar (eds.) (2003) *Readings in Human Development: Concepts, Measures and Policies for a Development Paradigm*, New Delhi: Oxford University Press.

Fukuyama, F. (2001) "Culture and Economic Development: Cultural Concerns," in *International Encyclopedia of the Social and Behavioral Sciences*, London: Elsevier Science.

Garnett, Robert F. Jr. (ed.) (1999) *What Do Economists Know? New Economics of Knowledge*, London: Routledge.

Geertz, Clifford (1963) *Peddlers and Princes: Social Change and Economic Modernization in Two Indonesian Towns*, Chicago: University of Chicago Press.

—— (1973) *The Interpretation of Cultures: Selected Essays*, New York: Basic Books.

—— (1978) "The Bazaar Economy: Information and Search in Peasant Marketing," *American Economic Review, Papers and Proceedings*, 68 (2): 28–32.

—— (1984) "Culture and Social Change: The Indonesian Case," *Man*, 19 (4): 511–532.

Ginsburgh, Victor A. and David Throsby (eds.) (2006) *Handbook of the Economics of Art and Culture*, Amsterdam: Elsevier North-Holland.

Goldschmidt, Nils and Bernd Remmele (2005) "Anthropology as the Basic Science Of Economic Theory: Towards a Cultural Theory of Economics," *Journal of Economic Methodology*, 12 (3): 455–469.

Goodwin, Craufurd (2006) "Art and Culture in the History of Economic Thought," in V. Ginsburgh and D. Throsby (eds.) *Handbook of the Economics of Art and Culture*, Amsterdam: Elsevier North-Holland, 25–68.

Gramsci, Antonio (1985) *Selections from Cultural Writings*, ed. David Forgacs and Geoffrey Nowell-Smith, trans. William Boelhower, Cambridge, MA: Harvard University Press.

Granato, Jim, Ronald Inglehart, and David Leblang (1996) "The Effect of Cultural Values on Economic Development: Theory, Hypotheses, and Some Empirical Tests," *American Journal of Political Science*, 40 (3): 607–631.

Granovetter, Mark (1985) "Economic Action and Social Structure: The Problem of Embeddedness," *American Journal of Sociology*, 91 (3): 481–510.

Gray, H. Peter (1996) "Culture and Economic Performance: Policy as an Intervening Variable," *Journal of Comparative Economics*, 23 (3): 278–291.

Greif, Avner (1994) "Cultural Beliefs and the Organization of Society: A Historical and Theoretical Reflection on Collectivist and Individualist Societies," *Journal of Political Economy*, 102 (5): 912–950.

Gudeman, Stephen (1986) *Economics as Culture: Models and Metaphors of Livelihood*, London: Routledge & Kegan Paul.

Guiso, Luigi, Paola Sapienza, and Luigi Zingales (2006) "Does Culture Affect Economic Outcomes?" *Journal of Economic Perspectives*, 20 (2): 23–48.

Hall, Stuart (1980) "Cultural Studies: Two Paradigms," *Media, Culture and Society*, 2: 57–72.

Halperin, Rhoda H. (1988) *Economies Across Cultures: Towards a Comparative Science of the Economy*, New York: St. Martin's Press.

Harcourt, Wendy (ed.) (1994) *Feminist Perspectives on Sustainable Development*, London: Zed Books.

—— (1995) "Gender and Culture," in *Our Creative Diversity*, The World Commission on Culture and Development Report, Paris: UNESCO, 129–149.

Harris, Marvin (1979) *Cultural Materialism: The Struggle for a Science of Culture*, New York: Random House.

Harrison Lawrence E. and Peter L. Berger (eds.) (2006) *Developing Cultures: Case Studies*, London: Routledge.

Hart, Keith (1973) "Informal Income Opportunities and Urban Employment in Ghana," *Journal of Modern African Studies*, 11(1): 61–89.

Harvey, David (1989) *The Condition of Postmodernity: An Enquiry into the Origins of Cultural Change*, Oxford: Blackwell.

Hay, Denys (1968 [1957]) *Europe: The Emergence of an Idea*, Edinburgh: Edinburgh University Press.

Hayami, Yujiro (1998) "Toward an East Asian Model of Economic Development," in Y. Hayami and Masahiko Akoi (eds.) *The Institutional Foundations of East Asian Economic Development*, London: Palgrave Macmillan, 3–38.

Higgins, Benjamin H. (1977) "Economic Development and Cultural Change: Seamless Web or Patchwork quilt?" in Manning Nash (ed.) *Essays on Economic Development and Cultural Change, in Honor of Bert F. Hoselitz*, Chicago: University of Chicago Press, 99–120.

Hirschman, Albert O. (1981) "The Rise and Decline of Development Economics," in *Essays in Trespassing: Economics to Politics and Beyond*, Cambridge: Cambridge University Press, 1–24.

Hodgson, Geoffrey M. (2007) "Evolutionary and Institutional Economics as the New Mainstream?" *Evolutionary and Institutional Economics Review*, 4 (1): 7–25.

Hofstede, Geert (2001) *Culture's Consequences: Comparing Values, Behaviors, Institutions, and Organizations across Nations*, London: Sage.

Hoselitz, Bert F. (1952) "Non-Economic Barriers to Economic Development," *Economic Development and Cultural Change*, 1 (1): 8–21.

Hutter, Michael and Ilde Rizzo (eds.) (1997) *Economic Perspectives on Cultural Heritage*, London: Macmillan.

Hutter, Michael and D. Throsby (eds.) (2008) *Beyond Price: Value in Culture, Economics, and the Arts*, Cambridge: Cambridge University Press.

Jackson, William A. (1996) "Cultural Materialism and Institutional Economics," *Review of Social Economy*, 54 (2): 221–244.

—— (1999) "Dualism, Duality and the Complexity of Economic Institutions," *International Journal of Social Economics*, 26 (4): 545–558.

—— (2009) *Economics, Culture and Social Theory*, Cheltenham: Edward Elgar.

Jennings, Ann L. (1993) "Public or Private? Institutional Economics and Feminism," in Marianne A. Ferber and Julie A. Nelson (eds.) *Beyond Economic Man: Feminist Theory and Economics*, Chicago: University of Chicago Press, 111–129.

—— (1999) "Dualisms," in Janice Peterson and Margaret Lewis (eds.) *The Elgar Companion to Feminist Economics*, Cheltenham: Edward Elgar, 142–153.

—— and Dell Champlin (1994) "Cultural Contours of Race, Gender, and Class Distinctions: A Critique of Moynihan and Other Functionalist Views," in Janice Peterson and Doug Brown (eds.) *The Economic Status of Women Under Capitalism: Institutional Economics and Feminist Theory*, Aldershot: Edward Elgar, 95–110.

—— and William Waller (1995) "Culture: Core Concept Reaffirmed," *Journal of Economic Issues*, 29 (2): 407–418.

Jones, Eric L. (2006) *Cultures Merging: A Historical and Economic Critique of Culture*, Princeton, NJ: Princeton University Press.

Kabeer, Naila (1991) "Cultural Dopes or Rational Fools? Women and Labour Supply in the Bangladesh Garment Industry," *The European Journal of Development Research*, 3 (November): 133–160.

—— (1994) *Reversed Realities: Gender Hierarchies in Development Thought*, London: Verso.

Katzner, Donald W. (2008) *Culture and Economic Explanation: Economics in the US and Japan*, London: Routledge.

Klamer, Arjo (1991) "Towards the Native's Point of View: The Difficulty of Changing the Conversation," in Don Lavoie (ed.), *Economics and Hermeneutics*, London: Routledge, 19–33.

—— (1996) *The Value of Culture: On the Relationship between Economics and Arts*, Amsterdam: Amsterdam University Press.

Kovács, János Mátyás (2006) "Which Past Matters? Culture and Economic Development in Eastern Europe After 1989," in Lawrence E. Harrison and Peter L. Berger (eds.) *Developing Cultures: Case Studies*, London: Routledge, 329–347.

Kroeber, A. L. and Clyde Kluckhohn (1952) *Culture: A Critical Review of Concepts and Definitions*, Peabody Museum of American Archeology and Ethnology, vol. 47, no. 1, Cambridge, MA: Harvard University Press.

Krugman, Paul (1995) *Development, Geography, and Economic Theory*, Cambridge, MA: MIT Press.

Lal, Deepak (1985) "The Misconceptions of 'Development Economics'," *Finance and Development*, 22 (June): 10–13.

Latouche, Serge (1993) *In the Wake of the Affluent Society: An Exploration of Post-Development*, London: Zed Books.

Lavoie, Don and Emily Chamlee-Wright (2000) *Culture and Enterprise: The Development, Representation and Morality of Business*, London: Routledge.

Lazear, Edward P. (1999) "Culture and Language," *Journal of Political Economy*, 107 (6): S95–S125.

Lewis, W. Arthur (1954) "Economic Development with Unlimited Supplies of Labour," *Manchester School*, (22): 139–191.

—— (1955) *The Theory of Economic Growth*, London: George Allen and Unwin.

—— (1984) "The State of Development Theory," *American Economic Review*, 74 (1): 1–10.

Lian, Brad and John R. Oneal (1997) "Cultural Diversity and Economic Development: A Cross-National Study of 98 Countries, 1960–1985," *Economic Development and Cultural Change*, 46 (1): 61–77.

Lucas, Robert E. Jr. (1988) "On the Mechanics of Economic Development," *Journal of Monetary Economics*, 22: 3–42.

Malinowski, Bronislaw (1930–31) "Culture," in *Encyclopaedia of the Social Sciences*, vol. 4, New York: The Macmillan Co, 621–646.

Mandel, Ernest (1975) *Late Capitalism*, trans. Joris De Bres, London: NLB.

Marglin, Stephen A. and Frédérique Apffel Marglin (eds.) (1990) *Dominating Knowledge: Development, Culture, and Resistance*, Oxford: Clarendon Press.

Marini, Matteo (2004) "Cultural Evolution and Economic Growth: A Theoretical Hypothesis with Some Empirical Evidence," *The Journal of Socio-Economics*, 33: 765–784.

Maseland, Robbert (2008) "Taking Economics to Bed: About the Pitfalls and Possibilities of Cultural Economics," in Wolfram Elsner and Hardy Hanappi (eds.) *Varieties of Capitalism and New Institutional Deals: Regulation, Welfare and the New Economy*, Cheltenham: Edward Elgar, 299–321.

Mason, Patrick L. (1996) "Race, Culture, and the Market," *Journal of Black Studies*, 26 (6): 782–808.

Mayhew, Anne (1980) "Atomistic and Cultural Analyses in Economic Anthropology: An Old Argument Repeated," in John Adams (ed.) *Institutional Economics: Contributions to the Development of Holistic Economics: Essays in Honor of Allan Gruchy*, Boston: Martinus Nijhoff Publishing, 72–81.

—— (1987) "Culture: Core Concept Under Attack," *Journal of Economic Issues*, 21 (2): 587–603.

—— (1994) "Culture," in G. Hodgson and W. Samuels (eds.) *The Elgar Companion to Institutional and Evolutionary Economics*, Cheltenham: Edward Elgar, 115–119.

McCain, Roger (2006) "Defining Cultural and Artistic Goods," in Victor Ginsburgh and David Throsby (eds.) *The Handbook of the Economics of Art and Culture*, vol.1, Amsterdam: Elsevier North-Holland, 148–167.

McCloskey, Donald N. (1985) *The Rhetoric of Economics*, Madison, WI: University of Wisconsin Press.

McKinley, Terry (1998) "Measuring the Contribution of Culture to Human Well-Being: Cultural Indicators of Development," in *The World Culture Report 1998*, Paris: UNESCO, 322–332.

Meier, Gerald M. (1984) *Leading Issues in Economic Development*, New York: Oxford University Press.

—— and Joseph E. Stiglitz (eds.) (2000) *Frontiers of Development Economics: The Future in Perspective*, Oxford: Oxford University Press.

Meillassoux, Claude (1972) "From Reproduction to Production: A Marxist Approach to Economic Anthropology," *Economy and Society*, 1(1): 93–105.

Mini, Piero V. (1974) *Philosophy and Economics: The Origins and Development of Economic Theory*, Gainesville, FL: University of Florida Press.

Mulhern, Francis (2009) "Culture and Society: Then and Now," *New Left Review*, 55 (January–February): 31–45.

Myrdal, Gunnar (1968) *Asian Drama: An Inquiry into the Poverty of Nations*, vols I, II. New York: Pantheon.

Neale, Walter C. (1990) "Absolute Cultural Relativism: Firm Foundation for Valuing and Policy," *Journal of Economic Issues*, 24 (2): 333–344.

Nelson, Julie A. (1992) "Gender, Metaphor, and the Definition of Economics," *Economics and Philosophy*, 8 (1): 103–125.

—— (1993) "The Study of Choice or the Study of Provisioning? Gender and the Definition of Economics," in Marianne A. Ferber and Julie A. Nelson (eds.) *Beyond Economic Man: Feminist Theory and Economics*, Chicago: University of Chicago, 23–36.

Nisbet, Robert A. (1969) *Social Change and History: Aspects of the Western Theory of Development*, London: Oxford University Press.

North, Douglass C. (1990) *Institutions, Institutional Change and Economic Performance*, Cambridge: Cambridge University Press.

Nudler, Oscar and Mark A. Lutz (eds.) (1996) *Economics, Culture and Society: Alternative Approaches: Dissenting Views from Economic Orthodoxy*, New York: Apex Press (for the United Nations University).

Nussbaum, Martha C. (1995) "Human Capabilities, Female Human Beings," in Martha Nussbaum and Jonathan Glover (eds.) *Women, Culture, and Development: A Study of Human Capabilities*, Oxford: Clarendon Press.

O'Neil, Daniel J. (1995) "Culture Confronts Marx," *International Journal of Social Economics*, 22 (9/10/11): 43–54.

Park, Tae-Kyu (1997) "Confucian Values and Contemporary Economic Development in Korea," in Timothy Brook and Hy V. Luong (eds.) *Culture and Economy: The Shaping of Capitalism in Eastern Asia*, Ann Arbor, MI: Michigan University Press, 125–136.

Peacock, Alan and Ilde Rizzo (eds.) (1994) *Cultural Economics and Cultural Policies*, Boston: Kluwer Publishers.

Pietrykowski, Bruce (1994) "Consuming Culture: Postmodernism, Post-Fordism, and Economics," *Rethinking Marxism*, 7 (1): 62–80.

Polanyi, Karl (1957) "The Economy as Instituted Process," in K. Polanyi, Conrad M. Arensberg, and Harry W. Pearson (eds.) *Trade and Market in the Early Empires: Economies in History and Theory*, Chicago: The Free Press, 243–270.

Rahnema, Majid (ed.), with Victoria Bawtree (1997) *The Post-Development Reader*, London: Zed Books.

Rao, J. Mohan (1998) "Culture and Economic Development," in *The World Culture Report 1998*, Paris: UNESCO, 25–48.

Reder, Melvin W. (1999) *Economics: The Culture of a Controversial Science*, Chicago: University of Chicago Press.

Reimers, Cordelia W. (1985) "Cultural Differences in Labor Force Participation Among Married Women," *American Economic Review, Papers and Proceedings*, 75 (2): 251–255.

Resnick, Stephen A. and Richard D. Wolff (eds.) (1985) *Rethinking Marxism: Struggles in Marxist Theory: Essays for Harry Magdoff and Paul Sweezy*, New York: Autonomedia.

—— (1987) *Knowledge and Class: A Marxian Critique of Political Economy*, Chicago: University of Chicago Press.

Ridley, F. F. (1983) "Cultural Economics and the Culture of Economists," *Journal of Cultural Economics*, 7: 1–18.

Rima, Ingrid Hahne (2001) *Development of Economic Analysis*, London: Routledge.

Romer, Paul M. (1993) "Idea Gaps and Object Gaps in Economic Development," *Journal of Monetary Economics*, 32: 543–573.

Rosenbaum, Eckehard F. (1999) "Against Naïve Materialism: Culture, Consumption and the Causes of Inequality," *Cambridge Journal of Economics*, 23 (3): 317–336.

Rostow, W. W. (1971 [1960]) *The Stages of Economic Growth: A Non-Communist Manifesto*, Cambridge: Cambridge University Press.

—— (1990) *Theorists of Economic Growth from David Hume to the Present: With a Perspective on the Next Century*, Oxford: Oxford University Press.

Ruttan, Vernon W. (1988) "Cultural Endowments and Economic Development: What Can We Learn from Anthropology?" *Economic Development and Cultural Change*, 36 (3) Supplement: 247–271.

Sachs, Wolfgang (ed.) (1992) *The Development Dictionary: A Guide to Knowledge As Power*, London: Zed Books.

Sahlins, Marshall (1976) *Culture and Practical Reason*, Chicago: University of Chicago Press.

Said, Edward W. (1979) *Orientalism*, New York: Vintage Books.

Schneider, Louis and Charles M. Bonjean (eds.) (1973) *The Idea of Culture in the Social Sciences*, Cambridge: Cambridge University Press.

Schoenberger, Erica (1997) *The Cultural Crisis of the Firm*, Oxford: Basil Blackwell.

Scitovsky, Tibor (1976) *The Joyless Economy: An Inquiry into Human Satisfaction and Consumer Dissatisfaction*, New York: Oxford University Press.

Sen, Amartya K. (1983) "Development Which Way Now?" *Economic Journal*, 93 (372): 745–762.

—— (1998) "Culture, Freedom and Independence," *World Culture Report 1998*, Paris: UNESCO, 317–321.

—— (2004) "How Does Culture Matter?" in Vijayendra Rao and Michael Walton (eds.) *Culture and Public Action*, Stanford, CA: Stanford University Press, 37–58.

Serageldin, Ismail and June Taboroff (eds.) (1994) *Culture and Development in Africa*, Washington, DC: The World Bank.

Stanfield, James Ronald (1980) "The Institutional Economics of Karl Polanyi," *Journal of Economic Issues*, 14 (3): 593–614.

Stiglitz, Joseph E. (1986) "The New Development Economics," *World Development*, 14 (2): 257–265.

Stocking, George W. Jr. (1968) *Race, Culture, and Evolution: Essays in the History of Anthropology*, Chicago: University of Chicago Press.

Strassmann, Diana (1993) "Not a Free Market: The Rhetoric of Disciplinary Authority in Economics," in Marianne Ferber and Julie Nelson (eds.) *Beyond Economic Man: Feminist Theory and Economics*, Chicago: University of Chicago Press, 54–68.

Strassmann, W. Paul (1974) "Technology: A Culture Trait, a Logical Category, or Virtue Itself?" *Journal of Economic Issues*, 8 (4): 671–687.

Streeten, Paul (2000) "Culture and Sustainable Development: Another Perspective," in J. D. Wolfensohn *et al.* (eds.) *Culture Counts: Financing, Resources, and the Economics of Culture in Sustainable Development*, Washington, DC: The World Bank, 41–46.

—— (2006) "Culture and Economic Development," in V.A. Ginsburgh and D. Throsby (eds.) *The Handbook of the Economics of Art and Culture*, vol. 1, Amsterdam: Elsevier, 400–412.

Sweezy, Paul M. (1970 [1942]) *The Theory of Capitalist Development: Principles of Marxian Political Economy*, New York: Monthly Review Press.

Tabellini, Guido (2005) "Culture and Institutions: Economic Development in the Regions of Europe," CESifo Working Paper No. 1492.

Temin, Peter (1997) "Is It Kosher to Talk about Culture?" *Journal of Economic History*, 57 (2): 267–287.

Throsby, David (1995) "Culture, Economics, and Sustainability," *Journal of Cultural Economics*, 19 (3): 199–206.

—— (2001) *Economics and Culture*, Cambridge: Cambridge University Press.

Towse, Ruth (ed.) (1997) *Cultural Economics: The Arts, the Heritage and the Media Industries*, Cheltenham: Edward Elgar, vols. I, II.

—— and Abdul Khakee (eds.) (1992) *Cultural Economics*, Heidelberg: Springer-Verlag.

Tylor, Edward Burnett (1883 [1871]) *Primitive Culture: Researches into the Development of Mythology, Philosophy, Religion, Language, Art and Custom*, New York: Henry Holt and Company.

UNESCO (1998) *World Culture Report 1998: Culture, Creativity and Markets*, Paris: United Nations Educational, Scientific and Cultural Organization.

—— (2000) *World Culture Report 2000: Cultural Diversity, Conflict and Pluralism*, Paris: United Nations Educational, Scientific and Cultural Organization.

Veblen, Thorstein (1898) "Why Is Economics Not an Evolutionary Science?" *Quarterly Journal of Economics*, 12 (2): 373–397.

Waller, William T. (Jr.) (1982) "The Evolution of the Veblenian Dichotomy: Veblen, Hamilton, Ayres, and Foster," *Journal of Economic Issues*, 16 (3): 757–771.

—— (1994) "Veblenian Dichotomy and its Critics," in G. Hodgson and W. Samuels (eds.) *The Elgar Companion to Institutional and Evolutionary Economics*, Cheltenham: Edward Elgar, 368–372.

—— (1999) "Institutional Economics, Feminism and Overdetermination," *Journal of Economic Issues*, 33 (4): 835–844.

—— and Ann Jennings (1990) "On the Possibility of a Feminist Economics: The Convergence of Institutional and Feminist Methodology," *Journal of Economic Issues*, 24 (2): 613–622.

Weber, Max (1958 [1930]) *The Protestant Ethic and the Spirit of Capitalism*, New York: Charles Scribner's Sons.

—— (2012 [1947]) *The Theory of Social and Economic Organization*, trans. A.M. Henderson and Talcott Parsons, Mansfield Centre, CT: Martino Publishing.

Wilk, Richard (1996) *Economies and Cultures: Foundations of Economic Anthropology*, Boulder, CO: Westview Press.

Williams, Raymond (1961) *Culture and Society: 1780–1950*, London: Penguin Books.

—— (1983 [1976]) *Keywords: A Vocabulary of Culture and Society*, New York: Oxford University Press.

Wolfensohn, James D., Lamberto Dini, Gianfranco Facco Bonetti, Ian Johnson, and J. Martin-Brown (2000) *Culture Counts: Financing, Resources, and the Economics of Culture in Sustainable Development*, Washington, DC: The World Bank.

Woodmansee, Martha and Mark Osteen (eds.) (1999) *The New Economic Criticism: Studies at the Intersection of Literature and Economics*, London: Routledge.

World Bank (1999) *Culture and Sustainable Development: A Framework for Action*, Washington, DC: World Bank.

—— (2000) *Entering the 21st Century, World Development Report 1999/2000*, New York: Oxford University Press.

World Commission on Culture and Development (1995) *Our Creative Diversity*, Paris: UNESCO.

Wyss, Brenda (1999) "Culture and Gender in Household Economies: The Case of Jamaican Child Support Payments," *Feminist Economics*, 5 (2): 1–24.

Young, Robert (1995) *Colonial Desire: Hybridity in Theory, Culture and Race*, London: Routledge.

Zein-Elabdin, Eiman O. (1998) "The Question of Development in Africa: A Conversation for Propitious Change," *African Philosophy*, 11 (2): 113–125.

—— (2001) "Contours of a Non-Modernist Discourse: The Contested Space of History and Development," *Review of Radical Political Economics*, 33 (3): 255–263.

—— (2003) "The Difficulty of a Feminist Economics," in Drucilla K. Barker and Edith Kuiper (eds.), *Toward a Feminist Philosophy of Economics*, London: Routledge, 321–338.

—— (2004) "Articulating the Postcolonial (with Economics in Mind)," in E. Zein-Elabdin and S. Charusheela (eds.) *Postcolonialism Meets Economics*, London: Routledge, 21–39.

—— (2009) "Economics, Postcolonial Theory, and the Problem of Culture: Institutional Analysis and Hybridity," *Cambridge Journal of Economics*, 33 (6): 1153–1167.

—— (2011) "Postcolonial Theory and Economics: Orthodox and Heterodox," in Jane Pollard, Cheryl McEwan, and Alex Hughes (eds.) *Postcolonial Economies*, London: Zed Books, 37–61.

—— and S. Charusheela (eds.) (2004) *Postcolonialism Meets Economics*, London: Routledge.

2 Classical political economy and the rise of Neoclassicism

The founding father of economics, Adam Smith, had a strong sense of the cultural matrix of economic phenomena. One of the most interesting of the unasked questions of intellectual history is how the science of economics should have lost this sense and become an abstract discipline void almost of any cultural context. The loss of interest within the economics profession in the cultural matrix of its own discipline is a fairly continuous process, almost from the days of Adam Smith.

(Boulding 1973: 47)

To understand the treatment of culture in Economics requires recalling the origins from which the discipline sprang, centuries ago, upon the dense foundation of European Enlightenment philosophy and industrial capitalism. Classical political economy (CPE) cemented two key principles of the humanist worldview: instrumental rationality—the means-to-ends expression of reason and capacities of the human mind; and historicism, the belief that 'history' represents an orderly realization of immutable laws of human progress defined by the record of European societies.[1] The construction of market rationality as a universal human impulse ensured the exclusion of cultural differences, while historicism prescribed the meaning of 'development' for all peoples around the globe.

In this chapter, I briefly outline the place of culture in the liberal tradition of CPE and the beginnings of Neoclassical theory, i.e., late eighteenth to early twentieth centuries. The outline is not by any chance meant to be comprehensive. I only comment on the most iconic figures—Smith, Ricardo, J.S. Mill, Bentham, Jevons, Menger, J.B. Clark, and Marshall—and pieces of literature to merely give a sense of the presence and absence of culture in the discipline's origins.[2] To the trained historian of economic thought, surely my coverage will appear sketchy. Nevertheless, I hope the outline helps illuminate discussions of Neoclassical and other schools of economics in the following chapters. What tentatively emerges from this outline is that classical and early Neoclassical treatments of culture were *partial and tangential*, and displayed the ontological separation of 'culture' from 'economy,' rooted in the Enlightenment dualism of ideal/material. My use of the word 'culture' here refers to broadly—but unevenly—shared sensibilities, habits, and lifeways of a society or a group, a social frame of reference that shapes even economic action and knowledge (see Chapter 1 and Appendix II for more on culture). I am interested in both the extent to which culture appeared in analyses of economic phenomena, and in the way the culture of the specific time and place was reflected in economic thought.

I will not devote much attention to classical theories of economic growth since these are well covered in the literature (Schumpeter 1954; Adelman 1961; Rostow 1990).[3] Classical Marxian thought is discussed in Chapter 6. Increasing debates surround the term Neoclassical economics (see Colander 2000; and Chapter 1 in this book). I use it broadly in reference to all those branches of the discipline that envision the economic problem as a series of individual-induced and centered optimizing choices (see Chapter 3).

Classical political economy (CPE)

There is a general perception that most classical political economists "were comfortable in using cultural explanations for economic phenomena" (Guiso *et al.* 2006: 26). This echoes Kenneth Boulding's (1973: 47) claim, quoted in this chapter's epigraph, that Adam Smith was keenly aware of "the cultural matrix of economic phenomena," though Boulding did not quite explain what this is.[4] In this chapter, I dig more deeply to find what specific awareness of and notions of culture and a 'cultural matrix' were present in CPE. What emerges is that there is almost no usage of the term 'culture' in classical economic literature, and more importantly, no causal link between culture—as a way of life—and economic behavior or action. In this sense, the treatment of culture was partial and tangential, that is, various parts of culture were recognized individually—more implicitly than explicitly—but not linked causally to economic phenomena. This treatment could be described as 'innocent' in that it lacked an understanding that economic action and knowledge were themselves culturally defined. As a result, culture remained simply an interesting tangent to the analysis.

In general, four major patterns characterize the classical approach to culture: (1) reliance on the philosophy of natural law in economic explanations. Here culture was absent; (2) use of the word 'culture' in the sense of "cultivation," this was almost exclusively confined to discussions of agriculture. Less often, the word 'cultivation' was invoked to denote learning and intellectual growth; (3) general awareness that social norms and affiliations surround economic activity. Here culture was implicitly present in the words "custom" and "habit"; and (4) making cross-cultural references to other world regions and peoples to support different economic claims based on the notion of "civilization."[5] These four patterns were present to different degrees and in multiple shades in the work of different authors. I will examine both when culture was named and when it was only implied.

The first reason for the scarcity of culture in the beginnings of systematic economic analysis is the dominance of natural law philosophy. The saturation of the second half of the eighteenth century to at least mid-nineteenth century with the belief in predestination and fatalistic attitudes that attributed human conditions to either God or Nature is well established in the literature (Schumpeter 1954; Nisbet

1969; Mini 1974).[6] According to A. Hirschman (1982), the notion of humanly devised social change was quite new, dating back only to the eighteenth century. Despite the move toward humanism, classical texts were variously infused with two natural law-based ideas. The first is that there exists a definite, recognizable human nature. In other words, all humans shared a certain innate character or set of traits, as in being 'self-interested,' for instance. The second natural law-based idea is that a predestined order—from God or Nature—determined the function-ing of society, including economic activity.

The second reason that the term culture did not frequently appear in the clas-sical era, of course, is that the concept in its contemporary usage did not become visible until late in the nineteenth century, with the rise of Anthropology. This is not to say there was no mention of the word prior to this time. J. Gottfried Herder's (1968) extensive musings on culture offer a notable example.[7] But this was an infrequent occurrence. The most common equivalent words to a concept of culture in the eighteenth century were "custom" (accepted social practice) and "civilization" (refined taste and habits, i.e., remove from brute 'nature'). References to elements of culture, such as education, law, or language, are readily found in CPE, but the word itself hardly appeared, except in association with agriculture. Adam Smith's work illustrates all four patterns of culture treatment suggested here: reliance on natural law explanations (culture is absent); use of the word 'cultivation' mostly for agriculture, and less so for learning and refine-ment; speaking of custom or habit (culture is present without being named); and employing the word 'civilization' to make cross-cultural comparisons.

The influence of natural law doctrine on Smith's thought is transparent, per-haps most in his belief in the natural progress of wealth and the existence of a natural price. Although he was well aware of the social context, Smith did not accord it a determining role in how economies operate. He attributed exchange and the division of labor—his most prized ideas—to nature more than culture. Accordingly, in *The Wealth of Nations*, he suggested that "the propensity to truck, barter, and exchange one thing for another" might be "one of those original prin-ciples in human nature, of which no further account can be given" (1976 [1776], vol. 1: 17). But Smith oscillated between natural and social causes in a rather indeterminate manner. The overwhelming emphasis by economists on the famous expression "a certain propensity in human nature to truck, barter, and exchange" has given disproportionate weight to his reliance on nature. However, in the same text, Smith immediately went on to state he was inclined to believe that this pro-pensity "seems more probable, [to] be the necessary consequence of the faculties of reason and speech" (ibid.), which could be seen as pointing toward mental and linguistic development, both highly conditioned by enculturation.[8]

The relative weight of nature and culture in Smith's thinking shifted back and forth, but nature tended to prevail as it did in his stages of growth theory asserted in more than one text. In *Lectures on Jurisprudence* (1978 [1762]), he conjec-tured that mankind had passed through four "ages," beginning with the chase, then shepherding, followed by agriculture (cultivation), then, through specialization, mankind reached the final stage when geographically limited exchange flourished into an age of worldwide commerce. A few years later, Smith elaborated this vision in what he called the "natural progress of opulence."

> Had human institutions, therefore, never disturbed the natural course of things, the progressive wealth and increase of the towns would, in every political society, be consequential, and in proportion to the improvement and cultivation of the territory or country ... According to the natural course of things, therefore, the greater part of the capital of every growing society is, first, directed to agricultures, afterwards to manufactures, and last of all to foreign commerce. This order of things is so very natural, that in every society that had any territory, it has always, I believe, been in some degree observed.
>
> (1976 [1776], vol. 1: 404–5)

In this passage he focused on progress since the arrival of agriculture, but his idea of a 'natural' course of change is clear. This belief in a naturally ordained, universal sequence of events set the theoretical stage for the absence of culture from discussions of economic activity.

The second pattern in which culture lurks in Smith's work is in the sense of cultivation. This appeared frequently in his discussions of colonialism. For example, he stated, "[i]n all European colonies the culture of the sugar-cane is carried on by negro slaves" (1976 [1776], vol. 2: 99). Here and in other passages commenting on the production of sugar-cane, the word 'culture' refers to crop cultivation (e.g., ibid.: 89, 102). Smith also used the term cultivation in the context of education and learning. Thus, according to him, "[w]hat are called Metaphysics or Pneumatics were set in opposition to Physics, and were cultivated not only as the more sublime, but, for the purposes of a particular profession as the more useful science of the two" (ibid.: 292–293). In other words, he recognized the meaning of culture as knowledge and intellectual growth. His thoughts on colonialism also contain this meaning as he argued that the colonizers brought to the colonies a knowledge of agriculture and other crafts, including government and law. In contrast, he claimed, the natives—members of "savage and barbarous nations"—lacked the "natural progress of law and government" that would allow them to defend their territories against foreign aggression (ibid.: 76).[9]

Third, the meaning of culture as social custom is also found in Smith's work, perhaps most emblematically in *The Theory of Moral Sentiments* (2009 [1759]). His thoughts on human psychology, expressed in passions and temper, have received the bulk of economists' scrutiny (Hirschman 1982; Sen 1987). Here, I am more concerned with how the meaning of culture as a social frame of reference appears in this text, where he discussed common social values and practices, including religion, creativity (arts), and education. Part V of the book is devoted to the "Influence of Custom and Fashion Upon the Sentiments of Moral Approbation and Disapprobation." Here, Smith argued that custom and fashion were "principles which extend their dominion over our judgments concerning beauty of every kind" (2009 [1795]: 227). They influence judgments about beauty in dress, music, poetry, architecture, and beauty in human—and even animal—features. In this argument, he used the word 'custom' in two senses: habituation, i.e., being or becoming accustomed to something over time by enculturation; and group practice, i.e., sharing a common social habit or set of values. The first meaning refers to a temporal sense of culture (tradition), while the second embodies the idea of culture as group sensibilities. In Boulding's terms, Smith did have a sense of a "cultural matrix" that shapes human action and sentiment. My point, however, is that Smith fell short of grasping or articulating the extent to which this 'matrix' also shapes economic behavior, outcomes, and knowledge. The significant result is that culture remained tangential to his theoretical system.

The fourth pattern of Smith's treatment of culture is embodied in the word 'civilization,' which surfaces in discussions of non-European societies. His views about other cultures may be gleaned from his comparisons of different world regions. In *The Wealth of Nations*, he named an extensive number of states and peoples within and beyond Europe, as well as other periods of history from ancient Egypt to the Americas. These discussions presented a mixed picture of caution and parochialism. On one hand, his statements were full of orientalism, the cultural prejudice of his time, referring to "tribes of naked and miserable savages" in America (1976 [1776], vol. 2: 70) and barbarous nations in Africa (ibid.: 297).[10] On the other hand, many of his claims were punctuated by qualifications and non-hierarchical descriptions of different peoples. He showed awareness of the tentative nature of historical knowledge in such statements as "the nations that, according to the best authenticated history, appear to have been first civilized, were those that dwelt around the coast of the Mediterranean sea" (ibid., vol. 1: 23). He attributed the "backwardness" of Africa to distance from coastal outlets and lack of navigable rivers rather than to cultural factors such as the absence of an economizing tendency, a presumption that would come to dominate twentieth-century development economics. Similarly, his descriptions of the Scottish Highlands, associating their "very small villages" "scattered about" (ibid.: 21) with a lower stage of economic progress, resemble depictions of "poor" countries in contemporary economic discourse.

David Ricardo shared Smith's worldview and pattern of treatment of culture, but he was less of a philosopher than Smith and other prominent contemporaries— J.S. Mill, Bentham, and Marx. Ricardo is generally blamed for being "one of the first culprits in the process of reducing economics to a culturally free abstraction" (Boulding 1973: 47) though the reasons behind this charge, as they relate to culture, are not particularly explored in the literature. Ricardo's *The Principles of Political Economy and Taxation* (1948 [1817]) is much more limited in scope, perhaps because his project was to merely elaborate and formalize some of Smith's specific ideas rather than comment on his general social philosophy. In a similar manner to Smith, throughout *The Principles*, Ricardo used the word 'cultivation' to refer to agriculture—cultivating the land —and to cultivation of industry (ibid.: 1). He invoked the word 'civilization' in comparative contexts. For example, he spoke of money "being the general medium of exchange between all civilized countries" (ibid.: 30), and suggested that trade took place among "the universal society of nations throughout the civilized world" (ibid.: 81). In laying out the principles of foreign trade, Ricardo referred to a variety of countries, in Europe as well as America and the East Indies. He fell in line with Smith in considering England to be rich, while poor nations were the likes of Poland, Spain, or Portugal, and largely agreed with Smith's discussion of relations between Europe and its colonies.

As a descendant of natural law philosophy, Ricardo held on to the notion of a natural price, which led him to believe that income distribution was dictated by "the natural course of rent, profit, and wages" (ibid.: 1). But his commitment to natural law doctrine was not unshakable. Late in his life he confessed substantial skepticism about an objective theory of value, and concluded that "there is not in nature any correct measure of value nor can any ingenuity suggest one, for what constitutes a correct measure for some things is a reason why it cannot be a correct one for others."[11] This statement, which exhibits a deeply relativist perspective, could have potentially opened the door for consideration of value itself as a culturally defined concept. Ricardo did take notice of some economic implications of culture but only in its sense as artistic creation. For example, he argued that the value of some works of art, e.g., rare paintings or sculptures, was determined more by demand ("the varying wealth and inclinations of those who are desirous to possess them") and scarcity than by the quantity of labor expended in their making (ibid.: 6). However, he considered this an exception to the general rule, and therefore did not devote much space to it in his economic analysis. This is an example of the partial and tangential treatment of culture.

John Stuart Mill presents a more complicated case with respect to evaluating the place of culture in CPE. Mill certainly shared the classical *Weltanschauung*, as manifested for instance in his references to 'nature' (e.g., 1994 [1848]: 66) and 'human nature' (ibid.: 127). Yet, he departed from prevailing wisdom in his normative evaluation of three major questions: the distribution of wealth, the social status of women, and the idea of progress. Mill argued that, while production was governed by "the laws of nature," the distribution of wealth "is a matter of human institution solely" (ibid.: 5–6). He was clearly far ahead of his time in objecting to the inferior status accorded to women in Victorian England. In *The Subjection of Women* (1970 [1869]), he recognized the role of social institutions and custom in the inequality of "the sexes." His firm appreciation of the cultural character of men's social superiority to women shines in the statement that "unnatural generally means only uncustomary, and that everything which is usual appears natural. The subjection of women to men being a universal custom, any departure from it quite naturally appears unnatural" (ibid.: 22–3). Such a statement reveals a remarkable grasp of the social construction of gender relations, and shows that his understanding of the idea of nature itself was more sophisticated than that of his classical peers. With respect to women at least, Mill clearly understood culture as shared, often taken-for-granted habits and sensibilities.[12]

The assessment of progress is where the term culture appears explicitly in Mill's work. Although he believed in the progressive improvement of production as a historical 'fact,' he was less than fond of economic progress for its own sake; the end goal for him was elevation in the "Art of Living" (1994 [1848]: 129). Accordingly, he drew a distinction between "human improvement" and mere growth in capital. In *The Principles of Political Economy*, he used the term 'cultivation' in reference to agricultural pursuits, reserving the word 'culture' for learning and intellectual endeavors—"to cultivate freely the graces of life" (ibid.: 128). Considering the need for public support of the arts, he stated: "[i]t is scarcely necessary to remark that a stationary condition of capital and population implies no stationary state of human improvement. There would be as much scope as ever for all kinds of *mental culture*, and moral and social progress" (ibid.: 129; emphasis added). This statement marks the first time in the work of this group of classical authors that one encounters the word 'culture' outside of agricultural production. Culture in the sense of elevation of human faculties, greater movement away from nature, is clearly present in Mill's philosophy. His statements about cultivation of the senses and other qualities are echoed today in the discourse of human development, where the goal is a higher, more developed state of human existence, instead of mere economic growth, namely, accumulation of capital (see Nussbaum 1995; Fukuda-Parr and Kumar 2003).

By contrast, J.S. Mill was far from ground-breaking in his discussions of other societies. His liberal position on women was hardly matched by a similarly open-minded stance on British colonialism. Others have noted his failure to extend the idea of liberty to non-European societies. As Edward Said (1979: 14) has pointed out, Mill not only "was extraordinarily well aware of the fact of empire," he was implicated in it on account of his employment by the East India Company.[13] Mill followed his predecessors in referring to other 'races' and peoples "in poor and backward societies, as in the East" (1994 [1848]) 76), similarly describing them as barbarous and savage, though—like Smith—his statements were often qualified. In the end, however, Mill did not draw a parallel between the subjection of women and that of other (non-European) societies. I call this pattern the *Mill syndrome*. Today, interestingly, this pattern is observable in Feminist economics discourse. Feminists have exposed androcentric bias in the discipline of economics, but many remain largely oblivious to, or silent on, the parallel prejudice by which other societies are marked as 'underdeveloped' and, in effect, are culturally devalued (see Chapter 8 in this book).

The above outline illustrates the partial and tangential treatment of culture in CPE, namely, a lack of recognition of culture at the level of holistic implications for economic phenomena.[14] The common anthropological meaning of culture—an entire way of life—was present, but too much emphasis on Nature did not allow a concept of culture, as a human creation causally integral to economic action, to emerge. This appears to be the case even in J. S. Mill's writings, which embody the greatest awareness of the cultural construction of identity and status. The tangential place of culture is reflected in that Mill based his objection to the unequal treatment of women on the undesirable consequences for the general progress of civilization, not on a particular detriment to the functioning of markets or national economies.

An argument could be made that in those formative years, the disciplinary imperative was to define 'the economic' as a subject of inquiry, and therefore the role of society at large had to be muted. This is a legitimate argument, but only up to a point because by this logic the role of culture need never be entertained. Craufurd Goodwin (2006) has suggested that the search for scientific status and universal laws of behavior by new disciplines such as Economics explains the absence of the word 'culture' from nineteenth-century economic thought. However, this absence does not seem to reflect a temporary analytical device for disciplinary development. Rather it seems to rest on an understanding of 'the economic' and 'the cultural' as two different ontological realms. That is to say, from the very beginning, political economy was substantively built on a dualistic conception of 'culture' and 'economy' (see Chapter 1).

The rise of Neoclassicism

The marginalist revolution of the 1870s represents the second major moment in the disciplinary formation of Economics, the first being the eighteenth-century birth of CPE. This section explores the place of culture at the beginnings of Neoclassical thought, and the cultural perspectives of some of its pioneers.[15] Early Neoclassicism shows a great deal of continuity from the classical era despite the impression of a deep philosophical break generated by the shift to a different theory of value. In the last section we saw that the treatment of culture in CPE was partial and tangential, that is, the classical authors did not see a significant causal link between 'cultural' and 'economic' phenomena. In the Neoclassical era, much of the same treatment continues, but eventually culture is completely erased from the theoretical space of economic analysis. In this section I dwell on the continuities between CPE and early Neoclassicism.

It is necessary to begin from Jeremy Bentham, given his foundational contribution to Neoclassical theory, and the fact that he has been blamed for having contributed to "the neglect of culture and the arts" in economic thought (Goodwin 2006: 45). Bentham's well-known utilitarian principle placed human motivation and welfare under the two impulses of pain and pleasure without discriminating between different types of activities. In the *Rationale of Reward*, he famously stated, "[p]rejudice apart, the game of push pin is of equal value with the arts and sciences of music and poetry" (1962: 253). Goodwin claims this equalizing treatment has had the effect of trivializing the arts in the eyes of economists. But, Bentham's universal calculus of value sought to transcend culture altogether, his theory is decidedly *acultural*. In other words, the hedonistic principle discounts culture in its broadest sense as shared sensibilities, habits, and practices of a society or a group, not only as art and other expressions of creativity. Yet, Bentham was deeply aware of the social cultural origins of individual tastes, as is clear from his remark that "[i]t is only from custom and prejudice that, in matters of taste, we speak of false and true" (ibid.: 254). The purpose of his statement on poetry was merely to underscore the sovereignty of taste. As Chapter 3 in this book shows, Bentham's brutal subjectivism as a basis for value determination is not followed closely today in the field of Cultural Economics, where 'the arts' appear to occupy a higher status than 'popular' culture.

Utilitarian philosophy permitted the nineteenth-century shift from an objective theory of value (labor) to a subjective one (utility). This seemed to entail a radical departure from CPE in that the labor theory of value admits a place for social variables since it assumes a measurable—therefore, amenable to being broadly accepted—standard of valuation, i.e., labor. In contrast, for subjectivists, individual utility (presumed to be independent of any social influences) is the final arbiter of value. The labor theory of value, with its emphasis on production—instead of exchange—as a source of value, favored a materialist view, in which production depends on tangible inputs such as physical capital. The utility theory of value lays more emphasis on the ideal side of the ideal/material dualism, as private and abstract desires and wishes govern economic transactions. Despite this major difference, the marginalists' approach to culture remained in agreement with the classical pattern to the extent that they continued to draw on natural law philosophy, and only tangentially acknowledge social custom and habit. Only occasionally was a causal link drawn between culture, in a general anthropological sense, and economic phenomena, and this occurred on the periphery of analysis (Menger 1950 [1871]; Marshall 1938 [1890]).

As some prominent economists have argued, utilitarian economics remained within the epistemic domain of natural law philosophy. Thorstein Veblen (1898: 378) claimed that natural law was the "ultimate term" in the Neoclassical attempt to systematize economic knowledge, while Joseph Schumpeter declared "utilitarianism was nothing but another natural-law system" (1954: 132).[16] A cursory look at the writings of William Stanley Jevons, Carl Menger, and John Bates Clark reveals the residue of this philosophy in Neoclassicism.

In his *Theory of Political Economy*, Jevons' discussion of economics and ethics, and his multiple references to language, family, friends, and honor reveal some attention to the social context, which repeats the classical pattern of noting elements of culture without mention of a unifying whole. His use of the term "customary gratification" (1965a [1871]: 25) in describing potential conflicts between desire and duty indicates a realization that taste is not free from social obligation and habit. Yet, Jevons held on to the idea of 'nature' as the force behind human action. He thought Bentham's words (that nature "has placed mankind under the governance of two sovereign masters— *pain* and *pleasure*") were "too full of truth to be mitted" (ibid.: 24). Similarly, Menger (1950 [1871]: 74) argued that consumption and production take place "within the limits set by natural laws"—individual actions exhibit "conformity to definite laws of phenomena that condition the outcome of the economic activity of men [that] are entirely independent of the human will" (ibid.: 48) rather than the result of social forces. More than twenty years later, J.B. Clark claimed that the distribution of wealth was explained by "a deep acting natural law at work amid the confusing struggles of the labor market" (1956 [1899]: 2).

The continuity between CPE and Neoclassical economic thought is further embodied in the marginalists' implicit references to culture in two related senses: first, as something that distances humans from nature, and Europeans from other peoples; and second, as custom and traditions. As in CPE, the first meaning was often wrapped up in the term civilization. Goodwin suggests that the marginalists' own social background and value judgments were transparent, for example, in Menger's references to "pagan people" and "those at lower levels of civilization" (Goodwin 2006: 57). Echoing Smith, Menger (1950) frequently referred to savagery in such places as Australia, and drew comparisons between civilized and barbarian countries. He used the word 'civilization' to mean progress, which he associated with the accumulation of goods. Jevons seems exceptional among his peers in spelling out the word 'culture' in the sense of refinement. In *The Methods of Social Reform*, he stated: "This want of *culture* greatly arises from the fact that the amusements of the masses, instead of being cultivated, and multiplied, and refined, have been frowned upon and condemned, and eventually suppressed, by a dominant aristocracy" (Jevons 1965b [1883]: 6; emphasis added). In this passage, which he made as a public policy advocate, culture refers to the arts—the embodiment of refinement and hence distance from nature. According to him, culture, whether in the shape of music or museums, had a civilizing effect (Goodwin 2006).

The meaning of culture as a group's shared practices and sensibilities can also be found—mostly in implicit form—in some texts of this period. In *Principles of Economics*, Menger thought "custom and practice" were the key factors in establishing a monetary exchange economy. In his judgment, "[t]he force of custom is so strong that the ability of a metal used as money to continue in this role is assured even when men are not directly aware of its character as an industrial metal" (1950: 320). This might be the first instance where culture, as social practices and tradition, not as agricultural cultivation, enters in direct causality with an economic phenomenon, in this case, money. Menger's discussion of the role of custom and convention in the emergence and functioning of money is so firm that some today claim him to be the original founder of institutional economics, instead of Veblen (Schotter 1981; Langlois 1986; see also Chapter 5 in this book).

Alfred Marshall was quite explicit in suggesting a significant correlation between culture—as beliefs and a way of life—and economic conditions, though this also remained tangential to his main contribution. The consideration he gave to cultural factors is revealed in the first appendix to *Principles of Economics* (1938), in which he described the rise of the industrial economy in England. He suggested this process was facilitated by the Reformation. According to him:

> The natural gravity and intrepidity of the stern races that had settled on the shores of England inclined them to embrace the doctrines of the Reformation; and these reacted on their habits of life, and gave a tone to their industry. Man was, as it were, ushered straight into the presence of his Creator, with no human intermediary; and now for the first time large numbers of rude and *uncultured* people yearned towards the mysteries of absolute spiritual freedom. The isolation of each person's religious responsibility from that of his fellows, rightly understood, was a necessary condition for the highest spiritual progress.
>
> (ibid.: 742; emphasis added)

Here, the word 'uncultured' overtly refers to lack of refinement of manners, senses, and intellect. He went on to state that through this "isolation of each person's religious responsibility," the Reformation sanctioned the idea of "individuality" which was a necessary quality for "the next stage upwards" (ibid.: 743), namely, growth of the industrial economy. The general implication is that religious beliefs had some hand in economic development. He therefore concluded that: "England's industrial and commercial characteristics were intensified by the fact that many of those who had adopted the new doctrines in other countries sought on her shores a safe asylum from religious persecution" (ibid.: 743). Thus Marshall seems to argue that the adoption of Protestantism—the new doctrine—was a significant factor in England's industrial and commercial success. To that extent, one could claim, Marshall anticipated Max Weber's (1958 [1930]) well-known thesis, but he did not dwell on this idea long enough to allow a more extended evaluation.

The upshot is that early Neoclassicists had more in common with the classical authors than markets and self-interest. Their treatment of culture was similarly partial and tangential. The concept was invoked most commonly to denote the arts and elevation of the human senses and intellect. Early Neoclassicists showed awareness of the relevance of custom and traditions in a similar manner to the classical authors. However, their discussions of culture in all the above-mentioned examples did not establish a significant causal relationship to economic activity in production, exchange, or growth. The major exceptions were Menger's view of money and Marshall's elementary connection between religious beliefs and economic development in Britain. However, these were only hints rather than a developed theory. The combination of the subjective value theory and residual adherence to natural law philosophy ensured the omission of an anthropological idea of culture from this period's economic analyses, even against the backdrop of considerable appreciation by utilitarian economists of the social dimensions of individual action.

Robinson Crusoe and the double erasure of culture

Apart from the few instances enumerated in the previous section, early Neoclassical economists largely avoided the concept of culture. In this section I argue this avoidance was facilitated by a literary device that made it rhetorically possible to adopt a substantively acultural economic model, without resort to the ambiguous and problematic idea of 'nature.' This device was Daniel Defoe's eighteenth-century tale, *Robinson Crusoe*. The novel holds a special pedagogical place in Economics, being commonly used in textbooks to illustrate the iconic 'economic man.'[17]

In the celebrated novel, an English sailor is shipwrecked and isolated on a remote island for more than 20 years. During this time he manages to build a 'civilization' on the new land, before he is eventually rescued and returned to England (Defoe 1993 [1719]). Economists have used this tale as a case study in economic behavior since the early days of CPE (Zein-Elabdin 2011). According to Michael

White (1982), heavy reliance on the novel as a pedagogical tool did not surface until the late nineteenth-century turn to the subjective theory of value. All major theorists of this period—Jevons (1965a), Menger (1950), Marshall (1938), and Clark (1956)—drew on the figure of the shipwrecked sailor to personify utility maximization and gains from trade, among other key principles. Several authors (White 1982; Grapard 1995; Hewitson 1999) have commented on this use of Crusoe, focusing mainly on the assumption of complete autonomy on the island, the novel's racial colonialist undertones, and the absence of women in the narrative. What has not been explored so far is the role the novel has played in framing the place of culture in Neoclassical economics, which is characterized by multiple levels of *erasure*, that is, removal from the space of economic knowledge.

I would argue that Crusoe made it possible to erase culture—in the sense of a common social frame of reference that shapes economic action and knowledge—from economic theory since his actions could be represented as the timeless responses of any human in the absence of 'civilization.' Of course, these actions could be also interpreted as displaying the 'nature' of humankind. However, this interpretation somehow does not arise because the figure of Crusoe *intervenes* such that 'nature' need not be invoked. Crusoe's ability to establish a 'civilized' human presence on the island provides a step away from nature.[18] Yet at the same time, being isolated on an island removes the need to speak of belonging to any particular culture. Thus, for instance, in the process of developing the basic principles of marginalist theory, Menger moved from explicit references to "natural laws" (1950: 74), which occur earlier in his book, to summarizing his entire theoretical framework by appeal to Crusoe, "an isolated economizing individual" motivated solely by satisfaction of his needs (ibid.: 134). The transformation in representation is quite noticeable in the way Menger's language migrated from nature to the individual human agent, describing him as "our Crusoe."

The figure of Robinson Crusoe enabled a shift away from Nature, while keeping culture, as a potential alternative explanation, at bay. But, this is not all. Defoe's novel helped in the occlusion of culture from discussions of economic phenomena, while at the same time it instituted the superiority of a particular culture. This is a quintessential example of the *double erasure* of culture in Economics, namely, the theoretical occlusion of cultures considered uncivilized or 'underdeveloped,' and at the same time the occlusion of the fact that economic analysis itself is culturally circumscribed (Zein-Elabdin 2004). The novel itself is commonly taken as a blueprint for European modernity, presenting the life that Crusoe (re)creates on the island as an ideal of modern European culture: individualist, autonomous, prudent, Christian, and—in this case—English-speaking. It is a culture so familiar to leading economists that in both classical and contemporary textbooks the story is never told, but only cryptic and quick references to it are given (Zein-Elabdin 2011). Familiarity with this canon of English literature is taken for granted. Indeed, the untold story itself becomes part of the taken-for-granted cultural core of Neoclassical economics.

Thus, *Robinson Crusoe* made possible two things at once: (1) the shift away from explicit reliance on natural law; and (2) the inscription of an idealized modern

European culture as the prototype of economic reason and action. Accordingly, no reference to culture needs to be made at all. I do not claim that the marginalists consciously deployed Crusoe with this effect in mind. Nonetheless, this does not negate the effectivity of the narrative as a rhetorical device in the erasure of culture from the dominant discourse of economics.

Conclusion

The treatment of culture by classical political economists of the liberal tradition was *partial* and *tangential*. Most were well aware of the social character of human life, and the influence of custom, habits, and education. However, they did not see a causal link between 'culture' and 'economy.' For the most part, they perceived economic activity to take place under the direction of natural laws, a perception that persisted into the early Neoclassical era. Although classical economists were aware of different peoples and world regions, this awareness did not translate into a self-critical reflection on their own cultural background. Smith, Ricardo, and J.S. Mill did not employ the term culture in the sense of a shared body of traditions and social norms since they were speaking within the context of their taken-for-granted world—eighteenth- to nineteenth-century middle-class Britain, and Europe's industrial modernity more broadly.

As we will see in later chapters, this path became the given cultural core of the twentieth-century discourse of economic development. In classical political economy, the epitome of the civilized world was England, the backward was other regions of Europe, and, at a great distance, was the rest of the globe, home of the savage and uncivilized. In contemporary Economics, the language has changed but the hierarchy persists, with some modification. The rest of Europe and its cultural extensions worldwide (the USA, Canada, Australia) have joined England on the pedestal of development (civilization), with Japan admitted later on. The territories beyond are now the underdeveloped, instead of barbarous or uncivilized.

The pioneers of Neoclassicism spoke occasionally of culture as different expressions of creativity. Their awareness of its meaning as a way of life showed little deviation from the pattern seen in classical thought. Most prominent Neoclassicists spoke of custom and habits without using the term culture, and referred to uncivilized nations and peoples outside of Europe. Neoclassical theory began in natural law philosophy, then shifted away from it with the rhetorical help of Daniel Defoe's *Robinson Crusoe*, which made possible the adoption of a universal—acultural—standard of valuation without having to resort to either 'nature' or 'culture.' The framing of Crusoe as a universal figure accomplished the double erasure of culture in Neoclassical economics.

The rise of Neoclassicism coincided with the emergence of Anthropology as a distinct field of inquiry, which was prompted by the late nineteenth-century European imperialist expansion and the need to subdue and manage colonial subjects worldwide. E.B. Tylor's book *Primitive Culture* as well as Jevons' and Menger's texts referred to earlier were all published in the same year, 1871 (Tylor 1883 [1871]). The contemporaneous rise of Anthropology and Neoclassical economics contained two counter-developments: culture was being erased from the subject matter of Economics at the very historical moment in which a new field of inquiry devoted to the study of culture was being launched. Economists offered a universal model of behavior while anthropologists were revealing cultural differences around the globe.

Notes

1 The concept of rationality—economic or otherwise—has been the subject of debates and critiques for a very long time. For some examples, see Mitchell (1910), Mini (1974), Sen (1977, 1987), Pujol (1992), Hodgson (1993), Ferber and Nelson (1993, 2003), and Maseland (2008). Polanyi (1957) and Weber (1961) locate the historical origins of instrumental rationalism in the rise of the market society in Western Europe. Enlightenment philosophy replaced the ancient meaning of rationality as proportion (*ratio*) with the notion of deliberative instrumentality, which acquired the quantitative character Weber described as formal rationality. See Wilk (1996), for struggles with the concept of rationality in Anthropology. For discussions of historicism in Economics, see Bury (1932), Nisbet (1969), and Zein-Elabdin (2004).

2 For discussions of cultural dimensions within CPE, see Hirschman (1982), Pujol (1992), Callari (2004), and Goodwin (2006), who include key figures not covered in this chapter. General histories of economic thought relied on here include Schumpeter (1954), Backhouse (1985), Rostow (1990), and Rima (2001). See Jackson (2009) for cultural critiques of classical economic thought.

3 Rostow's (1990) volume is most comprehensive in its focus on growth theories from pre-classical to twentieth-century contributions. Also see Furtado (1964), who gives a critical account of theories of development in the classical era.

4 See Jackson (2009) for a somewhat different view. He describes the relationship between culture and classical economists as "uneasy" (ibid.: 42).

5 See Stocking (1968) for a history of the concepts of culture and civilization. Also see Young (1995).

6 According to Schumpeter (1954: 107–142), in Greek philosophy, natural law was an ethico-legal concept referring to a narrow class of actions made necessary by Nature, though sometimes the idea was broadened without clarity. The Romans adopted the general meaning of a 'naturally just' order. In the hands of Thomas Aquinas, natural law also referred to socially necessary rules. Over time, the term natural law referred to all these meanings in addition to "dictates of reason," "the common good," and "primitive" conditions. Thus, Schumpeter stresses the confusing ambiguity and shifting meanings of the term. Here, I use the term to denote things that are ordained by some force or logic external to the parameters of human society.

7 Herder (1968) was deeply convinced of the equal worth of all human societies around the globe. He was highly critical of the idea that Europe had a superior culture to other world regions and peoples. It is important to bear in mind, however, that the notion of culture he used was often a synonym for society, and contained a strong sense of naturalism. See Williams (1983 [1976]) for a history of the term culture.

8 Smith ended this discussion by stating that whether the origin of exchange and the division of labor were the result of a natural propensity or the faculty of speech, this "belongs not to our present subject to enquire" (1976 [1776], vol. 1: 17). See Sen (1987) for a discussion of how economists have truncated Smith's ideas, particularly with respect to ethics.

9 Smith (2009 [1759]) did not support colonialism because, in his judgment, colonies were unjustified from a financial point of view. He also opposed the establishment of new colonies on moral grounds, objecting to what he considered a wrong and foolish enterprise. See

Bagchi (1996) on CPE and colonialism. It is worth recalling that the word 'culture' also means colonizing, namely, inhabiting a place (Williams 1983 [1976]).

10 For another example of orientalism in CPE, see Dimand (2004) on Nassau Senior's observations on 'the East,' which he recorded in a series of travel diaries.

11 This was stated in a letter to James Mill that Ricardo wrote in 1823 (Ricardo 1952: 387). Also see Mini (1974) on Ricardo's general ambivalence.

12 See Pujol (1992) on the sources of Mill's gender sensitivity, and on the general classical economic approach to women and women's social conditions. I am indebted to Kirsten Madden (pers. comm.) for alerting me to Pujol's discussion of the influence of J.S. Mill's women associates on his ideas concerning the status of women and his overall economic thought.

13 See Dimand (2004) on both John Stuart Mill and James Mill and the East India Company.

14 T.R. Malthus also displayed the classical treatment of culture—reliance on natural law, associating cultivation with agriculture, recognizing the weight of custom, and seeing the rest of the world as an inferior contrast to the level of civilization reached by modern Europe. For him, both in land productivity and sexual drive, Nature determined wealth. His discussions were speckled with references to customs, habits, and manners. To demonstrate his principle of population, he distinguished between "civilized nations" (1927 [1798]: 13), that is, different regions of modern Europe, and "less civilized" parts of the world, e.g., America, Africa, Persia, and Japan. He referred to "the progress of civilisation" (ibid.: 18), but did not use the word 'culture'. Boulding (1973: 47) claims Malthus had a "very strong" sense of the importance of culture.

15 This exploration leaves out many prominent thinkers—Walras, Böhm-Bawerk, among others. For more on early Neoclassical literature, see Schumpeter (1954), Backhouse (1985), Pujol (1992), and Rima (2001). Schumpeter (1954) reviews the influence of "neighboring fields," including Anthropology, on Economics during 1870 to 1914. See Callari (2004) on the factors behind the turn to subjectivism in Economics, which he sees at least in part, to be the result of the late nineteenth-century European imperial expansion and 'discovery' of non-European peoples worldwide.

16 Veblen (1898) especially targeted the language of naturalism in Marshall's work, and claimed that adherence to natural law philosophy was the reason why Economics could not be considered an evolutionary science.

17 The discussion in this section draws on a previous paper (Zein-Elabdin 2011), in which I commented on the novel from the point of view of a different cultural context. See Said (1993) on the political service of *Robinson Crusoe* and literature generally to modern Europe's imperialist expansion and construction of its own identity.

18 The civilization Crusoe builds on the island includes the production of simple and more sophisticated tools (table, chair, clothes, candles, a variety of food items), education (teaching language and religion to his slave companion, Friday), establishing property, and eventually marriage and family for the other inhabitants of his colony.

References

Adelman, Irma (1961) *Theories of Economic Growth and Development*, Stanford, CA: Stanford University Press.

Backhouse, Roger (1985) *A History of Modern Economic Analysis*, Oxford: Basil Blackwell.

Bagchi, Amiya Kumar (1996) "Colonialism in Classical Political Economy: Analysis, Epistemological Broadening and Mystification," *Studies in History*, 12 (1): 105–136.

Bentham, Jeremy (1962) *The Works of Jeremy Bentham*, vol. 2, ed. John Bowring, New York: Russell and Russell.

Boulding, Kenneth E. (1973) "Toward the Development of a Cultural Economics," in Louis Schneider and Charles Bonjean (eds.) *The Idea of Culture in the Social Sciences*, Cambridge, MA: Cambridge University Press, 47–64.

Bury, J.B. (1932) *The Idea of Progress: An Inquiry into Its Origin and Growth*, New York: The Macmillan Company.

Callari, Antonio (2004) "Economics and the Postcolonial Other," in E. Zein-Elabdin and S. Charusheela (eds.) *Postcolonialism Meets Economics*, London: Routledge, 113–129.

Clark, John Bates (1956 [1899]) *The Distribution of Wealth: A Theory of Wages, Interest and Profits*, New York: Kelley and Millman.

Colander, David (2000) "The Death of Neoclassical Economics," *Journal of the History of Economic Thought*, 22 (2): 127–143.

Defoe, Daniel (1993 [1719]) *Robinson Crusoe*, New York: Wordsworth Editions.

Dimand, Robert W. (2004) "Classical Political Economy and Orientalism: Nassau Senior's Eastern Tours," in E. Zein-Elabdin and S. Charusheela (eds.) *Postcolonialism Meets Economics*, London: Routledge, 73–90.

Ferber, Marianne A. and Julie A. Nelson (eds.) (1993) *Beyond Economic Man: Feminist Theory and Economics*, Chicago: University of Chicago Press.

—— (eds.) (2003) *Feminist Economics Today: Beyond Economic Man*, Chicago: University of Chicago Press.

Fukuda-Parr, Sakiko and A.K. Shiva Kumar (eds.) (2003) *Readings in Human Development: Concepts, Measures and Policies for a Development Paradigm*, New Delhi: Oxford University Press.

Furtado, Celso (1964) *Development and Underdevelopment*, Berkeley, CA: University of California Press.

Goodwin, Craufurd (2006) "Art and Culture in the History of Economic Thought," in V. Ginsburgh and D. Throsby (eds.) *Handbook of the Economics of Art and Culture*, Amsterdam: Elsevier North-Holland, 25–68.

Grapard, Ulla (1995) "Robinson Crusoe: The Quintessential Economic Man?" *Feminist Economics* 1 (1): 33–52.

Guiso, Luigi, Paola Sapienza, and Luigi Zingales (2006) "Does Culture Affect Economic Outcomes?" *Journal of Economic Perspectives*, 20 (2): 23–48.

Herder, Johann Gottfried von (1968) *Reflections on the Philosophy of the History of Mankind*, Chicago: University of Chicago Press.

Hewitson, Gillian J. (1999) *Feminist Economics: Interrogating the Masculinity of Rational Economic Man*, Northampton, MA: Edward Elgar Publishing.

Hirschman, Albert O. (1982) "Rival Interpretations of Market Society: Civilizing, Destructive or Feeble?" *Journal of Economic Literature*, 20 (4): 1463–1484.

Hodgson, Geoffrey M. (ed.) (1993) *The Economics of Institutions*, Aldershot: Edward Elgar Publishing.

Jackson, William A. (2009) *Economics, Culture and Social Theory*, Cheltenham: Edward Elgar.

Jevons, W. Stanley (1965a [1871]) *The Theory of Political Economy*, New York: Augustus M. Kelley.

—— (1965b [1883]) *Methods of Social Reform*, London: Macmillan and Company.

Langlois, Richard N. (ed.) (1986) *Economics as a Process: Essays in the New Institutional Economics*, Cambridge: Cambridge University Press.

Malthus, T.R. (1927 [1798]) *An Essay on Population*, vol. 1, London: J. M. Dent & Sons.

Marshall, Alfred (1938 [1890]) *Principles of Economics: An Introductory Volume*, London: Macmillan & Co.

Maseland, Robbert (2008) "Taking Economics to Bed: About the Pitfalls and Possibilities of Cultural Economics," in Wolfram Elsner and Hardy Hanappi (eds.) *Varieties of Capitalism and New Institutional Deals: Regulation, Welfare and the New Economy*, Cheltenham: Edward Elgar, 299–321.

Menger, Carl (1950 [1871]) *Principles of Economics*, trans. and ed. James Dingwall and Bert F. Hoselitz, Glencoe, IL: The Free Press.

Mill, John Stuart (1994 [1848]) *Principles of Political Economy, and Chapters on Socialism*, New York: Oxford University Press.

—— (1970 [1869]) *The Subjection of Women*, New York: Source Book Press.

Mini, Piero V. (1974) *Philosophy and Economics: The Origins and Development of Economic Theory*, Gainesville, FL: University of Florida Press.

Mitchell, Wesley C. (1910) "The Rationality of Economic Activity, I-II," *Journal of Political Economy*, 18 (3): 197–216.

Nisbet, Robert A. (1969) *Social Change and History: Aspects of the Western Theory of Development*, London: Oxford University Press.

Nussbaum, Martha C. (1995) "Human Capabilities, Female Human Beings," in Martha Nussbaum and Jonathan Glover (eds.) *Women, Culture and Development: A Study of Human Capabilities*, Oxford: Clarendon Press, 61–104.

Polanyi, Karl (1957 [1944]) *The Great Transformation*, Boston: Beacon Press.

Pujol, Michèle A. (1992) *Feminism and Anti-Feminism in Early Economic Thought*, Aldershot: Edward Elgar.

Ricardo, David (1948 [1817]) *Principles of Political Economy and Taxation*, London: J. M. Dent & Sons.

—— (1952) *The Works and Correspondence of David Ricardo*, vol. IX, ed. Piero Sraffa and Maurice Dobb, Cambridge: Cambridge University Press.

Rima, Ingrid Hahne (2001) *Development of Economic Analysis*, London: Routledge.

Rostow, W. W. (1990) *Theorists of Economic Growth from David Hume to the Present: With a Perspective on the Next Century*, Oxford: Oxford University Press.

Said, Edward W. (1979) *Orientalism*, New York: Vintage Books.

—— (1993) *Culture and Imperialism*, New York: Vintage Books.

Schotter, Andrew (1981) *The Economic Theory of Social Institutions*, Cambridge: Cambridge University Press.

Schumpeter, Joseph A. (1954) *History of Economic Analysis*, New York: Oxford University Press.

Sen, Amartya K. (1977) "Rational Fools: A Critique of the Behavioural Foundations of Economic Theory," *Philosophy and Public Affairs*, 6 (4): 317–344.

—— (1987) *On Ethics and Economics*, Oxford: Blackwell.

Smith, Adam (2009 [1759]) *The Theory of Moral Sentiments*, ed. Ryan Patrick Hanley, New York: Penguin Books.

—— (1978 [1762]) *Lectures on Jurisprudence*, ed. R.L. Meek, D.D. Raphael, and P.G. Stein, New York: Oxford University Press.

—— (1976 [1776]) *An Inquiry into the Nature and Causes of the Wealth of Nations*, ed. Edwin Cannan, Chicago: University of Chicago Press.

Stocking, George W. Jr. (1968) *Race, Culture, and Evolution: Essays in the History of Anthropology*, Chicago: University of Chicago Press.

Tylor, Edward Burnett (1883 [1871]) *Primitive Culture: Researches into the Development of Mythology, Philosophy, Religion, Language, Art and Custom*, New York: Henry Holt and Company.

Veblen, Thorstein (1898) "Why Is Economics Not an Evolutionary Science?" *Quarterly Journal of Economics*, 12 (2): 373–397.

Weber, Max (1958 [1930]) *The Protestant Ethic and the Spirit of Capitalism*, New York: Charles Scribner's Sons.

—— (1961) *General Economic History*, New York: Oxford University Press.

White, Michael V. (1982) "Reading and Rewriting: The Production of an Economic Robinson Crusoe," *Southern Review Australia*, 15 (2): 115–142.

Wilk, Richard (1996) *Economies and Cultures: Foundations of Economic Anthropology*, Boulder, CO: Westview Press.

Williams, Raymond (1983 [1976]) *Keywords: A Vocabulary of Culture and Society*, New York: Oxford University Press.

Young, Robert (1995) *Colonial Desire: Hybridity in Theory, Culture and Race*, London: Routledge.

Zein-Elabdin, Eiman O. (2004) "Articulating the Postcolonial (with Economics in Mind)," in E. Zein-Elabdin and S. Charusheela (eds.) *Postcolonialism Meets Economics*, London: Routledge, 21–39.

—— (2011) "How Does an African Student of Economics Make Sense of *Robinson Crusoe*?" in Ulla Grapard and Gillian Hewitson (eds.) *Robinson Crusoe's Economic Man: A Construction and Deconstruction*, London: Routledge, 215–231.

3 Neoclassical economics and culture

Is it necessary to modify the standard economic model in order to incorporate culture? The answer definitely is 'no.'

(Fernández 2008: 10)

Chapter 2 showed that during the nineteenth-century rise of Neoclassicism, as Anthropology was discovering 'culture' and cultural difference, economic marginalists were moving in the opposite direction by dismissing the influence of shared sensibilities, habits, and practices of a society—culture—on economic action and knowledge. Neoclassical economics offered individual utility maximization as a universal truth of human behavior; and the rhetorical device of *Robinson Crusoe* paved the way for the theoretical *erasure* of culture, that is, removing it from the space of economic knowledge.

In this chapter, I show that this state of affairs persisted for most of the twentieth century as most economists went on to assume any implications of cultural factors for economic behavior were at best negligible. Culture was bracketed away. George Stigler and Gary Becker finally formalized this general avoidance into an explicit guiding principle, which suggested:

On the traditional view, an explanation of economic phenomena that reaches a difference in tastes between people or times is the terminus of the argument: the problem is abandoned *at this point* to whoever studies and explains tastes (psychologists? anthropologists? phrenologists? sociobiologists?). On our preferred interpretation, one never reaches this impasse: the economist continues to search for differences in prices or incomes to explain any differences or changes in behavior.

(1977: 76)

Stigler and Becker instructed economists "not to abandon opaque and complicated problems" (ibid.: 89–90) in the hope that other behavioral sciences would one day supply the answers. This advice has, in effect, given economists license to defer consideration of the potential significance of culture for economic phenomena indefinitely.

The chapter shows that in the past three decades, the opening up of Economics to the 'cultural turn' in the humanities and social sciences has rendered adherence to the Stigler–Becker doctrine untenable for many (see Cowen 1989; Peacock 1992). Today, many admit that "modern neoclassical economics has, until recently, ignored the potential role of culture in explaining variation in economic outcomes" (Fernández 2008: 1). As a result, a vigorous effort to account for this role has begun across different fields, ranging from decision-making (Fershtman and Weiss 1993), international trade (Acheson and Maule 1999), to economic history (North 1990), to macroeconomic growth and development (Dieckmann 1996).

Currently, the volume of Neoclassical treatments of culture spans three overlapping research programs. The first is the Preferences Approach (PA), in which culture is theorized as a single variable in the preference function of an individual agent. The second program, Cultural Economics (CE), contains two strands: one takes a *'culture industry'* view by applying microeconomic theory to 'the arts' and other works of creativity. The other, which I call the *'cultural value'* view, embraces an anthropological meaning of culture as a way of life—including art— and attempts to understand the difference and relationship between economic and cultural value. This strand raises some legitimate questions about the universal applicability of Neoclassical theory (see Blaug 2001; Ginsburgh and Throsby 2006), but has not yet proposed a theoretical alternative. The third research program, the New Institutional Economics (NIE) represents cultural values and traditions as a general constraint on economic 'rationality.' In this chapter, I review the first two programs; NIE is discussed in Chapter 5.

This broad review of Neoclassicism warrants two observations. First, the primary goal of most authors has been to estimate the 'effect' of culture on economic outcomes (e.g., Guiso *et al.* 2006) within the paradigmatic context of a price system. In consequence, their analyses begin and end with the optimizing individual intact. This is clearly reflected in Raquel Fernández's statement that "incorporating culture" requires no modification to the standard model of individual preferences → choice → market equilibrium. It is not entirely clear what 'incorporating' culture means in this exercise, but I would argue that it is not possible to adequately understand the role of culture while claiming a universal mode of behavior—an innate human tendency—unless one assumes infinite cultural homogeneity. At best, this claim relegates culture to the margins such that 'normal' behavior is identified with utility-maximizing action, culture only gives rise to different 'tastes'—as in whether to use chopsticks or a knife and fork. When the very meaning of economic normality is so limited, there is effectively no theoretical space to 'incorporate' culture.[1]

Second, as I suggested in Chapter 1, the majority of economic thought is rooted in *dualistic ontology*, that is, a conception of 'reality' in a binary framework that leaves little to no conceptual room for cultural complexity and hybrid economic phenomena (see Chapter 9). This ontology is most foundationally embodied in the theoretical separation between 'culture' and 'economy' as two distinct realms— culture deals with the mental and symbolic, while economy signifies subsistence, provisioning, and resource management. This separation broadly follows from the old dualism of ideal/material, which is ultimately rooted in a more general existential dichotomy of desire/limits (see Chapter 1). The *paradigmatic dualism* of preferences/constraints manifests this dualistic ontology. This chapter shows that Neoclassical treatments of culture are dualistic in the same complex sense. The culture/economy dichotomy surfaces in two perceptions: first, that culture operates as an external force on existing economic reason and action (e.g., Guiso *et al.* 2006); and second, that there is a deep ontological and epistemological divide between 'culture' and 'economics' (e.g., Throsby 2001).

The first part of the chapter gives an overview of the Preferences Approach, as expressed in the work of Gary Becker, and samples some analyses of culture deriving from his thought. The second part reviews the field of Cultural Economics. Although PA and CE appear to be two different species, they are both rooted in dualism. This is true not equally or uniformly in every model or argument, but as the backdrop of most analyses. Following the panoramic method of this book, my discussion is not particularly concerned with the details of each text, including technical issues of modeling or measurement, as integral to the picture as these are. Instead, I highlight conceptual interpretations of culture and their philosophical premises, hoping that the relatively high level of generality does not get in the way of clarity (see Appendix II for a sample of interpretations of culture by economists).

Culture in Neoclassical theory

Neoclassical economics, though an increasingly contested term (see Colander 2000), captures most varieties of thought that perceive human behavior to be a reflection of individual-centered, instrumentally rational impulses, and consider an economy to be an aggregate of these impulses. One may differentiate between the Chicago and the Virginia Schools, or ponder where to place the Austrian School perspective. But, to different degrees, the three share this vision, which may be identified narrowly with "maximizing behavior, market equilibrium, and stable preferences" (Becker 1976: 5), or, more broadly, with "an appreciation of systematic market forces" (Boettke 1996: 35). This vision defines the philosophical boundary between Chicago, Virginia, and the Austrian Schools, on one hand, and Marxian and Veblenian Institutionalist approaches, on the other.[2] In this chapter, I take the Chicago tradition to represent Neoclassical thought because of its disciplinary influence, and the leading role of Chicago economists—most notably, B.F. Hoselitz (1952)—in establishing the journal *Economic Development and Cultural Change*, where a considerable literature on culture and development is published (see Appendices I and III). I focus on theoretical attempts to admit culture in the behavioral model.

The early twentieth century witnessed consolidation of the definition of economics as a science of scarcity and choice (Robbins 1946 [1932]), which explicitly placed the existential struggle between desire and limits at the heart of the economic problem.[3] Roger Backhouse (1985: 275) refers to the 1930s as a "turning point" toward abstraction in the discipline. This turn contributed to what

Amartya Sen (1987) has called a movement in approach from ethics to engineering. This approach was further cemented by ruling out interpersonal comparisons, and dispensing with the need for realism in economic analysis (Friedman 1953). Any interest in the social context of economic phenomena was channeled to the discourse of international development, which became the only permissible space for entertaining culture in an anthropological sense (see de Jong 2009). The launching of *Economic Development and Cultural Change* and the research center bearing the same name at the University of Chicago in the early 1950s institutionalized the isolation of culture discussions from the general stream of Neoclassical economics.

From the 1960s onward, one begins to see some intermittent discussions of culture as it is embodied in 'the arts' (Baumol and Bowen 1966). Culture also appeared periodically in discussions of the state of African Americans in the US economy (Dixon 1970, also see Chapter 1 in this book). However, both types of writings were very limited in scope and frequency. For the most part, the term culture was absent from the lexicon of most economists. Altogether, from the beginning of the twentieth century up to 1970, the words culture or cultural appeared in the titles of less than 10 books and journal articles in Economics, all written by Institutionalists (see Appendix I for a chronological list).

The first work to break this pattern was Tibor Scitovsky's book *The Joyless Economy* (1976), which was exceptional because of its broad treatment of culture, defining it as "the preliminary information we must have to enjoy the processing of further information" (ibid.: 226). In the essay "Our Disdain for Culture," he criticized "the American way of life" for harboring "an anti-cultural bias" (ibid.: 236). This, according to him, stemmed from the Puritan tradition's emphasis on work, rational economizing, and material comfort rather than mental stimulation. Drawing a correlation between religious beliefs and economic behavior is not new. As I discussed in Chapter 2, Alfred Marshall (1938 [1890]) had suggested that Protestantism played a positive role in England's industrial growth, but this line of thought did not occupy any significant place in marginalist economics. Max Weber's (1958 [1930]) thesis about capitalism and Protestant teachings is well known. Scitovsky extended the argument to American society, except he claimed that the general influence of religious beliefs was detrimental in that Americans ignored knowledge and "novelty" (1976: 11).[4] This is a debatable claim, but, more to the point, Scitovsky's broad treatment of culture remained an aberration for quite some time as the Stigler–Becker doctrine dominated Neoclassical thought.

The Preferences Approach: Becker's way

In this approach, culture enters as an influence on individuals' desire for tangible or intangible consumables. Thus, it is placed exclusively in the realm of psychic perception, which reflects an idealist perspective. This approach is associated with Gary Becker, who presents a rather complicated figure to examine in this regard. Becker played a key role in the disavowal of culture in economic analysis by claiming that all facets of human life may be explained by a universal principle of utility maximization (Becker 1976, 1981; Stigler and Becker 1977). Yet, in this same move, he also helped bring into the scope of economic inquiry topics of such high cultural content as marriage and family. His influential contribution legitimated the inclusion of culture in Neoclassical discussions, and inspired much of the current literature on the subject. This paradoxical role is reflected in Becker's own work, which spans an earlier phase in which cultural elements are only implicitly present—for example, as a factor in racial discrimination—and a later one in which he explicitly defines culture.[5]

The highlight of the earlier phase is the influential paper "*De Gustibus non est Disputandum*" (Stigler and Becker 1977), in which the word 'culture' did not appear. The purpose of the paper was to mathematically demonstrate that "widespread and/or persistent human behavior can be explained by a generalized calculus of utility-maximizing behavior, without introducing the qualification 'tastes remaining the same'" (76). In the paper, tastes were defined as the "unchallengeable axioms of man's behavior" (ibid.), though the concept was never unpacked beyond this characterization. But, even this minimal reference is rendered irrelevant by the treatment of "tastes as stable over time and similar among people" (ibid.). The first part of this assumption, i.e., the stability of tastes, discounts the movement embodied in all cultures, albeit to different degrees. This is not my main concern here. It is the second part, the similarity of 'tastes' among people, which poses a problem from a cross-cultural standpoint as it presumes a single universal culture, and accordingly suggests culture need not be entertained at all. Despite criticisms of the assumption of identical tastes (e.g. Cowen 1989), generally, in the literature, tastes came to serve as a surrogate for all presumably cultural influences.

Stigler and Becker advised economists to continue "to search for differences in prices or incomes to explain any differences or changes in behavior" (1977: 76), offering this approach as a superior explanation of economic phenomena than J.S. Mill's "maxims and traditions" (ibid.: 81). In their words, these traditions are nothing but a reflection of "investment of time and other resources in the accumulation of knowledge about the environment, and of skills with which to cope with it" (ibid.: 82). Behavior, action, and cultural artifacts could all be expressed as economic variables—for instance, "the stock of music capital" (ibid.: 80). The use of music as an example underscores that even such an emotive aspect of life may be explained by choice theory. As Eckehard Rosenbaum (1999) has pointed out, the main flaw of this strategy is that it misses the cultural significance of consumption; in this example, music constitutes a generic 'good' like any other, with no symbolic dimension or culturally specific meaning.

Becker's earlier work contains some explicit references to culture. However, he takes it as data, for instance, in his analysis of discrimination (1976), or minimizes its role as he does with respect to marriage and family relations. In *Treatise on the Family* (1981), he envisioned that each family maximizes a utility function that includes the quantity and quality of children and other goods. His model of "cultural selection" (ibid.: 95) assumed each household imparts to its offspring a certain "family culture" (ibid.: 113), that is, an endowment of beliefs and skills, as well as genes. He claimed this is "a simple way to incorporate the influence of the culture, or social capital, of all families" (ibid.: 117).[6] Although he realized that families influence each other, this influence is construed only in terms of different attitudes about education or success. This treatment reveals that the theoretical erasure of culture could be accomplished not only by never mentioning the word, as in the Stigler and Becker paper, but also—perhaps more effectively—by suggesting that culture could be easily accounted for with no disruption to the existing conceptual framework.

In the later phase of Becker's work, the term 'culture' appears prominently, as exemplified in *Accounting for Tastes* (1996). Here, he gives a definition:

> Culture and traditions are shared values and preferences handed down from one generation to another through families, peer groups, ethnic groups, classes, and other groups ... Culture exercises a sizable influence over preferences and individual behavior, whereas behavior has only a slow return influence on culture. Differences in culture cause considerable differences in preferences over goods ...
>
> (1996: 16)

This marks a shift from the earlier phase in terms of the space assigned to culture. A good deal could be said about this statement, but three observations are most pertinent. First, values and traditions are 'handed down' from one generation to the next. This is a static view that was abandoned in Anthropology long ago. As Clifford Geertz (1973) has remarked, the days of thinking about culture in this way are past. Second, there is some ambiguity in that culture is defined as values and preferences; at the same time, it exerts influence over preferences. The relationship between the two is unclear. Third, Becker maintains the optimal choice assumption for all contexts. That is, cultural difference only impacts preferences over goods—chopsticks or knife and fork. Therefore, his shift toward a more substantial discussion of culture did not entail any theoretical adjustments or revisions to the core of the Neoclassical model.

Generally, in Becker's approach preferences remain exogenous, i.e., their specific origin and the process by which they are formed remain unexplained.[7] What he did not realize is that the idea of preferences, which is predicated upon optimizing choice, is itself culturally defined. Thus 'incorporating' culture while assuming infinite homogeneity of economic behavior engenders no significant analytical consequences. Fernández's conclusion that there is no need "to modify the standard economic model in order to incorporate culture" (2008: 10) is unavoidable if one follows Becker's way.[8]

Modeling culture

Neoclassical writings on the role of culture are quite varied, but they follow a common strategy of defining it as "differences in beliefs and preferences that vary systematically across groups of individuals" (ibid.: 2). For instance, Cordelia

Reimers (1985) analyzes differences in labor force participation rates among married women in different "ethnic sub-cultures" in the USA. Christopher D. Carroll *et al.* study immigrants in Canada to find out whether "cultural factors influence saving behavior" (1994: 698). Other authors have used game theory and experiments to investigate the economic significance of gender (Croson and Buchan 1999) and cultural differences across countries (Henrich 2000).[9] Most of these studies infer the impact of culture residually from differences that could not be attributed to any other variables. In this section, I outline three papers that derive from Becker's work to model the economic implications of social status (Fershtman and Weiss 1993), parenting (Bisin and Verdier 2001), and religious beliefs (Guiso *et al.* 2006).[10]

C. Fershtman and Y. Weiss (1993: 947) start from the premise that "cultural differences may have important economic consequences" and, accordingly, they construct a general equilibrium model of the relationship between social status—defined as "effective claim for social esteem" (ibid.: 948)—and economic performance. They do not attach a specific meaning to culture, but approximate it by attitudes toward social status, and the relative weight different societies place on the prestige of an occupation. According to the authors, these attitudes may 'translate' into different occupational preferences and wage rates, and hence could be measured using a compensating wage differences model in which status represents non-wage income. Occupational status is represented as a function of the average skill level and wage rate; workers derive utility from status just as they do from consumption. This representation is based on evidence from sociological literature where surveys between 1947 and 1963 revealed a hierarchy of occupations in the USA. The most highly regarded jobs included judges and physicians; janitorial services were ranked at the bottom of the status ladder.

Assuming a two-sector economy, in which firms maximize profits by hiring one or two types of workers, high and low skilled, Fershtman and Weiss predict that societies with relatively high demand for social esteem will exhibit a bigger wage gap between low and high status occupations—"the larger is the demand for status the larger is the wage gap" (ibid.: 946). In conjunction, aggregate output will be lower in these societies because of the inefficiency created when workers are not hired and compensated according to skill. These predictions indicate a "trade off between cultural attitudes and economic performance" (ibid.: 955). Therefore, Fershtman and Weiss conclude that cultural differences can play a "role in determining economic development" in a manner similar to the role differences in tastes play in deciding "individual performance" (ibid.: 957). They recognize potential causality in the opposite direction, i.e., that the prestige of an occupation may derive from higher monetary compensation, but they leave this to be explored by future collaborative research between Economics and Sociology.

In the second study, Alberto Bisin and Thierry Verdier (2001) model the transmission of "cultural traits" from one generation to the next. They do not directly define culture, but use the terms preferences, norms, and traits interchangeably. Preferences include such things as religious values and attitudes toward education. Traits are transmitted rationally by "cultural parents" (ibid.: 299)!, and acquired through direct socialization within the family (vertical transmission), or imitation from the wider society (oblique transmission). The transmission mechanism could take different forms: (1) exclusive family environment, where socialization depends on the degree of a parent's tolerance of noncompliance with the family's cultural norms; (2) a parent's instruction regarding proper behavior in society, namely, "do not talk to strangers" (ibid.: 309); and (3) picking up traits from non-family members, aka "it takes a village" (ibid.: 310). Depending on the particular situation, the two mechanisms may complement or substitute for one another. The study finds that, because of externalities, "too many resources are individually invested by parents to affect the preferences of their children" (ibid.: 300). The model—as Bisin and Verdier realize—leaves out important elements, including the surrounding economic environment, which limits their ability to capture more of the complexity and nuances of cultural interaction and change. Nonetheless, this is an interesting effort to inject some realism into modeling culture.[11]

The above contributions illustrate attempts to handle the theoretical question: in what way, or ways, does 'culture matter'? Most studies are also preoccupied with the empirical task of quantitatively measuring its economic impacts. Stephen Woodbury expresses the difficulty confronted in both endeavors. Commenting within the context of human capital studies, he suggests that attributing causality to 'culture':

> throws the framework into chaos by stressing the importance of an unob-served variable … The proper response to omitted variables is not to give them a collective name, like culture, especially when we believe there may be systematic relationships involved. Rather, a serious response in an empirical context is to improve measurements or methods of estimation.
>
> (1993: 259)[12]

In other words, he disputes the validity of 'culture' as a generalized explanatory variable. For him, the solution lies in disaggregating it into smaller components through better estimation methods to capture individual cause–effect patterns. Economists should thus concentrate on improving measurement techniques.

The third example of PA attempts to both model and measure cultural impacts. In the widely cited paper, "Does Culture Affect Economic Outcomes?" Luigi Guiso, Paola Sapienza, and Luigi Zingales define culture as "customary beliefs and values that ethnic, religious, and social groups transmit fairly unchanged from generation to generation" (2006: 23). They suggest culture may be observed in beliefs and preferences, reflected in such things as fertility, family size, or 'trust.' The authors propose a three-step procedure for estimating the economic 'effect' of culture: first, show the direct impact of culture on preferences; second, locate an association between these preferences and economic outcomes; and third, infer a causal link between culture and outcomes. In particular, the paper explores the effect of religion and ethnic background on trust and the consequent effect on entrepreneurship (measured by self-employment). Guiso and his collaborators are aware of the complex nature of factors such as religion. Nonetheless, they go on to estimate their effect based on data from the US General Social Survey and the World Values Survey.[13] The results indicate that "culture as defined by religion and ethnicity affects beliefs about trust" (Guiso *et al.* 2006: 35). For instance, "trusting others increases the probability of being self-employed by 1.3 percentage points" (ibid.: 36).

Guiso *et al.*'s paper is quite rich, giving a historical review that reaches back into Classical Political Economy treatments of culture, and invokes Weber, Gramsci, and Polanyi to build a background to their own effort. Nevertheless, the paper illustrates several difficulties common to the Preferences literature. Others have questioned the adequacy of data and statistical techniques to support clear conclusions about culture and economic behavior (Lipset 1993; Adkisson 2014). Here, I am more concerned with theoretical issues. First, ambiguities about the meaning of key variables and their relationships to one another abound. In this case, Guiso *et al.* begin by defining culture as "customary beliefs and values," and end up with culture and beliefs being distinct from one another. Trust seems to act as both a belief and a preference, which is inconsistent with their initial suggestion that beliefs affect preferences. Second, the interpretation of culture remains static, following Becker's definition stated earlier, but goes further by claiming it is "transmitted fairly unchanged," thereby assuming away the degree to which cultural change takes place. Third, the word 'affect' intimates that culture is external, operating on pre-existing forms of economic rationality and action.[14] This conception is a common symptom of a dualistic separation of economy from culture, where each is considered a distinct ontological realm.

To summarize, Neoclassical economics—at least in rhetoric—has joined the cultural turn of the late twentieth century, with a substantial volume of studies offering claims about culture. The literature contains interesting discussions and ideas. Unfortunately, the conceptual effort to explore the relevance of culture is minimal, engendering no substantive revisions to the doctrine. This is exemplified in Guiso *et al.*'s assumption that "each individual has one identity and maximizes the utility of this identity" (2006: 29). In effect, the maximizing individual is theoretically intact and situated outside of culture.

The field of cultural economics

The term 'cultural economics' has several meanings. Institutional economists have used it to underscore their emphasis on the cultural embeddedness of economic phenomena (Boulding 1973; Mayhew 1994). Guiso *et al.* (2006: 29) describe their method discussed in the previous section as "a new cultural economics," a term that Robert Maseland (2008) also claims for a more radical project to rethink both "the cultural" and "the economic." In this section, I outline CE, the sub-set of Neoclassical discourse that is articulated in two overlapping views.[15] The *culture industry* view represents standard applications of microeconomic theory to 'the arts' and other products of creativity, while the *cultural value* perspective adopts an anthropological meaning of culture, in which creativity constitutes one element of a society's way of life. In the latter view, authors struggle with how the value of 'cultural goods' is, or might be, determined beyond the strict confines of price theory. Despite some differences, the two views share a fundamental similarity, that is, they remain within the theoretical boundaries of preferences → choice → equilibrium, and adopt a dualistic conception of culture/economy.

According to Ruth Towse (1997), CE is simply a new name for economics of the arts, having evolved from studies spurred by the 1960s "cultural boom" in New York City. These studies began with William Baumol and William Bowen's (1966: 4) project "to explain the financial problems of the performing groups and to explore the implications of these problems for the future of arts in the United States." Baumol and Bowen examined issues of pricing, organization, and public funding. They did not make a point of defining culture. Their discussion touched on cultural background only when audience characteristics such as education or gender were being examined. Since then, cultural economics has expanded to include all works of creativity.

Early work in the field includes Lionel Robbins' (1997 [1971]) call for public support of threatened artistic ventures, reflecting his belief that the state should make available "examples of the highest standards of cultural achievement in visual arts, music, theatre, and literary production" (ibid.: 4). As to be expected from his classic view that economics is a "neutral" science (1946 [1932]: 147), Robbins saw his position regarding the arts as a matter of value judgment that could not be settled on the basis of economic theory. Economists could only elucidate the consequences of such judgment. Mark Blaug's volume *The Economics of Arts* (1976), which brought together several papers analyzing the arts as an applied microeconomics problem, completes these early explorations. Since then, the literature has grown dramatically (Hendon and Shanahan 1983; Hendon *et al.* 1984; Shaw *et al.* 1988; Towse and Abdul Khakee 1992). Alan Peacock and Ilde Rizzo (1994) suggest that dwindling state budgets, especially in Europe, have contributed to this growth.[16]

The 'culture industry' view

This perspective, which dominated the field's formative years, is concerned with the "economics of the performing visual and literary arts" (Blaug 2001: 123). Its analytical domain is categorized in several related areas: taste and taste formation (some in this area are critical of Stigler and Becker's assumptions about the stability and exogeneity of tastes); the demand for and supply of cultural goods (including the media); industrial organization of museums, theaters, non-profits; art markets; economic history of the arts; labor markets; Baumol's cost disease; valuation; and public goods problems (Hutter 1996; Towse 1997; Blaug 2001).[17] It is generally agreed that the field relies on a "loose neoclassicism" in the "Adam Smith sense of self-interested individual action constrained by costs, incomes and the norms of economic institutions" (Blaug 2001: 124).

Peacock and Rizzo define the purview of CE as "economics of the creative process in painting, sculpture, architecture, and music and the consequential presentation of works of arts by display or performance in museums and galleries, theatres and concert halls" (1994: ix). Their justification for this somewhat narrow focus is that there is enough complicated subject matter to address without broadening the scope of inquiry to the more general meaning of culture as shared beliefs and traditions. Instead of offering an explicit interpretation of culture, they chose to simply name cultural activities in order to avoid what they thought would be "an arid debate" about the meaning of culture (ibid.). Their implicit reference clearly associates it with artistic activity and output, which is consistent with usage in early Neoclassical writings (e.g., Jevons 1965 [1883]).

In the culture industry view, price theory is applied to the arts in much the same way it is employed in environmental economics or other fields.[18] Authors deal with typical microeconomic problems of pricing and trade (Towse and Abdul Khakee 1992), imperfect information, and regulation (Peacock and Rizzo 1994). Still, one encounters departures and debates because of the idiosyncrasies and politics of the 'culture industry.' The most pronounced departure concerns the principle of consumer sovereignty, and whether economists should advocate state support for the arts except on the basis of externalities and public goods arguments. Peacock (1992) perceives the role of cultural economists, at least in Britain, to be gatekeeping, i.e., providing the proper theoretical rationale for public policy. In clear departure from Jeremy Bentham's strict subjectivism (see Chapter 2 in this book), Peacock calls for public support of art markets—via consumer vouchers rather than provider subsidies—to encourage the cultivation of taste and interest in the arts. He recognizes the difficulty of determining "the optimal level of investment" in taste cultivation (ibid.: 11), but leaves unaddressed the issue of which cultural diversions to support: poetry or a game of push pin, as Bentham (1962) put it.

Bruno Frey (1994a) distinguishes between an "economic aspect" of, and an "economic approach" to art. The first perspective studies mundane, more institutional concerns of the industry, e.g., organizational set-up and financial details. The second perspective, the economic approach, is based on a rational-choice premise that consumer decisions with respect to art represent a logical outcome of their preferences and the constraints they face. He advocates focusing on constraints as they are more empirically observable than preferences. This second, more behavioral, perspective is not unanimously endorsed. For example, F. Ridley (1983) argues that the idea of rational taste is incongruous with an appreciation of the arts, which cannot be subjected to strict market principles. Indeed, he feels, introducing rationality into the picture might alienate cultural economists from art communities. Expressing a similar sentiment, Michael Rushton (1999) adds that the "communitarian" character of cultural goods is incompatible with a methodological individualist approach to CE.

What currently unites the culture industry view is the idea of culture as a product that can be bought and sold—paintings, sculptures, music, and so on. However, there is a nagging concern that scholarship has been mostly empirical, occupied with estimating demand and supply elasticities of cultural goods, or documenting the institutional structure of art markets. Blaug (2001) has cautioned that CE has yet to develop a theoretical core in the manner of other fields in the discipline. He suggested that cultural economists had a choice to make:

maintain their loose Neoclassicism, or "scrap the entire neoclassical framework" (ibid.: 126) in favor of a case study approach. Sadly, he did not get a chance to see the verdict on this choice. Towse and Abdul Khakee (1992), who had earlier expressed the same concern about the lack of a theoretical core, are optimistic that this will develop in time.

The 'cultural value' view

This strand of CE is where the majority of more philosophical discussions currently take place. Authors here embrace culture as both "practices and products of cultural activity, including especially the arts," and "a set of attitudes, beliefs or values common to a group that somehow identifies and binds the group together" (Ginsburgh and Throsby 2006: 6). Blaug (2001) has criticized this broader outlook as an unwarranted attempt to stretch the field beyond the boundaries of Economics. The cultural value view is most prominently represented in the work of David Throsby and Roger McCain, who question the ability of microeconomic theory, at least in its current form, to fully account for the value of culture.[19] They explore the notion of cultural value in such depth as to raise the question of whether it could be represented without modifying some fundamentals of Neoclassicism.

The cultural value literature offers a good opportunity to observe the dualistic separation of 'culture' from 'economy' as it draws a sharp contrast of economic vis-à-vis cultural value. Discussions reveal a perception of deep ontological differences between 'the cultural'—as creativity and imagination—and 'the economic,' as behavior or a mode of thought, though it is not always clear which meaning of economic is under scrutiny.

David Throsby articulates the twofold interpretation of culture:

> [A]ll those activities undertaken within 'the arts' and more broadly within the so-called 'cultural industries', the latter term embracing areas such as publishing and the media as well as the core artistic fields. In short, culture in this functional sense can be thought of as being represented by the 'cultural sector' of the economy.

and

> [A]ttitudes, practices, and beliefs that are fundamental to the functioning of different societies. Culture in this sense is expressed in a particular society's values and customs, which evolve over time as they are transmitted from one generation to another.
>
> (Throsby 1995: 202)

This interpretation mirrors the ideal/material dualism, with beliefs and attitudes reflecting the ideal, and activities and industries referring to the material. The second meaning converges with PA to the extent that it represents culture as something frozen in time, with little change from one generation to another. Throsby goes further to draw a parallel between 'economics' and 'culture,' characterizing them both as "modes of thought" and "representations of human behavior ... the economic impulse can be described as individualistic, and the cultural impulse as collective" (2001: 13, 158). This is a peculiar framing, and it is not clear which meaning of culture he is referring to. However, what matters here is that the contrast assumes that economics is extraneous to culture, which is broadly similar to Guiso *et al.*'s treatment of culture in relation to economic outcomes.

Throsby's culture/economics dualism draws on the work of Arjo Klamer (1996), who has contributed to the CE literature (see Klamer and Throsby 2000) even though he is not typically counted among Neoclassicists. Klamer (1991) has called on economists to take culture seriously by recognizing ontological and methodological differences between economics and economists, on one side, and art and artists, on the other. According to him, economics is a modernist discourse governed by objectivity and reason, whereas art embodies the non-modernist sensibilities of romanticism, moralism, and subjectivity. To bridge the gap between the two, he proposes taking an anthropological standpoint that treats artists as 'natives' to be understood on their own terms. In *The Value of Culture*, Klamer extends this dualistic conception by describing economics and art as two different "worlds," each with its own set of "shared values" (1996: 11)—the first is guided by realism, the latter being rooted in romanticism. He argues that cultural economics, which seeks to identify commonalities between artistic and economic activities, inherently threatens the integrity of creative occupations by theoretically subsuming 'the world of art' into economics, for instance, by defining art as a commodity. Throsby thus endorses Klamer's comparison but broadens it further by moving from an economics/art to an economics/culture dualism.

One of Throsby's contributions has been an attempt to clarify the idea of cultural capital, which he defines as "an asset embodying cultural value" (1999: 3), with tangible and intangible components.[20] The first exists in 'things'—buildings, artworks, and so on. Culture here represents a stock of materials. The intangible component "comprises the set of ideas, practices, beliefs, traditions and values which serve to identify and bind together a group of people" (ibid.: 7). In effect, it is indistinguishable from his concept of culture quoted above (1995: 202). Throsby claims this idea of cultural capital clarifies the relationship between cultural and economic value—for instance, investment in certain heritage items or practices may be required for ecological sustainability—and allows for quantitative inclusion of culture in cost-benefit analyses. In his assessment, "cultural capital could take its place alongside other forms of capital in the production function" (1999: 9). The effort to develop a well-defined systematic economic approach to culture is commendable. However, Throsby's conceptual horizon remains within 'the standard economic model' of consumer–firm behavior. By treating culture as capital, he imports it with no revision of theoretical principles, which renders culture substitutable to or tradable with every other good or form of capital.[21] Thus, inadvertently, Throsby's effort risks being no more than the type of threat to 'the art world' that Klamer fears.

Throsby realizes that despite a substantially expanded understanding of the economic problem, the conventional approach remains restrictive in theoretical scope and assumptions. In *Economics and Culture* (2001), he takes up the problem of value, which, he believes, is at the heart of both 'culture' and 'economics.' He proposes three "objectively definable characteristics" (ibid.: 4) to identify cultural and artistic activities and their outcomes. These are creativity, symbolic meaning, and an existing or a potential form of intellectual property. He takes it as given that economic value is embodied in market price or some other form of willingness to pay, derived from the assumption of utility maximization. In contrast, he notes, cultural value is elusive, unstable, and more complex. 'Ordinary' goods and services generate only economic value, whereas 'cultural' goods and services generate both economic and cultural value. The difficulty is that the latter lacks a standard unit of account, and is therefore unquantifiable. He suggests cultural value could be understood only by disaggregating its constituent elements: "aesthetic, spiritual, social, historical, symbolic and authenticity value" (ibid.: 159). Leaving the details of each element unclear, Throsby concludes, "it is essential to admit a concept of cultural value alongside that of economic value in assessing the phenomena under study" (ibid.: 160). This is well and good, but throughout the discussion he seems to operate with only one concept of culture, that of artistic and other forms of creativity.

McCain (2006) is similarly preoccupied with establishing a consistent, defensible economic approach to cultural phenomena. He affirms that culture comprises "everything that people derive from their tradition and heritage, including folklore and kinship patterns, 'material culture', religion, and so on" (ibid.: 150). But he goes further by attempting to unpack the nature of creativity in culture. In the process he parses the meaning of different types of value, and contemplates issues of creativity, provenance, and intrinsic worth.[22] Like Throsby, McCain takes the Neoclassical meaning of economic value—a quantum determined by individual preferences—for granted. However, he points out that the matter-of-fact result of the common distinction between 'economic' and 'non-economic' value is that artistic and cultural goods are lumped together with all things thought to be of no value. He fears this distinction damages the communication channels between economists and those interested in the development of cultural policies. Therefore, he argues, the challenge is to find a meaningful, i.e., a non-trivializing, way of representing the distinction between economic and non-economic value. This distinction, which has a long history in social science discourse generally, is grounded in the dualistic differentiation between economy and culture.

To address the challenge of more properly conceptualizing different types of value, McCain argues, one must consider intrinsic value, which he defines as achieving "unity in diversity."[23] According to him, cultural goods "carry cultural value, in that they derive their meaning from the unity-in-diversity of some specific cultural group and from the fact that they symbolize, through their provenance, the unity and distinctness of that group" (ibid.: 154). In other words, art has value not because of some general notion of creativity, but for the specific meaning it achieves in conveying the diverse sensibilities of a particular group or artist. He, therefore, takes issue with Throsby's attempt to construct an objective measure of cultural value based on the criteria of creativity, symbolic meaning, and intellectual property. McCain is concerned that this measure would exclude cultural goods that have no artistic value (in a narrow sense) or potential to be protected as intellectual property. Most problematic, for him, is the claim of objectivity since it ignores the cultural specificity, i.e., intrinsic value, of art. In other words, for him, one must take into account the broader meaning of culture as a distinct way of life in order to appreciate its narrower meaning as artistic creativity.

McCain states that he has merely "suggested a broader conception of value, that allows distinction among economic, cultural, artistic and aesthetic values" (ibid.: 164). But, in the end, he concedes that distinctions between artistic, cultural and ordinary goods can be justified only on "pragmatic" grounds. Although he does not resolve these issues, his contribution is stimulating and could open the door for more profound questioning of the concept of value in Neoclassical economics generally. It is doubtful, however, whether such questioning can take place as long as McCain and others are willing to unpack 'cultural value' while taking 'economic value' as given.

Conclusion

This chapter has reviewed the treatment of culture in two research programs of Neoclassical economics: (1) the Preferences Approach, in which culture is conceptualized as mental states of desire or beliefs; and (2) Cultural Economics, where it is mostly represented as an industry amenable to understanding through the principles of cost, price, elasticity, and market structure. The Preferences Approach has been used to investigate the economic implications of social status, upbringing, and religious beliefs, among other phenomena. Some studies have found that culture has a quantitatively non-negligible 'effect' on economic outcomes. However, it is not clear how useful such findings are in terms of generality or insight. CE literature shows there are many interesting aspects of creativity and art markets to be learned, but in terms of theory, significant new insights beyond those already established in microeconomic theory have yet to emerge. A few cultural economists grapple with the issue of value more deeply by adopting a broader concept of culture, and seem willing to put at least some phenomena beyond the reach of conventional economic calculus, thereby admitting the limits of Neoclassical theory. However, the cultural value perspective is still in its theoretical infancy. More work remains to clarify the concept of culture, as well as value, and to flesh out the implications for economic analyses.

The chapter has advanced two related points. First, both research programs are grounded in the dualistic ontology of culture/economy. In PA, this could be seen in the construction of culture as an external force acting upon an established pattern of economic behavior. In CE, the dualism is apparent in an explicit ontological distinction between culture and economics, and between economic and non-economic value. Second, both research programs maintain the core assumption of a world populated by individual rational maximizers, with no departure or revision. Even highly thoughtful discussions of culture and value (such as McCain's) take this principle as data. The question, then, is: can Neoclassical economists meaningfully 'incorporate culture' without some paradigmatic alteration?

Notes

1 The Neoclassical behavioral model requires specific assumptions about the nature and parameters of the self and notions of individuality, autonomy, choice, and decision-making. Its premises have been disputed as far back as the rise of Neoclassicism itself. For a classic critique, see Veblen (1909). Some contemporary debates and critical discussions, including the issue of rationality, can be found in Mini (1974), Sen (1977, 1987), Hodgson (1993), and Ferber and Nelson (1993, 2003). For Sociology and Anthropology perspectives, see Granovetter (1985) and Wilk (1996). In this book I am particularly concerned with the model's applicability across different societies and cultures, see Zein-Elabdin (2003, 2004, 2009) on Economics and cultural hegemony.
2 According to Boettke (1996) and Chamlee-Wright (1997), what separates Neoclassical and Austrian economics is methodological disagreement. See Buchanan (1995) for a Virginia School perspective on culture and 'economic science.' For more on the paradigmatic composition and different classifications of Economics, see Chapter 1 in this book, Samuels (1993), Dow (1995), Foldvary (1996), Reder (1999), and Hodgson (2007).
3 See Goodwin (2006) and McCain (2006) on the impact of Robbins' definition on the treatment of culture, especially 'the arts,' in Economics. The early twentieth century also witnessed the development of welfare economics, further narrowing the scope of economic analysis (Sen 1987).
4 Scitovsky associated culture only with consumption, stating that "consumption skills, therefore, are part of culture, while production skills are not" (1976: 226). This dualistic treatment is common in Economics but it is not taken up in this book. For another example see Dieckmann (1996), who investigates the relationship between national culture and economic development. He maintains that certain cultural activity enhances utility (e.g., buying art) but does not affect production. The odd implication is that a rise in utility contributes nothing to one's productivity. See Pietrykowski (1994) for a look at the consumption and production problematic within a postmodernist context. Other critical economic analyses of culture and consumption can be found in Rosenbaum (1999), Koritz and Koritz (2001), and Fine (2002).
5 I am grateful to Sean Flaherty (pers. comm.) for helping to clarify both my understanding and critique of Becker's position with respect to culture, in addition to other very helpful comments on this chapter. Flaherty argues that Becker accounts for culture in a more profound way than I have suggested here. For critical discussions of reliance on preferences as an entry point for culture, see Rosenbaum (1999), Chamlee-Wright (1997), and Maseland (2008).
6 According to Becker (1981), this model is an improved synthesis of the Malthusian and Darwinian conceptions because Malthus overlooked the quality of children, while Darwin ignored other commodities beside children. Becker argues the evolution of 'the family' resulted in large part from changes in the benefits to costs ratio of having children. His assumptions, for example, an altruistic head of household, have drawn substantial critique, see Amsden (1980), Greenwood (1984), Folbre (1986), and Kabeer (1991).
7 For critical discussions of preference endogeneity, see Woolley (1993), Bowles (1998), and Blaug (2001). Akerlof and Kranton introduce a model of "identity-based preferences" (2000: 749) in an interesting paper that discusses subtle and complex aspects of individual identity and group interactions, including the role of such things as anxiety,

ambivalence, and guilt. Their model manages to give fairly convincing interpretations of gender wage gaps and occupational segregation on the basis of a utility-maximizing behavioral assumption. They make repeated references to "the dominant culture" but never unpack this term or give a direct interpretation of culture.

8 Stigler and Becker (1977: 89) extend their analysis cross-culturally, claiming that the utility-maximizing model predicts that people in low-income countries (India) would pay less attention to 'fashion' than those living in high-income countries (the USA) "even if tastes were the same in wealthy and poor countries."

9 Neither Reimers (1985), nor Carroll *et al.* (1994) found significant differences in behavior resulting from differences in culture. See Chapter 8 in this book for more Neoclassical analyses of gender.

10 In another example, Lazear (1999) studies the economic impact of language based on the premise that speaking a common language increases gains from trade, thereby constituting a primary motivation for learning a non-native language. Using US Census data for different groups of immigrants from 1900 to 1990, he finds that chauvinism may be an economically efficient attitude. See Cuesta (2004) and Fernández (2008) for more literature.

11 Compare this to Cozzi's (1998: 379) representation of culture as an asset taught from one generation to another, with a "*self-fulfilling* expectation of an ever-increasing price of this immaterial asset over its market fundamental." If price ceases to rise, demand for culture collapses.

12 Woodbury was concerned that bringing culture into discussions of wage differences might invite racialist arguments, whereas the preferred path should be to exhaust all possible economic explanations of these differences. This assessment is consistent with the Stigler–Becker approach. See Darity and Williams (1985) and Mason (1996) on culture, race, and labor markets in the USA. For a critical discussion of the neglect of culture in the Neoclassical approach to the labor market, see Austen (2000).

13 Several quantitative studies (Marini 2004; Tabellini 2005; Tadesse and White 2008) rely on the World Values Survey, self-described as "a global network of social scientists studying changing values and their impact on social and political life," see www.worldvaluessurvey.org/WVSContents.jsp. To date, five survey "waves" have been conducted, in which respondents are asked to name qualities or traits they teach their children. To establish the quality of 'trust,' respondents are asked "would you say that most people can be trusted or that you can't be too careful in dealing with people?" For more quantitative literature, see Granato *et al.* (1996), de Jong (2009), and Adkisson (2014). See Chapters 5 and 7 in this book for a discussion of other studies relying on the Survey, and the type of associated problems.

14 Scholars in other social sciences have explored this issue for a long time. Geertz (1984) criticizes both economists and anthropologists for externalizing culture. See DiMaggio (1994) for a discussion of the meaning and analytical requirements to establish a "cultural effect" on economic phenomena.

15 In the *Journal of Economic Literature*'s classifications of research and teaching areas, CE is identified as "economics of the arts and literature" (listed under Other Special Topics). This represents the traditional purview of UNESCO, which was influential in early economists' efforts to define the cultural industries (see Hendon *et al.* 1984). The agency has since broadened its interpretation of culture (see UNESCO 1998).

16 The *Journal of Cultural Economics* came into publication in 1977, and the first international conference of the Association of Cultural Economics was convened in 1980. The field's rapid growth is indicated by several sizable volumes such as Towse's (1997) *Cultural Economics: The Arts, the Heritage and the Media Industries*, which features over 70 articles, covering 8 different subject areas. Also see Hutter and Rizzo (1997). For more history, see Towse and Abdul Khakee (1992), Throsby (1994), and Frey (1994b).

17 Baumol's cost disease (Baumol and Bowen 1966) describes the phenomenon that technology in the arts lags behind, while wages keep pace with other sectors of the economy, resulting in "cost inflation in the arts" (Blaug 2001: 131). It appears to be the single concept uniquely identified with CE.

18 Indeed, cultural economists have borrowed the method of contingent valuation from environmental economics to examine art and cultural products. See Noonan (2003) and Throsby (2003).

19 The broad interpretation of culture is displayed in the *Handbook of the Economics of Art and Culture* (Ginsburgh and Throsby 2006), an extensive collection of articles, with sections on history, value, the law, international trade, and economic development, among other concerns. Also see the *Handbook of Cultural Economics* (Towse 2003), which contains over 60 entries, including cultural capital, sustainability, tourism, the Internet, and the value of culture. Hutter and Throsby (2008) give a brief account of the evolution of discourses on cultural and economic value.

20 In other literature cultural capital is defined more broadly. For instance, in development economics, W. Arthur Lewis defined it as "the background of knowledge accumulated by society" (1955: 29). See Chapter 7 in this book.

21 I am indebted to Neil Perry (pers. comm.) for the observation about the substitutability of culture. Perry makes this point with respect to the issue of ecological sustainability, where Neoclassical logic would equate the moral value of, say, an endangered species with any other economic value. This, of course, is a direct implication of Bentham's subjectivism noted above.

22 In the present discussion I have avoided debates about the nature of art, its genres, and movements. For contemporary discussions of these issues beyond the boundaries of Economics, see Williams (1983 [1976]), Harvey (1989), During (1993), and Eagleton (2000).

23 This interpretation is borrowed from the philosopher Robert Nozick's (1981) discussion in *Philosophical Explanation*.

References

Acheson, Keith and Christopher Maule (1999) *Much Ado About Culture: North American Trade Disputes*, Ann Arbor, MI: University of Michigan Press.

Adkisson, Richard (2014) "Quantifying Culture: Problems and Promises," *Journal of Economic Issues*, 48 (1): 89–107.

Akerlof, George and Rachel Kranton (2000) "Economics and Identity," *The Quarterly Journal of Economics*, 115 (3): 715–753.

Amsden, Alice H. (ed.) (1980) *The Economics of Women and Work*, New York: St. Martin's Press.

Austen, Siobahn (2000) "Culture and the Labor Market," *Review of Social Economy*, 58 (4): 505–521.

Backhouse, Roger (1985) *A History of Modern Economic Analysis*, Oxford: Basil Blackwell.

Baumol, William J. and William G. Bowen (1966) *Performing Arts: The Economic Dilemma*, New York: Twentieth Century Fund.

Becker, Gary S. (1976) *The Economic Approach to Human Behavior*, Chicago: University of Chicago Press.

—— (1981) *A Treatise on the Family*, Cambridge, MA: Harvard University Press.

—— (1996) *Accounting for Tastes*, Cambridge, MA: Harvard University Press.

Bentham, Jeremy (1962) *The Works of Jeremy Bentham*, vol. 2, ed. John Bowring, New York: Russell and Russell.

Bisin, Alberto and Thierry Verdier (2001) "The Economics of Cultural Transmission and the Dynamics of Preferences," *Journal of Economic Theory*, 97: 298–319.

Blaug, Mark (ed.) (1976) *The Economics of the Arts*, London: Martin Robertson and Company.

—— (2001) "Where Are We Now on Cultural Economics?" *Journal of Economic Surveys*, 15 (2): 123–143.

Boettke, Peter J. (1996) "What Is Wrong with Neoclassical Economics (and What Is Still Wrong with Austrian Economics)?" in F. Foldvary (ed.), *Beyond Neoclassical Economics: Heterodox Approaches to Economic Theory*, Cheltenham: Edward Elgar, 22–40.

Boulding, Kenneth E. (1973) "Toward the Development of a Cultural Economics," in Louis Schneider and Charles Bonjean (eds.) *The Idea of Culture in the Social Sciences*, Cambridge, MA: Cambridge University Press, 47–64.

Bowles, Samuel (1998) "Endogenous Preferences: The Cultural Consequences of Markets and Other Economic Institutions," *Journal of Economic Literature*, 36 (1): 75–111.

Buchanan, James M. (1995) "Economic Science and Cultural Diversity," *Kyklos*, 48 (2): 193–200.

Carroll, Christopher D., Byung-Kum Rhee, and Changyong Rhee (1994) "Are There Cultural Effects on Savings? Some Cross-Sectional Evidence," *The Quarterly Journal of Economics*, 109 (3): 685–699.

Chamlee-Wright, Emily (1997) *The Cultural Foundations of Economic Development: Urban Female Entrepreneurship in Ghana*, London: Routledge.

Colander, David (2000) "The Death of Neoclassical Economics," *Journal of the History of Economic Thought*, 22 (2): 127–143.

Cowen, Tyler (1989) "Are All Tastes Constant and Identical? A Critique of Stigler and Becker," *Journal of European Behavior and Organization*, 11: 127–135.

Cozzi, Guido (1998) "Culture as a Bubble," *Journal of Political Economy*, 106 (2): 376–394.

Croson, Rachel and Nancy Buchan (1999) "Gender and Culture: International Experimental Evidence from Trust Games," *American Economic Review, Papers and Proceedings*, 89 (2): 386–391.

Cuesta, José (2004) "From Economicist to Culturalist Development Theories: How Strong Is the Relation Between Cultural Aspects and Economic Development?" *The European Journal of Development Research*, 16 (4): 868–891.

Darity, William Jr. and Rhonda M. Williams (1985) "Peddlers Forever? Culture, Competition, and Discrimination," *American Economic Review*, 75 (2): 256–261.

De Jong, Eelke (2009) *Culture and Economics: On Values, Economics and International Business*, London: Routledge.

Dieckmann, Oliver (1996) "Cultural Determinants of Economic Growth: Theory and Evidence," *Journal of Cultural Economics*, 20 (4): 297–320.

DiMaggio, Paul (1994) "Culture and Economy," in Neil J. Smelser and Richard Swedberg (eds.) *The Handbook of Economic Sociology*, Princeton, NJ: Princeton University Press, 27–57.

Dixon, Vernon, J. (1970) "The Di-Unital Approach to 'Black Economics,'" *American Economic Review, Papers and Proceedings*, 60 (2): 424–429.

Dow, Sheila C. (1995) "The Appeal of Neoclassical Economics: Some Insights from Keynes's Epistemology," *Cambridge Journal of Economics*, 19 (6): 715–733.

During, Simon (ed.) (1993) *The Cultural Studies Reader*, London: Routledge.

Eagleton, Terry (2000) *The Idea of Culture,* Oxford: Blackwell.

Ferber, Marianne A. and Julie A. Nelson (eds.) (1993) *Beyond Economic Man: Feminist Theory and Economics*, Chicago: University of Chicago Press.

—— (eds.) (2003) *Feminist Economics Today: Beyond Economic Man*, Chicago: University of Chicago Press.

Fernández, Raquel (2008) "Culture and Economics," in Steven N. Durlauf and Lawrence E. Blume (eds.) *The New Palgrave Dictionary of Economics Online*, 2nd edition, Basingstoke: Palgrave Macmillan. Available at: www.dictionaryofeconomics.com/article?id=pde2008_E000282, doi:10.1057/9780230226203.0346.

Fershtman, Chaim and Yoram Weiss (1993) "Social Status, Culture and Economic Performance," *Economic Journal*, 103 (419): 946–959.

Fine, Ben (2002) *The World of Consumption: The Material and Cultural Revisited*, London: Routledge.

Folbre, Nancy (1986) "Cleaning House: New Perspectives on Households and Economic Development," *Journal of Development Economics*, 22 (1): 5–40.

Foldvary, Fred E. (ed.) (1996) *Beyond Neoclassical Economics: Heterodox Approaches to Economic Theory*, Cheltenham: Edward Elgar.

Frey, Bruno (1994a) "Art: The Economic Point of View," in A. Peacock and I. Rizzo (eds.) *Cultural Economics and Cultural Policies*, Boston: Kluwer Publishers, 3–16.

—— (1994b) "Cultural Economics and Museum Behavior," *Scottish Journal of Political Economy*, 41 (3): 325–335.

Friedman, Milton (1953) *Essays in Positive Economics*, Chicago: University of Chicago Press.

Geertz, Clifford (1973) *The Interpretation of Cultures: Selected Essays*, New York: Basic Books.

—— (1984) "Culture and Social Change: The Indonesian Case," *Man*, 19 (4): 511–532.

Ginsburgh, Victor A. and David Throsby (eds.) (2006) *Handbook of the Economics of Art and Culture*, Amsterdam: Elsevier North-Holland.

Goodwin, Craufurd (2006) "Art and Culture in the History of Economic Thought," in V. Ginsburgh and D. Throsby (eds.) *Handbook of the Economics of Art and Culture*, Amsterdam: Elsevier North-Holland, 25–68.

Granato, Jim, Ronald Inglehart, and David Leblang (1996) "The Effect of Cultural Values on Economic Development: Theory, Hypotheses, and Some Empirical Tests," *American Journal of Political Science*, 40 (3): 607–631.

Granovetter, Mark (1985) "Economic Action and Social Structure: The Problem of Embeddedness," *American Journal of Sociology*, 91 (3): 481–510.

Greenwood, Daphne (1984) "The Economic Significance of 'Woman's Place' in Society: A New-Institutionalist View," *Journal of Economic Issues*, 18 (3): 663–680.

Guiso, Luigi, Paola Sapienza, and Luigi Zingales (2006) "Does Culture Affect Economic Outcomes?" *Journal of Economic Perspectives*, 20 (2): 23–48.

Harvey, David (1989) *The Condition of Postmodernity: An Enquiry into the Origins of Cultural Change*, Oxford: Blackwell.

Hendon, William S. and James L. Shanahan (eds.) (1983) *Economics of Cultural Decisions*, Cambridge, MA: Abt books.

Hendon, William S., Douglas V. Shaw, and Nancy K. Grant (eds.) (1984) *Economics of Cultural Industries*, Akron, OH: Association for Cultural Economics.

Henrich, Joseph (2000) "Does Culture Matter in Economic Behavior? Ultimatum Game Bargaining among the Machiguenga of the Peruvian Amazon," *American Economic Review*, 90 (4): 973–979.

Hodgson, Geoffrey M. (ed.) (1993) *The Economics of Institutions*, Aldershot: Edward Elgar Publishing.

—— (2007) "Evolutionary and Institutional Economics as the New Mainstream?" *Evolutionary and Institutional Economics Review*, 4 (1): 7–25.

Hoselitz, Bert F. (1952) "Non-Economic Barriers to Economic Development," *Economic Development and Cultural Change*, 1 (1): 8–21.

Hutter, Michael (1996) "The Impact of Cultural Economics on Economic Theory," *Journal of Cultural Economics*, 20 (4): 263–268.

—— and Ilde Rizzo (eds.) (1997) *Economic Perspectives on Cultural Heritage*, London: Macmillan.

—— and D. Throsby (eds.) (2008) *Beyond Price: Value in Culture, Economics, and the Arts*, Cambridge: Cambridge University Press.

Jevons, W. Stanley (1965 [1883]) *Methods of Social Reform*, London: Macmillan and Company.

Kabeer, Naila (1991) "Cultural Dopes or Rational Fools? Women and Labour Supply in the Bangladesh Garment Industry," *The European Journal of Development Research*, 3 (November): 133–160.

Klamer, Arjo (1991) "Towards the Native's Point of View: The Difficulty of Changing the Conversation," in Don Lavoie (ed.) *Economics and Hermeneutics*, London: Routledge, 19–33.

—— (ed.) (1996) *The Value of Culture: On the Relationship between Economics and Arts*, Amsterdam: Amsterdam University Press.

—— and David Throsby (2000) "Paying for the Past: The Economics of Cultural Heritage," in *The World Culture Report 2000: Cultural Diversity, Conflict and Pluralism*, Paris: UNESCO, 130–145.

Koritz, Amy and Douglas Koritz (2001) "Checkmating the Consumer: Passive Consumption and the Economic Devaluation of Culture," *Feminist Economics*, 7 (1) March: 45–62.

Lazear, Edward P. (1999) "Culture and Language," *Journal of Political Economy*, 107 (6): S95–S125.

Lewis, W. Arthur (1955) *The Theory of Economic Growth*, London: George Allen and Unwin.

Lipset, Seymour Martin (1993) "Culture and Economic Behavior: A Commentary," *Journal of Labor Economics*, 11(1) Part 2: S330–S347.

Marini, Matteo (2004) "Cultural Evolution and Economic Growth: A Theoretical Hypothesis with Some Empirical Evidence," *The Journal of Socio-Economics*, 33: 765–784.

Marshall, Alfred (1938 [1890]) *Principles of Economics: An Introductory Volume*, London: Macmillan & Co.

Maseland, Robbert (2008) "Taking Economics to Bed: About the Pitfalls and Possibilities of Cultural Economics," in Wolfram Elsner and Hardy Hanappi (eds.) *Varieties of Capitalism and New Institutional Deals: Regulation, Welfare and the New Economy*, Cheltenham: Edward Elgar, 299–321.

Mason, Patrick L. (1996) "Race, Culture, and the Market," *Journal of Black Studies*, 26 (6): 782–808.

Mayhew, Anne (1994) "Culture," in G. Hodgson and W. Samuels (eds.) *The Elgar Companion to Institutional and Evolutionary Economics*, Cheltenham: Edward Elgar, 115–119.

McCain, Roger (2006) "Defining Cultural and Artistic Goods," in Victor Ginsburgh and David Throsby (eds.) *The Handbook of the Economics of Art and Culture*, vol. 1, Amsterdam: Elsevier North-Holland, 148–167.

Mini, Piero V. (1974) *Philosophy and Economics: The Origins and Development of Economic Theory*, Gainesville, FL: University of Florida Press.

Noonan, Douglas S. (2003) "Contingent Valuation and Cultural Resources: A Meta-Analytic Review of the Literature," *Journal of Cultural Economics*, 27 (3–4): 159–176.

North, Douglass C. (1990) *Institutions, Institutional Change and Economic Performance*, Cambridge: Cambridge University Press.

Nozick, Robert (1981) *Philosophical Explanation*, Cambridge, MA: Belknap Press.

Peacock, Alan (1992) "Economics, Cultural Values and Cultural Policies," in Ruth Towse and Abdul Khakee (eds.) *Cultural Economics*, Heidelberg: Springer-Verlag, 9–20.

—— and Ilde Rizzo (eds.) (1994) *Cultural Economics and Cultural Policies*, Boston: Kluwer Publishers.

Pietrykowski, Bruce (1994) "Consuming Culture: Postmodernism, Post-Fordism, and Economics," *Rethinking Marxism*, 7 (1) (Spring): 62–80.

Reder, Melvin W. (1999) *Economics: The Culture of a Controversial Science*, Chicago: University of Chicago Press.

Reimers, Cordelia W. (1985) "Cultural Differences in Labor Force Participation Among Married Women," *American Economic Review, Papers and Proceedings*, 75 (2): 251–255.

Ridley, F.F. (1983) "Cultural Economics and the Culture of Economists," *Journal of Cultural Economics*, 7: 1–18.

Robbins, Lionel (1946 [1932]) *An Essay on the Nature and Significance of Economic Science*, London: Macmillan and Co.

—— (1997 [1971]) "Unsettled Questions in the Political Economy of the Arts," in Ruth Towse (ed.) *Cultural Economics: The Arts, the Heritage and the Media Industries*, vol. I, Aldershot: Edward Elgar, 3–19.

Rosenbaum, Eckehard F. (1999) "Against Naïve Materialism: Culture, Consumption and the Causes of Inequality," *Cambridge Journal of Economics*, 23 (3): 317–336.

Rushton, Michael (1999) "Methodological Individualism and Cultural Economics," *Journal of Cultural Economics*, 23 (3): 137–147.

Samuels, Warren J. (ed.) (1993) *The Chicago School of Political Economy*, London: Transaction Publishers.

Scitovsky, Tibor (1976) *The Joyless Economy: An Inquiry into Human Satisfaction and Consumer Dissatisfaction*, New York: Oxford University Press.

Sen, Amartya K. (1977) "Rational Fools: A Critique of the Behavioural Foundations of Economic Theory," *Philosophy and Public Affairs*, 6 (4): 317–344.

—— (1987) *On Ethics and Economics*, Oxford: Blackwell.

Shaw, Douglas V., William S. Hendon and Virginia Lee Owen (eds.) (1988) *Cultural Economics 88: An American Perspective*, Akron, OH: Association for Cultural Economics.

Stigler, George J. and Gary S. Becker (1977) "*De Gustibus Non Est Disputandum*," *American Economic Review*, 67 (2): 76–90.

Tabellini, Guido (2005) "Culture and Institutions: Economic Development in the Regions of Europe," CESifo Working Paper No. 1492.

Tadesse, Bedassa and Roger White (2008) "Do Immigrants Counter the Effect of Cultural Distance on Trade? Evidence from US State-level Exports," *Journal of Socio-Economics*, 37 (6): 2304–2318.

Throsby, David (1994) "The Production and Consumption of the Arts: A View of Cultural Economics," *Journal of Economic Literature*, 32: 1–29.

—— (1995) "Culture, Economics, and Sustainability" *Journal of Cultural Economics*, 19 (3): 199–206.

—— (1999) "Cultural Capital," *Journal of Cultural Economics*, 23 (1–2): 3–12.

—— (2001) *Economics and Culture*, Cambridge: Cambridge University Press.

—— (2003) "Determining the Value of Cultural Goods: How Much (Or How Little) Does Contingent Valuation Tell Us?" *Journal of Cultural Economics*, 27 (3–4): 275–285.

Towse, Ruth (ed.) (1997) *Cultural Economics: The Arts, the Heritage and the Media Industries*, Cheltenham: Edward Elgar, vols. I, II.

—— (ed.) (2003) *A Handbook of Cultural Economics*, Cheltenham: Edward Elgar.

—— and Abdul Khakee (eds.) (1992) *Cultural Economics*, Heidelberg: Springer-Verlag.

UNESCO (1998) *World Culture Report 1998: Culture, Creativity and Markets*, Paris: United Nations Educational, Scientific and Cultural Organization.

Veblen, Thorstein (1909) "The Limitations of Marginal Utility," *Journal of Political Economy*, 17 (9): 620–636.

Weber, Max (1958 [1930]) *The Protestant Ethic and the Spirit of Capitalism*, New York: Charles Scribner's Sons.

Wilk, Richard (1996) *Economies and Cultures: Foundations of Economic Anthropology*, Boulder, CO: Westview Press.

Williams, Raymond (1983 [1976]) *Keywords: A Vocabulary of Culture and Society*, New York: Oxford University Press.

Woodbury, Stephen A. (1993) "Culture and Human Capital: Theory and Evidence or Theory Versus Evidence?" in William A. Darity Jr. (ed.) *Labor Economics: Problems in Analyzing Labor Markets*, Boston: Kluwer Academic Publishers, 239–267.

Woolley, Frances R. (1993) "The Feminist Challenge to Neoclassical Economics," *Cambridge Journal of Economics*, 17 (4): 485–500.

Zein-Elabdin, Eiman O. (2003) "The Difficulty of a Feminist Economics," in Drucilla K. Barker and Edith Kuiper (eds.), *Toward a Feminist Philosophy of Economics*, London: Routledge, 321–338.

—— (2004) "Articulating the Postcolonial (with Economics in Mind)," in E. Zein-Elabdin and S. Charusheela (eds.) *Postcolonialism Meets Economics*, London: Routledge, 21–39.

—— (2009) "Economics, Postcolonial Theory, and the Problem of Culture: Institutional Analysis and Hybridity," *Cambridge Journal of Economics*, 33 (6): 1153–1167.

4 Institutional economics

Veblen's tradition

> There is, therefore, no neatly isolable range of cultural phenomena that can be rigorously set apart under the head of economic institutions.
>
> (Veblen 1898a: 393)

The Original tradition of Institutional Economics (OIE) may be described as the economic philosophy most preoccupied with both 'culture' and 'development' ever since Thorstein Veblen envisioned this approach as "the theory of a process of cultural growth as determined by the economic interest" (ibid.). But as Institutionalism fell from professional prominence in the first half of the twentieth century, culture faded from the general discourse of Economics to such an extent that today some leading figures of the New Institutional Economics (NIE) lack basic familiarity with or appreciation of the principles and contributions of OIE (e.g., Coase 1984).[1]

In this chapter, I trace the treatment of culture and development in OIE, namely the body of thought that Veblen, John R. Commons, and Wesley Clair Mitchell established, and its interpretations and extension by many followers. Culture is a complex and elusive concept-phenomenon. Here, I take it to mean the broadly shared, though contested, sensibilities and lifeways of a society or group that authorize and censor different practices, in not always fully coherent and seamless ways (see Chapter 1 and Appendix II for more on culture). I am interested in culture both as a subject of economic inquiry and an operator, shaping economists' thoughts about social phenomena in their own and other cultures, often expressed in discussions of comparative economic development. To varying degrees, the majority of work discussed in this chapter assumes the dominant meaning of development, that is, as John K. Galbraith put it, achieving the levels of material well-being associated with "twentieth-century existence" (1964: 25). The standard for this has been set by the income levels and accompanying 'way of life' prevalent in affluent North Atlantic societies (see Chapter 7 in this book for more on development).

In Chapter 1, I argued that the majority of economic thought is rooted in *dualistic ontology*, that is, an apprehension of 'reality' in a binary framework that leaves little theoretical room for in-between or altogether different phenomena.

This is analytically reflected in the separation of 'culture' and 'economy' as two distinct realms, paralleling the philosophical dualism of ideal/material, which is itself rooted in an existential problem of desire/limits (see Chapter 1). In development economics, the parallel to the ideal/material dichotomy surfaces as authors either highlight ideas and beliefs, or emphasize 'material' factors such as savings and physical capital. The overwhelming tendency to reductively theorize culture as either an obstacle to or a driving force behind economic growth reflects the desire/limit dualism.

This chapter advances two points. First, while Institutionalists reject the dualism of culture/economy, as the quotation in this chapter's epigraph indicates, OIE rests on a *paradigmatic dualism* contained in the theoretical distinction between the ceremonial (institutional) and the instrumental (technological)—the famous Veblenian dichotomy (see Waller 1982, 1994).[2] This distinction seems to echo—though not in a straightforward way—the ideal/material dualism despite Veblen's and Clarence Ayres' attempts to transcend this construction.[3] William Waller (1999) has disputed the centrality of Veblen's dichotomy to OIE. In this chapter, I draw a different conclusion, and show that the dichotomy is mirrored in the presence of two lines of thought in contemporary Institutionalism: an *anthropological* (relativist) line and an *instrumentalist* (universalist) one. Second, in the fury of the twentieth-century discourse of international development, the concept of culture in OIE lost some of its theoretical significance to the idea of instrumental valuation. The result has been an estrangement from culture, where a universalist vision, converging with the rest of 'modernization' theory and development economics, took over. In this vision, development is associated with technological advance, and considered an ultimately inevitable mark of 'progress.'

In the first two sections, I outline the treatment of culture and development in OIE as represented in the major works of its three founding architects—Veblen, Commons, and Mitchell. In the third section, I turn to contemporary Institutional (aka neoinstitutional) economics.[4] The next section discusses the theory of development articulated by Clarence Ayres, and its applications by Gunnar Myrdal and William Kapp—all prominent figures of postwar Institutionalism. The final section examines the relationship between development economics and contemporary Institutionalist discourse on development. The body of Veblenian Institutionalist literature is vast. Most of the issues brought up in this chapter have been extensively studied and debated. I hope to highlight some major themes and draw some connections regarding culture and development without simply repeating or overworking existing scholarship. Following the panoramic approach employed throughout this book, I will not delve into the nuances and analytical details of each work, but limit the discussion to the level of a broad overview.

The paradigm

Veblen's primary critique of Neoclassical economics is that it failed to adopt a scientific perspective in a manner similar to Anthropology and Biology, the evolutionary sciences of his time; it had no theory for studying the "economic life process" (1898a: 387). Neoclassical theory adhered to a static, faulty conception of 'human nature' as immutable self-contained desire, instead of an outcome of "a given body of traditions, conventionalities, and material circumstances" (ibid.: 390). Veblen's main aim was to show that the complex body of 'modern' culture has emerged from centuries-long, even ancient, processes of social evolution. For him, economic reason and action were embedded in an intricate network of institutions, i.e., "habits of thought" (2006 [1904]: 318) and taken-for-granted social terms of reference. Thus, from the very beginning, Institutionalism departed from prevalent economic doctrine in conceptualizing an economy as a social evolving organism.

One text that sharply illustrates Veblen's emphasis on culture is "The Cultural Incidence of the Machine Process" (in *The Theory of Business Enterprise*, 2006 [1904]), in which he attributed a host of cultural phenomena to the introduction of machine technology. From his perspective, the technologically mandated conformity to standard units of time and output engendered new habits of thought, in particular a "matter-of-fact" attitude. For him, the wide adoption of machine technology and "workday ideals and skepticism of what is only conventionally valid—is the unequivocal mark of the Western culture of to-day as contrasted with the culture of other times and places" (ibid.: 323). He argued the cultural results of mechanization included the rise of trade unionism, decline in the desire for individual ownership, and erosion of the patriarchal family. Here, Veblen used the word 'culture' in an anthropological sense (way of life) that encompassed the use of technology.[5]

In comparing modern "Western culture" to other places, Veblen was cautious, showing a great deal of cross-cultural sensitivity and awareness. For example, he spoke of "those communities which we are in the habit of calling 'industrially backward'" (ibid.: 316). Yet, at other times, he referred to "the populace of half-civilized and barbarous countries" (ibid.: 349). Generally, in this comparative mode, Veblen's statements were similar to those frequently made by classical political economists, namely, exhibiting a mix of analytical savvy and orientalism (see Chapter 2 in this book).

In contrast to Veblen, Commons rarely used the word 'culture.' Instead, he opted for institutions, custom, and going concern, moving interchangeably from one to another. He defined institutions as "collective action in control, liberation and expansion of individual action" (1931: 649), which includes ordinary habits and rules codified in written law or unspoken lore. Institutions take the form of both custom and going concerns. Custom, typically unorganized, refers to established transactions between individuals who share similar social locations. Going concerns are more organized (e.g., the credit system).[6] Commons elaborated that:

> [a going concern] interjects between the state and the individual a complex of habits, practices, opinions, promises and customs which are both a substitute for state action and a highly intractable force which even the most powerful state cannot override, or will not if its officials care to hold their jobs.
>
> (1925: 376)

This statement shows that, even though it is typically more organized and specific than custom, a going concern does embody the concept of culture as diffuse, entrenched conventions. The depth of Commons' idea of custom allowed him to see that 'reality' is neither objective nor constant—"facts are facts as our habits, investigations and purposes deem them to be facts" (1968 [1924]: 359).

Wesley Mitchell also adopted the idea of institutions as "habits of thought and action" (1910: 112). Although he said very little explicitly about culture, the bulk of his work shows a firm hold on the concept. In "The Backward Art of Spending Money" (1912), he criticized economists' lack of attention to the social activity of consumption. While describing the division of labor in household spending habits, he uncovered important aspects of the cultural construction of gender relations and the patriarchal family. His understanding of culture more broadly is evident in his presidential address to the American Economic Association where he remarked that "economic institutions [are] the aspect of culture" that preoccupies economists (1925: 8). Mitchell's broad understanding is clearest in his statement that:

> [t]o find the basis of rationality, then, we must not look inside the individual at his capacity to abstract from the totality of experience the feeling elements, to assess their pleasant or unpleasant characters, and to compare their magnitudes. Rather must we look outside the individual to the habits of behavior slowly evolved by society and painfully learned by himself.
>
> (1916: 156)

Although he did not use the word 'culture' in this passage, his attributing such a significant role in the formation of 'rationality' to an extra-individual factor signals a strong belief in the constitutive role of cultural context.

Following Veblen, Commons, and Mitchell, Institutionalists' efforts went mostly into clarifying the meaning of institutions, especially, their relationship to culture. Walton Hamilton (1932: 84) notably defined an institution as a "cluster of social usages" that may take the shape of an informal body (common law), a formal organization (a corporation), or broad social arrangements (democracy). In all shapes, institutions structure and organize behavior, and thereby effectuate order and stability. Culture, on the other hand, represents a "synthesis—or at least an aggregation—of institutions" (ibid.), the unforeseen framework within which institutions appear and evolve.[7]

Development and change in original Institutionalism

The original Institutionalists understood an economy to be an evolving process within a specific culture and history. Veblen theorized this process as the cumulative result of two features of 'mankind:' an "instinct of workmanship," which he described as "a human trait necessary to the survival of the species" (1898b: 190); and a social nature of habit and emulation.[8] Accordingly, he drew a distinction between technological, or instrumental, types of action—matter-of-fact, workman-like or industrial pursuits—and ceremonial, or institutional, ones, i.e., those driven by invidious, atavistic sentiment, and predatory or pecuniary considerations (1994 [1899]). According to William Glade, this dichotomy is "the sum and substance of Veblen's work" (1952: 433).[9]

Veblen's discussions of evolution cannot be easily categorized into an idealist or a materialist perspective. He seems to take an idealist position when claiming that economic change "is always in the last resort a change in habits of thought" (1898a: 391). At other times, he emphasized "the material means of life" (ibid.: 387). Yet, he erases the distinction by claiming that when the instinct of workmanship is "enforced upon the group or the race by selective elimination," it can pass "from the status of habit to aptitude or propensity, to a transmissible trait" (1898b: 195). This conception (habit → aptitude → transmissible trait) contains a mutual reinforcement of 'material' and 'spiritual' in an inextricable joining of body–mind. In this attempt to fuse biology and anthropology in one evolutionary process, Veblen transcends ideal/material and nature/culture dualisms. Indeed, this effort anticipates current work in bio-anthropology (see Boyd and Richerson 2000), which interprets human cognition as the outcome of genetic and cultural evolution in one intricate process.

According to William Dugger (1989: 13), Veblen was an existentialist, for whom evolution represented "blind drift" rather than a knowable trajectory. Nonetheless, his position on change could be elusive. Despite his rejection of teleological thinking, Veblen spoke of "phases of civilization" and "sequence" where one stage of human society followed another (1909: 628).[10] At times, he adopted the common historicist view in which contemporary non-European societies theoretically stood for earlier periods in the 'development' of European cultures. This representation appears in his discussion of the post-WWI agreement between Pacific League countries concerning investment and trade in world regions such as Abyssinia, Persia, and Afghanistan—regions inhabited by "those backward peoples" (1998 [1932]: 374). In this text he used the term development to mean commercial exploitation. However, his general language—e.g., "peoples of the lower civilization" (ibid.: 373)—indicates that he had a broader context in mind, in which these societies belonged to an earlier stage of history. This is clearly inconsistent with an unteleological perspective, though it is not clear whether he used this staging lexicon in a normative sense or not. Overall, Veblen rarely made invidious cross-cultural comparisons, but at least on this occasion, his statements about 'other' cultures converge with the views of the mass of classical economists.

Commons' work contains hardly any references to regions beyond Europe and North America, but he was deeply preoccupied with time as a crucial dimension of economic phenomena. This is reflected in his belief that all transactions take place in the context of "perpetual change" such that the law simply provides insurance against the uncertainty of future transactions (1931: 657). He was particularly concerned about human adaptation to change, and therefore placed more emphasis on psychological factors, in critical contrast to what he saw as Veblen's and Marx's over-confidence in the role of technology (Gruchy 1947). Thus, when studying the US labor movement, Commons emphasized the problem of "cultural lag" (ibid.), that is, psychological adjustment to industrial growth. Sociologists have generally thought such lag occurs when parts of 'non-material' culture fall behind material culture (Glade 1952; also see Brinkman and Brinkman 1997).[11] Glade suggests cultural lag should be seen as a manifestation of the distance between technological advances and ceremonial attitudes. In other words, it illustrates the Veblenian dichotomy. Whether Commons' emphasis on psychological over technological aspects is specifically based on this interpretation is not clear.

Mitchell was similarly committed to the idea that economic phenomena are shaped by "the evolution of culture" (1925: 8). In comparative context, he used the vocabulary of his day, for instance, speaking of "the highly civilized nations of the world to-day" (1927: 174). In this group, he included the USA, Great Britain and its settler colonies, France, the Netherlands, Germany, and Scandinavia. At a "somewhat less mature stage of the money economy," he placed other countries of Europe, and Spanish and Portuguese-speaking peoples of South America, followed by 'the Orient.' He associated economic development with the presence of monetary exchange, but cautioned that his "statements are based upon rather vague and general impressions" (ibid.). He carefully noted "perhaps the grouping suggested is not quite fair in all cases; certainly it is subject to revision as conditions develop in the countries which we now count laggard" (ibid.). Nonetheless, the qualification indicates that the grouping may be revised only insofar as findings show that the money economy in some of these territories is more advanced than it was thought to be.

In short, the phenomenon of development was central to early Institutionalists—whether it referred to technological mastery, social evolution, or growth in commerce. For them, change was inherently tied to the cultural past and the present habits of society. When cross-cultural statements were made, they fell in line with the pattern seen in Classical Political Economy; namely, different societies fall along a developmental path set by the historical experience of Western Europe and North America.

Culture in contemporary Institutional Economics

Almost all neoinstitutionalists explicitly present culture as a key concept, albeit with different degrees of emphasis and shades of meaning (Ayres 1951; Junker 1968; Gruchy 1972, 1987; Mayhew 1987; Jennings and Waller 1995; Hodgson 2000; Waller 2003). Within this philosophical framework, it is possible to identify two overlapping lines of scholarship: anthropological and instrumentalist. The first highlights the relative and unteleological substance of culture; the second emphasizes the universally practical value of technological knowledge. The two lines, in effect, follow the ceremonial and technological sides of the Veblenian dichotomy. In this section, I broadly outline each line of scholarship, as expressed in a few salient contributions, cautioning that not all Institutional economics can or should be identified with one side or the other.[12]

Before reviewing the two literatures, it is worth elaborating on Veblen's dichotomy. As stated in the previous section, Veblen (1898b, 1994) distinguished between two aspects of human behavior: the instrumental is governed by technology with its dynamic character, whereas the ceremonial is embodied in slowly changing habits of thought. In *The Theory of the Leisure Class*, Veblen (1994) illustrated ceremonial behavior in an almost ethnographic tracing of the phenomenon of conspicuous consumption. Clarence Ayres (1962 [1944]) later formalized and elaborated the concepts of ceremonialism and instrumental valuation. According to him, ceremonialism—change-inhibiting habits of thought—requires the presence of a social hierarchy (e.g., class), conventions that define the behavior acceptable for each social stratum, and "tribal beliefs" that justify the given hierarchy, which acquires a mystical status as a result of early emotional conditioning and repeated performance of rituals (ceremonies).[13] On the other hand, instrumental valuation refers to the process by which individuals judge the serviceability of technology, defined as an indivisible combination of tools, knowledge, skills, and processes for accomplishing tasks. Technology serves as a universal "locus of value" (Gordon 1980: 41).[14]

Anthropological institutionalists may be described as those who most strongly believe in a *homo culturalis* (Gruchy 1987) representation of human action and knowledge. They adopt the broadest understanding and offer the most extensive treatments of culture (e.g., Benton 1982; Adams 1986; Mayhew 1987; Neale 1987; Waller 1987, 2003; Schaniel 1988). This is indicated, for example, by such interpretations of culture as: "an aggregation of past decisions made by people in something like the same circumstances" (Adams 1986: 279) or "a primary and therefore undefined rubric for all the rules and folkviews to which its members subscribe" (Neale 1990: 335). These statements are indeed anthropological in tone and substance. The influence of Anthropology resounds in W.C. Neale's call for "absolute cultural relativism" (ibid.), which, according to him, grasps the impossibility of full access to meaning and rationality of thought in other cultures, but does not preclude making moral judgments about them. This strand of Institutionalism also draws from the contributions of Karl Polanyi, particularly the idea of a "substantive economy," namely, actual processes of "material want satisfaction" (1957b: 243) in contrast to a "formal economy," which is predicated upon scarcity and choice.[15]

Instrumental Institutionalists also take culture seriously and present rich treatments of it (e.g., Hayden 1993).[16] However, relying on Veblen's stress on technology, instrumentalists privilege the problem-solving facet of human behavior (Junker 1968; Tool 1986, 1993; Bush 1988; Hayden 1988). Great weight is placed on "the instrumental use of knowledge" to further human life (Tool 1981: 576). Paul Bush offers the concept of ceremonial encapsulation to show that humans make use of technology as a criterion for evaluating "instrumental efficiency" (1988: 130) only to the extent allowed by the existing institutional value system. The emphasis on the importance of technology seems to have produced an idealist interpretation of culture. For instance, Gregory Hayden defines culture as "a collective systemic mental construct which contains a group's abstract ideas, ideals, and values from the superorganic and supernatural world and is found in legends, mythology, supernatural visions, folklore, literature, elaborated superstitions and sagas" (1993: 308). In consequence, culture is identified with myth and other products of imagination, ontologically opposite to technological, 'matter-of-fact' facets of life.

As Anne Mayhew has pointed out, "culture and instrumental valuation are the concepts from which all of the rest of institutional economics flows" (1987: 587). The anthropological line of thought emphasizes culture, the instrumentalist line stresses instrumental valuation. In comparative, cross-cultural terms, the two lines broadly overlap with relativist and universalist visions respectively—the anthropological calls for cultural relativism, while the instrumentalist prioritizes the universality of technological expediency. In the discourse of international development, the concept of culture lost some of its significance to instrumental valuation, which became a platform for norma-tive judgment and therefrom policy prescription.

Development Institutionalism

The twentieth-century discourse of international development engulfed most economists, including Institutionalists who sought to accommodate the agenda of 'third world development.' The work of Clarence Ayres (1962 [1944]), which laid the theoretical foundation for the OIE approach to development economics, is emblematic in this regard. The concept of culture became conflated with cer-emonialism, and a universalist outlook dominated. This could be seen in such well-known texts as Gunnar Myrdal's *Asian Drama* (1968), and less familiar ones as William Kapp's *Hindu Culture* (1963). This section examines the con-tributions of these three authors.[17]

Clarence Ayres' dilemma

Ayres, by all accounts, was the most influential figure in postwar OIE (Street 1987; Hodgson 2000), his work influenced many students of development economics (Adams 1993). Unfortunately, his attempt to adapt institutional analysis to the dis-course of international development contributed to the relegation of culture to the theoretical status of a ceremonial impediment to 'progress.'

The idea of culture impressed Ayres deeply as is clear in his wholehearted embrace of the principle that it is "a phenomenon *sui generis*" (1962 [1944]: 95), and in his multiple articulations of its meaning and significance, for instance:

> Cultural phenomena (including the economic) derive exclusively from other cultural phenomena and can be explained only in terms of other cultural phenomena—*"omnis cultura ex cultura."*
>
> (1944: 96)

> Culture has reference to the body of lore which pervades and sustains that system of relationships and which has been (in varying amounts) learned by all the members of the community.
>
> (1952: 11)

No other idea has made a greater contribution to our understanding of human nature.

(1961: 85)

In other words, he saw that 'human nature' itself is a cultural creation.[18]

Ayres' most extensive discussion of culture occurs in *Toward a Reasonable Society* (1961), in which he affirmed Veblen's view that all social relationships had two aspects: technological (tool-skill using, problem-solving) and ceremonial or institutionalized (arbitrary, power and status-driven). The biggest mistake, he cautioned, was to see technology as external to humans and to draw a distinction between material and nonmaterial culture, which in turn leads to "two serious misconceptions" (ibid.: 83): that the institutional network of a society constitutes its nonmaterial culture, and that the latter stands for the irrational. Ayres rejected metaphysical dualisms such as mind/body and spiritual/physical (Miller 1992), and argued that the technological and the ceremonial are "behavior functions" rather than "two separate realms of being"—"a dichotomy but not a dualism" (Ayres 1962 [1944]: 101). Nevertheless, he stated: "the enigma of culture is that ... man the tool user should also be man the mythmaker and the conjurer" (1961: 85–86). That he considered this a mystery suggests that Ayres could not break away from the dualism of ideal/material. His dilemma was that, on one hand, he had a profound understanding of the concept-phenomenon of culture, which admits no universal truths. On the other, he possessed an equally compelling insight into the concept-phenomenon of technology that—by his reckoning—contained its own universal logic. This seems to me an inevitable consequence of the ceremonial/technological paradigmatic dualism, which Ayres imparted to Institutionalist development thought.

In the second edition of *The Theory of Economic Progress* (1962), Ayres presented a universalist perspective on development, which entailed evaluating all cultures by what he perceived to be an objective criterion, namely, instrumental value. As James Street (1987) recognized, it was the postwar interest in international development that foregrounded the second edition of Ayres' book. The subtitle *A Study of the Fundamentals of Economic Development and Cultural Change* was added to signal the book's relevance to problems of 'underdevelopment.' Ayres articulated the rationale for this addition in a Foreword, stating that though the original edition published in 1944 was not written with an eye toward international development, in substance it contained a theory applicable to this problem. The main points of this theory are: first, the process of development is indivisible and irresistible because technology—"all human activities involving the use of tools" (1962: vii)—advances cumulatively through the combination of tools. Second, human capital is vital for economic growth. Third, technological advance proceeds in inverse ratio to institutional rigidity, that is, ceremonialism in the form of hierarchy, rituals, and tribal beliefs. Fourth, being science-based, the values accompanying technological change are universal.

Cross-cultural judgment in Ayres' work arises from this fourth point—that technological change mandates its own universal culture. Industry requires the adoption of a different way of life, with a different rhythm and a new set of habits, as Veblen had noted in describing the impact of the machine process. In short, economic development engenders cultural change. As a general observation, this is difficult to dispute. However, Ayres went on to offer his normative conclusion that "industrial society is the most successful way of life mankind has ever known" (1962: xxv), as measured by better nutrition, health, and accommodations, and wider availability of information. In effect, the twentieth-century postwar preoccupation with development allowed the instrumental value of technology to serve as a criterion for policy prescriptions for low-income societies. As Mayhew explained, Ayres' "goal is less to offer an evolutionary theory than to understand what can be done to hasten evolution, now clearly stated as a path toward progress" (1998: 459).[19] This became a guiding principle for postwar Institutionalism.

Culture as a ceremonial impediment

The scholarly agenda that Ayres left behind called for locating instances where ceremonialism hindered technological change. However, in the context of the development discourse, the term ceremonialism came to take the place of all beliefs and practices common in those countries classified as 'under' or 'less' developed; in other words, their cultures. This perspective appears in somewhat different ways in Myrdal's and so Kapp's work.[20] Their contributions contain many issues to comment on and some to dispute, so my discussion is kept to a minimally critical overview.

Myrdal (1957, 1968, 1970) was a leader in the modernization movement. In his preoccupation with the problem of 'world poverty,' he did not spell out a particular interpretation of culture, but his writings indicate he was mindful of it in a broad anthropological sense. In general, Myrdal was committed to two related tasks: the first was to challenge conventional development economics out of concern that 'Western' models were based on inaccurate assumptions about life in poor countries. The second task was to identify institutional obstacles to development. Both tasks were extensively displayed in *Asian Drama*, in which he produced a detailed account of cultural "inhibitors" of and "obstacles" to change (1968: 1505), commenting on every aspect of life in the region from education to health, marriage and religion, and institutional structures, whether moneylenders or the state. According to him, the challenge for development planning was to enable the 'Western outlook' of local elites to overrule 'traditional attitudes;' this required locating not only the observable "totality of beliefs and valuations" (ibid.: 102), which elites adhered to, but also those that lay dormant at a muted deeper level.

On the other hand, Myrdal was critical of the generalized notion of "Asian values" commonly used in the literature then to represent an intransigent handicap to modernization. He described this notion as a belief that "people of one religion, one country, or of the entire region—meaning usually all Asia—have the same fundamental cultural and personality traits and world outlook" (ibid.: 94). In this view, Asians were thought to be "more spiritual and less materialistic" than Europeans, intuitive more than rationalist, endowed with high regard for learning, and capable of enduring "extreme physical suffering" (ibid.: 95). These attributes were believed to be the fountain of higher wisdom and moral character. Myrdal dismissed this composite characterization as no more than a "stereotype" (ibid.) rooted in misconceptions and biased ideologies, whether colonialist or nationalist. Interestingly, today the somewhat similar idea of 'Confucian values' has surfaced in explanations of rapid economic growth in East Asia, except these values are seen as a catalyst for, rather than an obstacle to, development (see Chapter 7). Myrdal would likely reject this similarly reductive view.

Instead of speculating about Asian values, Myrdal suggested a list of "modernization ideals" required for development, emphatically expressing his partiality to European-like modernity (1968: 61–62). In his words, these ideals are:

- efficiency
- diligence
- orderliness
- punctuality
- frugality
- scrupulous honesty
- rationality in decisions on action
- preparedness for change
- alertness to opportunities
- energetic enterprise
- integrity and self-reliance
- cooperativeness
- willingness to take the long view.

According to him, these are the qualities of the "modern industrial man." Some of the ideals, e.g., punctuality, may be granted as characteristic of industrial discipline, while others carry the implication that (as a group) people in non-European societies lack such general attributes as rationality or honesty. However, Myrdal did not simply present broad qualities that may be conceived differently in different cultures. He was more specific, for example, defining rationality by "the rationally calculating 'economic man' of Western liberal ideology" (ibid.: 61), and cooperativeness as "acceptance of responsibility for the welfare of the community and the *nation*" (ibid.: 62; emphasis added).

Rather than a set of abstract qualities conducive to personal and social improvement, Myrdal was advocating the specific pattern of how certain qualities have—or are thought to have—emerged in modern European history to produce these nations' particular path of economic evolution. For instance, in the development literature, authors have commonly represented 'individualism' and 'collectivism' as opposite traits belonging to entirely different cultures (see Chapters 5 and 7 in this book). Myrdal did not think of these in the dualistic manner found in the literature most likely because he was trying to model an actual account, that is, a specific combination of behavior patterns (calculating, individual-centered, but cooperative, patient, and so on) seen in the history of development in Western Europe and North America.

Similarly interested in Asia, William Kapp attempted to locate cultural impediments to economic development. His monograph, *Hindu Culture: Economic
Development and Economic Planning in India* (1963) represents a classic example of orientalism in Economics.[21] Kapp defined "Hindu culture" to include
members of the religion and those who share "important value orientations and
behavior patterns of the Hindus" regardless of religion (ibid.: 9). He interpreted
culture generally to be:

> [T]he basic rules and patterns of human behaviour. As such it has refer-
> ence to the patterns of thought, emotions, values, ideas and categories often
> expressed in symbols which shape human awareness and human experience.
> These patterns influence the way in which man looks upon himself and his
> role in the universe ... Indeed, culture conditions our conscious and uncon-
> scious desires and feelings, gives meaning to behaviour and provides the
> rationale for living.
>
> (ibid.: 7)

This is an idealist perception, associating culture only with consciousness, meaning,
and symbols. According to Kapp, the "distinctive features of Hindu culture" were
"complexity and diversity" (ibid.: 9–10), unity of religious and social systems,
and group identification. Of particular import were the ideas of cyclical metaphysics, fate, and reincarnation; in short, the "iron law of inescapable retribution
(*Karma*)" (ibid.: 15).

Kapp claimed this set of beliefs led to renunciation of material wealth as it
"tends to lower the level of human aspiration but places a premium on passive
acceptance rather than amelioration of the human situation whether by hard work
or by social reform" (ibid.: 16). He characterized the coexistence of an ascetic
worldview with persistent search for material wealth among some followers of
Hindu teachings as one of "apparent paradoxes" (ibid.: 17) in the culture, instead
of seeing it as a manifestation of the complexity that he observed. He was aware
that religion was one factor among many—caste, family, village, and land tenure.
Nevertheless, he went on to conclude that Hindu culture "tends to retard India's
economic development" (ibid.: vi), and to call for a national development plan
to bring about more equal opportunities and economic mobility. For Kapp, the
impediment was not ceremonialism in a rigorous sense, it was 'Hindu culture' *en
masse*. This represents a departure from Ayres' articulation of the development
problem.[22]

To summarize, this brief overview of some contributions by Ayres, Myrdal,
and Kapp suggests that despite deep appreciation of the concept of culture,
which should lead to a relativist perspective on development, a universalist
position has dominated. But, there is a subtle difference between the three. For
Ayres, universalism resulted from a conviction that technology—the locus of
instrumental value—supplied its own cumulative supra-cultural logic such that
"the only remaining alternative is that of intelligent, voluntary acceptance of
the industrial way of life" (1962: xxiv–xxv). For Myrdal and Kapp, the cultural

superiority of European modernity seems to constitute its own rationale for advocating 'development' in other countries.

Institutionalism and development economics

With the exception of Myrdal, Institutionalist development thought is almost unknown in the general stream of Economics. Literature reviews typically do not refer to an Institutionalist theory of growth and development along with the Classical, Marxian, and Schumpeterian (Adelman 1961; Furtado 1964; Hunt 1989). What is also little known is the extent to which OIE has influenced development thought in its formative years. According to Adams (1993: 248), "Development economics has from its infancy embraced the study of institutions and its validity as a field must rest on the proposition that institutions matter." A look at the literature reveals broad convergence between Institutional and Neoclassical analyses in this field. (See Appendix III for more development literature.)

The influence of OIE was visible in prominent texts of early development economics. It was clearest in the work of W.A. Lewis, who, drawing on Veblen and various anthropological sources, stated: "First we must inquire which kinds of institutions are favourable to growth, and which are inimical to effort, to innovation or to investment" (1955: 11). Veblen was also cited in other classic texts of this period (e.g., Hirschman 1958; Nurkse 1962 [1953]). Major authors who took note of the potential implications of culture used the term "non-economic" barriers (Hoselitz 1952; Adelman and Morris 1965; Rostow 1971 [1960]), which became common shorthand for culture among development economists. The leading role of OIE in development thinking was summarized in Benjamin Higgins' remark that "Professor Ayres and his fellows, it is now clear, have long been doing the sort of thing all 'development economists' now find it necessary to do" (1960: 16).[23] Some Neoclassical economists (Bauer 1972) agreed with Myrdal's diagnosis of the development 'problem' in Asia though they thought he underestimated the difficulty of transforming entrenched cultural traditions.

Thus, despite the drastic general philosophical gulf between Neoclassical and Institutional economists, the two converged on the question of 'third world development.' Institutionalists have documented this convergence without noting anything incongruous about it (Klein 1977; Street 1987; Adams 1993; Strassmann 1993; Mayhew 1998). According to Philip Klein (1977: 785), "the most significant visible impact of American institutionalism has been in the field of what is now called development economics." He argued the development problem was the same for Institutionalists and mainstream economists, namely, how to raise per capita output through institutionally appropriate industrialization, and to address the consequences of economic and social transformation. Based on a comparison of the contents of two journals, *Economic Development and Cultural Change* (representing the mainstream) and the *Journal of Economic Issues* (the premiere Institutionalist venue) from 1968 to 1977, Klein concluded there was no difference in the treatment of growth and development. Articles in both publications were "essentially institutionalist" (ibid.: 792) in their preoccupation with the conflict between dynamic technology and institutional barriers—whether these are manifested in power structures or inadequate fiscal systems.

Looking at the bulk of OIE writings, it is clear that the universalist, instrumentalist line of thought dominated. The universalist contributions were instrumentalist in the added sense that their attention to culture was mostly a vehicle for deriving appropriate policy for development in low-income countries. In this regard, OIE was a full participant in the development discourse although Institutionalists usually cautioned about the social complexities of modernization.

Most OIE contributors were driven to locate cultural impediments to technological advance, with some variation in thematic or regional focus, and the force with which policies were prescribed (Dowd 1967; Junker 1967; Gordon 1973; Bolin 1984; De Gregori 1985). Commenting on Marxist analyses of Latin American economies, Street (1967: 61) went so far as to state "[i]t is the culture that must be updated, rather than merely a class to be overthrown." This trend continued into the 1990s, with Adams—otherwise of the anthropological brand of Institutionalism—claiming that 'underdeveloped' countries furnished "a laboratory case of the effects of inhibitory and inappropriate institutions on technological and economic progress" (1993: 261). For Africa, it was concluded, without much elaboration, that "ceremonialism in the Ayresian sense is impeding technological progress" (Schneider 1999: 328). In this literature, ceremonialism—the intransigence of certain traditions or elements of a way of life—is conflated with culture as a whole. This conflation is inconsistent with Ayres' theory according to which ceremonialism constitutes one aspect of culture that could engender different levels of and forms of impediment to economic development, depending on the specific context. In this sense, these works lack a rigorous application of his argument. What these authors took from Ayres is the universalist vision derived from emphasis on technological advance, which allowed the convergence between Institutional and Neoclassical analyses of development.

Today, the return to culture in development economics (see Chapter 7) has led to another convergence between Institutionalist and Neoclassical economists. The signs of this convergence resound in Vernon Ruttan's (1988: 253) praise of Myrdal for having carried out "[t]he most ambitious effort by an economist to employ cultural variables to interpret economic behavior, assess the prospects for growth, and prescribe economic policy." In turn, Adams (1993) commends Ruttan (1988) for bringing culture and institutions back into development economics. Some authors (Casson 1993; Stein 2008) combine OIE and NIE principles in an attempt to construct new theoretical interpretations of economic development. Given its Neoclassical basis, NIE's treatments of culture are narrow and static (see Chapter 5). But, this aside, the convergence between OIE and NIE is rooted in a common belief in the imperative of modernization as this process unfolded in Western Europe and North America. This is an outlook in which the present of underdeveloped countries represents—as Polanyi puts it—"a mere prelude to the true history of our civilization" (1957a [1944]: 45).

The anthropological line of Institutional economics holds a non-invidious view that adheres to Ayres' uncompromised understanding of culture (1962 [1944], 1952). In this line, institutions and other cultural phenomena are investigated without necessarily being theorized as ceremonial obstacles to be cleared by the appropriate set of development policies. Unfortunately, it is extremely rare to find examples of this line of thought in published work. Examples include analyses of British colonialism in Africa by W.J. Barber (1961) and W.C. Neale (1984), and William Schaniel's (1988) study of the cultural impacts of new technology on the Maori in New Zealand. Schaniel notes that because of their lack of knowledge of iron, the Maori initially used the nails brought over by Captain Cook as ornaments, instead of tools. Schaniel shows that in the process of technology borrowing, it is possible to adopt a technological product without "the system of thought that produced the technology" (ibid.: 493)—in this case, a piece of metal could serve as a nail or an ornament depending on the cultural context. Without calling for Maori culture to be 'updated,' he gives a parallel account of situations in which Europeans were in a similar position of cultural exchange—for example, borrowing gunpowder from 'the Orient.' Although his argument retains an element of ideal/material dualism, the paper offers the type of unteleological, non-invidious cultural perspective that challenges the development discourse.[24]

The dominance of the universalist perspective is exhibited in the dearth of such truly substantive economic analyses of specific cultural phenomena that honor Veblen's institutional method, that is, "a scrutiny of the details of their activities" (1898a: 391). The strength of original Institutionalism lies in its exceptional grasp of the complexity, entrenchedness, and internal contradictions of culture. However, this strength is often lost because of uncritical eagerness to spot ceremonialism and accordingly prescribe development policy. As Mayhew has suggested, Institutional economics contains a "duality" of coexistence between "pragmatic" judgment and "inherited and unquestioned beliefs" (1988: 27). Could it be that the emphasis on instrumental valuation and 'development' has itself acquired the status of an inherited, unquestioned tribal belief?

Conclusion

The original tradition of Institutional economics is premised on the inseparability of 'economy' from 'culture.' Economic action is diffused through any given culture, within a labyrinth of institutions and power dynamics, all evolving in a historically specific and unpredictable manner that precludes an uncomplicated reading of the future of other cultures from the past of European modernity. Yet, OIE is also built on the belief in a pervasive human ability or inclination to instrumentally use technology. This dualistic framework is embodied in the dichotomy between the ceremonial and the instrumental, expressed in the presence of an *anthropological* (relativist) line of thought and an *instrumentalist* (universalist) line within OIE. The problem with dualism is that it confines the analytical horizon to either one or the other of two poles, and therefore limits the ability to grasp in-betweenness and alterity.

Whenever contemporary Institutionalists have delved into analyses of different societies, the universalist position seems to dominate. This became clear in the twentieth-century discourse of international development as Ayres generalized from industrial economies to the entire world, leaving behind his belief in culture as a phenomenon *sui generis*. In general, examining social change in a comparative context, without immediately theorizing the societies classified as under or less developed (subaltern cultures) as inherent objects for modernization, has been the exception in OIE. In William Waller's apt words, it has been "our culture, all the way down" (2003: 44).

Notes

1 Mirowski (1991) argues that Institutional economics receded partly because of the decline of pragmatist philosophy in the USA. For other accounts of OIE, see Dorfman (1949, 1959), Gruchy (1947), Samuels (1988), Mayhew (1988, 1989), Tool (1988), Rutherford and Samuels (1997), and Hodgson (1998, 2000). See Chapter 5 in this book for NIE. For discussions of the two institutionalisms, see Hutchison (1984), Hodgson (1993, 2007), Rutherford (1994), and Castellano and García-Quero (2012).

2 The dichotomy has been a source of debate within OIE (see Mayhew 1987; Samuels 1988, vol. III; Tool 1990). Dyer (1986) has proposed that making habit the unifying concept of Veblen's theory avoids the dualism of technological versus ceremonial behavior. Miller (1992) suggests the dichotomy reveals "ambivalence" among Institutionalists about the notion of progress.

3 Others have debated the question of dualism in OIE. According to Waller (1994), the charge that Institutional theory suffers from a dualism of individual/society is false, though he admits that some writings do bear a dualistic interpretation. I do not believe that OIE contains a dualism in this regard. For more on dualism and related questions, see Miller (1992), Adams (1993), Hayden (1993), Jennings (1999), Waller (1999), Jackson (2009), and Chapter 1 in this book. For Institutionalist critiques of dualism, see Jennings (1993), Jennings and Champlin (1994), and Champlin (1997).

4 The term neoinstitutional (sometimes also neo-institutional) was introduced by Marc Tool (Gruchy 1969, 1972; Junker 1968; Mayhew 1988). Some NIE authors (Schotter 1981; Eggertsson 1990) have adopted the term without seeming familiarity with its previous usage. Contemporary OIE encompasses a vast volume of scholarship produced within the parameters of the Association for Evolutionary Economics and the Association for Institutional Thought that is only partially covered in this chapter.

5 The variety of meanings and usages that culture assumes throughout Veblen's work may be indicated by a simple—though not comprehensive—enumeration of the ways in which he identified culture and the range of phenomena he characterized as cultural. In the first instance, he referred to specific cultures: archaic, savage, predatory, peaceable, nomadic, modern, pecuniary, human, and Western. In the second, he used the word 'cultural' to describe: value, structure, traits, regions, environment, beauty, history, growth, change, lag, drift, trend, advance, sequence, and development. Goodwin (2006) blames Veblen for partly derailing interest in arts and culture in Economics because he characterized 'the arts' as instruments of conspicuous consumption. Goodwin is obviously referring to the narrow meaning of culture as creativity.

6 Commons defined a transaction as "the means, under operation of law and custom, of acquiring and alienating legal control of commodities" (1931: 656). This is one of his major influences on NIE proponents, especially Williamson, who adopts "the transaction" as his "basic unit of analysis" (1985: 387).

7   Another contributor to early Institutionalist thought is Dixon (1941). Although he cited Veblen and Hamilton, Dixon is rarely mentioned in OIE literature (Waller, 1982, is an exception). See Rutherford and Samuels (1997, vols. I–IV) for additional early contributors.

8   Much debate surrounds Veblen's use of the term instinct, see Adams (1980) and Tool (1986). Jennings and Waller (1994) have proposed discarding the term altogether, given its lack of clarity.

9   For an early application of the dichotomy, see Hamilton's (1957) criticism of the mythical place of the entrepreneur in Neoclassical economics. He argued the entrepreneur's role is merely ceremonial, whereas economic advance depends on the state of science and technology.

10 Veblen thought man's actions are teleological in the sense of being purpose-driven, but without a foreseeable end result (1898a, 1994). Jennings and Waller (1994: 998) call this "small-t teleology" to distinguish it from the teleology of Neoclassical theory.

11 Brinkman and Brinkman (1997) review the literature and offer some contemporary applications of cultural lag, for example, the discrepancy between technological impacts on the environment and human attitudes toward ecological damage.

12 "Radical" institutionalists, who profess an affinity with Marxian thought, present one example (see Dugger 1989; Stanfield 1995). Contributions to Feminist economics also form a distinct perspective, though some could be placed with the anthropological line (Jennings 1993; Waller and Jennings 1990; Zein-Elabdin 1996; Waller 1999; Hopkins 2007; see Chapter 8 in this book). For more on culture in OIE, see Strassmann (1974), Waller (1982), Hill (1989), Jackson (1993, 1996), Mayhew (2008), and Zein-Elabdin (2009).

13 Tribal beliefs in Ayres' usage strictly refer to old, purely ceremonial habits in any context—"Hindu priests" as well as "the Christian Church" in Europe (1962 [1944]: xxiv). According to Waller (1982), Ayres (1952) substituted the term ceremonial for institutional to identify aspects of culture or behavior that resisted change. Also see Adams (1993) on Ayres' use of these two terms.

14 The relationship of technology to culture and institutions is not always clear in OIE literature. Some consider technology an aspect of culture (Ayres 1961; Junker 1967; Lower 1988; De Gregori 2001), others conceptualize evolutionary cultural change itself as an outcome of technological choices (Bush 1988).

15 One outcome of Polanyi's dichotomy has been the association of the substantive meaning only with non-market, or 'primitive,' economies, see Halperin (1988) for a critique. For more on Polanyi and OIE, see Gordon (1980), Stanfield (1980, 1995), Neale (1987), Lower (1988), Adams (1993), and Hayden (1993).

16 Hayden models the relationship of culture to society, institutions, and values in his idea of a "social fabric matrix"—an "integrated process" of interaction between seven components: cultural values, social beliefs, attitudes about specific objects, tastes, the natural environment, technology, and social institutions (1993: 312). He characterized dualistic thought as a Western cultural value but did not elaborate.

17 In this and the following section I concentrate on theoretical work in which a philosophical discussion of culture and development is transparent. A good part of the empirical literature is referenced in Klein (1977, 1998), Adams (1993), and Mayhew (1998). More recent work tends to be limited to specific issues or problems without much reference to culture or development generally. See Castellano and García-Quero (2012) for a helpful review of current development debates within OIE and NIE.

18 For more on Ayres and culture, see Gruchy (1972), Strassmann (1974), Hill (1989), and Miller (1992).

19 Mayhew (1998) made this point in reference to *Toward a Reasonable Society* (Ayres 1961), which, she suggests, represented a note of optimism in response to prevalent critiques of the American industrial capitalist way of life, for example, by Galbraith (1958).

20 For more of these two authors' work, see Myrdal (1978), Kapp (1965, 1968), Gruchy (1972), and Steppacher *et al.* (1977). See Bergeron (2004) for a critique of Myrdal's modernism. Galbraith has also contributed to the subject of development although more generally. In *Economic Development* (1964), a collection of lectures he delivered as US Ambassador to India, he stated that the causes of 'national poverty' depended on culture and history. Unlike Myrdal and Kapp, he was skeptical of the very purpose of development.
21 See Dimand (2004) and Olmsted (2004) for other examples of orientalism in classical and contemporary economic literature.
22 In other work, Kapp (1965) cited Ayres (1962 [1944]) to argue that resource allocation based on ceremonial goals hinders development in many underdeveloped countries. Accordingly, development policy should be based on rational planning and practical scientific considerations.
23 Higgins (1960) was "recanting" his criticism of Ayres (1944) for drawing on Anthropology, Psychology, and other fields outside of Economics.
24 The dualism is apparent in the theoretical distinction between the product (material) and the systems of thought within which technology originated (ideas).

References

Adams, John (ed.) (1980) *Institutional Economics: Contributions to the Development of Holistic Economics: Essays in Honor of Allan Gruchy*, Boston: Martinus Nijhoff Publishing.
—— (1986) "Peasant Rationality: Individuals, Groups, Cultures," *World Development*, 14 (2): 273–282.
—— (1993) "Institutions and Economic Development: Structure, Process, and Incentives," in Marc Tool (ed.) *Institutional Economics: Theory, Method, Policy*, Boston: Kluwer Academic Publishers, 245–269.
Adelman, Irma (1961) *Theories of Economic Growth and Development*, Stanford, CA: Stanford University Press.
—— and Cynthia Taft Morris (1965) "A Factor Analysis of the Interrelationship between Social and Political Variables and Per Capita Gross National Product," *The Quarterly Journal of Economics* 79 (4): 555–578.
Ayres, Clarence E. (1951) "The Co-ordinates of Institutionalism," *American Economic Review*, 41 (2): 47–55.
—— (1952) *The Industrial Economy: Its Technological Basis and Institutional Destiny*, Boston: Houghton Mifflin.
—— (1961) *Toward A Reasonable Society: The Values of Industrial Civilization*, Austin, TX: University of Texas Press.
—— (1962 [1944]) *The Theory of Economic Progress: A Study of the Fundamentals of Economic Development and Cultural Change*, New York: Schocken Books.
Barber, William J. (1961) *The Economy of British Central Africa: A Case Study of Economic Development in a Dualistic Society*, Stanford, CA: Stanford University Press.
Bauer, Peter T. (1972) *Dissent on Development: Studies and Debates in Development Economics*, Cambridge, MA: Harvard University Press.
Benton, Raymond Jr. (1982) "Economics as a Cultural System," *Journal of Economic Issues*, 26 (2): 461–469.
Bergeron, Suzanne (2004) *Fragments of Development: Nation, Gender, and the Space of Modernity*, Ann Arbor, MI: University of Michigan Press.

Bolin, Meb (1984) "An Institutionalist Perspective on Economic Development," *Journal of Economic Issues*, 18 (2): 643–650.

Boyd, Robert and Peter J. Richerson (2000) "Climate, Culture, and the Evolution of Cognition," in Cecilia M. Heyes and Ludwig Huber (eds.) *The Evolution of Cognition*, Cambridge, MA: MIT Press, 66–82.

Brinkman, Richard L. and June E. Brinkman (1997) "Cultural Lag: Conception and Theory," *International Journal of Social Economics*, 24 (6): 609–627.

Bush, Paul D. (1988) "The Theory of Institutional Change," in M. Tool (ed.) *Evolutionary Economics*, vol. 1: *Foundations of Institutional Thought*, Armonk: M.E. Sharpe, 125–166.

Casson, Mark (1993) "Cultural Determinants of Economic Performance," *Journal of Comparative Economics*, 17: 418–442.

Castellano, Fernando López and Fernando García-Quero (2012) "Institutional Approaches to Economic Development: The Current Status of the Debate," *Journal of Economic Issues*, 46 (4): 921–940.

Champlin, Dell (1997) "Culture, Natural Law, and the Restoration of Community," *Journal of Economic Issues*, 31(2): 575–584.

Coase, Ronald H. (1984) "The New Institutional Economics," *Journal of Institutional and Theoretical Economics*, 140: 229–231.

Commons, John R. (1968 [1924]) *Legal Foundations of Capitalism*, Madison, WI: University of Wisconsin Press.

—— (1925) "Law and Economics," *Yale Law Journal*, 34 (February): 371–382.

—— (1931) "Institutional Economics," *American Economic Review*, 21 (December): 648–657.

De Gregori, Thomas R. (1985) *A Theory of Technology: Continuity and Change in Human Development*, Ames, IA: Iowa State University Press.

—— (2001) "Does Culture/Technology Still Matter to Institutionalists?" *Journal of Economic Issues*, 35 (4): 1009–1017.

Dimand, Robert W. (2004) "Classical Political Economy and Orientalism: Nassau Senior's Eastern Tours" in E. Zein-Elabdin and S. Charusheela (eds.) *Postcolonialism Meets Economics*, London: Routledge, 73–90.

Dixon, Russell A. (1941) *Economic Institutions and Cultural Change*, New York: McGraw-Hill.

Dorfman, Joseph (1949) *The Economic Mind in American Civilization*, vol. 3, *1865–1918*, New York: Viking Press.

—— (1959) *The Economic Mind in American Civilization*, vol. 4, *1918–1933*, New York: Augustus M. Kelley.

Dowd, Douglas F. (1967) "Some Issues of Economic Development and of Development Economics," *Journal of Economic Issues*, 1 (3): 149–160.

Dugger, William M. (ed.) (1989) *Radical Institutionalism: Contemporary Voices*, New York: Greenwood Press.

Dyer, Alan W. (1986) "Semiotics, Economic Development, and the Deconstruction of Economic Man," *Journal of Economic Issues*, 20 (2): 541–549.

Eggertsson, Thráinn (1990) *Economic Behavior and Institutions*, Cambridge: Cambridge University Press.

Furtado, Celso (1964) *Development and Underdevelopment*, Berkeley, CA: University of California Press.

Galbraith, John Kenneth (1958) *The Affluent Society*, Boston: Houghton Mifflin Company.

—— (1964) *Economic Development*, Cambridge, MA: Harvard University Press.

Glade, William P. (1952) "The Theory of Cultural Lag and the Veblenian Contribution," *American Journal of Economics and Sociology*, 11 (4): 427–437.

Gordon, Wendell (1973) "Institutionalized Consumption Patterns in Underdeveloped Countries," *Journal of Economic Issues*, 7 (2): 267–287.

—— (1980) *Institutional Economics: The Changing System*, Austin, TX: University of Texas Press.

Gruchy, Allan G. (1947) *Modern Economic Thought: The American Contribution*, New York: Prentice-Hall.

—— (1969) "Neoinstitutionalism and the Economics of Dissent," *Journal of Economic Issues*, 3 (1): 3–17.

—— (1972) *Contemporary Economic Thought: The Contribution of Neo-Institutional Economics*, Clifton, NJ: Augustus M. Kelley.

—— (1987) "The Subject Matter of Institutional Economics," in *The Reconstruction of Economics: An Analysis of the Fundamentals of Institutional Economics*, New York: Greenwood Press, 1–19.

Halperin, Rhoda H. (1988) *Economies Across Cultures: Towards a Comparative Science of the Economy*, New York: St. Martin's Press.

Hamilton, David (1957) "The Entrepreneur as a Cultural Hero," *The Southwestern Social Science Quarterly*, 38 (3): 248–256.

Hamilton, Walton H. (1932) "Institution," in Edwin R. A. Seligman and Alvin Johnson (eds.) *Encyclopaedia of the Social Sciences*, vol. 8, London: Macmillan & Co.

Hayden, F. Gregory (1988) "Values, Beliefs, and Attitudes in a Sociotechnical Setting," *Journal of Economic Issues*, 22 (2): 415–426.

—— (1993) "Institutionalist Policy Making," in M. Tool (ed.) *Institutional Economics: Theory, Method, Policy*, Boston: Kluwer Academic Publishers. 283–331.

Higgins, Benjamin H. (1960) "Some Introductory Remarks on Institutionalism and Economic Development," *The Southwestern Social Science Quarterly*, 41 (1): 15–21.

Hill, Lewis E. (1989) "Cultural Determinism or Emergent Evolution: An Analysis of the Controversy between Clarence Ayres and David Miller," *Journal of Economic Issues*, 23 (2): 465–471.

Hirschman, Albert O. (1958) *The Strategy of Economic Development*, New Haven, CT: Yale University Press.

Hodgson, Geoffrey M. (1993) "Institutional Economics: Surveying the 'Old' and the 'New'," *Metroeconomica*, 44 (1): 1–28.

—— (ed.) (1998) *The Foundations of Evolutionary Economics, 1890–1973*, vols. 1, 2, Cheltenham: Edward Elgar.

—— (2000) "What Is the Essence of Institutional Economics?" *Journal of Economic Issues*, 34 (2): 317–329.

—— (2007) "Evolutionary and Institutional Economics as the New Mainstream?" *Evolutionary and Institutional Economics Review*, 4 (1): 7–25.

Hopkins, Barbara E. (2007) "Western Cosmetics in the Gendered Development of Consumer Culture in China," *Feminist Economics*, 13 (3–4): 287–306.

Hoselitz, Bert F. (1952) "Non-Economic Barriers to Economic Development," *Economic Development and Cultural Change*, 1 (1): 8–21.

Hunt, Diana (1989) *Economic Theories of Development: An Analysis of Competing Paradigms*, Savage, MD: Barnes & Noble Books.

Hutchison, Terence W. (1984) "Institutionalist Economics Old and New," *Journal of Institutional and Theoretical Economics*, 140: 20–29.

Jackson, William A. (1993) "Culture, Society and Economic Theory," *Review of Political Economy*, 5 (4): 453–469.

88 *Institutional economics: Veblen's tradition*

—— (1996) "Cultural Materialism and Institutional Economics," *Review of Social Economy*, 54 (2): 221–244.

—— (2009) *Economics, Culture and Social Theory*, Cheltenham: Edward Elgar.

Jennings, Ann L. (1993) "Public or Private? Institutional Economics and Feminism," in Marianne A. Ferber and Julie A. Nelson (eds.) *Beyond Economic Man: Feminist Theory and Economics*, Chicago: University of Chicago Press, 111–129.

—— (1999) "Dualisms," in Janice Peterson and Margaret Lewis (eds.) *The Elgar Companion to Feminist Economics*, Cheltenham: Edward Elgar, 142–153.

—— and Dell Champlin (1994) "Cultural Contours of Race, Gender, and Class Distinctions: A Critique of Moynihan and Other Functionalist Views," in Janice Peterson and Doug Brown (eds.) *The Economic Status of Women Under Capitalism: Institutional Economics and Feminist Theory*, Aldershot: Edward Elgar, 95–110.

—— and William Waller (1994) "Evolutionary Economics and Cultural Hermeneutics: Veblen, Cultural Relativism, and Blind Drift," *Journal of Economic Issues*, 28 (4): 997–1030.

—— and William Waller (1995) "Culture: Core Concept Reaffirmed," *Journal of Economic Issues*, 29 (2): 407–418.

Junker, Louis J. (1967) "Capital Accumulation, Savings-Centered Theory, and Economic Development," *Journal of Economic Issues*, 1 (1): 25–43.

—— (1968) "Theoretical Foundations of Neo-Institutionalism," *American Journal of Economics and Sociology*, 27 (2): 197–213.

Kapp, K. William (1963) *Hindu Culture: Economic Development and Economic Planning in India: A Collection of Essays*, Bombay: Asia Publishing House.

—— (1965) "Economic Development in a New Perspective: Existential Minima and Substantive Rationality," *Kyklos*, 17 (1): 49–79.

—— (1968) "In Defense of Institutional Economics," *The Swedish Journal of Economics*, 70 (1): 1–18.

Klein, Philip A. (1977) "An Institutionalist View of Development Economics," *Journal of Economic Issues*, 11 (4): 785–807.

—— (1998) "Rethinking American Participation in Economic Development: An Institutionalist Assessment," *Journal of Economic Issues*, 32 (2): 385–393.

Lewis, W. Arthur (1955) *The Theory of Economic Growth*, London: George Allen and Unwin.

Lower, Milton D. (1988) "The Concept of Technology within the Institutionalist Perspective," in M. Tool (ed.) *Evolutionary Economics*, vol. 1, Armonk, NY: M.E. Sharpe, 197–226.

Mayhew, Anne (1987) "Culture: Core Concept Under Attack," *Journal of Economic Issues*, 21 (2): 587–603.

—— (1988) "The Beginnings of Institutionalism," in M. Tool (ed.) *Evolutionary Economics*, vol. 1: *Foundations of Institutional Thought*, Armonk, NY: M.E. Sharpe, 21–48.

—— (1989) "Contrasting Origins of the Two Institutionalisms: The Social Science Context," *Review of Political Economy*, 1 (3): 319–333.

—— (1998) "On the Difficulty of Evolutionary Analysis," *Cambridge Journal of Economics*, 22 (4): 449–461.

——(2008) "Institutions, Culture and Values," in John B. Davis and Wilfred Dolfsma (eds.) *The Elgar Companion to Social Economics*, Cheltenham: Edward Elgar, 28–43.

Miller, Edythe S. (1992) "The Economics of Progress," *Journal of Economic Issues*, 26 (1): 115–124.

Mirowski, Philip (1991) "The Philosophical Bases of Institutionalist Economics," in Don Lavoie (ed.) *Economics and Hermeneutics*, London: Routledge, 76–112.

Mitchell, Wesley C. (1910) "The Rationality of Economic Activity, I-II," *Journal of Political Economy*, 18 (3): 197–216.

—— (1912) "The Backward Art of Spending Money," *American Economic Review*, 2 (2): 269–281.

—— (1916) "The Role of Money in Economic Theory," *American Economic Review*, 6 (1): 140–161.

—— (1925) "Quantitative Analysis in Economic Theory," *American Economic Review*, 15 (1): 1–12.

—— (1927) *Business Cycles: The Problem and Its Setting*, New York: National Bureau of Economic Research.

Myrdal, Gunnar (1957) *Economic Theory and Under-Developed Regions*, London: Gerald Duckworth & Co.

—— (1968) *Asian Drama: An Inquiry into the Poverty of Nations*, vols. I, II. New York: Pantheon.

—— (1970) *The Challenge of World Poverty: A World Anti-Poverty Program in Outline*, New York: Pantheon Books.

—— (1978) "Institutional Economics," *Journal of Economic Issues*, 12 (4): 771–783.

Neale, Walter C. (1984) "The Evolution of Colonial Institutions: An Argument Illustrated from the Economic History of British Central Africa," *Journal of Economic Issues*, 18 (4): 1177–1187.

—— (1987) "Institutions," *Journal of Economic Issues*, 21 (3): 1177–1206.

—— (1990) "Absolute Cultural Relativism: Firm Foundation for Valuing and Policy," *Journal of Economic Issues*, 24 (2): 333–344.

Nurkse, Ragnar (1962 [1953]) *Problems of Capital Formation in Underdeveloped Countries*, New York: Oxford University Press.

Olmsted, Jennifer (2004) "Orientalism and Economic Methods: (Re)reading Feminist Economic Discussions of Islam," in E. Zein-Elabdin and S. Charusheela (eds.) *Postcolonialism Meets Economics*, London: Routledge, 165–182.

Polanyi, Karl (1957a [1944]) *The Great Transformation*, Boston: Beacon Press.

—— (1957b) "The Economy as Instituted Process," in K. Polanyi, Conrad M. Arensberg, and Harry W. Pearson (eds.) *Trade and Market in the Early Empires: Economies in History and Theory*, Chicago: The Free Press, 243–270.

Rostow, W. W. (1971 [1960]) *The Stages of Economic Growth: A Non-Communist Manifesto*, Cambridge: Cambridge University Press.

Rutherford, Malcolm (1994) *Institutions in Economics: The Old and the New Institutionalism*, Cambridge: Cambridge University Press.

—— and Warren Samuels (eds.) (1997) *Classics in Institutional Economics: The Founders, 1890–1945*, vols. I–V, London: Pickering & Chatto.

Ruttan, Vernon W. (1988) "Cultural Endowments and Economic Development: What Can We Learn from Anthropology?" *Economic Development and Cultural Change*, 36 (3) Supplement: 247–271.

Samuels, Warren J. (ed.) (1988) *Institutional Economics*, vols. I–III, Brookfield, VT: Edward Elgar.

Schaniel, William C. (1988) "New Technology and Culture Change in Traditional Societies," *Journal of Economic Issues*, 22 (2): 493–498.

Schneider, Geoffrey E. (1999) "An Institutionalist Assessment of Structural Adjustment Programs in Africa," *Journal of Economic Issues*, 33 (2): 325–334.

Schotter, Andrew (1981) *The Economic Theory of Social Institutions*, Cambridge: Cambridge University Press.

Stanfield, James Ronald (1980) "The Institutional Economics of Karl Polanyi," *Journal of Economic Issues*, 14 (3): 593–614.

—— (1995) *Economics, Power and Culture: Essays in the Development of Radical Institutionalism*, New York: St. Martin's Press.

Stein, Howard (2008) *Beyond the World Bank Agenda: An Institutional Approach to Development*, Chicago: University of Chicago Press.

Steppacher, Rolf, Brigitte Zogg-Walz, and Hermann Hatzfeldt (eds.) (1977) *Economics in Institutional Perspective: Memorial Essays in Honor of K. William Kapp*, Lexington, MA: Lexington Books.

Strassmann, W. Paul (1974) "Technology: A Culture Trait, a Logical Category, Or Virtue Itself?" *Journal of Economic Issues*, 8 (4): 671–687.

—— (1993) "Development Economics from a Chicago Perspective," in W. J. Samuels (ed.) *The Chicago School of Political Economy*, London: Transaction Publishers, 277–294.

Street, James H. (1967) "The Latin American 'Structuralists' and the Institutionalists: Convergence in Development Theory," *Journal of Economic Issues*, 1 (1): 44–64.

—— (1987) "The Institutionalist Theory of Economic Development," *Journal of Economic Issues*, 21 (4): 1861–1887.

Tool, Marc R. (1981) "The Compulsive Shift to Institutional Analysis," *Journal of Economic Issues*, 15 (3): 569–592.

—— (1986) *Essays in Social Value Theory: A Neoinstitutionalist Contribution*, Armonk, NY: M.E. Sharpe.

—— (ed.) (1988) *Evolutionary Economics*, vols. 1, 2, Armonk, NY: M.E. Sharpe.

—— (1990) "Culture Versus Social Value? A Response to Anne Mayhew," *Journal of Economic Issues*, 24 (4): 1122–1133.

—— (1993) "The Theory of Instrumental Value: Extensions, Clarifications," in Marc Tool (ed.) *Institutional Economics: Theory, Method, Policy*, Boston: Kluwer Academic Publishers, 119–159.

Veblen, Thorstein (1898a) "Why Is Economics Not an Evolutionary Science?" *Quarterly Journal of Economics*, 12 (2): 373–397.

—— (1898b) "The Instinct of Workmanship and the Irksomeness of Labor," *American Journal of Sociology*, 4 (2): 187–201.

—— (1994 [1899]) *The Theory of the Leisure Class*, New York: Dover Publications.

—— (2006 [1904]) "The Cultural Incidence of the Machine Process," in *The Theory of Business Enterprise*, New Brunswick, NJ: Transaction Publishers, 302–373.

—— (1909) "The Limitations of Marginal Utility," *Journal of Political Economy*, 17 (9): 620–636.

—— (1998 [1932]) "Outline of a Policy for the Control of the 'Economic Penetration' of Backward Countries and of Foreign Investments," in Leon Ardzrooni (ed.) *Essays in Our Changing Order*, New Brunswick, NJ: Transaction Publishers, 361–382.

Waller, William T. Jr. (1982) "The Evolution of the Veblenian Dichotomy: Veblen, Hamilton, Ayres, and Foster," *Journal of Economic Issues*, 16 (3): 757–771.

—— (1987) "Ceremonial Encapsulation and Corporate Cultural Hegemony," *Journal of Economic Issues*, 21 (1): 321–328.

—— (1994) "Veblenian Dichotomy and its Critics," in G. Hodgson and W. Samuels (eds.) *The Elgar Companion to Institutional and Evolutionary Economics*, Cheltenham: Edward Elgar, 368–372.

—— (1999) "Institutional Economics, Feminism and Overdetermination," *Journal of Economic Issues*, 33 (4): 835–844.

—— (2003) "It's Culture All the Way Down," *Journal of Economic Issues*, 37 (1): 35–45.
—— and Ann Jennings (1990) "On the Possibility of a Feminist Economics: The Convergence of Institutional and Feminist Methodology," *Journal of Economic Issues*, 24 (2): 613–622.
Williamson, E. Oliver (1985) *The Economic Institutions of Capitalism: Firms, Markets, Relational Contracting*, New York: The Free Press.
Zein-Elabdin, Eiman O. (1996) "Development, Gender, and the Environment: Theoretical or Contextual Link? Toward an Institutional Analysis of Gender," *Journal of Economic Issues*, 30 (4): 929–947.
—— (2009) "Economics, Postcolonial Theory, and the Problem of Culture: Institutional Analysis and Hybridity," *Cambridge Journal of Economics*, 33 (6): 1153–1167.

5   The New Institutional Economics

'Culture' is still largely a black box.

The New Institutional Economics (NIE) constitutes the third Neoclassical research program that attempts to account for culture, the first two being the Preferences Approach and Cultural Economics (see Chapter 3). NIE is preoccupied with how institutions arise and how they 'determine' or 'affect' economic growth. Interest in the role of social context from a Neoclassical point of view has been underway for a long time (e.g., Coase 1937). However, the early literature mostly examined institutions in the narrow sense of organizations with specific roles. Concern with a broader notion of institutions, as they shape economic behavior and change, gained visibility and momentum in the 1980s (e.g., Coase 1984), at about the same time as attention to culture began to pervade Economics generally. This chapter examines Neoclassical Institutionalism, while pointing out the divergences and continuities between this perspective and the original Institutionalist tradition (OIE) (see Chapter 4).[1]

A broad survey of NIE literature shows that, like most current economic concern with culture, there is a genuine effort to account for its presence and economic ramifications. There are thoughtful as well as shallow inquiries. This is reflected, for instance, in the significant distance between cautious discussions of the dynamics of technological and organizational change (North 1981, 1991) and hasty opportunistic interpretations of different patterns of 'development' (Greif 1994; Tabellini 2005). Despite this diversity, NIE literature shares a certain conception of culture that permits three general observations.

First, NIE demonstrates the *dualistic ontology* of culture/economy found in most economic thought that theoretically splits the two into fundamentally different realms (see Chapter 1), with culture represented as an external force acting upon pre-formed individual economic agency. NIE concentrates on the second half of the Neoclassical *paradigmatic dualism* of preferences/constraints, which, as I have argued, is rooted in the deeper existential dichotomy of desire/limits. Second, cultural values and traditions are understood primarily as a general curb on 'rational' individual self-seeking. This reduces culture to a one-dimensional entity, and ensures that 'incorporating' it into economic analysis engenders no threat to the standard model of individual preferences → choice → equilibrium (see Chapter 3). Third, NIE literature on development draws a distinction between cultural 'beliefs' or 'traits' that constrain economic growth and those that facilitate it. As such, not all culture or cultural 'variables' are conceptualized as a constraint and, hence, an obstacle to development. Only some are held in this 'negative' light.

The following two sections outline the basic principles of NIE and its treatment of culture, focusing on the work of three major articulators: Andrew Schotter, Oliver Williamson, and Douglass North. The next section discusses NIE analyses of development. The final section reviews two widely read studies of the role of cultural beliefs and traits in development: Avner Greif's (1994) historical account of Maghribi and Genoese traders along the Mediterranean, and Guido Tabellini's (2005) assessment of regional development patterns in Europe. The two studies deploy the dichotomy between 'individualist' and 'collectivist' cultures or attitudes, thereby illustrating one of the dualisms of development economics.

My approach in this book is panoramic. Since my goal is to map out the treatment of culture in different schools of economics, I identify general patterns and common themes instead of delving deeply into the specific details and analytical nuances of each work. Culture and development are two complicated and contested terms. I interpret culture as the generally shared, often taken-for granted, sensibilities and practices—including economic ones—of a society or group, which provide an implicit frame of reference, though not in a fully coherent and harmonious manner that predates and explains all. Institutions exist and operate within the common framework of a culture. In Economics, development has been generally identified with economic growth, this is also the case in NIE discourse. The literature reviewed in this chapter contains many claims that warrant more critical scrutiny, but my discussion is limited to a general overview.

Institutionalism in Neoclassical theory

The coalescence and flourishing of this research program owe a great deal to contemporary upheavals in the former Soviet Union and Eastern Europe as they revealed the extent to which social change—in this case, 'transition' to a market economy—depends on institutional infrastructure. This finding was reinforced during the 1990s financial crisis in East Asia, leading Williamson (1996: 338) to criticize the World Bank for paying little attention to "the institutional environment—culture, politics, and history."[2] NIE quickly grew into several fields of inquiry, with different methodological and substantive focal points: transaction(s) cost, evolutionary game theory, general analysis of contemporary capitalism, economic history, and development. In this section, I outline the theoretical contributions of Schotter, Williamson, and North, who have done most to articulate the Neoclassical brand of Institutionalism.

NIE has been identified variously. According to Richard Langlois (1986), it is based on three assumptions: (1) economic agents are rational but without full knowledge of optimizable alternatives; (2) learning takes place over time in an evolutionary manner; and (3) an array of institutions coordinates economic activity. These assumptions "extend" the empirical reach of Neoclassical theory, while maintaining "the tenets of orthodox marginalism" (Furubotn and Richter 1991: 1).[3] The extended list of concerns includes transaction costs and property rights; political economy and public choice; quantitative economic history; and cognition, ideology, and path dependence (Drobak and Nye 1997). John Harriss *et al.* (1995: 2) affirm that this approach "retains the neo-classical axioms of methodological individualism but rejects certain very restrictive assumptions in the notion of 'the market.'" In short, NIE "has little in common with the older Institutionalists" (Drobak and Nye 1997: xv), who reject the premise of a universal economic rationality.[4] Schotter and Williamson theorize institutions narrowly as policing devices and mechanisms of governance, while North envisions them very broadly to be rules of the social 'game.' The three authors converge on taking optimizing rationality to be a universal basis of human behavior. I outline their key ideas in turn.

In his widely cited book, *The Economic Theory of Social Institutions*, Schotter (1981) gives one of the earliest and most direct theoretical accounts of institutions from a Neoclassical standpoint.[5] He first defines economics as "the study of *how individual economic agents pursuing their own selfish ends evolve institutions as a means to satisfy them*" (ibid.: 5). It is the study of how institutions emerge from atomistic welfare maximization, i.e., the pursuit of subjective desires and wishes. For Schotter, the main drawback of the standard Neoclassical approach is that it places exclusive emphasis on competitive markets, when these are only one set of institutions. In general, institutions constitute "information mechanisms that supplement the information contained in competitive prices" (ibid.: 118). He points out that his concept of economics goes beyond the conventional definition (Robbins 1946 [1932]) by considering non-competitive markets, and recognizing coordination between individuals.

According to Schotter, a "social institution" is "a regularity in social behavior that is agreed to by all members of society, specifies behavior in specific recurrent situations, and is either self-policed or policed by some external authority" (1981: 11). This concept clearly emphasizes the constraining facet of institutions, though it is not entirely clear who is policing whom or what is being policed. Regardless of the ambiguity, and, even though he admits that social institutions are nebulous, Schotter attempts to formalize this concept mathematically in order to predict equilibrium outcomes from recurring circumstances. Formally, an institution is:

A regularity R in the behavior of members of a population P when they are agents in a recurrent situation Γ is an *institution* if and only if it is true that and is common knowledge in P that (1) everyone conforms to R; (2) everyone expects everyone else to conform to R; and (3) either everyone prefers to conform to R on the condition that the others do, if Γ is a coordination problem, in which case uniform conformity to R is a coordination equilibrium; or (4) if anyone ever deviates from R it is known that some or all of the others will also deviate and the payoffs associated with the recurrent play of Γ using these deviating strategies are worse for all agents than the payoff associated with R.

(ibid.)

Here, institutions are mainly regulative. This is an extremely restricted interpretation, but it may be necessary to render the phenomenon more mathematically pliable and productive. Thus, Schotter wishes to broaden the Neoclassical framework by recognizing coordination problems and imperfect markets; yet, by mathematically grounding the concept of institutions, he also restricts the scope of this framework.

Schotter relies on evolutionary game theory to conceptualize institutions as solutions to past problems. In particular, he investigates the emergence of institutions in response to the repeated problems of coordination, inequality, cooperation, and the prisoners' dilemma.[6] According to him, the optimality of institutions requires a set of social rules such as anti-trust or minimum wage legislation. Since problems change over time, institutions also change and, therefore, could only be understood in light of the original exigencies that led to their creation. Although highly structured, Schotter's treatment leaves at least two related questions unanswered: could institutions arise through mechanisms or efforts beside individual action? and could they arise unintentionally?

Williamson's approach differs considerably. Borrowing from J.R. Commons (see Chapter 4 in this book), Williamson describes his own work as "a comparative institutional approach to the study of economic organization in which the transaction is made the basic unit of analysis" (1985: 387). Commons (1931) had argued that the smallest unit of economic analysis is not labor, utility, or commodity. It is the transaction—an activity between individuals. He categorized transactions into three main types: managerial, bargaining, and rationing, each containing conflict, dependence, and order. For him, transactional, more than technological, considerations explain firm structure and behavior. This conceptual foundation has clearly influenced Williamson's idea of "transaction cost economics" (1985: Chapter 1). Commons' focus on the law (1925, 1931) has also broadly left its mark in Williamson's emphasis on governance. Williamson (1996) compares three institutional settings: market contracting, hierarchical organizations, and "hybrids," which are mixed contractual arrangements that ensure autonomy and protection more so than the first two settings.[7] He claims his approach retains a key role for the individual agent. Its departure lies in adding the assumptions of bounded rationality and opportunism—that is, borrowing Herbert Simon's language, "behavior is *intendedly* rational, but only *limitedly* so," and agents are opportunistic, "self-interest seeking with guile" (Williamson 1985: 30). On the basis of these assumptions, Williamson defines institutions (e.g., corporations, organized labor, and anti-trust regulation) as "mechanisms of governance" (1996: 5), and the corporation as a governance structure, rather than an executor of a production function.

A broad view guides the work of Douglass North, according to whom, institutions represent "a set of rules, compliance procedures, and moral and ethical behavioral norms *designed* to constrain the behavior of individuals in the interest of maximizing the wealth or utility of principals" (1981: 201–2; emphasis added). The overall impact of institutions on economic performance stems from their effect on the costs of production and exchange. North distinguishes between institutions, "rules of the game in a society" (1990: 3), and organizations, that is, "purposive entities designed by their creators to maximize wealth, income, or other objectives defined by the opportunities afforded by the institutional structure of the society" (ibid.: 73). He considers this an attempt to build "a theory of institutions" on the basis of "the choice theoretic approach" (ibid.: 5). The hallmark of this theory is emphasis on intentionality (design) and constraints: institutions, whether formal (rules) or informal (conventions), represent "humanly devised constraints" (1991: 97) that limit the set of individual choices.

Culture as a constraint

As the previous section shows, NIE upholds the philosophical core of Neoclassicism, that is, individual maximizing behavior. Institutions—whether theorized as policing devices, governance mechanisms, or social rules—represent a curb on individual reason and action.[8] Unlike OIE, authors here rarely give direct interpretations of, or even explicitly mention, culture as a concept-phenomenon (e.g., Schotter 1981; Langlois 1986; Eggertsson 1990; Harriss *et al.* 1995). Instead, it is left implied in the term institutions or various other surrogates of it such as norms and custom. As a result, the relationship between culture and institutions is often unclear.

Schotter's work offers an example of this pattern, as the word 'culture' makes no appearance in his book. His preferred expression is "rules of thumb" (1981: 118), conceptualized as guides to individual action. The absence of the word 'culture' from his text mirrors the general state of Neoclassical discourse, where the word rarely appeared—except in reference to 'the arts'—until the 1990s (see Appendix I). Schotter's faint awareness of culture in an anthropological sense crops up in his statement "we behave the way we do because in many of our social and economic encounters we know what type of behavior is expected of us and others, and behaving that way is the 'equilibrium thing to do'" (ibid.: 143). In other words, there is such a thing as socially normal behavior. However, the norm is individual welfare maximization, which, in effect, negates culture by suggesting that each person processes social norms based on a uniform impulse of cost-benefit calculation. Culture follows from willful choice in a unidirectional manner. Schotter's text says nothing about cultural differences or whether the individually driven nature of institutions is characteristic of all societies.

In Williamson's work, the word 'culture' is rare, though more visible. In *The Economic Institutions of Capitalism*, it enters the discussion conspicuously once, in the course of explaining transaction cost economics: "[t]he social context in which transactions are embedded—the customs, mores, habits, and so on—have [*sic*] a bearing, and therefore need to be taken into account, when moving from one culture to another" (1985: 22). Culture here is an aggregate of customs, mores, and habits. Williamson notes the presence of different cultures, but it is not clear whether he is referring to sub-cultures within a capitalist economy or to different societies altogether. Unlike Schotter, he invokes many aspects of sociality, including family, power, and even more ambiguous and such culturally circumscribed notions as trust and dignity; and draws on sociology (Granovetter 1985) to produce a more complex profile of both individual agents and firms than is normally encountered in Neoclassical economics. For him, agents are "both less and more calculative," while the firm is an economizer on transaction cost (Williamson 1985: 391).[9] The image enriches the tapestry, but does not threaten the core paradigm.

Williamson's more philosophical thoughts on culture unfold in later work, where he makes extended statements on the subject, though leaving the relationship of culture to individual behavior somewhat unclear. He argues that the "main import of culture, for the purposes of economic organization, is that it serves as a check on opportunism" (1996: 268). That is to say, it acts as a constraint. But, I wonder, would not this be true only if one assumes a culture that is intolerant of opportunism? It seems that having made it an element of 'human behavior,' opportunism would be constituent of the cultural make-up. Williamson appears to recognize this, as he adds "[s]ocial conditioning into a culture that condones lying and hypocrisy limits the efficacy of contract" (ibid.). He further realizes "[c]ulture applies to very large groups, sometimes an entire society, and involves very low levels of intentionality" (ibid.). The difficulty for him is how to productively bring this complexity into economic analysis.

To maneuver this difficulty, Williamson (1996) proposes distinguishing between two levels of analysis: the institutional environment, and the institutions of governance. The first contains norms and rules, including political regimes and the law; this seems to be the equivalent of culture in a broad sense. The second level encompasses the mechanisms of governance: markets, hierarchies, and hybrids. The two levels of analysis are related in that changes in the institutional environment alter the cost of governance. Williamson's analytical strategy is to take the institutional environment as given, and focus on governance because he deems it more capable of producing refutable claims. His strategy dictates that a concept of institutions must be amenable to approximation by observable variables. In consequence, he is critical of "soft"' ideas such as "corporate culture" (ibid.: 270) because it discounts intentionality in favor of spontaneous action.[10] Overall, Williamson skirts around culture rather than take it on as the subject of inquiry.

In comparison, North appears willing to step into the quicksand of culture discourse. In his early descriptions of the feudal system in medieval Europe (North and Thomas 1971, 1973), North did not use the word 'culture,' opting instead for "arrangements" (e.g., 1973: 6) and "custom." For instance, "customs of the manor" (ibid.: 11) referred to specific details of mutual obligations such as the type of tenants considered acceptable to a landlord. In more recent work, he spells out a concept of culture: "the transmission from one generation to the next, via teaching and imitation, of knowledge, values, and other factors that influence behavior" (1990: 37).[11] This interpretation acknowledges culture as a group process, but leans toward a static conception of it that agrees with the Preferences Approach (see Chapter 3 in this book). For North, culture is the incentive structure for society. His emphasis on "sanctions," "taboos," and "codes of conduct"

(1991: 97) places almost exclusive weight on repressive aspects that restrict the maximizingly rational impulses of its members.

North's perspective has been criticized. As Steven Heydemann (2008) has remarked, the constraint interpretation is essentializing as it assigns to culture a single predictable function instead of recognizing it as a composite of multiple and shifting parts. Others have noted that, in North's interpretation, culture limits but does not change the basic portfolio of individual "motivations or desires" (Castellano and García-Quero 2012: 925). The main tension in North's position is that he recognizes the influence of shared principles and traditions; yet, he also wishes to retain "the choice theoretic approach that underlies microeconomics" (1995: 17). This leaves the Neoclassical self in place, and hence forecloses the possibility of significant cultural differences.

The upshot is that, in NIE, culture acts as a constraint on individual self-seeking. This by itself reduces it to a one-dimensional entity and moreover, it ensures that the rational choice model remains theoretically outside of any cultural context except if one assumes an infinitely homogeneous society of utility maximizers. This clearly follows Gary Becker's way (e.g., 1976, 1996; also see Chapter 3 in this book). Going further, NIE analyses repeat the same dualism found in most economic thought by theoretically separating 'economy' from 'culture' as two ontologically distinct realms, with the latter constructed as an external force, acting upon fully formed individual agency.

New Institutionalism and development

The strongest appeal of NIE for development economists has been the claim of a "grand theory of social and economic change" (Harriss *et al.* 1995: 1). On the other hand, some believe New Institutionalist theory "adds nothing to what we already have" (Toye 1995: 64). A decade ago, this wide range of opinion prompted Ha-Joon Chang (2003: 15) to declare institutions "the new battleground in development economics." Today, he believes, NIE has won (Chang 2011). The debate, however, goes on concerning the nature of institutions and the direction of causality between them and economic development (see de Jong 2011; Castellano and García-Quero 2012). This section discusses NIE ideas on development. I dwell more on North's work, as he has offered the most extensive theoretical statements on the subject, particularly, the role of the state, property rights, and technological change.[12]

Visible NIE engagement with the field of development is relatively recent, dating back to Williamson's (1996) remarks to the World Bank's 1994 annual conference on development economics that though NIE was in its theoretical infancy, its core ideas were applicable to the study of transition and development in Eastern Europe and Asia (also see Stein 2008). The applications include analysis of firms, market organization, and governance structures, whether narrowly or broadly specified, e.g., the judiciary vs. the nation-state (Williamson 1996). Amplifying his analytical framework discussed in the previous section, Williamson (2000: 596) argues that social analysis takes place on four levels: social embeddedness ("norms, customs, mores, traditions"), the institutional environment, institutions of governance, and the micro level of optimizing decisions. According to him, what NIE could contribute to the understanding of development is the micro-analytic, "bottom-up" approach. The clear implication is that development economics should steer away from grand theorizing.

North has taken the grand, sweeping approach. He is critical of conventional Neoclassical theory for its failure to shed light on economic performance over time, especially why and how institutions rise and evolve (1991). He argues understanding historical change requires dealing with demographic shifts, growth in knowledge, and the nature of institutions, which in turn requires examining the role of ideology, the state, and property rights (1981). The fundamental challenge is "to account for the evolution of political and economic institutions that create an economic environment that induces increasing productivity" (1991: 98). This, for him, is the way to answer the nagging questions of divergence in human history—why did many societies take such different turns? Why did institutional inefficiency persist for so long in so many regions? In short, why have all societies not been able to replicate the affluence of the few industrially mature ones?

Despite the enormity of these questions, North claims explaining economic development in the 'Western' world is "straightforward" (North and Thomas 1973: 1)— institutions determine the opportunities, efficient organizations (the actors) take advantage of them. The problem, he adds, is that the actors often operate with incomplete information or incorrect world models to process information (North 1981). These models resemble ideology, which he defines as "an economizing device by which individuals come to terms with their environment and are provided with a 'world view' so that the decision-making process is simplified" (ibid.: 49). Ideologies have significant implications for economic theory because they impose limits on individual maximizing choices.[13] In this sense, economic history is nothing more than "a theory of the evolution of constraints" (ibid.: 209). This is a grand theory, but without much clarity about the relationship(s) between norms, institutions, ideologies, and other elements of culture.

Much of NIE literature stresses the role of the state, taking its cue from North's statement that "the heart of development policy must be the creation of polities that will create and enforce efficient property rights" (1995: 25) because inadequacy of ownership arrangements could delay the realization of new ideas and inventions. In broader terms, Pranab Bardhan (2005) points out that the major obstacle to development is exemplified in state failures whether manifested in violence, corruption, or generally feeble political institutions. Accordingly, he calls for a more rigorous concept of power. This theoretical framework of polity and property rights has been applied to a host of countries and contexts (see Harriss *et al.* 1995). On the other hand, several authors have cautioned against excessive simplification and application of limited economic principles to political issues (Hutchison 1984). Howard Stein (1995) argues that adherence to core microeconomic postulates has led to an over-emphasis on efficiency and a narrowly construed concept of property rights, precluding in-depth examination of culturally complex facets of development. Chang (2011) also points out that the presumed positive correlation between governance and economic growth lacks historical evidence.[14]

Another theme in North's contribution to the development discourse concerns the role of technology. According to him (North 1981), when technological change is discussed in Neoclassical economics, the focus is typically on single events or inventions (namely, the Industrial Revolution) rather than the series of institutional adjustments that had to be made in order to move from a nascent idea to a marketable product. The time distance between invention and diffusion may be centuries long as was in the case of the steam engine. The lag, he asserts, could be explained by the absence of adequate property rights or knowledge. A given institutional setting might lead to technological lock-in, which occurs when—because of logistical circumstances, politics, or mere accident—an inferior technology is selected even though an equally serviceable or superior one exists. The most celebrated example is the QWERTY typewriter. Technological lock-in constitutes a root cause of path dependence (see Hodgson 1994). North (1991) argues that competition takes place not between technologies but between the organizations that adopt or block them. Hence, the practical predominance of a particular technology over superior ones is less critical for development than the institutional rigidities that hold back its implementation (Drobak and Nye 1997).

These views on the role of technology represent the main point of convergence between NIE and OIE. North's (1981) remarks on the complex and reciprocal relationship between technological change and economic organization echo Veblen's distinction between technological (instrumental) and ceremonial (institutional) aspects of culture (see Chapter 4 in this book). However, it is important to remember that in OIE technology is more broadly defined and situated within a fundamentally different theory of value. Although both Institutionalisms are preoccupied with the major problematics of development (change, technology, institutions), these are embedded in different philosophical frameworks. The unifying thread in North's thought on economic history, the state, and technology is the idea of property rights as they constrict individual decisions, which renders his perspective much more limited than Veblen's.

Cultural beliefs and traits in development

In this section I discuss two widely read attempts to model a relationship between culture and development. The first, by Avner Greif (1994), uses game theory to interpret the economic influence of 'cultural beliefs' in two medieval societies. The second, by Guido Tabellini (2005), quantitatively estimates the role of 'cultural traits' in the development of different regions in Europe. The two studies are consistent with the general return to culture in development economics (see Chapter 7). However, they diverge in their concern with this subject in the context of Europe, a region that has historically escaped the gaze of the development discourse.[15] Greif and Tabellini illustrate the dualistic construction of culture/economy, where cultural variables externally act upon economic phenomena. The two authors also employ the dichotomy between 'individualist' and 'collectivist' (or obedience, group-oriented) attributes, thought to characterize entirely different cultures, and carry opposite implications for economic growth.

Greif's (1994) paper "Cultural Beliefs and the Organization of Society" seeks to demonstrate the significance of culture in the history of development. He defines cultural beliefs as "the ideas and thoughts common to several individuals that govern interaction—between these people, and between them, their gods, and other groups" (ibid.: 915). According to him, such beliefs are unverifiable, but they do provide a basis for social expectations and communication, and form part of "the institutional framework of each group" (ibid.: 925). Most significantly, they determine the costs and benefits of economic action. Greif is particularly interested in what he calls "rational cultural beliefs" (ibid.: 915) because they are amenable to incorporation within a formal game theoretic explanation of individual decisions.

This notion of cultural beliefs provides the conceptual basis for Greif's account of two "premodern" societies and their respective economies: Maghribi Jewish traders of the eleventh century, who traded widely across North Africa and the Mediterranean, and the twelfth-century Italian merchants of Genoa. The basis of comparison is that "the Maghribis and the Genoese faced a similar environment, employed comparable naval technology, and traded in similar goods" (ibid.: 917). Culturally, Greif claims, the Maghribis and the Genoese belonged to two different worlds—the Maghribis "were part of the Muslim world" that had collectivist cultural beliefs, whereas the Genoese inhabited "the Latin world," with its individualist tradition (ibid.: 914). He draws on a variety of sources and interpretations from religious texts, traders' correspondences, and histories of medieval Europe to establish the historical and theological bases of his account.

Greif's premise is that different cultural beliefs are manifested in different modes of socio-economic organization. In collectivist societies, people are divided into different groups by religion or family, for example, and they interact with outsiders from within these groups. This belief set is characterized by group responsibility and enforcement mechanisms. In contrast, individualist societies organize interactions between individual members. Each group's beliefs defined its economic behavior and organization. This was reflected, for instance, in the decision to hire agents as a way to cut down the transactions cost of overseas trading. Employing agents was more efficient because of greater specialization, but whether this was done or not depended on the presence of supporting institutions that lowered the probability of cheating. Cultural beliefs, thus, had an impact on efficiency, profitability, and ultimately the emergence of specific forms of economic organization. According to Greif, the Maghribis, reflecting their collectivist culture, formed information-sharing networks; the Genoese, instead, developed formal institutions such as the bill of lading to offset the lack of such networks and informal group arrangements, which their culture discouraged.

On the basis of this account, Greif asserts that "the medieval Latin individualist society may have cultivated the seeds to the 'rise of the West'" (ibid.: 943). Then extrapolating to the present time, he claims the Maghribis' social organization is similar to contemporary "developing countries," in contrast, the Genoese society parallels the "developed West" (ibid.). Given today's record of economic development, he argues, social organization based on individualist beliefs seems to be more efficient over time. He goes on to conclude "[t]o the extent that the division of labor is a necessary condition for long-run sustained economic growth, formal enforcement institutions that support anonymous exchange facilitate economic development" (ibid.). This leap from a historical narrative of two medieval communities to a sweeping generalization about a vast swath of contemporary societies is quite jarring. It is not difficult to conclude that historical 'data' have been conveniently assembled to arrive at a preformed conclusion.

Leaving this methodological concern aside, Greif's line of thought also exudes essentialism. Heydemann (2008: 35) takes him to task for assuming a "uniform and coherent Muslim collectivist culture" and, even more, for subsuming secular Jewish traders into 'the Muslim world.' As Chang (2011) has noted, cultures are not monolithic entities; they contain different, and often, contradictory teachings so that it is possible to simultaneously observe signals that appear to foster economic growth and others that seem to weigh against it. He points out, for example, that NIE writers have been highly selective in crediting Confucianism with East Asia's economic success by hailing this tradition's emphasis on education and frugality, while ignoring its heavy bureaucratic leaning and near contempt for commerce (for more on East Asia literature, see Chapter 7). Greif's paper shows how NIE explanations "can easily degenerate into *ex post* justifications" (Chang 2011: 491).

Taking a somewhat different road, Guido Tabellini's (2005) paper, "Culture and Institutions: Economic Development in the Regions of Europe," aims to "show that specific indicators of culture, that can be interpreted either as social norms or as individual values, are correlated both with historical patterns and with current economic development" (ibid.: 3), as indicated by per capita income levels for 1995–2000. Following North (1981, 1990) and Schotter (1981), Tabellini differentiates between institutions in the narrow sense of "formal rules of the game that shape individual incentives and constraints," and the broader meaning of "systems of belief or social norms that sustain specific equilibria" (2005: 1–2). He defines culture as: "the social norms and the individual beliefs that sustain Nash equilibria as focal points in repeated social interactions" (ibid.: 2). Although these explanations are given from the outset, the difference between culture and institutions, especially in the broad sense of the latter, is unclear. He suggests a causal sequence of: Historical institutions → Culture → Economic development. But this just magnifies the ambiguity since culture seems to refer to present institutions only. According to him, culture is an endogenous variable, shaping and shaped by development, and transmitted inter-generationally through family instruction and social contact. Therefore, history may be used as an estimation instrument for culture.

To verify his proposed sequence, Tabellini looks for cultural 'traits' that are rooted in history and exert an impact on "current economic performance" (ibid.: 3). To construct the traits, he chooses the categories of "trust," "individual confidence," "respect for others," and "obedience" from the World Values Survey.[16] The first three traits—trust, individual confidence, and respect for others—are expected to positively correlate with economic development. A high level of trust reduces transactions cost and, thereby, promotes the spread of markets, while confidence that individual effort will be rewarded enhances motivation for success. The trait of 'respect for others' is based on the notion that a person's moral commitment extends beyond their family, friends, and acquaintances, though Tabellini does not explain the association between "respect" and "morality." The last trait, obedience, is assumed to have a negative impact on development.

The study estimates the relationship between the four cultural traits and economic development for 69 regions in Belgium, France, Germany, Italy, the Netherlands, Portugal, Spain, and the UK. The econometric results show that, despite regional variations, "there is a strong and significant correlation between all measures of culture and current development, after controlling for country fixed effects and for school enrollment in 1960" (ibid.: 14).[17] Taking historical factors into account—literacy in 1800 and political institutions in 1600–1850—the results indicate that culture and institutions have an 'impact' on the level of income. For example, "If Southern Italy had the same culture as Lombardy, its average yearly growth rate would have been higher by ½%" (ibid.: 26). Southern Italy's current income turns out to be 17 percent below that of Lombardy because political institutions in the former are correlated with a low level of trust, respect for others, and individual confidence, and with high regard for obedience in children. Overall, the study concludes that "the effect of culture on economic development is always large and statistically significant" (ibid.: 23).

Tabellini is slightly less speculative than Greif, cautioning that the "precise interpretation of these cultural indicators is difficult" (ibid.: 31) and requires more detailed study. Nevertheless, both are ambiguous about the differences between culture and institutions and between other key variables; Tabellini uses the terms traits and beliefs interchangeably, with no elaboration on their meanings. The two studies share the problem of dualism in the perception of cultural 'indicators' in relation to economic outcomes. As I discussed in Chapter 3 with respect to the Preferences Approach (e.g., Guiso *et al.* 2006), the ontological rift between culture and economy is palpable in the idea that culture 'affects' economy. In Greif's paper, cultural beliefs are treated as an external constant, exerting a single impact on economic organization. Moreover, dualism is carried further in the assumption of two types of characteristics, individualist and collectivist, belonging to different societies or regions. Greif envisions two altogether different worlds—Muslim and Latin. In Tabellini's paper, though the dichotomy is subtler, it is discernible in the contrast between 'individual confidence' and 'obedience,' where the latter is implicitly associated with a group-oriented, or collectivist, society.

Unlike the broader NIE paradigm, in which culture assumes the role of an abstract blanket constraint on rational choice and, therefore, a curb on economic growth, Greif and Tabellini distinguish between two sets of cultural characteristics, with positive or negative growth implications. This strategy is common in NIE explanations of comparative development, where—in a neo-Weberian fashion—industrial growth in Britain and the USA has been attributed to "Anglo-Saxon individualism" (Temin 1997: 267). With the contemporary success of East Asian economies, this argument has been slightly modified. Temin adds that Japan's success, built on a "more collective culture" (ibid.) with its own different institutions and management style, suggests that the 'Western' culture of individual freedom may not be equally productive everywhere. In fact, some authors have taken this argument a step further by asserting that 'Western individualism' is not at all ideal for superior economic performance (Casson 1993). Peter Gray (1996) has compared economic growth rates in the USA and five East Asian economies (Hong Kong, Japan, South Korea, Singapore, and Taiwan) between 1965 and 1987, and concluded that a culture of individual autonomy and self-interest has had a negative effect on US growth.[18]

Regardless of which side of the argument authors take, these interpretations are premised on a perceived opposition between two types of cultures—individualist and collectivist—mapped geographically as West and East. For Greif and Tabellini, only group-oriented cultures are unfavorable to growth, and these turn out to be those of societies or regions that have already been classified as 'under' or 'less' developed, whether in the Maghrib or southern Italy. This perspective follows a long line of development economists across different schools of thought (e.g., Lewis 1955; Fei and Ranis 1969), with Peter Bauer expressing the boldest verdict that the "cultures of large parts of the less developed world are uncongenial to economic achievement and advance" (1984: 86). New Institutionalists have not gone this far, but their cultural representations are consistent with an orientalist outlook. It is not clear what the two papers by Greif and Tabellini add to mid-twentieth-century development economics or Anthropology. The only difference between then and now seems to be the illusion of accuracy and rigor conveyed by the use of game theory and econometric estimation techniques.[19]

Conclusion

The New Institutional Economics maintains the substantive and methodological principles of Neoclassical theory by occupying one side of the preferences/ constraints dichotomy. Culture plays the role of a general constraint on individual optimizing rationality, with institutions serving as policing devices and mechanisms of governance. In a similar manner to the Preferences Approach and Cultural Economics, NIE reproduces the dualism of culture/economy, where the latter resides in individual decisions upon which the former acts. In the context of development analyses, NIE studies replicate and extend this dualistic ontology by adding an opposition between individualism and collectivism according to which they divide cultures into growth promoters and growth inhibitors. NIE treatment of culture and development—as represented in the two papers by Greif and Tabellini—falls in line with the interpretation of culture in Economics, as either a liberating or a limiting force, in direct parallel to the existential problem of desire/limits. NIE literature on development draws a distinction between cultural beliefs or traits that constrain economic growth and those that facilitate it. As such, not all culture is represented as a constraint on individual maximizing behavior and, hence, an inherent growth inhibitor.

The conception and treatment of culture in NIE are more limited than in OIE. For instance, in NIE, the concepts of cultural beliefs and traits are handled at a superficial level, without much digging into the nature, origins, meaning, and dynamics of each. To this extent, Tabellini is correct: culture remains an unpacked "black box." More importantly perhaps is that in NIE, the 'effect' of culture on economic behavior is tested against a universal model of rationality. This diverges fundamentally from OIE. Despite seemingly genuine concern with accounting for the role of culture in economic analyses, most NIE efforts end up lacking depth, and resorting to opportunistic mining of historical and statistical data to support *a priori* conclusions. The reason for this opportunism is partly conceptual, that is, authors insist on preserving the core behavioral model; and partly methodological, they seek to identify measurable variables in order to quantify the role of culture. Others choose to avoid 'culture' altogether. Williamson exemplifies this strategy as he recognizes the complexity involved in any attempt to analytically approach culture, then responds by simply bypassing it instead of taking up the actual task of articulating the specific economic ramifications of this complexity.

Despite deep philosophical differences, the two Institutionalisms converge on the twentieth-century question of international development—both theorize institutions as an obstacle to desired economic growth. In NIE, whether conceived broadly as beliefs or narrowly as property rights regimes, culture constrains 'rational choice.' In OIE, culture—in the form of past-binding institutions and ceremonialism—arrests technological change. In the former, the curb is placed on human desire (preferences); in the latter, what is suppressed is human ingenuity (technology). The result in both cases is a universalist perspective preoccupied with removing institutional impediments to development, or 'modernization,' in countries classified as under/less developed. In other words, for both, 'development' constitutes a supra-cultural imperative normatively defined by the historical experience of industrial modernity.

Notes

1 Langlois (1986) considers Carl Menger—rather than Thorstein Veblen—the 'father' of Institutional Economics. Schotter (1981) and Hutchison (1984) also note Menger's recognition of the institutional origins of money. For reviews of NIE, see Furubotn and Richter (1991), Harriss *et al.* (1995), Drobak and Nye (1997), and Williamson (2000). For surveys of Institutional Economics of both types, see Hutchison (1984), Hodgson (1993), and Rutherford (1994). Hodgson (2007) discusses the blurring boundaries between OIE and NIE. For critical analyses of Institutional economics generally, see Jones (2006) and Zein-Elabdin (2009).
2 Some writings predate these events, for instance, North and Thomas (1971, 1973). However, NIE did not come to prominence until later. North was awarded the Nobel Memorial Prize in Economic Sciences in 1993.
3 See Chapters 1 and 3 in this book for the parameters of Neoclassical economics and debates about the term itself in economic literature.
4 Mayhew (1989: 326) has suggested that the fundamental difference between the new and old approaches is that the latter is grounded in the twentieth-century "culture-based social sciences," which Neoclassical economics "was never really part of." For some theoretical attempts to reconcile the two traditions, see Casson (1993) and Stein (2008).
5 The book has been cited by Langlois (1986), Furubotn and Richter (1991), Greif (1994), Williamson (1996), Tabellini (2005), and Hodgson (2007).

6 Citing Veblen and J.R. Commons, Schotter offers his ideas as a "neo-institutional approach to economics" (1981: 144), with no indication of familiarity with the usage of the term in OIE. See Hodgson (1998, 2007) for more on evolutionary economics.

7 Fafchamps (2004) applies Williamson's taxonomy to analyze African economies. See Zein-Elabdin (2009) and Chapter 9 in this book on economic hybridity.

8 This strategy was spelled out by Coase (1984), who is commonly identified as a founding member of NIE though he has not articulated significant thoughts on the economic implications of culture (see also his 1998 speech). See Chamlee-Wright (1997), Wyss (1999), and Maseland (2008) for critical discussions of the constraint approach to culture. Adams (1993) comments on this approach from an OIE viewpoint.

9 Agents "are less calculative in the capacity to receive, store, retrieve and process information. They are more calculative in that they are given to opportunism" (Williamson 1985: 391). Sociologists have criticized the NIE approach, with Granovetter (1985) describing it as "undersocialized" because it reduces concrete social relations to overly "stylized" patterns, and DiMaggio (1994) pointing out that Williamson's analytical framework is too narrow, while North's is too broad.

10 Kreps (1990) used the idea of corporate culture to suggest that learning and social conditioning play an important role in the formation of a firm's reputation and trading relations. See Waller (1987) for an analysis of the corporation from an OIE perspective.

11 This language is quoted from Robert Boyd and Peter Richerson's *Culture and the Evolutionary Process* (1985).

12 NIE principles have been vigorously applied to many issues, ranging from commodity market structures to structural adjustment programs. This empirical literature is not discussed here. For more, see Harriss *et al.* (1995), Meier and Stiglitz (2000), and Bardhan (2005). Castellano and García-Quero (2012) give a helpful review of recent NIE and OIE scholarship and debates on development.

13 In more recent work, North takes this concern with ideology further by emphasizing the role of human cognition, and concludes that development in the USA and similar countries has been the result of a "rich cultural heritage" (2005: 36), the basis of which is human consciousness.

14 Chang (2011) criticizes the NIE approach to development for being simplistic and static because it ignores the cost of institutional change for policy and assumes an even and constant relationship between institutions and development. In addition, he argues, it relies almost exclusively on cross-section analysis, when time series studies are more appropriate, given the length of time institutional change takes. He classifies New Institutionalists into: "fatalists" or those holding a "climate-culture" vision, in which a country's future is predetermined; and "voluntarists," who believe that better institutions can readily be adopted by rational policy-makers. Chang himself gives no clear interpretation of either culture or institutions.

15 Writing on culture and development in the context of Europe is a relatively recent trend, with some very interesting discussions. For example, Kovács (2006) comments on the complex cultural milieu within which Eastern European countries are pursuing economic development. He disputes the dominant narrative that surviving cultural traditions from the distant past explain differences in current economic performance. Instead, he suggests, diversity in the way communism was instituted in Europe accounts, at least partially, for these differences. Also see the European Task Force on Culture and Development (1997).

16 The survey data were collected for 1990–91 and 1995–97. Responses to survey questions determine each trait or category. For example, for trust, the question is "Would you say that most people can be trusted or that you can't be too careful in dealing with people?" (Tabellini 2005: 9); individual confidence: "How much freedom of choice and control in life [do] you have over the way your life turns out?" (ibid.: 10); respect and obedience: "Which qualities that children can be encouraged to learn at home ... do you consider to be especially important?" (ibid.: 11). The questions are quite vague

and over-simplified. Tabellini admits he chose traits that could be more easily 'measured.' See www.worldvaluessurvey.org/index_surveys, and Chapter 3 in this book for more on the World Values Survey. See Marini (2004), Guiso *et al.* (2006), and Tadesse and White (2008) for other economic studies that rely on the survey. Granato *et al.* (1996) give an example of similar usage of it in political science studies.

17 Controlling for fixed effects here refers to removing the impact of formal and legal institutions that are common to different countries. Tabellini also controlled for the level of education and urbanization in each country since they are likely to be correlated with economic growth.

18 Kunio (2006: 83) claims Japan's postwar growth is rooted in its "appropriate culture" that values hard work, saving, and education, but these values had to be supplemented with the "appropriate institutions" to accelerate growth.

19 See Chapters 3 and 7 in this book for more attempts to estimate the role of culture. See Rao (1998) for a critical discussion of quantitative economic analyses of culture. Adkisson (2014) gives a helpful review of the quantitative literature.

References

Adams, John (1993) "Institutions and Economic Development: Structure, Process, and Incentives," in Marc Tool (ed.) *Institutional Economics: Theory, Method, Policy*, Boston: Kluwer Academic Publishers, 245–269.

Adkisson, Richard (2014) "Quantifying Culture: Problems and Promises," *Journal of Economic Issues*, 48 (1): 89–107.

Bardhan, Pranab (2005) *Scarcity, Conflicts, and Cooperation: Essays in the Political and Institutional Economics of Development*, Cambridge, MA: MIT Press.

Bauer, Peter T. (1984) *Reality and Rhetoric: Studies in the Economics of Development*, Cambridge, MA: Harvard University Press.

Becker, Gary S. (1976) *The Economic Approach to Human Behavior*, Chicago: University of Chicago Press.

—— (1996) *Accounting for Tastes*, Cambridge, MA: Harvard University Press.

Boyd, Robert and Peter Richerson (1985) *Culture and the Evolutionary Process*, Oxford: Oxford University Press.

Casson, Mark (1993) "Cultural Determinants of Economic Performance," *Journal of Comparative Economics*, 17: 418–442.

Castellano, Fernando López and Fernando García-Quero (2012) "Institutional Approaches to Economic Development: The Current Status of the Debate," *Journal of Economic Issues*, 46 (4): 921–940.

Chamlee-Wright, Emily (1997) *The Cultural Foundations of Economic Development: Urban Female Entrepreneurship in Ghana*, London: Routledge.

Chang, Ha-Joon (ed.) (2003) *Rethinking Development Economics*, London: Anthem Press.

—— (2011) "Institutions and Economic Development: Theory, Policy and History," *Journal of Institutional Economics*, 7 (4): 473–498.

Coase, Ronald H. (1937) "The Nature of the Firm," *Economica*, 4 (16) November: 386–405.

—— (1984) "The New Institutional Economics," *Journal of Institutional and Theoretical Economics*, 140: 229–231.

—— (1998) "The New Institutional Economics," *American Economic Review*, 88 (2): 72–74.

Commons, John R. (1925) "Law and Economics," *Yale Law Journal*, 34 (February): 371–382.

—— (1931) "Institutional Economics," *American Economic Review*, 21 (December): 648–657.

De Jong, Eelke (2011) "Culture, Institutions, and Economic Growth," *Journal of Institutional Economics*, 7 (4): 523–527.

DiMaggio, Paul (1994) "Culture and Economy," in Neil J. Smelser and Richard Swedberg (eds.) *The Handbook of Economic Sociology*, Princeton, NJ: Princeton University Press, 27–57.

Drobak, John N. and John V.C. Nye (eds.) (1997) *The Frontiers of the New Institutional Economics*, San Diego, CA: Academic Press.

Eggertsson, Thráinn (1990) *Economic Behavior and Institutions*, Cambridge: Cambridge University Press.

European Task Force on Culture and Development (1997) *In from the Margins: A Contribution to the Debate on Culture and Development in Europe*, Strasbourg: Council of Europe Publishing.

Fafchamps, Marcel (2004) *Market Institutions in Sub-Saharan Africa: Theory and Evidence*, Cambridge, MA: MIT Press.

Fei, John C.H. and Gustav Ranis (1969) "Economic Development in Historical Perspective," *American Economic Review, Papers and Proceedings*, 59 (2): 386–400.

Furubotn, Eirik G. and Rudolf Richter (eds.) (1991) *The New Institutional Economics: A Collection of Articles from the Journal of Institutional and Theoretical Economics*, College Station, TX: Texas A&M University Press.

Granato, Jim, Ronald Inglehart, and David Leblang (1996) "The Effect of Cultural Values on Economic Development: Theory, Hypotheses, and Some Empirical Tests," *American Journal of Political Science*, 40 (3): 607–631.

Granovetter, Mark (1985) "Economic Action and Social Structure: The Problem of Embeddedness," *American Journal of Sociology*, 91 (3): 481–510.

Gray, H. Peter (1996) "Culture and Economic Performance: Policy as an Intervening Variable," *Journal of Comparative Economics*, 23 (3): 278–291.

Greif, Avner (1994) "Cultural Beliefs and the Organization of Society: A Historical and Theoretical Reflection on Collectivist and Individualist Societies," *Journal of Political Economy*, 102 (5): 912–950.

Guiso, Luigi, Paola Sapienza, and Luigi Zingales (2006) "Does Culture Affect Economic Outcomes?" *Journal of Economic Perspectives*, 20 (2): 23–48.

Harriss, John, Janet Hunter, and Colin M. Lewis (eds.) (1995) *The New Institutional Economics and Third World Development*, London: Routledge.

Heydemann, Steven (2008) "Institutions and Economic Performance: The Use and Abuse of Culture in New Institutional Economics," *Studies in Comparative International Development*, 43 (1): 27–52.

Hodgson, Geoffrey M. (1993) "Institutional Economics: Surveying the 'Old' and the 'New'," *Metroeconomica*, 44 (1): 1–28.

—— (1994) "Lock-in and Chreodic Development," in Geoffrey Hodgson and Warren Samuels (eds.) *The Elgar Companion to Institutional and Evolutionary Economics*, Aldershot: Edward Elgar, 15–19.

—— (ed.) (1998) *The Foundations of Evolutionary Economics: 1890–1973*, 2 vols., Cheltenham: Edward Elgar.

—— (2007) "Evolutionary and Institutional Economics as the New Mainstream?" *Evolutionary and Institutional Economics Review*, 4 (1): 7–25.

Hutchison, Terence W. (1984) "Institutionalist Economics Old and New," *Journal of Institutional and Theoretical Economics*, 140: 20–29.

Jones, Eric L. (2006) *Cultures Merging: A Historical and Economic Critique of Culture*, Princeton, NJ: Princeton University Press.

Kovács, János Mátyás (2006) "Which Past Matters? Culture and Economic Development in Eastern Europe After 1989," in Lawrence E. Harrison and Peter L. Berger (eds.) *Developing Cultures: Case Studies*, London: Routledge, 329–347.

Kreps, David M. (1990) "Corporate Culture and Economic Theory," in James E. Alt and Kenneth A. Shepsle (eds.) *Perspectives on Positive Political Economy*, Cambridge: Cambridge University Press, 90–143, 240–241.

Kunio, Yoshihara (2006) "Japanese Culture and Postwar Economic Growth," in L.E. Harrison and P.L. Berger (eds.) *Developing Cultures: Case Studies*, London: Routledge, 83–100.

Langlois, Richard N. (ed.) (1986) *Economics as a Process: Essays in the New Institutional Economics*, Cambridge: Cambridge University Press.

Lewis, W. Arthur (1955) *The Theory of Economic Growth*, London: George Allen and Unwin.

Marini, Matteo (2004) "Cultural Evolution and Economic Growth: A Theoretical Hypothesis with Some Empirical Evidence," *The Journal of Socio-Economics*, 33: 765–784.

Maseland, Robbert (2008) "Taking Economics to Bed: About the Pitfalls and Possibilities of Cultural Economics," in Wolfram Elsner and Hardy Hanappi (eds.) *Varieties of Capitalism and New Institutional Deals: Regulation, Welfare and the New Economy*, Cheltenham: Edward Elgar, 299–321.

Mayhew, Anne (1989) "Contrasting Origins of the Two Institutionalisms: The Social Science Context," *Review of Political Economy*, 1 (3): 319–333.

Meier, Gerald M. and Joseph E. Stiglitz (eds.) (2000) *Frontiers of Development Economics: The Future in Perspective*, Oxford: Oxford University Press.

North, Douglass C. (1981) *Structure and Change in Economic History*, New York: W.W. Norton & Co.

—— (1990) *Institutions, Institutional Change and Economic Performance*, Cambridge: Cambridge University Press.

—— (1991) "Institutions," *Journal of Economic Perspectives*, 5 (1): 97–112.

—— (1995) "The New Institutional Economics and Third World Development," in John Harriss, Janet Hunter, and Colin M. Lewis (eds.) *The New Institutional Economics and Third World Development*, London: Routledge, 17–26.

—— (2005) "Belief Systems, Culture, and Cognitive Science," in *Understanding the Process of Economic Change*, Princeton, NJ: Princeton University Press, 23–37.

—— and Robert Paul Thomas (1971) "The Rise and Fall of the Manorial System: A Theoretical Model," *The Journal of Economic History*, 31 (4): 777–803.

—— and —— (1973) *The Economic Rise of the Western World: A New Economic History*, Cambridge: Cambridge University Press.

Rao, J. Mohan (1998) "Culture and Economic Development," in *The World Culture Report 1998*, Paris: UNESCO, 25–48.

Robbins, Lionel (1946 [1932]) *An Essay on the Nature and Significance of Economic Science*, London: Macmillan and Co.

Rutherford, Malcolm (1994) *Institutions in Economics: The Old and the New Institutionalism*, Cambridge: Cambridge University Press.

Schotter, Andrew (1981) *The Economic Theory of Social Institutions*, Cambridge: Cambridge University Press.

Stein, Howard (1995) "Institutional Theories and Structural Adjustment in Africa," in John Harriss, Janet Hunter, and Colin M. Lewis (eds.) *The New Institutional Economics and Third World Development*, London: Routledge, 109–132.

—— (2008) *Beyond the World Bank Agenda: An Institutional Approach to Development*, Chicago: University of Chicago Press.

Tabellini, Guido (2005) "Culture and Institutions: Economic Development in the Regions of Europe," CESifo Working Paper No. 1492.

Tadesse, Bedassa and Roger White (2008) "Do Immigrants Counter the Effect of Cultural Distance on Trade? Evidence from US State-level Exports," *Journal of Socio-Economics*, 37 (6): 2304–2318.

Temin, Peter (1997) "Is It Kosher to Talk About Culture?" *Journal of Economic History*, 57 (2): 267–287.

Toye, John (1995) "The New Institutional Economics and its Implications for Development Theory," in John Harriss, Janet Hunter, and Colin M. Lewis (eds.), *The New Institutional Economics and Third World Development*, London: Routledge, 49–68.

Waller, William T. Jr. (1987) "Ceremonial Encapsulation and Corporate Cultural Hegemony," *Journal of Economic Issues*, 21 (1): 321–328.

Williamson, E. Oliver (1985) *The Economic Institutions of Capitalism: Firms, Markets, Relational Contracting*, New York: The Free Press.

—— (1996) *The Mechanisms of Governance*, New York: Oxford University Press.

—— (2000) "The New Institutional Economics: Taking Stock, Looking Ahead," *Journal of Economic Literature*, 38 (3): 595–613.

Wyss, Brenda (1999) "Culture and Gender in Household Economies: The Case of Jamaican Child Support Payments," *Feminist Economics*, 5 (2): 1–24.

Zein-Elabdin, Eiman O. (2009) "Economics, Postcolonial Theory, and the Problem of Culture: Institutional Analysis and Hybridity," *Cambridge Journal of Economics*, 33 (6): 1153–1167.

6 Marxian economics

From modern to postmodern

> Capitalism finds various sections of mankind at different stages of development, each with its own profound internal contradictions ... it brings about their *rapprochement* and equalizes the economic and cultural levels of the most progressive and the most backward countries.
>
> (Mandel 1975: 23)

'Culture' and 'development' are the two fronts on which Marxist philosophy has been challenged most in the last few decades. On the first front, critics argued that Marx's theoretical framework marginalized culture by conceptualizing it as superstructure, and by analytically centering capitalism, thereby sidelining, as it were, modern Europe's cultural Others. On the second front, critics targeted determinism and historicism, where Marx's vision that industrial societies only represented the future of those less industrialized was recalled again and again to endorse industrial modernity as an inescapable historical necessity. Theoretical critiques of Marxism, together with political developments in socialist states, have prompted major revision efforts such as the US-based project of Rethinking Marxism (Resnick and Wolff 1985) to eliminate determinism in Marxian analyses.[1]

This chapter examines the treatment of culture and development in Marxian economics, I hope, without simply repeating or belaboring the extensive critical body of Marxian thought. The first section briefly looks at modernist Marxism as manifested in the classic texts by Marx and Engels, and their twentieth-century interpretations and applications to the question of development, expressed in the work of Paul Sweezy (1970 [1942]) and Ernest Mandel (1968, 1975).[2] Here, I believe that the occlusion of culture in modernist Marxism was the result of what I call *tactical omission*—that is, prioritizing the 'material' (base) over the 'ideal' (superstructure)—rather than a simple oversight of the import of culture. The second section shows that this analytical move cast a long epistemological shadow over Marxian thought, demonstrated in the near absence of culture from major writings on economic development (Dobb 1951; Frank 1966, 1967; Baran 1973 [1957]; Amin 1974, 1976). This section takes a brief look at Samir Amin's critique of

Eurocentrism (2009 [1989]), which offers a rare attempt at grappling with cultural problematics in this tradition.

The last two sections of the chapter focus on postmodernist revisions of Marxian political economy with respect to the relative positions of culture and class, first outlining the theoretical interventions by Stephen Resnick and Richard Wolff (1987, 1996) and others in the Rethinking Marxism tradition (Amariglio *et al.* 1988, 1996). Following the work of Louis Althusser (1970), this body of thought theorizes class, together with the remainder of the social world, as processes, thereby avoiding the essentialism of labor/capital. I then review some applications of this intervention to the context of economic policy and development in contemporary India by Anjan Chakrabarti, Stephen Cullenberg, and Ajit Chaudhury (Chakrabarti and Cullenberg 2001; Chakrabarti *et al.* 2009), who present a non-determinist, non-teleological conception of social change.

In Chapter 1, I argued that economic thought is mostly rooted in *dualistic ontology*, that is, a binary apprehension of social 'reality' that leaves little conceptual room for alterity, in-betweenness, and hybridity. This ontology is embodied in the theoretical split between culture and 'economy,' which ultimately rests on the archaic dualism of ideal/material. Dualistic ontology in classical Marxism is apparent in the much-criticized schema of base and superstructure. The last two sections in this chapter examine the extent to which postmodernist economic revisions have transcended this framework. I argue that despite the theoretical shift away from the schema of base/superstructure, the postmodern solution ends up erecting a dichotomy of *class/nonclass*. Some may see this as a merely analytical distinction. However, as has been learned from Marx's tactical omission of culture, analytical decisions engender epistemological consequences. In the postmodernist case, since class forms the "guiding thread" of analysis (Amariglio *et al.* 1988: 488), culture remains secondary to—or to put it more strongly, a theoretical negative of—class. The consequences of this construction crop up in the applications discussed in the last section of the chapter.

Like the rest of this book, the following discussion concentrates on the literature within Economics, though I am mindful of the inherent multidisciplinarity of Marxian discourse. The present study is only a first step toward greater understanding of a complex terrain. In line with the panoramic method of this book, many relevant details, concerning such things as the theory of value and issues of distribution are not entertained in this chapter as integral to the Marxian conception of economy and society as they are. I will primarily isolate statements on culture or cultural phenomena for illustration more than present an extended holistic analysis of certain ideas or arguments. As stated in Chapter 1, my concept of culture in this book is rather inclusive, referring to the conglomeration of broadly shared, though contested, beliefs and lifeways of a community that sanction and censor its members' ideas and practices, including economic action and knowledge, in multiple ways that are not necessarily fully coherent, and are never complete. (See Chapter 1 for more on culture, and Appendix II for a sample of economists' interpretations of it.)

Culture in modernist Marxism

The classical tradition

The place of culture in Marxism is complex, indeed, paradoxical. Tom Bottomore points out that Marxist philosophy rejects the bourgeois view of culture as high art and an alternative to materialist readings of society. In this sense, he argues, culture "is not an indigenously Marxist concept" (1983: 109). At the same time, Marxism has a profound cultural dimension in the problem of consciousness and ideology. In Marxian political economy, however, this complexity was glossed over in favor of simpler determinist treatments. Although there is much debate over the extent to which this determinism is present in Marx's own writings (e.g., Resnick and Wolff 1987). In addition to the established contributions of Antonio Gramsci (1985) and Louis Althusser (1970), two contemporary views help frame this debate: Raymond Williams' assessment of the impact of Marxism on the place of culture in British thought, and—for a specifically economic viewpoint—Immanuel Wallerstein's perspective on the "crisis of Marxism."[3]

In "Marxism and Culture," Williams (1961) thought Marx did not possess a developed theory of culture, only an outline. According to Williams, even though Marx emphasized complexity and cautioned against over-simplification, his 'formula' of base and superstructure had the effect of diminishing the place of culture in his philosophy. Williams argued this was not because Marx did not respect "intellectual and imaginative creation," but because he did not think it was the decisive factor in "human development" (ibid.: 266). According to him, in Marx's scheme, the hierarchy between the economic and the cultural was clear. Thus, for Williams:

> A Marxist theory of culture will recognize diversity and complexity, will take account of continuity within change, will allow for chance and certain limited autonomies, but, with these reservations, will take the facts of the economic structure and the consequent social relations as the guiding string on which a culture is woven, and by following which a culture is to be understood. This, still an emphasis rather than a substantiated theory, is what Marxists of our own century received from their tradition.
>
> (ibid.: 261–2)

In this tradition, he claimed, cultural interpretations followed a rigid causality from base to superstructure, and economic analyses of any situation had to precede cultural ones.

Wallerstein's view of the 'crisis of Marxism' is that, like all thinkers, Marx was subject to a tension between theory (abstraction) and history (concreteness), which he dealt with by emphasizing one over the other at different times. Unfortunately, Marx's followers ignored "his qualifications, his prudences, his ambiguities" (Wallerstein 1985: 387), and chose to stress the reductive moments in his thought. This argument does not answer the question of why Marxists took this particular route, but the answer is not crucial. What is most pertinent is that reductionism came to define Marxian discourse.

In their classic writings, Marx and Engels reflected both reductionism and complexity. On one hand, there is a streak of strong deterministic materialism, most sharply observed in polemic texts. In the *Communist Manifesto*, where they discuss culture mainly in the context of the abolition of private property, they state:

> All objections urged against the communistic mode of producing and appropriating material products, have, in the same way, been urged against the communistic mode of producing and appropriating *intellectual products*. Just as, to the bourgeois, the disappearance of class property is the disappearance of production itself, so the disappearance of *class culture* is to him identical with the disappearance of *all culture*. That *culture*, the loss of which he laments, is, for the enormous majority, a mere training to act as a machine. But don't wrangle with us so long as you apply, to our intended abolition of bourgeois property, the standard of your bourgeois notions of freedom, *culture*, law, etc. Your very ideas are but the outgrowth of the conditions of your bourgeois production and bourgeois property, just as your jurisprudence is but the will of your class made into a law for all, a will, whose essential character and direction are *determined* by the economical conditions of existence of your class.
>
> (1998 [1848]: 55; emphases added)

First, the term 'culture' is used in a superstructural meaning, i.e., in opposition to 'economic' conditions; but also more narrowly in reference to a specific element of the superstructure, namely, "intellectual products," separate from law or politics. Second, material conditions—the "economical conditions of existence"—"determine" other elements of society. This determinism is showcased in the famous Preface to *The Critique of Political Economy*, in which Marx referred to "the economic structure of society, the real foundation, on which arises a legal and political superstructure and to which correspond definite forms of social consciousness" (1970: 20).

On the other hand, Marx clearly recognized culture in a broader sense, as a way of life. In *Grundrisse*, for instance, he described "the cult of money" among English Puritans and Dutch Protestants, with its values of "asceticism," "frugality," and "contempt for mundane, temporal and fleeting pleasures" (1973 [1939]: 232). Here, he revealed a keen grasp of an intricate cultural phenomenon and recognition of the cultural (cult) forms of human existence and economy. In the end, however, Marx relegated these aspects to the superstructure. Although he placed man within society, he considered any social commitments that fell beyond the demands of capital to belong to an earlier stage of historical development. "[T]hey are founded either on the immaturity of man as an individual, when he has not yet torn himself loose from the umbilical cord of his natural species-connection with other men, or on direct relations of dominance and servitude" (1977 [1867]: 173); these kinds of commitments belong to an age when man had not gained control over "the process of production" (ibid.: 175). Therefore, he theorized kinship and other communal commitments as remnants of pre-capitalist epochs of history.[4]

In short, cultural moments in classical Marxism were muted by the 'decision' to prioritize the material. I see this occlusion of culture as a case of tactical omission, the result of an analytical move. Its consequence has been that Marxism played a substantial part in centering 'the economic'—as ontologically distinct from culture—in social analysis, with the concepts of class and capitalism theoretically exhausting this realm.

Twentieth-century discourse

In this section I take two iconic texts to represent modernist articulations of Marx's philosophy: Sweezy's *The Theory of Capitalist Development* (1970 [1942]) and Mandel's *Late Capitalism* (1975). This is a very limited selection, but discussions of culture are not prevalent in this brand of Marxian economic scholarship (see Appendix I). These two well-studied texts illustrate the deterministic approach to history and change, and the superstructural status of culture. (See Howard and King 1992, for more literatures.)

Although generally associated with the determinist brand of Marxism, Sweezy's book is moderated by qualifications and prudences. He painstakingly explains the role of abstraction in Marx's philosophy, and shows that his decision to exclude elements such as use-value from the study of political economy did not amount to banishing them from the causal background of economic activity. Sweezy's critique of Neoclassical economics for its disregard of the social context gives some indication of his sensitivity to reductionism. All the same, he left this sensitivity behind to focus on narrowly construed economic factors. The result is that his explanation of such knotty questions as colonialism and nationalism reduces them to instruments for "directing attention away from class struggle" (1970 [1942]: 311), and suggests that subaltern opposition is motivated almost solely by material concerns. Sweezy might have believed there were other motivations for these phenomena but he did not consider them significant enough to entertain. This is an epistemological consequence of the classical omission of culture.

The only instance where Sweezy possibly refers to a cultural context occurs in the course of explaining the impact of capitalist expansion on 'native' peoples:

> [I]t must not be supposed that capital finds everything in readiness to receive it in the backward regions. The native populations have *their own accustomed ways of making a living* and are far from eager to enlist in the service of capital at meager wages. Consequently the areas must be brought under the jurisdiction of the capitalist state and conditions favorable to the growth of capitalist relations of production must be forcibly created.
>
> (ibid.: 304; emphasis added)

Here historical materialism requires the premise that development takes place in certain stages such that one could speak of 'backward regions.' The spectrum of world history is divided into four economic systems: (1) well-developed capitalist; (2) rapidly becoming capitalist; (3) hardly touched by capitalism; and

(4) pre-capitalist. Accordingly, capital 'finds' societies in one stage or another, and operates on them in predictable ways. More pertinently, the expression "accustomed ways of making a living" seems to suggest that people in the colonies had their own lifeways (culture), but this is only a vague hint with no analytical follow-up or implications.

In a similar manner, Mandel's analysis in *Late Capitalism* (1975) is grounded in the "laws of motion of capital" (ibid.: 13). His reference to the "successive historical stages of capitalist development" (ibid.: 9) embodies the teleological perspective. Echoing Sweezy, he categorizes the "capitalist world economy" into a "system of capitalist, semi-capitalist and pre-capitalist relations of production" (ibid.: 48). Thus, world history and economic, social phenomena and movement are reduced to predictable elements in the dynamics of capitalism. Mandel's statement—following Trotsky—that capitalism 'finds' mankind at different stages of development renders capitalism a force that stands beyond human society altogether, i.e., outside of culture.

Unlike Sweezy, Mandel devotes substantial space to cultural features of life in 'advanced' economies. He argues that the culture of late capitalism turns all super-structural activities such as popular art and the media, which are all part of the "sphere of consumption," into industries. The defining characteristic of late capitalist culture is consumer society. Mandel advises Marxists that the rise of the consumer society must be seen as part of "the cultural achievements of the proletariat" (ibid.: 393), which include increased consumption of books, papers, sports, and other habits of leisure and refinement. The "services sector," he notes, expands according to the higher demand for non-food consumption, social pressures created by advertising, and displacement of the producing proletariat family by the market. The expansion of the services sector involves, among other things, the "possibilities for developing the cultural and civilizing needs of the working population" (ibid.: 401). Here, culture refers to intellectual and creative activity as well as distance from 'nature.' Following Marx (1973), Mandel argues that the general diversified increase in consumption results from the civilizing character of capital—a "genuine extension of the cultural needs" of the proletariat (Mandel 1975: 394–395).[5]

Marxism and international development

Marxism is inherently preoccupied with development, that is, social movement from a meager human existence to a more materially secure plain, with all the types of enrichment that are thought to accompany this security. Marx's entire enterprise was devoted to the explanation of this historical process as it unfolded in Western Europe. Marxism—as philosophy, method, and political force—has played an inspirational and a practically supportive role in anti-colonial struggles and the nation-building efforts of many societies worldwide. This section addresses only its academic contributions on the question of economic development in reference to former European colonies.[6]

The first main feature of Marxian discourse on international development is its exclusive emphasis on the impact of capitalism on 'peripheral' economies, with little attention to their internal dynamics, especially, the role of culture. Commonly, cultural factors are acknowledged, together with social and political ones, before they are quickly set aside. The second feature is the idea of unequal or uneven development (Mandel 1975), which denotes the inability of capitalism to move forward in a uniform fashion worldwide. Conceptually, the international economic structure consists of a few dominant 'advanced' (well-developed capitalist) countries, and many 'satellite' economies lagging behind. Both features underscore that agency is invested in capitalism.

The dependency perspective

The Dependency School contended that capitalist intervention through European colonialism had reduced once vibrant and autonomous societies to the state of inferiority and 'underdevelopment' observed in the mid-twentieth century. A quick look at key contributors to the dependency discourse shows their consistency with the general Marxist view of this period, namely, a broad recognition of the social/cultural context that, in the end, cannot overrule material forces. Furthermore, it shows that on the question of 'third world development,' the Marxian position—despite some diversity—converged with the developmentalist view of mainstream economics (see Chapter 7).[7]

Paul Baran put the matter most starkly:

> Economic development is at the present time the most urgent, most vital need for the overwhelming majority of mankind. Every year lost means the loss of millions of human lives. Every year spent in inaction means further weakening, further exasperation of the peoples vegetating in the backward countries.
>
> (1973: 399)

He went on to explain that development was first and foremost a narrowly economic task. However, he also claimed that "[a] peaceful transplantation of Western culture, science, and technology to the less advanced countries would have served everywhere as a powerful catalyst of economic progress" (ibid.: 299). The meaning of culture here is not quite clear. It might signify a way of life, as in frugality, or it could refer to art and literature in their 'civilizing' capacity. What is clear is that this statement suggests that culture—irrespective of how it is understood—could play an important role in economic development, which somewhat departs from materialist logic.

André Gunder Frank criticized the exclusive focus among historians on the experience of "developed metropolitan countries" (1966: 17), which produced a truncated European-centered account. He disputed the Neoclassical economic 'misconception' that underdevelopment was an internally induced original state that could be removed by the diffusion of Western capital and technology. Here he disagrees with Baran's above-noted argument. Instead, Frank argued that underdeveloped countries experienced their greatest economic growth during periods of isolation from the 'metropolis,' and hence their contemporary development was

118

limited by their satellite position in the world economy. Development and under-development constituted "an integral part" of one historical process (1967: 242). His position was strongly materialist as he stated:

> Both in the metropolis and the satellites, the economic policy pursued and the resulting economic development and underdevelopment were produced by the underlying economic structure and must be traced to that structure.

> Whatever role Calvinist or Catholic morality, 'true bourgeois,' 'pseudo-bourgeois' or 'feudal' mentality, 'expansionist drive' or not, may have played in producing development and underdevelopment, such factors were not determinant or decisive but at best derivative and secondary.

> (ibid.: 96)

Economic structure is determinant. Although he did not spell out a particular meaning of culture, Frank's statement clearly indicates the direction of causality runs from economy to culture as the latter is embodied in religion or other mental states.

These early dependency arguments sustained criticism from Marxian scholars for lack of theoretical rigor (see Kanth 1992). As a result, a second wave of writings emerged to address some of the issues raised. This group included contributions by T. Dos Santos (1970) and F.H. Cardoso (1972), among others. Of this second wave, Samir Amin has been the most prolific, managing to synthesize three disparate lines of neo-Marxian political economy: world system, unequal exchange, and modes of production (Ruccio and Simon 1992). He also struggles more explicitly with the problem of culture.

Amin's central thesis (1974, 1976) is that two different, but complementary, forms of capitalist accumulation exist—in the center (Europe, North America, Japan) and in the periphery. The center operates on the basis of a "necessary" relationship between the rate of surplus value and the level of development of productive forces; that is, production is driven by domestic demand. In contrast, peripheral capitalism is driven by the production of goods for export. Capital emigrates from the center in pursuit of higher returns, which are ensured by the lower cost of labor in the periphery. This, Amin argued, is the "framework for the essential theory of *unequal exchange*" (1974: 13).[8] Underdevelopment is maintained by the "functional" relationship between the "autocentric" center, and the dependent, "extraverted" periphery (1976: 202–3). In general, Amin kept close to the letter of historical materialism, seeing capitalism as a "pre-requisite for socialism" (1974: 16). Nevertheless, he did not advocate waiting for capitalism to work itself out, while—in Baran's terms—people vegetate in the periphery. Amin argued that because of the world systemic contradiction where capitalism creates objective conditions for development, and simultaneously bars it from being fully realized, the periphery cannot 'catch up,' rather it has to "transcend the capitalist model" (ibid.: 18). Transition to socialism meant altering priorities in order to shift from a primary export economy to one capable of producing capital goods.

Culture in dependency economics

Dependency theorists made only sporadic and gestural references to cultural 'factors.' Explicit mentions of culture appeared in three overlapping patterns. The first is cursory treatment, namely, listing it among other factors, each separate from the 'economic,' without further elaboration, e.g., there are "[c]lose economic, political, social and cultural ties between each metropolis and its satellites" (Frank 1967: 147). The second pattern acknowledges culture in the limited sense of intellectual creativity and personal refinement—underdevelopment is a condition of poverty and "lack of culture" (ibid.: 136). The third pattern discounts the significance of culture to economic phenomena as we have just seen in Frank's remark about religion. Overall, the cultural and the economic appear to be two ontologically distinct realms, the bulk of emphasis being laid on the latter.

The reason for this analytical absence of culture is that all economies outside of industrial Europe have been theorized as pre-capitalist modes of production. As Claude Meillassoux has argued, Marx was interested in such modes only to the extent of their location in his historical sequence; as a result, he did not analyze pre-capitalist formations "from within." What he did was to "take the basic institutions and features of capitalism as it existed at his time and to try to trace their past evolution" (Meillassoux 1972: 97).[9] This insight goes some way to explain why dependency analyses of underdevelopment contained little discussion of the cultural substance of 'pre-capitalism.' Following the late cultural awakening in Economics generally (see Chapter 1), Marxian-inspired discussions of development have paid more attention to culture in more recent work (Amin 2009 [1989]; Wallerstein 1990a, 1990b). In this section, I highlight Amin's attempt to address a cultural problem.[10]

Notwithstanding a strong materialist emphasis, Amin often wove cultural concerns into the fabric of his economic inquiry (1974, 1976). For instance, he referred to cultural "mechanisms of domination" (1974: 15), though, reflecting the cursory treatment noted earlier, he gave no explanation. He pointed out that 'objective reality' was the driver of change, but stressed that this reality included "social, ideological, cultural, and political" problems (ibid.: 25). He interpreted all local and regional cultural phenomena as reactions to the expansion of the world economic system. At the same time he argued the transition to socialism must respect the "cultural and ethnic homogeneity" of certain regions (ibid.: 19). Again, he did not elaborate on the nature and specific implications of this directive.

Amin's attempt to address cultural problematics appears in a critique of Marxism rather than a direct analysis of economic processes. In his book *Eurocentrism*, first published in 1989, he set out to contribute "to the construction of a paradigm freed from culturalist distortion" (2009: 99). According to him:

[Culturalism is] an apparently coherent and holistic theory based on the hypothesis that there are cultural invariants able to persist through and beyond possible transformations in economic, social, and political systems.

Cultural specificity, then, becomes the main driving force of inevitably quite different historical trajectories.

(ibid.: 7)

For him, this type of 'theory' is symbolized in Max Weber's (1958 [1930]) well-known thesis, and other discourses such as "the culture of poverty."[11] This is clearly a criticism of static notions of culture commonly found in Economics (see Chapter 3 in this book). He goes on to draw a distinction between three types of cultures: capitalist, peripheral tributary, and pre-capitalist. The culture of capitalism, according to him, is Eurocentrism—a modern ideological construct diachronic with the rise of this mode of production in Europe, and a cultural form that goes beyond mere ethnocentrism. He argues that, contrary to Marx's own precautions, Marxism developed in a Eurocentric fashion that could be displaced only by a theory of politics and of culture. Thus, instead of dismissing this phenomenon of Eurocentrism, he maps it onto capitalism, its economic counterpart. In doing so, unlike Mandel and most modernist Marxian economists, Amin is willing to speak of a specifically European culture, instead of only an abstract culture of capitalism. It is unfortunate that, in all this, he does not offer a direct interpretation of culture, which makes it difficult to grasp which concept he has in mind.

Despite his questioning of cultural hegemony, implicit in Eurocentrism, Amin aspires to a "universalist" (2009 [1989]: 206) social theory based on his argument about unequal exchange. Within the contradictory global dynamic of capitalism, he suggests, "cultural life" is "the mode of organization for the utilization of use values," though "culture itself" is homogenized when use values are homogenized "by their submission to a generalized exchange value" (ibid.). Unfortunately, because of the absence of an explicit meaning of culture, the word is highly opaque and the ambiguity carries multiple meanings. Does it mean the 'sphere of consumption' (following Mandel)/the observance of tradition/consumption as a way of life/or intellectual and artistic output? This is all left unclear.

Still, Amin goes farther than any of his cohort in the level of attention and space devoted to the problem of culture. His seemingly unfinished contribution lies in a struggle to reconcile a culturally aware sense—that allowed him to see culture as integral to the workings of specifically European capitalism—with his universalist Marxist vision. I would also argue that he realized, even if not quite explicitly, that the major achievement of the Dependency School—that of turning the gaze of development theorizing to the global stage—inherently invites questions of a cross-cultural nature, which other dependency theorists did not dwell on.

Postmodern Marxism: culture and class

Postmodern Marxism draws on a rich history of critical scholarship, most notably the contributions of Gramsci and Althusser. Both had complex, unsealed interpretations of Marx's philosophy, albeit with different outlooks and emphases. Althusser's (1970) attempt to excise determinist interpretations of this philosophy has provided the theoretical backbone for postmodern Marxian thought. In this section I examine the place of culture in this strand of contemporary Marxian economics, focusing on a few leading authors of the Rethinking Marxism project (Resnick and Wolff 1987, 1996; Amariglio *et al.* 1988, 1996).[12]

Many contemporary Marxists have denounced crude materialist and historicist pronouncements on social change. Yet, the ghost of determinism has not been fully exorcised. Resnick and Wolff (1996: 170) write:

> It has become obligatory for many Marxists to affirm, in one way or another, a principled rejection of determinism in all its guises: economic determinism, structuralism, humanism, historicism, empiricism, rationalism, positivism, and foundationalism. Yet despite such affirmations, most Marxist discourses find it difficult and ultimately unacceptable to formulate consistently nondeterminist arguments. They thus commingle determinist and antideterminist formulations in paradoxical, contradictory discourses, inviting both criticism and resolution.

This statement realizes that a stated rejection of determinism by itself is not sufficient to remove its substance. I believe the same could be said of the treatment of culture; i.e., announcing that it is no longer simply a mirror of material forces does not automatically alter its superstructural conception in the theoretical framework of Marxian economics. Postmodern Marxists have introduced two related major revisions. The first has been to rid class of the essentialism of labor/capital by interpreting it as a process rather than a group with a shared consciousness (Resnick and Wolff 1987). The second revision consists of a self-conscious rejection of the idea that cultural phenomena are predetermined in the base structure (Amariglio *et al.* 1988). I elaborate on these two revisions.

In their (1987) landmark book, *Knowledge and Class: A Marxian Critique of Political Economy*, Resnick and Wolff seek to recover Marx, the non-determinist by enlisting the notion of overdetermination (Althusser 1970), where each element of the social world is constituted by other elements. Since "all entities are in ceaseless change" (Resnick and Wolff 1996: 175), "the process" becomes the basic analytical unit, which requires a non-essentialist concept of class. Resnick and Wolff define two class processes: (1) a fundamental process where the production and appropriation of surplus labor take place; and (2) a subsumed one, in which surplus labor is distributed. The same individual may participate in both.[13] The combination of fundamental and subsumed processes makes up a class structure. In particular, a capitalist enterprise is conceptualized as an "overdetermined site of contradictory tensions and conflicts among all the individuals occupying different class and nonclass positions, both internal and external to the enterprise, over both class and nonclass processes" (Resnick and Wolff 1987: 170).

The second revision has to do with the theoretical position of culture vis-à-vis class. Since the process is the basic unit of analysis, one can no longer speak of culture as such, but only of "*cultural processes*," defined as "the diverse ways in which human beings produce meanings for their existence" (ibid.: 20), or "processes of the production and circulation of meaning" (Amariglio *et al.* 1988: 487).

In contrast, economic processes are concerned with "the production and distribution of goods and services" (Resnick and Wolff 1996: 175). Amariglio *et al.* (1988) argue that cultural processes exist along with other 'nonclass' processes, which include those pertaining to natural and political conditions. Cultural processes performed within a capitalist enterprise include marketing strategies and any other procedures that establish and justify the firm's existence and operation (Resnick and Wolff 1987). Cultural processes external to the firm encompass institutions and activities (e.g., educational, artistic, religious) "necessary" to receive and distribute surplus value in the enterprise.

This formulation opens up more theoretical space beside the traditionally economic. At the same time, however, it raises at least two concerns. First, class remains "the guiding thread from and with which a particularly Marxist knowledge is constructed" (Amariglio *et al.* 1988: 488). What follows analytically is the distinction between class and nonclass processes, with culture being located within the nonclass universe. The very term nonclass renders all other processes (including cultural ones) a negative of class. Yet, if one takes seriously the concept of overdetermination, it seems as arbitrary to begin from class as it is to begin from culture. Second, since it is conceptualized as a realm of meaning, culture retains some superstructural residue; it remains in the sphere of the symbolic and ideal. This could be seen in the statement that "the specific forms in which art, music, literature, and history exist are the combined result of forms of economic processes (including the class processes) and forms of political processes" (ibid.). In effect, there is culture, and there is economy; and, with class being the initial guiding thread, and so long as class is located in the economic, culture can only be secondary or derivative.

Of course, overdetermination implies that there is no precedent—the economic is as much constituted by the cultural as the other way around. Therefore, class and nonclass could be seen as mere analytical categories, working at a discursive, rather than an ontological level.[14] This may well be. The problem, as I have argued with regard to Marx's tactical omission of culture, is that analytical decisions do carry epistemological consequences. Postmodernists insist that class processes do not necessarily authorize cultural processes; rather, the latter arise and continue "in certain locations with specific conditions of existence. As the conditions of existence vary from location to location, cultural processes are dispersed and differentiated" (Amariglio *et al.* 1988: 488). But, these processes are assumed to exist in mutual dependence "alongside" natural, economic, and political processes (ibid.: 487). This analytical separation between economic and cultural processes, in effect, maintains the *de facto* secondary status of culture, and allows class to eclipse it in translations of this theoretical framework to concrete applications.

The postmodernist revision responds to Williams' critique of classical Marxism by rendering cultural problematics more visible in the theoretical model. Clearly, the position of culture here is not a product of omission. On the contrary, it is a self-conscious move to reverse the classical error. Nor does this treatment bear any resemblance to the determinist stance of dependency economics. Yet, I wonder about possible unintended fallout from the class/nonclass distinction, especially for studying different cultural contexts. Could this convenient analytical dichotomy lead back to the modernist habit of slighting culture?

Culture and development in postmodern Marxism

The concerns stated above have considerable implications for analyses of socio-economic change in different cultures. I conclude this chapter by looking at some applications of the analytical framework outlined in the previous section. These applications pay more attention to cultural themes than is common in modernist Marxian literature. But, the culture—i.e., nonclass—side in these analyses is characteristically dimmer than the class side. Of course, this could simply mean that these particular texts have not lived up to the full potential of the postmodernist theoretical vision. However, I think, at least in part, the dimness of the culture side signals an epistemological consequence of the class/nonclass divide.

Richard McIntyre has adopted Resnick and Wolff's framework to offer a model of development. In a grid form, the model combines a series of "modes of production (capitalist, feudal, ancient, communal) down the side and their various conditions of existence (economic, political, cultural, natural) across the top" (McIntyre 1992: 91). In each 'cell' within the grid the overdetermined interaction between a particular mode of production and its conditions of existence produces a particular form or level of development, with the result being uneven development. McIntyre argues development is "a contingent process in which the effect of any force cannot be specified in general but only in a particular context" (ibid.), which includes "*cultural conditions of existence*" (ibid.: 92). He suggests one example of these conditions is that cultural and economic processes articulate in a slogan such as "own your own business" (ibid.), which acquires cultural significance and provides an emotional impetus for entry into economic action. Yet, these cultural threads are never unpacked, their own meanings seem to be taken for granted. Accordingly, relationships—such as between class and cultural processes—beg clarification. For example, does his description of capitalism itself as a class process mean that cultural processes are contained within the class process instead of existing alongside it as Amariglio *et al.* (1988) have suggested?

The centrality of capitalism has been an issue for postmodernist economic thought. As S. Charusheela has argued, the conception of the "material domain of exploitation" (2004: 48) in postmodern Marxian economics is exclusively construed within the theoretical boundaries of a capitalist economy, which forecloses the possibility of other modes of social organization. The re-articulation of class as a process does little to resolve this problem because "the very definitional constitution of the class categories disallows the non-capitalist from entering the terrain except as the obverse of capitalist-modernity's self-narrative" (ibid.: 49). This point is illustrated in J.K. Gibson-Graham and David Ruccio's paper critiquing the post-development discourse (e.g., Escobar 1995) for being centered on capitalism. The paper calls for "anticapitalocentric economic politics" to allow the possibility of 'noncapitalist' futures (Gibson-Graham and Ruccio 2001: 179). Unfortunately, a pre-analytic commitment to the concept of class precludes potential noncapitalist visions. For example, the paper enumerates different class processes (feudal, ancient, communal, slave, and capitalist) in order to insert noncapitalist class processes into the analysis. Gibson-Graham and Ruccio argue this could be accomplished by decoupling the concepts of markets, commodities, and enterprise from the capitalist mode of production, and allowing the process of surplus labor distribution, i.e., class, to incorporate an ever wider circle of constituencies affected by development interventions—"local communities, retrenched workers, traditional landowners, ..." and others who claim "environmental or cultural restitution" (ibid.: 177). In effect, instead of moving beyond capitalism, this analysis ends up enabling capitalism-centered theoretical categories—such as surplus labor—to swallow entire other cultural horizons of communities impacted by development.

In the remainder of this section, I concentrate on two studies of economic social change in contemporary India by Chakrabarti and Cullenberg (2001) and Chakrabarti *et al.* (2009). Chakrabarti and Cullenberg (2001) argue that post-independence perspectives on development in India, including Marxist ones, shared an underlying vision of social reality as a pre-given totality that experiences change as one homogeneous unit within a predictable path of history. According to them, orthodox Marxian theories of transition suffer from three problems: a macro vision, in which one social totality replaces another; a belief that change is teleological and "diachronic;" and a commitment to the idea of progress as irreversible change. In contrast, Chakrabarti and Cullenberg aim to offer a "multidirectional" and "decentered" notion of transition in which multiple class processes and modes of production coexist, thereby allowing the "possibility of alternative (noncapitalist) development paths" (2001: 184).

Using the same grid as McIntyre's, Chakrabarti and Cullenberg (ibid.) introduce 12 class sets categorized by mode of production (capitalist, feudal/slave, and communal); the form of access to surplus labor; remuneration (wage or non-wage); and the type of output distribution (commodity, noncommodity). Each class set rests on certain economic and "non-economic conditions of existence," and the combination of class sets and conditions makes up the "class structure of society" (ibid.: 188). This approach, they claim, disaggregates society and precludes a teleological reading of change since it is possible, for instance, to move from capitalism to feudalism. At this point in the analysis, cultural processes are not mentioned explicitly.

Chakrabarti and Cullenberg apply this framework to examine the impact of liberalization policies—privatization, subsidy cutting, and promotion of a profit orientation across the board—on India's class structures. They argue, these policies have produced a social knock-on effect that has drastically altered the "social totality" in the country. In particular,

> The once torpid economic, cultural, and political aspects of society are now undergoing rapid transformation and hitherto accepted ideas regarding development, progress, the proper role for central and state governments, the meaning of democracy, and embedded cultural values are in a state of profound turmoil.
>
> (ibid.: 190)

This description gives explicit attention to cultural "aspects" and "embedded values." But, whatever they are, these are mentioned without further explanation, in a way resembling the cursory treatment of culture seen earlier in the dependency literature. Moreover, in this statement, causality runs from economy to culture in that liberalization policies have induced cultural change; the turmoil in cultural values follows from economic processes. This might well be the case, but it cannot be assumed. If it is, then cultural processes remain theoretically derivative from class processes, a perception that falls short of the overdeterminist method.

The secondary status of culture crops up in Chakrabarti and Cullenberg's assessment of the impacts of liberalization policies on three sectors: agriculture, the state, and households. The discussion of the first two sectors focuses strictly on prices and surplus value appropriation. Culture makes an explicit appearance only in the household sector, which Chakrabarti and Cullenberg describe as having a complex class structure with feudal and patriarchal features. Where and how cultural phenomena enter the analytical terrain reveal their secondary place in the discussion, which occurs on multiple levels.

First, Chakrabarti and Cullenberg argue government policies have led to greater use of more efficient appliances in domestic work, and "[a]long with the adoption of these means of production has come changed cultural perceptions of what the socially necessary basket of commodities for a household unit might be" (ibid.: 197). As pointed out already, the statement reinforces the causality: economic → cultural, i.e., from the means of production to cultural perceptions. Second, in addition to the changed cultural perceptions brought about by the introduction of new consumption patterns, they remark:

> [t]he household sector is a significant site of production, appropriation, and distribution of surplus labor. It is, moreover, an arena where many of the social and cultural transformations taking place in Indian society are being discussed and struggled over.
>
> (ibid.: 198)

Of the three sectors discussed in the paper, the household is the only one where culture is invoked. In effect, the household serves as the repository of cultural processes. Third, culture is theoretically associated only with consumption. Cultural perceptions seem to influence consumption, the composition of the socially necessary basket of goods, but not production or, at least, they have no influence worth pointing out.[15] The authors do not seem to think that cultural perceptions also shape the amount of "socially necessary labor," which would in turn impact the amounts of surplus labor and surplus value themselves.

Chakrabarti, Chaudhury, and Cullenberg (2009) carry this analytical framework further with a "class-focused" analysis of the impact of India's New Economic Policy of liberalization on the small-scale sector. Following Resnick and Wolff, they take a view that decenters and disaggregates 'the economy' such that all processes—class and "non-class"—are overdetermined by other processes. There is a great deal in the paper to comment on. Here, I only wish to point out the occlusion of culture. The term 'cultural' appears explicitly once, without elaboration, as the authors argue that small-sector entities exist together with "different kinds of property structure and power structure, equal or unequal income distribution, and differentiated cultural forms depending upon such processes as race, gender, and caste" (Chakrabarti *et al.* 2009: 1172). The meaning of cultural forms is left unexplained, which echoes the dependency treatment—economic, political, cultural, and so on. Chakrabarti *et al.* allude to culture in the argument that capitalism is a "symbolic order" (ibid.: 1170), a system of representation that redefines all sociality in reference to itself. It would have been much more illuminating if the elements of this cultural process (the production and circulation of meaning) were laid out. For example, how is the meaning of capitalism interpreted and reappropriated by those in the small-scale sector? And, what are the specific economic ramifications? Overall, the non-class universe is dim, it is never clear how exactly the class processes are 'overdetermined' by non-class processes. Indeed, almost nothing is said in this regard.

Postmodern Marxian economics is far more alert to cultural dynamics than modernist Marxism. Yet, I believe the class/nonclass divide—even if thought of as merely analytical—has the effect of privileging class, albeit not in the same way and extent that classical Marxism did. Class processes may be prioritized as an entry point to Marxian political economy, but the term cultural processes itself cannot substitute for actual analysis of these phenomena.

Conclusion

Classical Marxism made a tactical decision to prioritize 'the material,' which cast a long epistemological shadow over Marx's legacy in Economics as represented in the work of such capable analysts and critics as Sweezy, Mandel, Baran, Frank, and Amin, among others. The Dependency School's treatment of culture was cursory, gestural, and sporadic. Later attempts, such as Amin's, to pay more attention to cultural problematics were still confined by the universalist foundation of modernist philosophy.

Postmodernist efforts have led to insightful revisions and greater visibility of culture in Marxian analytics. The most fundamental revision has been to move from the fixed (class as a group) to the fluid (class as a process). But so far, this has done little to change the theoretical hierarchy of class and culture. The astute postmodernist reformulation of Marxian political economy offers a different notion of class but leaves culture bracketed within the 'nonclass' universe. This framing—even if understood to be operative only at an analytical level—has the effect of maintaining culture in a secondary place to class. Looking from a different (perhaps subaltern) cultural perspective, if the interpretation of culture as processes of the production and circulation of meaning is granted, then the meaning and significance of class itself are 'up for grabs.'

Notes

1 See www.rethinkingmarxism.org/aesa.html for the Association for Economic and Social Analysis (AESA), which sponsors the publication *Rethinking Marxism*.
2 I have discussed the main elements and problematics of modernity, modernism, and postmodernism elsewhere, see Zein-Elabdin (2001, 2003, 2009), and Charusheela

and Zein-Elabdin (2003). For more on Marxism and modernity/modernism, see Banuri (1990), Amariglio and Ruccio (1994), Resnick and Wolff (1996), and Bartolovich and Lazarus (2002). I focus on academic Marxian publications, especially twentieth-century postwar literature. For earlier periods, see Howard and King (1992), Gurley (1979), and McIntyre (1992). See Furtado (1964) for the classical Marxian theory of development.

3 In "Questions of Culture," Gramsci was concerned with whether the proletariat was capable of creating its own "conception of the world," a "proletarian civilization or culture" (1985: 41). He saw culture as consciousness, creativity, and a general way of life. Althusser (1970) cautioned against trying to locate Marx's entire philosophy in any one of his texts. Also see his discussion of dualisms in Marxist literature (essence/phenomena, necessity/contingency, and economic/non-economic), which he calls "fallacies" because each is based on a comparison between two incomparable things, for example, knowledge with the object of knowledge (Althusser and Balibar 1970: 110–111). See O'Neil (1995) for a critical discussion of culture in the Marxian and Weberian traditions. See Eagleton (2000) for more perspectives on Marxism and culture.

4 I am grateful to Antonio Callari (pers. comm.) for alerting me that this reading limits Marx's vision to "the circuit of capital," when he did offer a "critical take on the reduction of society to capital." In other words, one could choose a more enabling one of Marx's legacies.

5 Also see Mandel's classic text *Marxist Economic Theory* (1968, vol. I). His account converges with the pattern of Classical Political Economy discussed in Chapter 2 in this book, in which the word 'culture' was used only in the context of agriculture— cultivation.

6 Other authors have criticized Marx's stance on colonialism, see Said (1979). For an analysis of colonialism in Classical Political Economy, including Marx, see Bagchi (1996).

7 I have not devoted space to other varieties of Marxian-inspired texts on development. A notable example is Dobb's (1951) India lectures, in which he did not spell out the term 'culture,' but identified institutional variables as growth limiting factors. For other literature, see Randall (1964), Dos Santos (1970), Cardoso (1972), Cardoso and Faletto (1979), Bardhan (1985), Howard and King (1992), Wilber and Jameson (1992 [1973]), Kanth (1992), and Ruccio and Simon (1992).

8 Amin (1976) claimed real wage differences were greater than productivity differences between the center and the periphery, and, therefore, the prices at which exchange took place resulted in a transfer of surplus from periphery to center. See Ruccio and Simon (1992) for some challenging questions to this argument.

9 Meillassoux criticized Marxian anthropologists for uncritically adopting this approach. Instead of examining actual social formations, which might combine several modes of production, they envisioned hypothetical 'pre-capitalist formations'——ancient, peasant, domestic household, or colonial. For more on the modes of production literature, see Geertz (1984), Ruccio and Simon (1992), and Wilk (1996).

10 In a somewhat brief discussion, Wallerstein has characterized culture as "the ideological battleground of the modern world-system" (1990a: 31); indeed, he added, it "is the world-system" (1990b: 63). See Appendix II in this book for his full statement.

11 For other Marxist-leaning critiques of this discourse, see Darity and Williams (1985) and Mason (1996).

12 Other prominent contributors include Amariglio and Ruccio (1994), Callari *et al.* (1995), Callari and Ruccio (1996), and Gibson-Graham *et al.* (2001). See Zein-Elabdin (2001) for an articulation of points of agreement and divergence between postmodern and postcolonial (also non-modernist) perspectives. See Zein-Elabdin and Charusheela (2004: Introduction) for more on a non-modernist postcolonial approach.

13 According to Resnick and Wolff (1987), Marx used the concept of class process (in *Capital, Theories of Surplus Value*, and *Grundrisse*) to analyze situations in a partial sense, i.e., when the same person both produces and appropriates surplus labor such as in the 'ancient' class structure.
14 I am indebted to Antonio Callari (pers. comm.) for pointing that in this theoretical framework there are no separate spheres, "only dimensions of a process."
15 The association of culture almost exclusively with consumption, while assuming production to be a separate sphere is common in Economics (e.g., see Chapter 3). For critical discussions of culture and consumption, see Pietrykowski (1994), Rosenbaum (1999), Koritz and Koritz (2001), and Fine (2002). For Feminist economic criticisms of the conventional Marxian approach to the 'household,' see Humphries (1977), Hartmann (1981), Folbre (1982, 1986), and Chapter 8 in this book.

References

Althusser, Louis (1970) "Contradiction and Overdetermination," in *For Marx*, trans. Ben Brewster. New York: Vintage Books.
—— and Etienne Balibar (1970) *Reading Capital*, London: Verso.
Amariglio, Jack L., Antonio Callari, Stephen Resnick, David Ruccio, and Richard Wolff (1996) "Nondeterminist Marxism: The Birth of a Postmodern Tradition in Economics," in Fred Foldvary (ed.) *Beyond Neoclassical Economics: Heterodox Approaches to Economic Theory*, Cheltenham: Edward Elgar, 134–147.
Amariglio, Jack L., Stephen A. Resnick, and Richard D. Wolff (1988) "Class, Power, and Culture," in Cary Nelson and Lawrence Grossberg (eds.) *Marxism and the Interpretation of Culture*, Urbana-Champaign, IL: University of Illinois Press, 487–501.
Amariglio, Jack L. and David F. Ruccio (1994) "Postmodernism, Marxism, and the Critique of Modern Economic Thought," *Rethinking Marxism*, 7 (3): 7–35.
Amin, Samir (1974) "Accumulation and Development: A Theoretical Model," *Review of African Political Economy*, 1 (1): 9–26.
—— (1976) *Unequal Development: An Essay on the Social Formations of Peripheral Capitalism*, trans. Brian Pearce, New York: Monthly Review Press.
—— (2009 [1989]) *Eurocentrism: Modernity, Religion, and Democracy—A Critique of Eurocentrism and Culturalism*, trans. Russell Moore and James Membrez, New York: Monthly Review.
Bagchi, Amiya Kumar (1996) "Colonialism in Classical Political Economy: Analysis, Epistemological Broadening and Mystification," *Studies in History*, 12 (1): 105–136.
Banuri, Tariq (1990) "Modernization and Its Discontents: A Cultural Perspective on the Theories of Development," in Stephen Marglin and Frédérique Marglin (eds.) *Dominating Knowledge: Development, Culture, and Resistance*, Oxford: Clarendon Press, 73–101.
Baran, Paul A. (1973 [1957]) *The Political Economy of Growth*, Harmondsworth: Penguin Books.
Bardhan, Pranab (1985) "Marxist Ideas in Development Economics: A Brief Evaluation," *Economic and Political Weekly*, 20 (13): 550–555.
Bartolovich, Crystal and Neil Lazarus (2002) *Marxism, Modernity and Postcolonial Studies*, Cambridge: Cambridge University Press.
Bottomore, Tom (ed.) (1983) *A Dictionary of Marxist Thought*, Cambridge, MA: Harvard University Press.
Callari, Antonio, Stephen Cullenberg, and Carole Biewener (eds.) (1995) *Marxism in the Postmodern Age: Confronting the New World Order*, New York: The Guilford Press.

Callari, Antonio, and David F. Ruccio (eds.) (1996) *Postmodern Materialism and the Future of Marxist Theory: Essays in the Althusserian Tradition*, Hanover, NH: Wesleyan University Press.

Cardoso, Fernando Henrique (1972) "Dependency and Development in Latin America," *New Left Review*, 1 (74): 83–95.

—— and Enzo Faletto (1979) *Dependency and Development in Latin America*, trans. Marjory Mattingly Urquidi, Berkeley, CA: University of California Press.

Chakrabarti, Anjan and Stephen Cullenberg (2001) "Development and Class Transition in India: A New Perspective," in J.K. Gibson-Graham, S. Resnick, and R. Wolff (eds.) *Re/Presenting Class: Essays in Postmodern Marxism*, Durham, NC: Duke University Press, 182–205.

Chakrabarti, Anjan, Ajit Chaudhury, and Stephen Cullenberg (2009) "Global Order and the New Economic Policy in India: The (Post)Colonial Formation of the Small-Scale Sector," *Cambridge Journal of Economics*, 33 (6): 1169–1186.

Charusheela, S. (2004) "Postcolonial Thought, Postmodernism, and Economics: Questions of Ontology and Ethics," in E. Zein-Elabdin and S. Charusheela (eds.) *Postcolonialism Meets Economics*, London: Routledge, 40–58.

—— and Eiman Zein-Elabdin (2003) "Feminism, Postcolonial Thought, and Economics," in Marianne A. Ferber and Julie A. Nelson (eds.) *Feminist Economics Today: Beyond Economic Man*, Chicago: University of Chicago Press, 175–192.

Darity, William Jr. and Rhonda M. Williams (1985) "Peddlers Forever? Culture, Competition, and Discrimination," *American Economic Review*, 75 (2): 256–261.

Dobb, Maurice (1951) *Some Aspects of Economic Development: Three Lectures*, Delhi: The Delhi School of Economics.

Dos Santos, Theotonio (1970) "The Structure of Dependence," *American Economic Review, Papers and Proceedings*, 60 (2): 231–236.

Eagleton, Terry (2000) *The Idea of Culture*, Oxford: Blackwell.

Escobar, Arturo (1995) *Encountering Development: The Making and Unmaking of the Third World*, Princeton, NJ: Princeton University Press.

Fine, Ben (2002) *The World of Consumption: The Material and Cultural Revisited*, London: Routledge.

Folbre, Nancy (1982) "Exploitation Comes Home: A Critique of the Marxian Theory of Family Labour," *Cambridge Journal of Economics*, 6 (4): 317–329.

—— (1986) "Cleaning House: New Perspectives on Households and Economic Development," *Journal of Development Economics*, 22 (1): 5–40.

Frank, André Gunder (1966) "The Development of Underdevelopment," *Monthly Review*, 18 (4): 17–31.

—— (1967) *Capitalism and Underdevelopment in Latin America: Historical Studies of Chile and Brazil*, New York: Monthly Review Press.

Furtado, Celso (1964) *Development and Underdevelopment*, Berkeley, CA: University of California Press.

Geertz, Clifford (1984) "Culture and Social Change: The Indonesian Case," *Man*, 19 (4): 511–532.

Gibson-Graham, J.K. and David F. Ruccio (2001) "'After' Development: Re-Imagining Economy and Class," in J.K. Gibson-Graham, Stephen Resnick, and Richard Wolff (eds.), *Re/Presenting Class: Essays in Postmodern Marxism*, Durham, NC: Duke University Press, 158–181.

Gibson-Graham, J.K., Stephen Resnick, and Richard D. Wolff (eds.) (2001) *Re/Presenting Class: Essays in Postmodern Marxism*, Durham, NC: Duke University.

Gramsci, Antonio (1985) *Selections from Cultural Writings*, ed. David Forgacs and Geoffrey Nowell-Smith, trans. William Boelhower, Cambridge, MA: Harvard University Press.

Gurley, John G. (1979) "Economic Development: A Marxist View," in Kenneth P. Jameson and Charles K. Wilber (eds.) *Directions in Economic Development*, Notre Dame, IN: University of Notre Dame Press, 183–251.

Hartmann, Heidi I. (1981) "The Family as the Locus of Gender, Class, and Political Struggle: The Example of Housework," *Signs: Journal of Women, Culture and Society*, 6 (3): 366–394.

Howard, M.C. and J.E. King (1992) *A History of Marxian Economics*, vol. 2, *1929–1990*, Princeton, NJ: Princeton University Press.

Humphries, Jane (1977) "Class Struggle and the Persistence of the Working-Class Family," *Cambridge Journal of Economics*, 1 (3): 241–258.

Kanth, Rajani (1992) *Capitalism and Social Theory: The Science of Black Holes*, Armonk, NY: M.E. Sharpe.

Koritz, Amy and Douglas Koritz (2001) "Checkmating the Consumer: Passive Consumption and the Economic Devaluation of Culture," *Feminist Economics*, 7 (1) March: 45–62.

Mandel, Ernest (1968) *Marxist Economic Theory*, vol. 1, trans. Brian Pearce, London: The Merlin Press.

—— (1975) *Late Capitalism*, trans. Joris De Bres, London: NLB.

Marx, Karl (1970 [1859]) *A Contribution to the Critique of Political Economy*, ed. Maurice Dobb, trans. S.W. Ryazanskaya, Moscow: Progress Publishers.

—— (1977 [1867]) *Capital: A Critique of Political Economy*, vol. 1, trans. Ben Fowkes and Friedrich Engels, New York: Vintage Books.

—— (1998 [1848]) *The Communist Manifesto: A Modern Edition*, London: Verso.

Mason, Patrick L. (1996) "Race, Culture, and the Market," *Journal of Black Studies*, 26 (6): 782–808.

—— (1973 [1939]) *Grundrisse: Foundations of the Critique of Political Economy*, trans Martin Nicolaus, New York: Vintage Books.

McIntyre, Richard (1992) "Theories of Uneven Development and Social Change," *Rethinking Marxism*, 5 (3): 75–105.

Meillassoux, Claude (1972) "From Reproduction to Production: A Marxist Approach to Economic Anthropology," *Economy and Society*, 1(1): 93–105.

O'Neil, Daniel J. (1995) "Culture Confronts Marx," *International Journal of Social Economics*, 22 (9/10/11): 43–54.

Pietrykowski, Bruce (1994) "Consuming Culture: Postmodernism, Post-Fordism, and Economics," *Rethinking Marxism*, 7 (1) (Spring): 62–80.

Randall, Laura (ed.) (1964) *Economic Development, Evolution or Revolution?* Boston: D.C. Heath & Co.

Resnick, Stephen A. and Richard D. Wolff (eds.) (1985) *Rethinking Marxism: Struggles in Marxist Theory: Essays for Harry Magdoff and Paul Sweezy*, New York: Autonomedia.

—— and —— (1987) *Knowledge and Class: A Marxian Critique of Political Economy*, Chicago: University of Chicago Press.

—— and —— (1996) "The New Marxian Political Economy and the Contribution of Althusser," in Antonio Callari and David Ruccio (eds.) *Postmodern Materialism and the Future of Marxist Theory: Essays in the Althusserian Tradition*, Hanover, NH: Wesleyan University Press, 167–192.

Rosenbaum, Eckehard F. (1999) "Against Naïve Materialism: Culture, Consumption and the Causes of Inequality," *Cambridge Journal of Economics*, 23 (3): 317–336.

Ruccio, David F. and Lawrence H. Simon (1992) "Perspectives on Underdevelopment: Frank, the Modes of Production School, and Amin," in Charles K. Wilber and Kenneth P. Jameson (eds.) *The Political Economy of Development and Underdevelopment*, New York: McGraw-Hill, 119–150.

Said, Edward W. (1979) *Orientalism*, New York: Vintage Books.

Sweezy, Paul M. (1970 [1942]) *The Theory of Capitalist Development: Principles of Marxian Political Economy*, New York: Monthly Review Press.

Wallerstein, Immanuel (1985) "Marx and Underdevelopment," in Stephen Resnick and Richard Wolff (eds.) *Rethinking Marxism: Struggles in Marxist Theory: Essays for Harry Magdoff and Paul Sweezy*, New York: Autonomedia, 379–395.

—— (1990a) "Culture as the Ideological Battleground of the Modern World-System," in Mike Featherstone (ed.) *Global Culture: Nationalism, Globalization and Modernity*, London: Sage Publications, 31–55.

—— (1990b) "Culture Is the World-System: A Reply to Boyne," in Mike Featherstone (ed.) *Global Culture: Nationalism, Globalization and Modernity*, London: Sage Publications.

Weber, Max (1958 [1930]) *The Protestant Ethic and the Spirit of Capitalism*, New York: Charles Scribner's Sons.

Wilber, Charles K. and Kenneth P. Jameson (eds.) (1992 [1973]) *The Political Economy of Development and Underdevelopment*, New York: McGraw-Hill.

Wilk, Richard (1996) *Economies and Cultures: Foundations of Economic Anthropology*, Boulder, CO: Westview Press.

Williams, Raymond (1961) *Culture and Society: 1780–1950*, London: Penguin Books.

Zein-Elabdin Eiman O. (2001) "Contours of a Non-Modernist Discourse: The Contested Space of History and Development," *Review of Radical Political Economics*, 33 (3): 255–263.

—— (2003) "The Difficulty of a Feminist Economics," in Drucilla K. Barker and Edith Kuiper (eds.) *Toward a Feminist Philosophy of Economics*, London: Routledge, 321–338.

—— (2009) "Economics, Postcolonial Theory, and the Problem of Culture: Institutional Analysis and Hybridity," *Cambridge Journal of Economics*, 33 (6): 1153–1167.

—— and S. Charusheela (eds.) (2004) *Postcolonialism Meets Economics*, London: Routledge.

7   Development economics
Three stances on culture

Professional opinion in economics has not dealt kindly with the reputations of those development economists who have made serious efforts to incorporate cultural variables into development theory or into the analysis of the development process.

(Ruttan 1988: 255)

Economic development, commonly described as "wide and deep improvements in welfare for the masses of the population" (Higgins 1977: 100), constitutes the twentieth century's most important mandate. While each term in this description is subject to debate, the dominant vision of 'development' has been premised on the modern European experience, with all its historical cultural constituents—large-scale industry, market system, nation-state. Economic historians (e.g., Kuznets 1965) understood that this experience required command over vast reservoirs of natural materials, a massive build-up of productive capacity, and a great deal of human dislocation. Nonetheless, development economists took up the task of comprehending and articulating how this historical episode could be replicated on a global scale across different societies and cultures.[1] This chapter focuses on the Neoclassical discourse on economic development.

The theoretical parameters of Neoclassical development thought are debatable, but they are generally drawn around a normative perception that human behavior reflects individual-centered, instrumentally rationalist impulses; an economy (or economic system) represents the aggregate expression of these impulses (see Chapter 3). Some have distinguished between *development economics* (DE)—"economics with a particular view of developing countries and the development process"—and *the economics of developing countries*, defined as "the mere application of orthodox economics to the study of developing countries" (Lal 1985: 10). Drawing this distinction misses the significance of culture as a shaper of economic action and knowledge. If culture is understood as the broadly—though contestedly—shared, sensibilities and practices of a society or group, which give meaning to life, albeit in less than fully coherent and definitive ways, then orthodox economics is nothing more than a particular view of social phenomena. Regardless of which one of the two definitions is adopted, both are culturally defined. (See Chapter 1 for more on culture, and Appendix II for a sample of economists' interpretations of it.)

In this chapter, I review the place of culture in post-WWII, sometimes loose, applications of Neoclassical principles to the question of economic and social change in countries classified as 'under' or 'less' developed. The literature shows that, since its inception, development economics has displayed three stances toward culture: *hospitality*, *retreat*, and *return*. The first generations of development theorists were hospitable to the idea that cultural beliefs and habits played a role in the development process, though these were mostly perceived as obstacles to economic growth. This perception persisted well into the 1970s and early 1980s. Since then, the field has forked into two divergent directions. One gathers around the New Development Economics (NDE), which takes the view that superior modeling is all that is required to decode the development process. I describe this view as a retreat from culture. The other direction, partly informed by the New Institutional Economics (see Chapter 5), marks a return to culture that began to surface with Vernon Ruttan's article "Cultural Endowments and Economic Development: What Can We Learn from Anthropology?" (1988), published within a climate of eagerness to explain the economic ascendency of East Asia. This literature seeks to model and quantify a presumed relationship between culture and development. What distinguishes the return from the hospitality stance, aside from differences in method, is that culture is no longer seen as an obstacle. Indeed, in the case of East Asia, it is considered a source of superior economic performance.

My claim in this chapter is that, like the majority of economic thought, all three perspectives, from hospitality to retreat to return, are rooted in *dualistic ontology*, that is, an apprehension of 'reality' in a binary framework that leaves no conceptual space for in-betweenness or alterity. This is most foundationally manifested in the theoretical separation between 'culture' and 'economy' as two distinct realms, a move originating in the defunct Enlightenment dualism of ideal/material, which is further rooted in an existential problem of desire/limits (see Chapter 1). Dualistic ontology in the development discourse appears on multiple levels. First, the decoupling of economy and culture is expressed in the language of cultural 'barriers,' 'determinants,' and 'effects' that are presumed to operate on a pre-existing economic agency or mode of organization. The dualism of culture/economy broadly parallels the dichotomy between 'ideal' and 'material' as authors either highlight ideas and beliefs, or emphasize tangible (material) factors such as savings and physical capital. Second, there is an overwhelming tendency to reductively theorize culture as either a driving force behind, or an obstacle to economic growth, reflecting the rootedness of development thinking in desire/limits metaphysics.[2] Going further, the culture/economy dualism is interlocked—explicitly and implicitly—with a set of hierarchical, mutually reinforcing *development dualisms*, the most salient of which are modern/traditional, individualist/collective, universal/particular, and, ultimately, developed/under(less)developed.[3] The problem with this dualistic framework is its analytical inadequacy in the face of the *economic hybridity* that characterizes contemporary societies. I leave this discussion to the final chapter of the book (see also Zein-Elabdin 2009).

This chapter begins by outlining classical development economics (CDE) as represented in the iconic work of W. Arthur Lewis (1954, 1955), W.W. Rostow (1971), and Albert Hirschman (1958, 1965). The second section briefly comments on the treatment of culture in NDE based on the work of Robert Lucas (1988) and Paul Krugman (1995). This is a very limited selection relative to the body of classical and contemporary development thought. Nevertheless, it captures the paradigmatic core of each literature. The final section reviews current discussions of culture and development (CAD), beginning with prevalent interpretations of East Asia's contemporary economic record, then more closely examines two broader studies. In the first, Oliver Dieckmann (1996) investigates the implications of 'national culture' for development. In the second, Matteo Marini (2004) suggests an evolutionary relationship between 'economic culture' and growth. Both studies illustrate the problem of ontological dualism.

Given the vast scope of this review, it is necessary to emphasize the panoramic approach employed in this book. My main aim is to reveal key conceptual themes with respect to the treatment of culture, rather than delve into the details and analytical nuances of each work. Conventionally in Economics, growth and development have been treated as two separate fields; the former belongs in macroeconomics, the latter is its own enigmatic realm.[4] In DE, the two have been used synonymously since economic growth is considered a necessary—though not necessarily sufficient—condition for development or 'modernization.' The literature reviewed in this chapter contains many issues that could be engaged in more critical depth. My observations, which do not apply equally to all texts or authors, are confined to the level of general overview.[5]

Classical development economics: hospitality

Early development economists were open to the idea that culture carried significant implications for economic performance. This is to be expected given the prominence of Anthropology and the dominance of Institutionalist thinking in Economics at the time. Alertness to the role of culture, while seeing it as an impediment to overcome, dominated the formative years of development thought.[6]

The hospitality stance was institutionalized when the journal *Economic Development and Cultural Change* and the research center bearing the same name were launched at the University of Chicago in the early 1950s. Bert Hoselitz, who played a leading role in this effort, advanced the concept of 'non-economic barriers' to development, for example, the absence of "a spirit of venturesomeness" (1952: 10). These types of representations served as shorthand for all references to culture in the literature. The distinction between economic and non-economic factors, indicative of the culture/economy dualism, set the terms of discourse well into the 1960s and beyond. In this section, I trace the treatment of culture by three giants of CDE. Lewis and Rostow were major architects of early development thinking, Hirschman was the leading critic within the orthodoxy.[7] I will not discuss well-known, extensively debated parts of these authors' work—e.g., surplus labor, take-off, or linkages—but only indicate their openness to the idea of culture, which must be measured against its general erasure in Neoclassical theory (see Chapters 2 and 3).

Although defined by the concept of surplus labor, Lewis was interested in a more profound understanding of development. In *The Theory of Economic Growth* (1955), he set out to explore the reasons behind the causes of growth, which he reduced to three factors: (1) the "will to economize," i.e., to "seek out and exploit economic opportunities" (ibid.: 23); (2) the growth of knowledge; and (3) the increase in capital and other resources. For him, the question was: what social environments and institutions were consistent with these three factors, and why? He believed that the ultimate benefit of economic development resided in expanding "the range of human choice" (ibid.: 420). At the same time, he thought that development imposed some costs in the form of excessively acquisitive, individualistic, and rationalist attitudes. In the end, however, Lewis was a modernist who believed that low-income countries suffered from the persistence of "economic darkness" surrounding "one or two modern towns" (1954: 6). This juxtaposition furnished a theoretical basis for the dualism of modernity/tradition.

Lewis' thoughts on culture unfold primarily in his explanation of 'the will to economize.' In his judgment, taboos or "limited horizons" (1955: 29) restricted the use of resources and prohibited some societies from exerting the effort required to propel development, for instance, some communities in Asia and Africa take a "non-commercial attitude toward livestock" (ibid.: 43). Here, Lewis is clearly referring to culture as a way of life. Anticipating much of today's discussions, he argued that the ability to raise consumption levels depends on the stock of "cultural capital," defined as "the background of knowledge accumulated by society" (ibid.: 29). In consequence, he claimed: "The expandability of wants increases as physical equipment increases, as the culture becomes more complex, as the hold of convention weakens, and as knowledge of new goods is spread" (ibid.: 31). Even though his criterion for judging the complexity of a culture is not clear, the statement suggests a reciprocal, sequential view: knowledge and a certain way of life determine economic behavior and outcomes, which in turn influence culture. There is much to quarrel with in this statement, but the point is that what has endured from Lewis' argument, aside from the ontological division between culture and economy, is that cultural norms and habits constitute an impediment to development efforts.

This impediment perspective was reinforced in Rostow's stages of growth thesis. As is well known, Rostow posited a five-stage growth path—the traditional society, preconditions for take-off, take-off, drive to maturity, and the age of high mass consumption. This blueprint has received substantial criticism for its teleological premise and Eurocentrism, among other deficiencies. Here, I am interested in the extent to which Rostow acknowledged the import of cultural 'variables' for economic growth. Rostow's description of the different stages is punctuated with references to cultural background, he concluded the discussion of each stage with a brief comment on the role of "non-economic" aspects, processes, or change. Although he stipulated that the take-off required a savings rate of over 10 percent of national income (1971: 39), he made it clear that it also entailed a change in thinking, knowledge, and institutions. Such change, he noted, was more often induced by external forces, most commonly colonialism, that "shocked the traditional society and began or hastened its undoing; ... and initiated the process by which a modern alternative to the traditional society was constructed out of the *old culture*" (ibid.: 6; emphasis added). The familiar perception of development as the leap from 'tradition' to 'modernity,' conceptualized as both sociality and states of mind, cemented this hierarchical dualism in DE (also see Higgins 1956, on dualistic development theory).

Contrasting his analyses with the Marxian viewpoint, Rostow claimed it was primarily in the drive to maturity stage that social change was governed by material considerations. Yet, each society experienced this "in terms of its own culture, social structure and political process" (1971: 152); and, once the age of high mass consumption is reached, social and cultural factors become more prominent. Societies with mature economies shift their attention to 'non-economic' goals, such as imperial domination and social welfare, depending on "geography, the old culture, resources, values, and the political leadership" (ibid.: 74). Rostow's thesis is classic both in its hospitality to the idea of culture, and hostility to what is thought to be the 'old culture'—an expression that served to signify contemporary life in any low-income country.

In contrast to the majority of early development economists, Hirschman is now characterized as something of an anti-culture figure. Ruttan (1988) suggests that Hirschman's (1965) questioning of the idea of cultural barriers played a role in shifting attention away from culture in DE. What Ruttan misses is that Hirschman criticized ethnocentrism among economists rather than dismiss the role of culture in development. Hirschman (1965) challenged the reliance on the notion of "obstacles"—obstructive beliefs and attitudes—as a generalized framework for development analysis. His alternative strategy was to disaggregate such perceived obstacles into those that, upon more scrutiny, turn out to be assets or motivators, not hindrances; those that it may not be necessary to eliminate at all; and those that could be circumvented by adopting a different logical sequence or priority ordering. Hirschman's position was more nuanced, but otherwise, it fitted within the hospitality stance of his time. He readily acknowledged differences in "the pattern of values and attitudes" between eighteenth-century Western European societies and today's 'underdeveloped' countries, throughout which one finds "strongly entrenched customs" and attitudes—e.g., staunch family orientation and lack of a "growth mentality"—that are inconsistent with competitive markets (1958: 135–137).

What separates Hirschman from the rest is that he found the development process to be highly complicated, combining many factors at the levels of individual psychology, social values, and institutions, whereas other economists tended to focus on one factor or one direction of causality. This view was most clearly pronounced in his assessment of the implications of "dualism," which he defined as "the prolonged coexistence and cohabitation of modern industry and of preindustrial, sometimes neolithic, techniques" (ibid.: 125). Rather than agree with the general opinion at the time, he did not see this as a problem that should capture the attention of policy-makers. On the contrary, he argued it should be seen as a necessary, and comparatively more efficient, feature of transition from under-development. This was the basis of his skepticism of the theoretical dichotomy between traditional and modern sectors.

Hirschman's major departure lay in a co-extensive view of the relationship between culture and development, as he stated:

> [C]ertain values and institutionalized behavior patterns that are conducive to successful development such as Max Weber's rationality and discipline, or Parsons' universalism and functional specificity, or McClelland's achieve-ment motivation must be induced in most of today's underdeveloped countries by the process of development itself.
>
> (ibid.: 137)

Here Hirschman agreed with Lewis and Rostow that certain attributes—rationality, discipline, and achievement motivation—are absent in underdeveloped countries. However, he believed that cultural change could accompany development:

> Ever since Max Weber, many social scientists looked at the 'right' cultural attitudes and beliefs as necessary conditions ('prerequisites') for economic progress, just as earlier theories had emphasized race, climate, or the presence of natural resources ... According to my way of thinking, the very attitudes alleged to be preconditions of industrialization could be generated on the job and 'on the way,' by certain characteristics of the industrialization process.
>
> (1992: 19–20)

This argument suggests a co-extensive view, instead of a unidirectional causality from 'culture' to 'economy' (Rostow) or sequential reinforcement between the two realms (Lewis). Therefore, to the extent that Hirschman did not see moder-nity/tradition as an immediate problem, he has less of a binary conception than most of his fellow developmentalists. However, ontological dualism remains in his 'way of thinking' since he saw the co-existence of tradition and modernity only as a transient phenomenon instead of being a part of coeval hybridity.

To summarize, classical development thought, represented in the work of Lewis, Rostow, and Hirschman, was hospitable to the idea of culture even though the majority emphasized the presence of attitudes and beliefs that were thought to prohibit or retard economic growth. Despite their recognition of cultural dif-ferences, the three shared a universalist wish to extend the 'benefits' of European modernity to the rest of 'mankind.'

The new development economics: retreat

From the 1960s onward, the bulk of development analysis took a narrower focus, concentrating on sectoral or thematic problems, e.g., migration and technology transfer, though interest in culture did not disappear (see Ruttan 1988). By the early 1980s, slower growth rates and multiple criticisms of DE had brought about a cascade of critical reflections (Hirschman 1981; Sen 1983; Bhagwati 1984; Lewis 1984; Streeten 1985) and repudiation of the early development thinkers by 'counter-revolution' authors, most harshly Deepak Lal (1985) and Peter Bauer (1972, 1984).[8] This tumultuous period culminated in the announcement of a 'new development economics' (Stiglitz 1986), which took a markedly different stance on culture from classical development thought. NDE highlights the role of institutions and knowledge, typically conceived as human capital. On the other hand, it emphasizes the ability of superior modeling to grasp the process of development, without the need to account for cultural specificity. In this sense, NDE simply retreats into the economy side of the culture/economy dualism. This section takes a broad look at this perspective.

According to Ruttan (1988: 251), the economics profession has held the early generation of development economists in low regard because of their conviction that "cultural endowments exerted major impact on behavior." Lal (1985) rebuked this generation for having denied the 'economic principle' of individual welfare maximizing behavior, in favor of cultural explanations. For him, the most serious misconception of early development economists was their perception that people in the 'third world' had "peculiar preferences," for example, regarding work and leisure, whereas "[n]umerous empirical studies from different cultures and climates" show that people everywhere "respond to changes in relative prices much as neoclassical theory would predict" (1985: 11).[9] Lal and other counter-revolutionaries did not offer a new theory of development; all they did was prepare the ground for the field's retreat from culture.

The 'new' development thinking dispenses with some Neoclassical assumptions, and claims to adopt an empirical approach (Kanbur 2005).[10] It takes its theoretical footing from the "new" (or endogenous) growth theory (Romer 1994; see also Ruttan 1998) motivated by dissatisfaction with the Solow growth model, in which technology is famously held constant. By endogenizing technological change, dropping the assumption of constant returns to scale, and admitting the presence of input complementarities and coordination failure between economic agents, the new growth theory opened the door to the presence of multiple equilibria, where a poor country might end up lodged in an inferior (low-income) equilibrium. This finding vindicated some early development theorists' arguments such as the need for a "big push" (Rosenstein-Rodan 1943). Indeed, Krugman (1995) concedes that CDE's pivotal ideas of external economies and complementarities had "anticipated" many of NDE's arguments.[11] The main theoretical break between the 'new' and the 'old' DE lies in their different stances toward culture.

Despite NDE's acknowledgment of the role of knowledge and institutional structures, the word culture—or any surrogate of it such as norms or values—is absent from major texts (e.g., Meier and Stiglitz 2000; Kanbur 2005). For instance, Paul Romer has advanced the notion of "idea gaps" versus "object gaps," arguing that poor countries suffer from a deficit of ideas, as opposed to physical objects. Fortunately, he claims, this knowledge gap could be closed at a relatively low cost by transnational corporations' ability to transfer "disembodied ideas" (1993: 548) to poor countries, provided good infrastructure, well-functioning financial institutions, and secure property rights are in place. Romer (1994) characterizes this as a neo-Schumpeterian perspective, in which institutional conditions for technological change, innovation, and knowledge are considered crucial ingredients. The framework of ideas/objects itself points to an ideal/material conception. But, more pertinently, Romer says nothing about the cultural contexts and channels within which ideas are developed, communicated, learned and applied. In the following paragraphs, I highlight two influential contributions by Lucas (1988) and Krugman (1995) because each offers an explicit, albeit extremely brief, statement regarding culture.

Lucas's (1988) article "On the Mechanics of Economic Development" formalizes the field's departure from the Solow model, noting its inability to explain income variation between countries and to predict international factor movements. Lucas addresses this flaw by incorporating human capital, which he defines as a person's "general skill level" (1988: 17). He recognizes the accumulation of human capital constitutes a "*social* activity, involving *groups* of people" (ibid.: 19), and acknowledges the difficulty in attempting to analytically capture its amorphous nature. To manage this difficulty, he suggests using related measurable variables such as earning differentials, instead of fixating on unobservable factors. Thereby, he suggests, one could make use of "microeconomic foundations" (ibid.: 36) to answer questions of macroeconomic trends. Based on a modified Solow model, Lucas predicts that labor will flow from poor to rich countries, though he admits the model could not support the 'convergence hypothesis,' i.e., it could not explain sustained income and growth differences between countries.

Despite this result, Lucas quickly brushes aside other potential explanations, particularly any having to do with culture. Referring to lower growth rates in India relative to East Asian countries, he asks "What is it about the 'nature of India' that makes it so?" (ibid.: 5). The 'nature' of India could possibly be associated with its geography or cultural make-up. However, without any elaboration on the term 'nature,' Lucas discounts the significance of cultural specificity.[12] Pointedly, he remarks:

> [S]ocieties differ in many easily observed ways, and it is easy to identify various economic and cultural peculiarities and imagine that they are keys to growth performance. For this ... we do not need economic theory: '[p]erceptive tourists will do as well.' The role of theory is not to catalogue the obvious, but to help us to sort out effects that are crucial, quantitatively, from those that can be set aside.
>
> (ibid.: 13)

This passage, which contains the sole reference to culture in the article, suggests 'cultural peculiarities' could be ignored. This is perhaps understandable once one accepts that economic development is "simply the problem of accounting for the observed pattern, across countries and across time, in levels and rates of growth of per capita income" (ibid.: 3), which could be understood with "a system of differential equations" that "imitate" observed economic behavior (ibid.: 39).

Krugman follows Lucas's emphasis on model building over substantive explanations. In *Development, Geography, and Economic Theory*, he explains the 'fall' of DE by the failure of its pioneers "to turn their intuitive insights into clear-cut models." In particular, they did not know how to explicitly model market structure because of their "adherence to a discursive, nonmathematical style" (1995: 24). In his opinion, Lewis's work was influential only because the idea of surplus labor was easy to formalize. Hirschman offered no more than "some hints about development planning;" his idea of forward and backward linkages was just "an evocative phrase" (Krugman 1995: 21–22). Thus, in opposition to Lal (1985), who attributes the weakness of DE to reliance on cultural explanations, Krugman blames methodological deficiencies.

Krugman believes "*Homo economicus*" remains the most "productive" theoretical alternative (ibid.: 78) for understanding development:

> It is common for those who haven't tried the exercise of making a model to assert that underdevelopment traps must necessarily result from some complicated set of factors—irrationality or short-sightedness on the part of investors, cultural barriers to change, inadequate capital markets, problems of information and learning, and so on. Perhaps these factors play a role, perhaps they don't: what we now know is that a low level trap can arise with rational entrepreneurs, without so much as a whiff of cultural influences, in a model without capital, and with everyone fully informed.
>
> (ibid.: 82)

The meaning of barriers in the statement is unclear, and there is some ambivalence about the implications of cultural influences. However, Krugman cares little whether these play a role or not. What is clear is the dualistic construction of economy vs. culture, where 'rational entrepreneurs' are theoretically placed beyond cultural boundaries. It is not surprising that Krugman sees no reason to 'drag' culture into economic analysis. In other words, he agrees with Lucas that cultural specificities could be set aside. The only reason to do otherwise is failure to construct an appropriate model.

In short, NDE marks a retreat from the hospitality stance of CDE. Yet, the theoretical split between culture and economy remains since NDE thinkers perceive themselves to be engaged in "the mere application of orthodox economics" (Lal 1985: 10) to the problem of development, armed with superior modeling tools.

Culture and development: return

The third stance on culture and development (CAD) appears in two varieties of literature. The first, embedded in international policy agendas, broadly acknowledges its relevance (both as creativity and values) to development outcomes (World Commission on Culture and Development 1995; World Bank 1999).[13] This view is exemplified in the human development and capabilities discourse (Sen 1993, 1998; Fukuda-Parr and Kumar 2003; UNDP 2004). The second variety of literature consists of more analytical studies that identify cultural 'determinants' of economic performance—mostly in East Asia—or model and quantify a relationship between culture and economic growth.

Human development is a decidedly universalist perspective, in which the goal is to cultivate certain innate capabilities in all human beings (Sen 1993; Nussbaum 1995). Even though proponents of this approach claim to honor the diversity of human experiences, so far in Economics, they have not devoted significant space to systematic analyses of the economic import of culture. The tension between the universal development agenda and the struggle to accommodate cultural difference is discernible in the writings of Amartya Sen, the most prominent advocate of this perspective. Sen's wide-ranging body of work has dealt with many themes of great cultural content and implications, including rationality and gender relations (e.g., 1977, 1990). However, his arguments have been mostly cast in terms of ethics rather than culture as such. Although the two are inextricably linked, the role of culture in economic phenomena has not been at the forefront of his writings. Sen's direct contributions on culture and development (e.g., 1998, 2004), though typically insightful, have been quite general.[14] In this section, I concentrate on the second variety of CAD literature as it more sharply illustrates the problem of ontological dualism, not only by theoretically severing culture from economy, but also by constructing 'individualism' and 'collectivism' as two fundamentally opposed cultural attitudes and modes of social organization that characterize different societies and engender different economic outcomes.[15]

Most studies of East Asian economies directly or indirectly adopt Max Weber's (1958) well-known thesis that the rise of capitalism was historically facilitated by Protestant teachings. Gustav Papanek names some of the 'cultural factors' that have been credited with rapid economic growth in Hong Kong, Japan, Singapore, South Korea, and Taiwan: "discipline, respect for authority and for education, thrift, this-worldliness, cultural homogeneity, and the fluidity of class structures" (1988: 75). In South Korea, according to Tae-Kyu Park, a "Confucian value system" (1997: 125) that stresses "faith, loyalty, filial piety, harmony and intellectualism" allowed public compliance with a "growth first" strategy; the country therefore represents a model of "Confucian capitalism" (ibid.: 130–131). Yujiro Hayami (1998: 15) claims that Japan benefited from "an admixture of Confucianism, Buddhism, and Shintoism," which cultivated Smithean values of "frugality, industry, honesty, and fidelity," though he notes that other 'traditional' cultures, for example, Islam and Buddhism, also contain the behavioral prerequisites of economic development.[16] These studies are generally premised on a static notion of culture as an endowment or heritage from the past.

Other studies have compared the role of cultural background in East Asian and Western economies. Peter Gray (1996) examines the USA vis-à-vis Hong Kong, Japan, Singapore, South Korea, and Taiwan from 1965 to 1987 to identify the 'effects' of 'cultural traits' on their divergent growth rates. He divides these effects into direct components, e.g., observed in saving rates, and indirect ones embodied in institutional arrangements and public policy. To capture the direct impacts, he uses Geert Hofstede's (2001) sociological study comparing 'cultural values' across countries based on an international survey of business organizations.[17] Hofstede has generated various categories of values from which Gray chose 'individualism,' namely, individual autonomy and self-interest; and 'Confucian dynamism,' defined as "the legitimacy of hierarchy and the value of perseverance and thrift, all without undue emphasis on tradition and social obligations which could impede business initiative" (1996: 280). He concludes that higher growth rates in the five Asian economies were the result of Confucian dynamism, while slower growth in the USA at least partly reflects its more individualistic culture. There are different views about the macroeconomic implications of 'individualism' (see Casson 1993; Temin 1997). What is most relevant here is the dualistic perception of two fundamentally different East and West cultures.

The discourse of culture and development in East Asia raises a host of issues that I can only point to here (see also Chapter 5). This discourse clearly converges with CDE in its hospitality to a society's shared values as a potential explanatory variable. Unfortunately, it shows no more sophistication or contemporaneity in perspective, often proposing arguments that have been abandoned in Anthropology or transcended by Cultural Studies (see Chapter 1). First, the descriptions of 'Asia' and 'Confucian values' carry an orientalist outlook, representing entire societies as collective and obedience-driven, among other depictions. Long ago, even such an avowed modernist as Gunnar Myrdal (1968) had criticized the notion of 'Asian values' as a mere stereotype. Second, none of the studies cited above give a clear concept of culture. What could be gleaned from the discussions is a shallow understanding that glosses over complexities within each society and the hazards of cross-cultural interpretation. As Ha-Joon Chang (2011) has pointed out, every belief system—namely, Confucianism—contains teachings that may be seen as conducive to economic growth, and others that could be read in an opposite light. CAD studies take a selective approach, singling out aspects that seem consistent with their *ex post* explanations (ibid.: 491).[18] Third, Feminist economists (Sen and Grown 1987) have also long ago questioned the wholesale valorization of 'tradition,' which tends to overlook negative gendered impacts.

Leaving all these issues aside, the remainder of this chapter highlights two broader studies by Dieckmann (1996) and Marini (2004). The first models the implications of 'national culture' for economic growth, the second presents a concept of 'economic culture' in an evolutionary model of growth.

Modeling culture and economic growth

Dieckmann begins with the hypothesis that "cultural aspects are an important determinant of the rate of economic growth" (1996: 304). According to him, "the total way of life of a people" (ibid.: 297) forms a national culture that filters through individual behavior to determine savings and productivity; some cultures are more conducive to growth than others. He does not name any specific 'nations,' but refers in passing to an Asian vis-à-vis a European "tradition" and to differences in values and ethics between Mediterranean Catholics and the Protestants of Northern Europe (ibid.: 300). He constructs a Lucas–Romer-inspired growth model premised on the assumptions that most traditions change infrequently and that participation in "standard cultural activity" (ibid.: 299) generates no utility. The implication is that one derives no comfort from belonging to a particular community and sharing a way of life, for instance, taking part in a wedding ritual (see Danby 2014, for an insightful articulation of the concept of community). On the contrary, Dieckmann asserts, "culture is costly" (1996: 299). He acknowledges that some cultural activity, such as buying a piece of art for one's home, enhances utility, but his main concern is "necessary" activity, which presumably affects production, without impacting utility.

Dieckmann suggests that disposable income depends on the share of gross income that goes toward compulsory spending on culture. He then incorporates "cultural determinants" in an aggregate Cobb-Douglas production function:

$$y = B \, k^\alpha \, h^{1-\alpha}$$

where total output (y) is determined by private capital (k) and society's cultural activity (h). In accounting terms:

$$y = c + k + h$$

which is to say, output is the sum of consumption (c), investment in private capital (k), and spending on cultural activity (h). Therefore, economic growth depends on consumption and the ratio of private capital to the cost of necessary cultural spending. Devoting time or money to comply with group ethos acts merely as a constraint on individual welfare maximization, and the corresponding penalty at the macro level is that "[s]ocieties for which culture is very important use only a small fraction of their inputs for production of consumer goods and capital" (ibid.: 301), which in turn slows economic growth down.[19]

Following Robert Barro's (1991) method of cross-country regression, Dieckmann goes on to estimate the economic impacts of six cultural determinants chosen from Hofstede's study referred to above:

- Individualism (working for personal goals).
- Masculinity (emphasis on "earnings, recognition, advancement and challenge").
- Power distance (hierarchy and degree of power inequality within an organization).
- Uncertainty avoidance (attitude toward uncertainty).
- Political culture (efficiency of the bureaucracy and degree of corruption).
- Ethnolinguistic fractionalization (diversity) (Dieckmann 1996: 306–307).

Regression results for 82 (unnamed) countries indicate that the determinants most correlated with economic growth are individualism (positive) and uncertainty avoidance (negative). The remaining determinants are statistically significant only with manipulation of the sample size. Dieckmann concludes that, even though questions remain, "economic growth experiences are culturally bounded" (ibid.: 316). Several issues could be raised about each 'determinant,' but the more important general conclusion that emerges from these results is that there is a "growth maximizing" culture of risk taking and individualism (as specified in this study), and, in effect, inferior cultures that lack these qualities.

To explore the policy implications of these findings, Dieckmann proposes two scenarios: in the first, individuals are aware of their national culture; in the second, they are oblivious to it. With no further elaboration on this distinction, he claims the first scenario is more growth-enhancing because policy measures would be taken to offset the cost of engagement in necessary cultural activity. In other words, some countries achieve high growth rates *in spite of* their cultural make-up. In this scenario, the task for economic advisors is to determine the "optimal cultural policy." In the second scenario, the challenge is to identify the "optimal cultural background" (ibid.: 304), a far more difficult task. In consequence, the growth implications for an 'inferior' culture depend on the extent of a country's awareness of this inferiority. This is all highly debatable, but in any event, Dieckmann's analysis converges with CDE in its general stance toward culture.

While most CAD literature has focused on geographical differences, Marini (2004: 776) offers an "evolutionary model," hoping to resolve the debate over which cultural characteristic is more crucial to economic growth: individual drive (McClelland's achievement motivation) or social connectedness (Fukuyama's notion of trust). Arguing that both are vital, Marini periodizes the primacy of each in a Rostow stages-of-growth type model centered on the concept of economic culture. Without offering a particular definition of culture itself, he states that:

> Economic culture, as any other aspect of culture, passes through stages of development. In the early stages, the prevailing attitudes toward wealth are concerned with the problem of its distribution, while in the following stages priority is given to its growth. During this latter stage, *both* the achievement motivation and a sense of generalized trust among impersonal actors of the market become the critical values for economic growth to occur.
>
> (ibid.: 768)

This concept moves away from the common static treatment of culture as an inert mass of lore handed down from one generation to another. Unfortunately, Marini ends up negating cultural specificity by envisioning a universal set of attitudes and ideas of achievement and trust.

Marini claims that human history has exhibited a continuum between "individual autonomy" and "collective identification" along one dimension, and a movement from equality to inequality on another dimension. For him, this represents a process of cultural evolution that has accompanied economic growth: "every stage of economic growth corresponds to a stage of economic culture that expresses society's prevailing attitudes at the time" (ibid.: 773). The direction of causality is unclear but, given his Weberian inspiration, one could infer that it flows from culture to economic growth. In this model, traditional societies exhibit the "limited good syndrome"—a belief that "economic stagnation is the norm" (ibid.: 773). In modern times, this view gives way to a mixture of trust and achievement. Currently, the prevalent economic culture mirrors a "post-materialistic syndrome," where people are more concerned with "spiritual" dimensions of life (ibid.: 775). Overall, the idea of economic culture attempts to avoid the dichotomy between the ideal and the material, and accordingly, the cultural and the economic. Marini's failure to recognize that economic growth itself is a cultural phenomenon signals that the ontological dualism of culture/economy might be at work in his analysis.

To quantify the role of culture, Marini turns to the World Values Survey (Granato *et al.* 1996), which offers a cultural index made of four "syndromes" of economic culture:

- the limited good (obedience, tolerance);
- achievement (independence, thrift, determination);
- generalized trust (responsibility);
- post-materialism (imagination, usefulness).[20]

Without much digging into the meanings and complexity of any of these 'syndromes,' he goes on to measure their significance to economic growth, expecting it to be correlated negatively with the limited good syndrome, and positively with achievement and trust, while showing a neutral relationship to post-materialistic values. The econometric results for 17 OECD countries and 8 lower-income countries suggest that every 1 percent increase in teaching achievement motivation to children is accompanied by a 1.88 percent rise in GDP. If both achievement and responsibility are taught to children, GDP rises by 2.07 percent for every 1 percent increase in teaching the two values (Marini 2004: 780). He also finds that achievement has a significantly greater impact on economic growth than that of trust.[21]

To summarize, CAD literature marks a 'return' to culture in development economics. Its major departure from the hospitality stance lies in emphasizing cultural values that are thought to enhance economic growth, and in attempting to model and quantify the role of these values, something that CDE authors did not do probably because they considered it neither feasible, nor desirable. CAD authors are commendable to the extent that they undertake more extended discussions of culture in a manner that unpacks it slightly more than CDE and NDE. Yet, the CAD project is beset with substantive and methodological difficulties, perhaps the least of which are quality and scope of data and interpretation of statistical correlations.

What concerns me more is the conceptual framing of cultural 'variables,' be they individualism, Confucian dynamism, achievement, or trust. First, analyses are steeped in dualism: culture is construed as either an obstacle or a driving force, and the perception of cultural difference (across contemporary societies and over time) is trapped within the modern/traditional and individualist/collective oppositions. Second, there is a glaring lack of explanations and awareness of the analysts' own cultural location. The two modeling efforts discussed in this section illustrate this lack, as one claims to consider national culture while assuming individual-centered, optimizing behavior as a global norm; and the other sees movement toward a 'modern' economic way of life as a historical inevitability. In both cases, culture is theoretically erased by the presumption of an innate 'economic' impulse (Dieckmann) or a universal pattern of 'responsible' and 'achievement'-oriented behavior (Marini).

Conclusion

This chapter has offered a broad overview of Neoclassical economic thought on development, based on which it is possible to identify three distinct stances toward culture: *hospitality, retreat,* and *return.* CDE economists were hospitable to the idea that cultural factors hold significant, albeit mostly detrimental, implications for economic growth. NDE economists retreated from this stance by taking the position that development problems could be understood with better mathematical modeling. Here, culture is willfully ignored. The return to culture by CAD authors resurrects its theoretical significance, mostly without the negative connotations. Indeed, citations of classical development texts in CAD literature give the field a 'retro' feel. What distinguishes CAD from CDE is boldness in methods, with statistical estimates conveying an appearance of more clarity and rigor. Yet, in terms of substantive analysis and critical insights into the development process and discourse, especially its cultural assumptions, not much has been added. If anything, there seems to be less awareness of the cultural nature of development knowledge itself.

Common to all three stances toward culture is an ontologically dualistic perception that reverberates on multiple levels. The most foundational is the theoretical severing of 'culture' from 'economy.' In the hospitable period, this dichotomy surfaced in the idea of non-economic barriers to development. In CAD writings, it survives in the language of cultural 'determinants,' which act upon economic activity from an external perch. The parallel to the dualism of ideal/material is traceable in a tendency to emphasize either ideas and beliefs, or material factors such as savings and physical capital. Culture itself is theorized as either a liberator of or a barrier to growth potential, hence following the Neoclassical dualism of preferences/constraints, with its rootedness in the existential problem of desire/limits. CAD writers emphasize cultural habits and values that they think are more conducive to economic growth, the vehicle to the fulfillment of human wishes of all kinds. In contrast, for early development theorists, culture played a limiting role, holding back 'the will to economize' and, as a result, lowering prospects for development. This dualistic ontology confined the vision of even such a shrewd critic as Albert Hirschman, who could see the economic hybridity of underdeveloped societies only as an interim state on the way to modernity.

Dualistic ontology is extended through a set of four hierarchical and mutually reinforcing *development dualisms*:

Modern	Traditional
Individualist	Collective(Collectivist)
Developed	Under(less)developed
Universal	Particular

The left side of each pair parallels the realm of economy, with its 'universal' (global) logic—individual utility-maximizing behavior—thought to characterize the modern European path of development. The right-hand side serves as the repository of the non-economic, the traditional, collective, local, and therefore underdeveloped, signified both in Lewis' "economic darkness" and Marini's "limited good syndrome." The left side of each dualism is valorized. Movement from the right (subaltern) side to the left is achievable through compliance with a universally applicable pattern of behavior—individualistic, economizing, and achievement-oriented. In this framework, there is no conceptual space for cultural horizons that do not comply, or which hybridize and, thereby, disrupt the dichotomies.

The early generation of development economists recognized cultural difference, while simultaneously advocating a culturally specific vision of development, which they took to be a desired natural process. Today, the culture and development economists are equally committed to the universalist perspective; their main, untenable, departure lies in attempting to theoretically accommodate different cultural sources for its realization. The return to culture has done much to repair the reputations of early development economists. It is not clear that it has made significant improvements on their efforts.

Notes

1 Like Adam Smith, most classical economists saw the growth of output as part of the natural "progress of opulence" (1976 [1776]: 401), though a few, for example, Dugald Stewart (1793), believed it was more the result of unique historical circumstances than an inevitable outcome of the course of 'nature.' The twentieth-century departure was that progress should not be left to nature. Instead, it should be planned. I have discussed the philosophical roots and cultural premises of the development discourse elsewhere, see Zein-Elabdin (1998, 2001).

2 Other social scientists have criticized such simplistic conceptions of culture. In particular, Geertz (1984: 513) has noted that both the "culture-as-obstacle" approach (predominant in Economics) and the "culture-as-stimulus" viewpoint (economic Anthropology) externalize culture. See Escobar (1995) for a discussion of the relationship between Anthropology and the twentieth-century project of international development. See Fukuyama (2001) for a review of the Sociology literatures on culture and development.

3 For more on universalism, ethnocentrism, and relativism, see Nussbaum (1995) and Charusheela (2001). Other common dualisms in economic analyses include formal/informal, market/state, and market/household. These are not taken up in this book. See Jennings (1993, 1999) for more on dualisms.

4 For more on the difference and relationship between these two bodies of thought, see Hirschman (1981), Lucas (1988), Ruttan (1998), and Jomo and Fine (2006). See Arndt (1981) for a history of the terms development and growth, and Myrdal (1968) on underdevelopment and related terminology.

5 I have not dedicated any space here to the record of economic development, though I am mindful of its essential relevance. For general reviews of DE, see Adelman (1961), Meier (1984), Arndt (1987), Hunt (1989), Rostow (1990), Bardhan (1993), and Meier and Rauch (2005). Hirschman (1981) discusses prominent early development economists not covered in this chapter. Wall (1972) and Strassmann (1993) review the work of Chicago School economists in particular. I have not included early twentieth-century thought on development, for examples, see Knowles (1924), Schumpeter (1934), and

Clark (1940). Appendix III in this book gives a chronological bibliography of development texts in Economics, including non-Neoclassical work. For critiques of the development discourse by economists, see Marglin and Marglin (1990), Wilber and Jameson (1992 [1973]), Sachs (1992), Latouche (1993), Kabeer (1994), Harcourt (1995), Nudler and Lutz (1996), and Rahnema (1997). Despite much rhetoric, discussions of women and gender relations are not usually integrated into the main current of DE, see Chapter 8 in this book for literature.

6 Schumpeter's (1934) theory of development, which was not offered in reference to 'underdeveloped countries,' had a substantial influence on the field. He suggested that the value of the entrepreneur resides in *his* willingness to act against the grain of established traditions of business and society. See Beugelsdijk (2007) for an attempt to quantitatively measure the impact of 'entrepreneurial culture' on economic growth.

7 The work of other prominent development economists of this period reflects their awareness of the relevance of social context and cultural influences even when they did not address these directly, for example, see Rosenstein-Rodan (1944) and Nurkse (1962 [1953]). More explicit attention to culture appears in Adelman and Morris (1965) and Fei and Ranis (1969).

8 The majority of criticism came from Marxian, Institutionalist, and Feminist scholars (e.g., Frank 1966; Myrdal 1968; Benería 1982; Boserup 1989 [1970]). For more on the counter-revolution, see Toye (1987), Krugman (1993), and de Jong (2009). Chang (2011), de Jong (2011), and Castellano and García-Quero (2012) offer helpful overviews of current literature and debates in the field.

9 Bauer, on the other hand, asserted "the presence in many underdeveloped countries of long-standing and interrelated attitudes, beliefs and cultural traditions uncongenial to material advance" (1984: 78). However, he believed market rationality could be implanted through institutional change, and open contact with 'Western culture.' Lal (1998) has since admitted the neglect of culture in Economics, but he remains convinced of the universal validity of the 'economic principle.'

10 Stiglitz (1986: 257) suggested that this paradigm is grounded in three main assumptions: individuals are rational in the sense of acting consistently and adapting to change, information is costly and imperfect, and institutions are endogenous and changing along with changes in information. Under these circumstances Pareto efficiency is not guaranteed and, therefore, governments do have a 'potential role' to play.

11 Bardhan (1993) and Fine (2003) have pointed out a lack of new insights in the new growth theory. For more discussion, see Jomo and Fine (2006).

12 Lucas's manner of alluding vaguely to the 'nature' of being in a particular country or region as an all-purpose holder of unexplained variables has been adopted in the literature, e.g., in Barro's widely cited study of growth in a large cross-section of countries. Citing Lucas, he refers to "the nature of being in Africa or Latin America" (1991: 435), also absent any explanation of the terms 'nature' or 'being.' This suggestive ambiguity, combined with his conclusion that the study could not explain a substantial part of growth patterns in Africa and Latin America, opened the door to explorations of the potential role of culture in economic growth (Dieckmann 1996; Lian and Oneal 1997; Cuesta 2004). See Dieckmann (1996) and Cuesta (2004) for reviews of empirical studies.

13 So far, the most concrete outcome of the UN's awakening to the significance of culture for development has been the construction of cultural indicators of development (as measured by expenditure on creative products, the number of languages spoken, the means of communication within a country, and so on), based on which countries are ranked at reasonable, modest, or low cultural development (McKinley 1998; Fukuda-Parr 2000). Also see UNESCO (1998, 2000). The World Bank has also designated culture as "one of the core areas to be addressed" (Wolfensohn *et al.* 2000: 10).

14 There is not enough space here for a meaningful discussion of Sen's extensive record of critical contributions to economic thought (e.g., 1977, 1987, 1990, 1999). See

Rosenbaum (1999) and Jackson (2005) for critical but sympathetic readings of Sen's capabilities approach with respect to culture. For more on human development, see Streeten (1994) and Nussbaum and Glover (1995).

15 The distinction between these two 'values' or 'traits' is not new. Lewis (1955) drew a comparison between individualistic and collective action. Fei and Ranis defined individualism as "individual initiative based on market discipline," and collectivism as "collaborative effort at the community and grass-roots level" (1969: 398). In most of the literature, 'individualism' has been associated with "advanced Western countries" (Casson 1993), Britain and the USA (Temin 1997), or certain societies and regions in Europe (Greif 1994; Tabellini 2005). See also Chapter 5 in this book.

16 See also Landes (2000) for another perspective on the significance of culture to economic growth. See Berger and Hsiao (1988) and Ozawa (1994) on debates on the "Asian economic miracle." Brook and Luong (1997) offer critical multidisciplinary views of culture and capitalism in postcolonial East Asia. For discussions of culture and development in reference to other regions, see Cuesta (2004) and Hojman (2006) for Latin America, Kovács (2006) on Eastern Europe, and Zein-Elabdin (2009) with respect to Africa.

17 This is a survey of IBM employees in 72 countries carried out in 1968 and 1972, on the basis of which Hofstede proposed what he characterized as five most fundamental "dimensions" in every culture: power distance, uncertainty avoidance, individualism or collectivism, masculinity versus femininity, and a long-term versus a short-term outlook. The survey was designed for business organizations rather than entire societies.

18 Chang's remarks were made in particular reference to New Institutionalist studies. More judicious treatments of culture and development can be found in Banuri (1990), Latouche (1993), Sen (2004), and Streeten (2006). See Zein-Elabdin and Charusheela (2004) on Economics and cultural hegemony.

19 The only way to make sense of this statement is to assume that Dieckmann is referring to the narrower meaning of culture as art and other expressions of creativity, which indicates that he shifts back and forth between different meanings without noting it. Furthermore, the paper does not state how the fraction of inputs used for production, which is an empirical issue, has been determined.

20 Though fraught with conceptual and methodological issues, the World Values Survey has become popular among economists. See Chapters 3 and 5 for more on the Survey, and references to the literature.

21 For another example of quantitative studies, see Lian and Oneal (1997) who find that cultural diversity, indicated by religion or language, has no significant effect on growth rates. Cuesta (2004) estimates the role of trust and community participation in Honduras. See Rao (1998) for a critique of attempts to quantify the role of intangibles such as trust in economic growth. Adkisson (2014) gives a helpful review of quantitative economic studies of culture.

References

Adelman, Irma (1961) *Theories of Economic Growth and Development*, Stanford, CA: Stanford University Press.

—— and Cynthia Taft Morris (1965) "A Factor Analysis of the Interrelationship between Social and Political Variables and Per Capita Gross National Product," *The Quarterly Journal of Economics*, 79 (4): 555–578.

Adkisson, Richard (2014) "Quantifying Culture: Problems and Promises," *Journal of Economic Issues*, 48 (1): 89–107.

Arndt, H.W. (1981) "Economic Development: A Semantic History," *Economic Development and Cultural Change*, 29 (3): 457–466.

—— (1987) *Economic Development: The History of an Idea*, Chicago: University of Chicago Press.

Banuri, Tariq (1990) "Modernization and Its Discontents: A Cultural Perspective on the Theories of Development," in Stephen Marglin and Frédérique Marglin (eds.) *Dominating Knowledge: Development, Culture, and Resistance*, Oxford: Clarendon Press, 73–101.

Bardhan, Pranab (1993) "Economics of Development and the Development of Economics," *Journal of Economic Perspectives*, 7 (2): 129–142.

Barro, Robert J. (1991) "Economic Growth in a Cross Section of Countries," *The Quarterly Journal of Economics*, 106 (2): 407–443.

Bauer, Peter T. (1972) *Dissent on Development: Studies and Debates in Development Economics*, Cambridge, MA: Harvard University Press.

—— (1984) *Reality and Rhetoric: Studies in the Economics of Development*, Cambridge, MA: Harvard University Press.

Benería, Lourdes (ed.) (1982) *Women and Development: The Sexual Division of Labor in Rural Societies*, New York: Praeger Publishers.

Berger, Peter L. and Hsin-Huang Michael Hsiao (eds.) (1988) *In Search of an East Asian Development Model*, Oxford: Transaction Books.

Beugelsdijk, Sjoerd (2007) "Entrepreneurial Culture, Regional Innovativeness and Economic Growth," *Journal of Evolutionary Economics*, 17 (2): 187–210.

Bhagwati, Jagdish N. (1984) "Development Economics: What Have We Learned?" *Asian Development Review*, 2 (1): 23–38.

Boserup, Ester (1989 [1970]) *Woman's Role in Economic Development*, London: Earthscan Publications.

Brook, Timothy and Hy V. Luong (eds.) (1997) *Culture and Economy: The Shaping of Capitalism in Eastern Asia*, Ann Arbor, MI: University of Michigan Press.

Casson, Mark (1993) "Cultural Determinants of Economic Performance," *Journal of Comparative Economics*, 17: 418–442.

Castellano, Fernando López and Fernando García-Quero (2012) "Institutional Approaches to Economic Development: The Current Status of the Debate," *Journal of Economic Issues*, 46 (4): 921–940.

Chang, Ha-Joon (2011) "Institutions and Economic Development: Theory, Policy and History," *Journal of Institutional Economics*, 7 (4): 473–498.

Charusheela, S. (2001) "Women's Choices and the Ethnocentrism/Relativism Dilemma," in S. Cullenberg, J. Amariglio, and D. Ruccio (eds.) *Postmodernism, Economics and Knowledge*, London: Routledge, 197–220.

Clark, Colin (1940) *The Conditions of Economic Progress*, London: Macmillan & Co.

Cuesta, José (2004) "From Economicist to Culturalist Development Theories: How Strong Is the Relation Between Cultural Aspects and Economic Development?" *The European Journal of Development Research*, 16 (4): 868–891.

Danby, Colin (2014) "How Is Community Made?" in Robert F. Garnett, Paul Lewis, and Lenore T. Ealy (eds.) *Commerce and Community: Ecologies of Social Cooperation*, London: Routledge.

De Jong, Eelke (2009) *Culture and Economics: On Values, Economics and International Business*, London: Routledge.

—— (2011) "Culture, Institutions, and Economic Growth," *Journal of Institutional Economics*, 7 (4): 523–527.

Dieckmann, Oliver (1996) "Cultural Determinants of Economic Growth: Theory and Evidence," *Journal of Cultural Economics*, 20 (4): 297–320.

Escobar, Arturo (1995) *Encountering Development: The Making and Unmaking of the Third World*, Princeton, NJ: Princeton University Press.

Fei, John C.H. and Gustav Ranis (1969) "Economic Development in Historical Perspective," *American Economic Review, Papers and Proceedings*, 59 (2): 386–400.

Fine, Ben (2003) "The New Growth Theory," in Ha-Joon Chang (ed.) *Rethinking Development Economics*, London: Anthem Press.

Frank, André Gunder (1966) "The Development of Underdevelopment," *Monthly Review*, 18 (4): 17–31.

Fukuda-Parr, Sakiko (2000) "In Search of Indicators of Culture and Development: Progress and Proposals," in *The World Culture Report 2000*, Paris: UNESCO Publishing, 278–283.

—— and A. K. Shiva Kumar (eds.) (2003) *Readings in Human Development: Concepts, Measures and Policies for a Development Paradigm*, New Delhi: Oxford University Press.

Fukuyama, F. (2001) "Culture and Economic Development: Cultural Concerns," *International Encyclopedia of the Social and Behavioral Sciences*, London: Elsevier Science.

Geertz, Clifford (1984) "Culture and Social Change: The Indonesian Case," *Man*, 19 (4): 511–532.

Granato, Jim, Ronald Inglehart, and David Leblang (1996) "The Effect of Cultural Values on Economic Development: Theory, Hypotheses, and Some Empirical Tests," *American Journal of Political Science*, 40 (3): 607–631.

Gray, H. Peter (1996) "Culture and Economic Performance: Policy as an Intervening Variable," *Journal of Comparative Economics*, 23 (3): 278–291.

Greif, Avner (1994) "Cultural Beliefs and the Organization of Society: A Historical and Theoretical Reflection on Collectivist and Individualist Societies," *Journal of Political Economy*, 102 (5): 912–950.

Harcourt, Wendy (1995) "Gender and Culture," in *Our Creative Diversity*, The World Commission on Culture and Development Report, Paris: UNESCO, 129–149.

Hayami, Yujiro (1998) "Toward an East Asian Model of Economic Development," in Y. Hayami and Masahiko Akoi (eds.) *The Institutional Foundations of East Asian Economic Development*, London: Palgrave Macmillan, 3–38.

Higgins, Benjamin H. (1956) "The 'Dualistic Theory' of Underdeveloped Areas," *Economic Development and Cultural Change*, 4 (2): 99–115.

—— (1977) "Economic Development and Cultural Change: Seamless Web or Patchwork Quilt?" in Manning Nash (ed.) *Essays on Economic Development and Cultural Change, in Honor of Bert F. Hoselitz*, Chicago: University of Chicago Press, 99–120.

Hirschman, Albert O. (1958) *The Strategy of Economic Development*, New Haven, CT: Yale University Press.

—— (1965) "Obstacles to Development: A Classification and a Quasi-vanishing Act," *Economic Development and Cultural Change*, 13 (4): 385–393.

—— (1981) "The Rise and Decline of Development Economics," in *Essays in Trespassing: Economics to Politics and Beyond*, Cambridge: Cambridge University Press, 1–24.

—— (1992) *Rival Views of Market Society and Other Recent Essays*, Cambridge, MA: Harvard University Press.

Hofstede, Geert (2001) *Culture's Consequences: Comparing Values, Behaviors, Institutions, and Organizations across Nations*, London: Sage Publications.

Hojman, David E. (2006) "Economic Development and the Evolution of National Culture: The Case of Chile," in Lawrence E. Harrison and Peter L. Berger (eds.) *Developing Cultures: Case Studies*, London: Routledge, 267–286.

Hoselitz, Bert F. (1952) "Non-Economic Barriers to Economic Development," *Economic Development and Cultural Change*, 1 (1): 8–21.

Hunt, Diana (1989) *Economic Theories of Development: An Analysis of Competing Paradigms*, Savage, MD: Barnes & Noble Books.

Jackson, William A. (2005) "Capabilities, Culture and Social Structure," *Review of Social Economy*, 63 (1): 101–124.

Jennings, Ann L. (1993) "Public or Private? Institutional Economics and Feminism," in Marianne A. Ferber and Julie A. Nelson (eds.) *Beyond Economic Man: Feminist Theory and Economics*, Chicago: University of Chicago Press, 111–129.

——— (1999) "Dualisms," in Janice Peterson and Margaret Lewis (eds.) *The Elgar Companion to Feminist Economics*, Cheltenham: Edward Elgar, 142–153.

Jomo, K.S. and Ben Fine (eds.) (2006) *The New Development Economics: After the Washington Consensus*, London: Zed Books.

Kabeer, Naila (1994) *Reversed Realities: Gender Hierarchies in Development Thought*, London: Verso.

Kanbur, Ravi (ed.) (2005) "New Directions in Development Economics: Theory or Empirics?" A symposium, in *Economic and Political Weekly*.

Knowles, Lilian C.A. (1924) *The Economic Development of the British Overseas Empire*, London: George Routledge & Sons.

Kovács, János Mátyás (2006) "Which Past Matters? Culture and Economic Development in Eastern Europe After 1989," in Lawrence E. Harrison and Peter L. Berger (eds.) *Developing Cultures: Case Studies*, London: Routledge, 329–347.

Krugman, Paul (1993) "Toward a Counter-Counterrevolution in Development Theory," in *Proceedings of the World Bank Annual Conference on Development Economics*, Washington, DC: The World Bank, 15–38.

——— (1995) *Development, Geography, and Economic Theory*, Cambridge, MA: MIT Press.

Kuznets, Simon (1965) *Economic Growth and Structure: Selected Essays*, New York: W.W. Norton & Company.

Lal, Deepak (1985) "The Misconceptions of 'Development Economics'," *Finance and Development*, 22 (June): 10–13.

——— (1998) *Unintended Consequences: The Impact of Factor Endowments, Culture, and Politics on Long-Run Economic Performance*, Cambridge, MA: MIT Press.

Landes, David. S. (2000) "Why Some Are So Rich and Others So Poor: The Role of Culture," in J.D. Wolfensohn *et al.*, *Culture Counts: Financing, Resources, and the Economics of Culture in Sustainable Development*, Washington, DC: The World Bank, 27–30.

Latouche, Serge (1993) *In the Wake of the Affluent Society: An Exploration of Post-Development*, London: Zed Books.

Lewis, W. Arthur (1954) "Economic Development with Unlimited Supplies of Labour," *Manchester School*, 22: 139–191.

——— (1955) *The Theory of Economic Growth*, London: George Allen and Unwin.

——— (1984) "The State of Development Theory," *American Economic Review*, 74 (1): 1–10.

Lian, Brad and John R. Oneal (1997) "Cultural Diversity and Economic Development: A Cross-National Study of 98 Countries, 1960–1985," *Economic Development and Cultural Change*, 46 (1): 61–77.

Lucas, Robert E. Jr. (1988) "On the Mechanics of Economic Development," *Journal of Monetary Economics*, 22: 3–42.

Marglin, Stephen A. and Frédérique Apffel Marglin (eds.) (1990) *Dominating Knowledge: Development, Culture, and Resistance*, Oxford: Clarendon Press.

Marini, Matteo (2004) "Cultural Evolution and Economic Growth: A Theoretical Hypothesis with Some Empirical Evidence," *The Journal of Socio-Economics*, 33: 765–784.

McKinley, Terry (1998) "Measuring the Contribution of Culture to Human Well-Being: Cultural Indicators of Development," in *The World Culture Report 1998*, Paris: UNESCO, 322–332.

Meier, Gerald M. (1984) *Leading Issues in Economic Development*, New York: Oxford University Press.

—— and James E. Rauch (2005) *Leading Issues in Economic Development*, New York: Oxford University Press.

—— and Joseph E. Stiglitz (eds.) (2000) *Frontiers of Development Economics: The Future in Perspective*, Oxford: Oxford University Press.

Myrdal, Gunnar (1968) *Asian Drama: An Inquiry into the Poverty of Nations*, vols. I, II. New York: Pantheon.

Nudler, Oscar and Mark A. Lutz (eds.) (1996) *Economics, Culture and Society: Alternative Approaches: Dissenting Views from Economic Orthodoxy*, New York: Apex Press (for the United Nations University).

Nurkse, Ragnar (1962 [1953]) *Problems of Capital Formation in Underdeveloped Countries*, New York: Oxford University Press.

Nussbaum, Martha C. (1995) "Human Capabilities: Female Human Beings," in Martha Nussbaum and Jonathan Glover (eds.) *Women, Culture and Development: A Study of Human Capabilities*, Oxford: Clarendon Press, 61–104.

—— and Jonathan Glover (eds.) (1995) *Women, Culture, and Development: A Study of Human Capabilities*, Oxford: Clarendon Press.

Ozawa, Terutomo (1994) "Exploring the Asian Economic Miracle: Politics, Economics, Society, Culture and History—A Review Article," *Journal of Asian Studies*, 53 (1): 124–131.

Papanek, Gustav (1988) "The New Asian Capitalism: An Economic Portrait," in Peter Berger and Hsin-Huang Hsiao (eds.) *In Search of an East Asian Development Model*, Oxford: Transaction Books, 27–80.

Park, Tae-Kyu (1997) "Confucian Values and Contemporary Economic Development in Korea," in Timothy Brook and Hy V. Luong (eds.) *Culture and Economy: The Shaping of Capitalism in Eastern Asia*, Ann Arbor, MI: Michigan University Press, 125–136.

Rahnema, Majid (ed.), with Victoria Bawtree (1997) *The Post-Development Reader*, London: Zed Books.

Rao, J. Mohan (1998) "Culture and Economic Development," in *The World Culture Report 1998*, Paris: UNESCO, 25–48.

Romer, Paul M. (1993) "Idea Gaps and Object Gaps in Economic Development," *Journal of Monetary Economics*, 32: 543–573.

—— (1994) "The Origins of Endogenous Growth," *Journal of Economic Perspectives*, 8 (1): 3–22.

Rosenbaum, Eckehard F. (1999) "Against Naïve Materialism: Culture, Consumption and the Causes of Inequality," *Cambridge Journal of Economics*, 23 (3): 317–336.

Rosenstein-Rodan, P. N. (1943) "Problems of Industrialization of Eastern and South-Eastern Europe," *The Economic Journal*, 53 (210/211): 202–211.

—— (1944) "The International Development of Economically Backward Areas," *International Affairs*, 20 (2): 157–165.

Rostow, W. W. (1971 [1960]) *The Stages of Economic Growth: A Non-Communist Manifesto*, Cambridge: Cambridge University Press.

—— (1990) *Theorists of Economic Growth from David Hume to the Present: With a Perspective on the Next Century*, Oxford: Oxford University Press.

Ruttan, Vernon W. (1988) "Cultural Endowments and Economic Development: What Can We Learn from Anthropology?" *Economic Development and Cultural Change*, 36 (3) Supplement: 247–271.

—— (1998) "The New Growth Theory and Development Economics: A Survey," *Journal of Development Studies*, 35 (2): 1–26.

Sachs, Wolfgang (ed.) (1992) *The Development Dictionary: A Guide to Knowledge as Power*, London: Zed Books.

Schumpeter, Joseph A. (1934) *The Theory of Economic Development: An Inquiry into Profits, Capital, Credit, Interest, and the Business Cycle*, Cambridge, MA: Harvard University Press.

Sen, Amartya K. (1977) "Rational Fools: A Critique of the Behavioural Foundations of Economic Theory," *Philosophy and Public Affairs*, 6 (4): 317–344.

—— (1983) "Development, Which Way Now?" *Economic Journal*, 93 (372): 745–762.

—— (1987) *On Ethics and Economics*, Oxford: Blackwell.

—— (1990) "Gender and Cooperative Conflict," in Irene Tinker (ed.) *Persistent Inequalities: Women and World Development*, Oxford: Oxford University Press, 123–149.

—— (1993) "Capability and Well-Being," in *The Quality of Life*, edited with Martha C. Nussbaum, Oxford: Clarendon Press, 30–53.

—— (1998) "Culture, Freedom and Independence," in *World Culture Report 1998*, Paris: UNESCO, 317–321.

—— (1999) *Development as Freedom*, New York: Alfred Knopf.

—— (2004) "How Does Culture Matter?" in Vijayendra Rao and Michael Walton (eds.) *Culture and Public Action*, Stanford, CA: Stanford University Press, 37–58.

Sen, Gita and Caren Grown (1987) *Development, Crises, and Alternative Visions: Third World Women's Perspectives*, New York: Monthly Review Press.

Smith, Adam (1976 [1776]) *An Inquiry into the Nature and Causes of the Wealth of Nations*, ed. Edwin Cannan, Chicago: University of Chicago Press.

Stewart, Dugald (1793) "The Life and Writings of Adam Smith, 1854–1860," in *The Collected Works of Dugald Stewart*, vol. 10, Edinburgh: Thomas Constable and Co., Hamilton, Adams and Co., pp. 1–98,

Stiglitz, Joseph E. (1986) "The New Development Economics," *World Development*, 14 (2): 257–265.

Strassmann, W. Paul (1993) "Development Economics from a Chicago Perspective," in W. J. Samuels (ed.) *The Chicago School of Political Economy*, London: Transaction Publishers, 277–294.

Streeten, Paul (1985) "A Problem to Every Solution: Development Economics Has Not Failed," *Finance and Development*, 22 (2): 14–16.

—— (1994) "Human Development: Means and Ends," *American Economic Review, Papers and Proceedings*, 84 (2): 232–237.

—— (2006) "Culture and Economic Development," in V.A. Ginsburgh and D. Throsby (eds.) *The Handbook of the Economics of Art and Culture*, vol. 1, Amsterdam: Elsevier, 400–412.

Tabellini, Guido (2005) "Culture and Institutions: Economic Development in the Regions of Europe," CESifo Working Paper No. 1492.

Temin, Peter (1997) "Is It Kosher to Talk About Culture?" *Journal of Economic History*, 57 (2): 267–287.

Toye, John (1987) *Dilemmas of Development: Reflections on the Counter-Revolution in Development Theory and Policy*, Oxford: Blackwell.

UNDP (United Nations Development Program) (2004) *The Human Development Report 2004: Cultural Liberty in Today's Diverse World*, New York: UNDP.

UNESCO (1998) *World Culture Report 1998: Culture, Creativity and Markets*, Paris: United Nations Educational, Scientific and Cultural Organization.

—— (2000) *World Culture Report 2000: Cultural Diversity, Conflict and Pluralism*, Paris: United Nations Educational, Scientific and Cultural Organization.

Wall, David (ed.) (1972) *Chicago Essays in Economic Development*, Chicago: University of Chicago Press.

Weber, Max (1958 [1930]) *The Protestant Ethic and the Spirit of Capitalism*, New York: Charles Scribner's Sons.

Wilber, Charles K. and Kenneth P. Jameson (eds.) (1992 [1973]) *The Political Economy of Development and Underdevelopment*, New York: McGraw-Hill.

Wolfensohn, James D., Lamberto Dini, Gianfranco Facco Bonetti, Ian Johnson, and J. Martin-Brown (2000) *Culture Counts: Financing, Resources, and the Economics of Culture in Sustainable Development*, Washington, DC: The World Bank.

World Bank (1999) *Culture and Sustainable Development: A Framework for Action*, Washington, DC: World Bank.

World Commission on Culture and Development (1995) *Our Creative Diversity*, Paris: UNESCO.

Zein-Elabdin, Eiman O. (1998) "The Question of Development in Africa: A Conversation for Propitious Change," *African Philosophy*, 11 (2): 113–125.

—— (2001) "Contours of a Non-Modernist Discourse: The Contested Space of History and Development," *Review of Radical Political Economics*, 33 (3): 255–263.

—— (2009) "Economics, Postcolonial Theory, and the Problem of Culture: Institutional Analysis and Hybridity," *Cambridge Journal of Economics*, 33 (6): 1153–1167.

—— and S. Charusheela (eds.) (2004) *Postcolonialism Meets Economics*, London: Routledge.

8   Feminist Economics

Women, culture, and development

> We are now faced with the serious challenge of developing agendas that avoid the
> dual pitfalls of ethnocentrism and Western bias on the one hand, and unprincipled
> forms of cultural relativism that deny women their basic human rights in the name
> of "difference," on the other.
>
> (Harcourt 1995: 131)

The second half of the twentieth century witnessed a remarkable level of attention to
women and gender relations in academic discourse and international development
policy agendas. This attention has expressed itself in two different perspectives.
First, since the 1970s, academic and policy literature, working within the framework of modernization theory, has taken up the issue of women's role in economic
development. Feminists in Europe and North America focused on the conditions
of 'third world' women, commonly seen as characteristic of patriarchal oppression. Second, over the same time span, gender emerged as a central theme in
postmodernist discourse although, unlike the first perspective, this has been
largely confined to academic circles. Thus, in the twentieth century, women and
gender came to be the site of the philosophical battle between modernism and
postmodernism. In Economics, these two perspectives have been manifested in
the field of women/gender and development (WGAD) and in the rise of Feminist
Economics (FE) as its own branch of the discipline.[1]

This chapter advances two main observations. First, FE has contributed tremendously to boosting the profile of culture in Economics (Ferber and Nelson
1993, 2003; Barker and Kuiper 2003; Benería et al. 2011). In general, Feminist
analyses offer broader, more extensive treatments of culture than the majority
of economic approaches discussed in the preceding chapters. Several authors
(Harcourt 1994; Jennings 1993; Kabeer 1994) have questioned the dichotomy
between 'economy' and 'culture,' thus departing from the *dualistic ontology* common in the discipline (see Chapter 1).

Second, despite these achievements, FE continues to be limited by the paradigmatic centrality of gender, which results in a *partial* approach to culture. By this I
mean FE scrutinizes gender relations, but does not sufficiently address the broader
role of culture in framing the discourse on women, gender, and development.

Although FE scholars have rejected dualism in economic epistemology and models (Nelson 1992, 1993; Jennings 1993, 1999), many have not fully recognized the divide between 'developed' and 'under(less)developed' countries as a hierarchical cultural dualism (see Chapter 7). Some texts have challenged the discursive power of 'development' and its associated cultural bias within FE itself (Charusheela and Zein-Elabdin 2003; Wood 2003; Bergeron 2004), or drawn a parallel between orientalism and androcentrism in economic discourse (Olson 1994; Grapard 1995). But this task remains tangential to the project of FE. In this chapter I suggest that the partial treatment of culture may have hindered FE from having an even bigger impact on the discipline than it has already. Therefore, FE might have to adopt a broader, more direct, and bolder approach to culture.

Culture and development are two of the most complicated and perennially disputed concept-phenomena. In this book, I use the term 'culture' to denote broadly shared, though often contested, sensibilities and practices of a society or a group, which sanction and censor its participants in multiple ways that are not always fully coherent. In turn, culture is shaped by individual idiosyncrasies, and changes in accord with social gaps and ruptures, as well as interaction with other cultures (see Chapter 1 for more on culture, and Appendix II for a sample of economists' interpretations of it). Economic development, on the other hand, has predominantly referred to high levels of material consumption, socially organized after the modern European experience: large-scale industry, a market system, urban agglomerations, and a rapid pace of life; in short, the culture of industrial modernity. The twentieth-century discourse of international development, which has served to universalize this prototype, constitutes a part of the cultural core of Economics, which FE shares, but must also contest.

The first two sections of the chapter outline FE and review the treatments of culture in this field. This is a general survey primarily intended to contribute to the book's goal of mapping out the place(s) of culture in Economics. The third section traces the evolution of economic thought on women, gender, and development from exclusive focus on women, to making gender relations the appropriate target of analysis. The expression women/gender and development captures this evolution. The last section examines an attempt to theorize the intersection of women, culture, and economic development by Emily Chamlee-Wright, based on her fieldwork in Ghana. In her book, *The Cultural Foundations of Economic Development* (1997), Chamlee-Wright adopts an Austrian School perspective to argue that Ghana's 'indigenous' cultural milieu puts female entrepreneurs in the best position to lead the country's development. Chamlee-Wright manages to avoid the culture/economy dualism and some other common dichotomies of social science. However, she takes an uncritical approach to the development discourse, which stands in contrast to her sound critique of Neoclassical theory.

This chapter follows the panoramic approach used throughout this book by pointing out major themes and common threads in the conceptual treatment of culture, without delving into the nuances and analytical details of different texts. The literature surveyed is limited to the discipline of economics, even though I realize the inherent multidisciplinarity of feminist inquiry.[2] This limited view is only intended as groundwork for more in-depth critical study.

Feminist Economics

A distinct Feminist perspective in Economics emerged in the 1990s though scholarship on women's economic conditions could be found at least since the early twentieth century (see Barker and Kuiper 2009). Lourdes Benería (1995) identifies two phases in the evolution of this scholarship. The first dates back to the 1930s debates over wage differences between men and women; the second refers to the 1970s appearance of the New Home Economics (Becker 1976). What sets FE apart from these earlier writings is that gender—instead of women—constitutes "a central category of analysis" (Benería 1995: 1842).[3]

The 'inaugural' event of FE is generally associated with the publication of *Beyond Economic Man: Feminist Theory and Economics* (Ferber and Nelson 1993), which summarized the feminist case against Economics, as practiced primarily in the US and Western European academy. The authors highlighted androcentric bias in the economics profession, where men dominate faculty and student bodies, as well as private sector practice and public policy advising. Furthermore, the majority of economic theory is derived from narrow concepts of rationality and value that exclude or underestimate the worth of household production and unpaid work in general; namely, the realm of social care and maintenance historically provided by women.

Since its emergence, FE research has drawn critically on Neoclassical, Marxian, and Institutionalist thought, the major economic traditions examined in this book, as well as other disciplines to examine the ways in which gender frames economic action and knowledge. (See Chapter 1 for more on the paradigmatic composition and different scholarly spheres of Economics.) As a result, FE literature is diverse. The bulk of it has concentrated on 'integrating'—aka 'mainstreaming'—gender in economic analysis (Herz 1989; Benería 2003; Jackson and Pearson 1998; Momsen 2008), which may take the form of scrutinizing 'the family,' re-valuing 'work,' or examining the position of women in 'development.' At another level, FE scholarship is concerned with a more profound rethinking of Economics itself, and therefore challenges the androcentric bias in disciplinary models and epistemologies instead of simply absorbing women into preconceived analytical categories. The following outline emphasizes theoretical contributions as they relate to the three schools of economics discussed in this book.[4]

The majority of FE work has uneasily relied on the Neoclassical theory derived from the Stigler–Becker doctrine (see Chapter 3). Gary Becker's relationship with feminism is complicated by his role in bringing economic attention to 'the family' (Becker 1976, 1981), while at once claiming that highly cultural phenomena such as marriage and parenting could be explained by market rationality rather than social relations or institutional, historical factors. Though rejecting his assumptions (e.g., the altruistic patriarch), many authors retained the underlying principles.[5] For example, Barbara Bergmann explained the massive entry of women into paid employment since WWII in pure 'economic man' logic: a woman "considers the financial reward of outside work, and also how much she values the leisure and housework she would have to forego" (2005 [1987]: 15).

Other authors have questioned the very premise of free choice, which envisions an autonomous unencumbered agent in calculated pursuit of 'self-interest.' They argue this vision precludes many forms of human interaction, particularly, family relationships and care giving (Strassmann 1993; Hewitson 1999).

Feminists have also challenged classical Marxian philosophy, for instance, by call-ing for the working-class family to be theorized on 'non-material' as well as 'material' grounds (Humphries 1977). Heidi Hartmann (1979) criticized Marxists for relying on three deficient approaches to 'the woman question.' The first assumes that capitalism erodes patriarchy such that the path to liberation inescapably passes through wage labor. The second approach theoretically subsumes the household, and all that has to do with women, into the process of capitalist reproduction; the third simply extends the concept of surplus value to household work, where women are conceived to labor "for capital and not for men" (Hartmann 1979: 4). In all three approaches, the pri-mary analytical category is capital rather than gender. As Alice Amsden (1980: 24) has pointed out, even though "[c]ustoms, culture, and consciousness" are part of Marx's theoretical framework, conventional Marxism failed to account for gender (also see Hartmann 1981; Folbre 1982; Albelda 1997).

By comparison, Institutional economics has received little criticism from Feminists. This is not surprising. To the extent that it is preoccupied with the social values that establish gender hierarchy and the institutional structure and practice of economics, all FE scholarship is Institutionalist. Thorstein Veblen had long ago shown that gender pervaded all economic relations (1894, 1899). Yet, despite this intellectual heritage, there has been a lack of contributions on women and gender in contemporary Institutional economics (Greenwood 1984). It was not until the 1990s that authors began to present systematic treatments of gender (e.g., Waller and Jennings 1990). Most notably, Ann Jennings (1993) traced the gendered dis-tinction between 'market' and 'household' to the historical evolution of European capitalism, which produced public/private and other related cultural dualisms.[6]

To be sure, not all FE is amenable to classification as reliant on Neoclassical, Marxian, or Institutionalist theory, or should be thought of in this way. Nancy Folbre has criticized Neoclassicism and Marxism for adopting idealized versions of coop-eration and conflict, and New Institutional Economics for overlooking the role of power. In *Who Pays for the Kids?* (1994), Folbre offers an alternative interpretation of economic development in Western Europe and the Americas based on four ana-lytical categories: structural factors (assets, norms, preferences), agents (individuals, groups), processes (coercion, exchange, coordination), and sites (states, markets, families). These categories are combined in the idea of "structures of constraint:" "sets of asset distributions, rules, norms, and preferences that empower given social groups. These structures locate certain boundaries of choice, but do not assign indi-viduals to a single position based on the ownership of productive assets" (ibid.: 51). This conceptual framework allows Folbre to show that the history of development has demonstrated both the softening and resilience of patriarchal structures. Unlike Bergmann, Folbre does not attribute the 'economic emergence' of women singu-larly to individual choice and technological change. She also sees it as an outcome of "collective identity and action" (ibid.: 7).

Additional FE work that stands as its own perspective includes critiques of Cartesian dualisms (Nelson 1992; Jennings 1993, 1999), post-structuralist analyses of the gendered construction of Neoclassical economic agency (Grapard 1995; Hewitson 1999), and interrogations of cultural hegemony and orientalism in Economics, including FE texts (Wood 2003; Zein-Elabdin 2003; Charusheela 2004; Olmsted 2004). This wide range of subject matter and perspectives underscores Feminists' desire to produce "a body of knowledge more accountable to the diversity of human lives" (Strassmann 1999: 364), which necessarily calls for culturally situated and aware theories and methods.

Culture in Feminist Economics

Culture—as both a concept and an operator—is central to the economic study of women and gender, not because this subject is more culturally defined than any other, but because Feminists are paradigmatically concerned with the role of cultural precepts in shaping economic action and knowledge. Unfortunately, the centrality of gender has resulted in a partial treatment of culture in FE. A quick indicator of this partial view is that such an extensive reference book as the *Elgar Companion to Feminist Economics* (Peterson and Lewis 1999) did not contain a specific entry on culture among its almost 100 subject areas. In the following pages, I review Feminist economic analyses of culture in a sample of texts.

A survey of the journal *Feminist Economics* reveals that culture is present to one degree or another throughout the literature. Articles with explicit references to it range from the incidental (Drago 2001) to those in which cultural themes form the primary subject. This latter category includes, for instance, analysis of cultural change in paid domestic work in Australia (Meagher 1997); discussion of the Neoclassical devaluation of culture (as consumption practices) despite the high theoretical status accorded the notion of consumer sovereignty (Koritz and Koritz 2001); and the revelation that the old economic debate about 'productive' versus 'unproductive' labor was settled by appeals to "select and shifting cultural norms" rather than to 'science' (Brennan 2006: 403). None of these contributions offers a definition of culture. Indeed, generally in FE literature many writers do not use the term at all, opting instead for surrogates such as habits, institutions, custom, norms, tradition, or patriarchy (e.g., Folbre 1994; Agarwal 1997; Bergmann 2005 [1987]). This is consistent with the long-held practice in most of Economics.

An early attempt to identify the economic implications of culture is Cordelia Reimers' (1985) analysis of labor force participation rates among married women from different "ethnic sub-cultures" in the USA. Reimers began from the premise that "'cultural' differences may give rise to systematic differences in utility functions that lead to systematic differences in behavior by women in different ethnic or nativity groups who face the same constraints or opportunity set" (ibid.: 251). This follows a common analytical strategy in which culture is interpreted as difference (e.g., Fernández 2008). Reimers examined Asian, Black, Hispanic, and White non-Hispanic groups, divided into native and foreign-born, based on 1976 US Census data. The cultural differences in question are attitudes about gender roles, working outside the home, and the desired number of children, which are thought to have direct (time allocation) and indirect (fertility) effects on women's labor supply. Reimers distinguished between "culturally conditioned" variables ("language, family size and age structure, and education") and "characteristics" (age, health, location, income) (ibid.: 252). Although she realized that cultural attitudes might be also present in these characteristics, she proceeded to measure how much each characteristic and attitude contributed to differences in labor force participation. She concluded that for Hispanic and foreign-born White wives, "traditional beliefs per se are unimportant for behavior" (ibid.: 255). On the other hand, for Black and Asian women, there were "direct cultural effects" (ibid.) that could not be explained by family circumstances and individual characteristics. Reimers' paper is one of the earliest attempts to quantitatively measure the 'impact' of cultural differences on economic decisions, an exercise that has become quite popular since then (see the Preferences Approach in Chapter 3).[7]

While Reimers attempted to measure intra-gender differences, Rachel Croson and Nancy Buchan (1999) explored whether gender itself makes a difference in economic behavior. Using trust game experiments in the USA, Japan, China, and South Korea, they looked for differences between men and women in giving, trust, and reciprocation.[8] The study covered 136 male and 50 female college students distributed evenly among the four countries, with women being more represented among US participants. The results showed that both genders gave similar portions of the money allotted to them, indicating no substantial difference in trusting behavior. In contrast, there was a significant difference in reciprocation across the four samples. Men returned an average of 28.6 percent of the amounts given to them, women returned 37.4 percent (ibid.: 389). Croson and Buchan took this outcome as an indicator of a higher sense of obligation to give back among women. However, they did not offer any hypotheses on the possible reasons behind the gender discrepancy. In fact, culture never entered their analysis because it was treated as a "nuisance variable" and was, therefore, "controlled for" (ibid.: 387).

On the more critical side of Economics, Feminist scholarship informed by Marxian philosophy has developed through two phases, each broadening the scope of Marxism while retaining its materialist approach. In the first phase this was accomplished by assimilating the concept of patriarchy, defined as a materially based "set of social relations between men ... that enable them to dominate women" (Hartmann 1979: 11). This phase led to the gender-class approach, which made possible analyses of non-class forms of exploitation (Humphries 1977; Benería and Sen 1981; Folbre 1982). The second phase broadened Marxism further by bringing in racial/ethnic difference as another instrument of capitalist oppression, thereby producing the race-gender-class perspective (Amott and Matthaei 1991; Matthaei 1996). Although enriching, these additions did not represent a theoretical shift since the premise is that gender and race are necessary categories for understanding capital. As such, Marxian contributions made it possible to include the impacts of capitalism on women and dominated ethnic groups but did not address the location of culture in the theoretical Marxian framework (Zein-Elabdin 2003).[9] More recent literature (Brewer *et al.* 2002) realizes the limitations of this additive approach. Nevertheless, it goes on to add 'caste' as another category. So far, the current efforts to rethink culture in Marxian political economy have not been reflected in FE scholarship even though there is work to be done (see Chapter 6).

Feminist authors who draw on the Veblenian Institutionalist tradition are most explicit in their approach to culture, defining it as "a system of symbolic interpretation that unites human thought and action" (Jennings 1993: 113). Jennings presents a strong culture-centered agenda "[to] *challenge the very definition of 'economic pursuits,' question cultural interpretations that prioritize 'the economic,' explore the historical origins of modern cultural beliefs and practices, and describe the gender dimensions of existing distinctions between 'economic' and 'noneconomic' pursuits" (ibid.: 119).* This holistic vision clearly rejects the dualism of culture/economy. In the same vein, authors here have criticized functionalist essentializing views in both Economics and feminism—the former prioritizes economy, the latter privileges culture as it materializes in gender relations (Jennings and Champlin 1994). Theoretical Institutional writings on culture have primarily dealt with issues of epistemology and method (Waller and Jennings 1990; Waller 1999), but there is also some attention to empirical contexts, for example, the development of gendered consumer culture in China (Hopkins 2007).

Critical analyses of different cultural contexts necessarily take a broad perspective on culture. In her paper, "Cultural Dopes or Rational Fools?" Naila Kabeer (1991) examined women's participation in the garment industry in Bangladesh, pointing out that analyses of Muslim women in the export-manufacturing sector typically adopted either a culturalist or an economic approach. The first simply compiled inventories of constraints, e.g., *purdah* or *hijab*, leaving no room for women's agency, whereas the second dismissed the cultural context in favor of rationalist individual-centered explanations. She called for a theoretical middle that does not thinly conceptualize women as prisoners to culture or hollow utility maximizers. Instead, this intermediate position would investigate the complex range of motivations and strategies behind Muslim women's entry into paid work. Kabeer (1994) has also called for a 'reversal' of analytical hierarchies in economic thought that privilege the 'economic' over the 'cultural.' Similarly, in her contribution to the first report of the World Commission on Culture and Development (1995), Wendy Harcourt suggested that the "links between cultures and economies are poorly understood and require systematic study" (1995: 148).

Some authors have made use of Postcolonial Theory to understand different contemporary economic experiences. This may be seen in Brenda Wyss' (1999) study of "household economies" in Jamaica, in which she incorporates the idea of hybridity, namely, situations of deep cultural mixing such as those created through colonialism (see Zein-Elabdin 2009).[10] Wyss begins by defining culture as "socially constructed meaning systems made up of ideas and processes that represent the world, that create cultural entities (like 'family,' or 'marriage,' or 'church'), that direct individuals to do certain things, and that evoke certain feelings" (1999: 1).

She claims that the hybridity of Jamaican households is reflected in 'distinct' patterns of kinship, conjugal arrangements, and resource pooling and management in which people mix altruism with selfishness, and high regard for individual autonomy and desire for material gain with contempt for self-serving calculating behavior. She describes this as a blend of "collective and private interests" (ibid.: 16). Of course, inconsistency in feelings or behavior patterns is not unique to Jamaica. However, the common practice in Economics has been to draw a dualistic theoretical opposition between so called 'individualist' and 'collectivist' attitudes, with each thought to characterize entirely different cultures (see Chapters 5 and 7 in this book). Wyss shows that both are found, not only in one society, but also within the mental states and daily practices of one household or person.

To summarize, Feminist economists offer substantial and diverse treatments of culture. Some take a shallow or minimal approach that imports it into conventional models without much thought, for instance, as a variable in a utility function. Reimers' study of labor force participation differences offers an example of the minimal treatment, which Wyss has described as "the least ambitious approach" to culture in Economics (1999: 2). As outlined above, other FE contributions combine different approaches from within and outside the discipline to chart unique theoretical courses.

Women/gender and development

According to the United Nations, "[o]ne of the defining movements of the twentieth century has been the relentless struggle for gender equality" (UNDP 1995: 1). This struggle has been mapped onto the discourse of development, the frame of thought that has governed international relations since the end of WWII. In this section, I trace the evolution of economic discourse on women, gender, and development from its initial preoccupation with women as a group to the recognition that it is the institutional set-up that produces gender inequality. The literature cuts across many disciplines in the humanities and social sciences, this section reviews a small selection of field-defining contributions within Economics to show that throughout this evolution, the treatment of culture—to varying degrees, implicitly or explicitly—has been partial, that is, it overlooks the cultural construction of the development discourse even though it is the framework within which all analyses and interpretations of gender dynamics take place.[11]

By all accounts, the inspiration of this field was Ester Boserup's book *Woman's Role in Economic Development*, published in 1970. Boserup documented that, in predominantly agrarian world regions, economic growth has been accompanied by an increasing gap between men and women in income, land ownership, formal education, and use of more advanced technology, for which she blamed both colonial and national administrators. Although she adopted a narrow economic theory, focusing on the concepts of efficiency, human capital, and market exchange, Boserup dealt with inherently cultural phenomena. For example, she discussed polygyny in Africa, suggesting that it persisted because of a wife's value as an agricultural asset. She identified "tradition" and a variety of "culture patterns"—whether "indigenous" or "imported" (1989: 179)—as catalysts in women's loss of economic status. Among those she named Arab, Chinese, Hindu, British, and Dutch cultural influences. Boserup potentially opened the theoretical door to an earnest study of culture in Economics, but her work was not recognized in this broad light, perhaps because she herself did not unpack the idea of culture.

The revelation that development had 'marginalized' women formed the basis for the women-in-development movement (WID) and the UN and World Bank agenda of "bringing women into the economic mainstream" (Herz 1989: 22). The World Bank (1990: 3) announced that "cultural traditions" and "barriers" lowered women's productivity and hence presented an obstacle to their full participation in development. Guidelines were issued for World Bank staff to be "sensitive to the role of culture" (ibid.: 4). The specific meaning of this directive is not clear, but it is worth noting that the idea of cultural barriers to development surfaced here at about the same time that the culture and development (CAD) literature began to take off in Economics generally (see Chapter 7). However, in CAD discussions, cultural values are mostly thought to have a positive influence, e.g., in the case of East Asia. These two discourses (WGAD and CAD) run parallel to one another, with almost no cross-over, and CAD shows no evidence of gender 'mainstreaming' (see Serageldin and Taboroff 1994; World Bank 1999; Wolfensohn *et al.* 2000; Harrison and Berger 2006).

As groundbreaking and influential as Boserup's book was, it had its shortcomings. Acknowledging Boserup's contribution, Lourdes Benería and Gita Sen (1981) contended that the lack of a feminist grounding rendered her study arbitrary, in effect, using "cultural values as filler for conceptual holes in the analysis" (ibid.: 285). Boserup paid little attention to the role of reproduction and treated capitalism as the natural path of development. Instead, they argued, women were "subordinated" as a gender, and at least in part this subordination served capitalist purposes. Furthering this argument, Diane Elson and Ruth Pearson (1981) examined the role of female workers in the export-manufacturing sector across newly industrializing countries, where low wages and "nimble fingers" have driven the high demand for women's labor since the 1980s. Elson and Pearson pointed to the gendered roots of these market-treasured 'female' skills, and suggested that capitalist development articulates with patriarchy to produce multiple outcomes: some "decompose" existing forms of gender subordination, while others "intensify" them or "recompose" new forms (ibid.: 99). The word 'culture' did not appear in their discussion.

The subordination thesis contributed to the theoretical shift toward a gender-focused perspective. Amartya Sen called for "treating gender as a force of its own in development analysis" (1990: 123) rather than subsuming its impact under the rubric of poverty. He offered his cooperative conflicts model in which gender inequality results from perceived interests and contributions and from the bargaining positions of different household members. He put forward the ideas of well-being and capabilities as more 'objective' welfare criteria than utility. Sen did not dwell on culture. Indeed, he was arguing against the tendency to perceive all gender-related things as "purely 'cultural phenomena'" (ibid.: 129). The shift from WID was solidified with Elson's call to adopt a male bias approach. According to her, male bias represents a social tendency that "operates in favour of men as a gender, and against women as a gender" (1991: 3); it is firmly grounded in the social institutional psyche and could be demonstrated in development outcomes.[12]

The contributions discussed above reflect partial treatments of culture in that they concentrate on women or gender relations without bringing on board the cultural specificity of development both as a historical process and discourse. They take the goal of 'development' as a given. Even though Benería and Sen pointed out Boserup's lapse in this respect, they were mainly concerned with capitalist development. Elson insightfully questioned development theory and policy, but her critique was confined to its assumptions about women and gender. Thus, in different ways and to varying degrees, these contributions represent a common pattern of omission of the role of culture in framing economic discourse on women, gender, and development. As Drucilla Barker (1998) has pointed out, feminist scholarship has missed the rootedness of the development discourse in European Enlightenment philosophy, with its dualistic epistemologies and culturally hegemonic concept of progress. In this regard, FE suffers from what I have called the *Mill syndrome* (see Chapter 2), namely, rejection of the social devaluation of women, but an inability to connect it to and systematically challenge the parallel phenomenon with respect to devalued (other) cultures.

It is relatively easy to see the partial treatment of culture in the context of the development literature. However, my argument applies to the general body of Feminist economic analysis where powerful critiques of dualisms (Nelson 1992; Jennings 1993) did not also point to hierarchical *development dualisms* such as modern/traditional and universal/particular, or universal/relative (see Chapters 1 and 7 in this book). This omission is not simply a function of the division of labor between the field of development and other areas of specialization, which FE inherited. On an abstract level, many authors do realize that gender is bound up with and exists in the company of multiple dimensions of othering and oppression. Jennings (1999: 151), who includes universal/particular in her general critique of dualism, has noted that the dichotomy of market/non-market leads to the devaluation and exclusion of "non-Western societies" from development theory and policy. Yet, this type of argument remains tangential to the project of FE. That Jennings did not include the universal/particular dichotomy in her list of cultural dualisms underscores this point. As I have suggested elsewhere (Zein-Elabdin 2003), FE has the difficulty of negotiating the paradigmatic centrality of gender, with the residue of modernist economic philosophy, and the related power of the development discourse. Below I give three examples to indicate the complexity of this position.

In the context of earlier WGAD debates, the DAWN Collective (Development Alternatives with Women for a New Era) took a broader approach by questioning the legitimacy of the development discourse on cultural grounds. DAWN described a global "crisis of culture" (Sen and Grown 1987: 74) in which the pursuit of economic growth proceeded alongside oppressive trends of inequality, militarization, and religious "fundamentalism." In this crisis, women were held as "pawns" in the battle between forces of 'modernity' and 'tradition.' Modernists tolerated the sexual objectification of women in the name of liberation, whereas traditionalists called for cultural purity, often masking a desire to assert male sovereignty. In effect, DAWN placed the discussion of women in a cultural framework that shapes ideas and practices of development. Yet, DAWN went on to advocate what they called the vantage point of "the poorest" and "most oppressed" women worldwide as a source of alternative visions for development (ibid.: 23). This alternative represents an essentializing reversal of hierarchies within the global dualisms of developed/under(less)developed, North/South, or rich/poor.

Wendy Harcourt has recognized the project of international development as a complex of knowledge-power that defines "reality" for those living in different parts of the world (1994: 22). She argues that the emphasis on economic growth as a universal goal implicitly dismisses culture. At the same time, she notes, questioning development does not require adherence to an idealized notion of tradition. Harcourt (1995) suggests the challenge is to find a middle ground between 'Western bias' and 'unprincipled' cultural relativism; the latter is demonstrated, for example, when one defends polygyny in the name of Islam, but ignores inheritance laws that guarantee women's rights to property under *Shari`a* law. This is a sound example. Harcourt claims a middle ground is achievable by protecting reproductive freedom, promoting gender-aware and culturally sensitive planning, and increasing women's presence in the mainstream. However, unless it is understood that ideas such as reproductive freedom are already circumscribed within the cultural parameters of WGAD discourse, i.e., they are defined on the basis of its global hierarchy of cultures, this proposition goes nowhere. As S. Charusheela (2001) has pointed out, the presumed necessary choice between ethnocentric universalism and cultural relativism leaves no theoretical space for 'non-Western' (subaltern) cultures.

Cynthia Wood's (2003) analysis of paid and unpaid work shows that the partial approach to culture has significant implications for FE generally. Wood discusses the project of accounting for women's work (Benería 1982, 2003), which problematizes the distinction between paid and unpaid labor. She points out a tendency in FE research to treat unpaid domestic work in 'developed' countries as equivalent to non-market work performed by women in 'less developed' ones. According to her, by not considering differences in the sexual division of labor and types of work between the two groups of countries, Feminist economists have instituted a "'first-world' bias" (2003: 305). She traces the roots of this bias to ideas of backwardness in early development economics (Lewis 1954) that became central to discussions of the household and domestic production in WID literature (Boserup 1989 [1970]), which FE seems to have uncritically inherited. The implication, Wood argues, is that—given the discursive hierarchy of development—FE writings end up 'marginalizing' unpaid domestic labor in general.

The upshot is that the treatment of culture in the discourse of women/gender and development has varied, but, for the most part, has remained partial, overlooking the cultural construction of development knowledge itself, and by extension all contemporary global problematics. Avoiding the conceptual pitfalls outlined above requires constant vigilance to the embeddedness of the cultural premises and history of European modernity in economic thought.

Theorizing women, culture, and development

In the remainder of this chapter I examine Emily Chamlee-Wright's book *The Cultural Foundations of Economic Development: Urban Female Entrepreneurship in Ghana* (1997), in which she presents a theoretico-empirical account of women, culture, and development. This is the most explicit, extended study of this confluence that I have encountered in economic literature. The book's central thesis is that economic development depends, at least partially, on the "cultural resources" (ibid.: 18) available to a community. In Ghana, she claims, these resources are already present within the 'indigenous' private sector, where female entrepreneurs are particularly poised to play a leading role in the country's development. In this study, Chamlee-Wright shows considerable alertness to cultural dynamics; yet, the concept of 'development' seems to exist beyond her analytical horizon. Her study raises many interesting questions that could be critically engaged in depth, my discussion is confined to a broad overview.

The book weaves together New Institutional and Austrian economics, with method and insights from Anthropology (Gudeman 1986; Ensminger 1992), into what might be called a Weberian, neo-Schumpeterian perspective. Chamlee-Wright begins by criticizing Neoclassical theory for conceptualizing culture as either a constant part of individual preferences or a constraint on 'rational' behavior. For her, culture is "the context in which meaning is negotiated and renegotiated" (1997: 24) through language, history, and learned practices. Therefore, she advocates the "radical subjectivist" (ibid.: 19) Austrian approach, which retains the centrality of individual choice and free markets, but maintains that because of uncertainty and little information, decision-making is a subjectively interpretive process. According to her, although Neoclassical and Austrian economics are both descendants of marginalism, the former focuses on the result (equilibrium), whereas the latter underscores the process, i.e., human interpretation of the physical world, which demands attention to the cultural milieu (also see Boettke 2001).

For Chamlee-Wright, economic development refers to a society's success in adapting to new circumstances and managing increasing orders of complexity. This success is achieved by the evolutionary accumulation of knowledge, which surpasses any one person's or political regime's cognitive abilities. Although this argument favors planning instead of uncoordinated market decisions, she goes on to suggest it was planning—rather than corruption or poor implementation—that lay behind the failure of national development efforts in Ghana. She adds that her analysis of development focuses both on the role of the entrepreneur and "the rules, institutions, morals, and cultural foundations which evolve to support the market" (ibid.: 55). Entrepreneurial attentiveness to new opportunities is crucial, but success in maximizing profit turns on the ability to interpret the available market data within a specific culture. To assess a business opportunity in the Ghanaian context, an entrepreneur might have to examine written evidence of credit history, a network of acquaintances, or someone's kinship status.

Chamlee-Wright then describes this cultural context, claiming that indigenous societies have long had institutions of property rights and well-defined procedures for arbitration and conflict resolution, e.g., the council of elders and the market queen. Emphasis on conflict resolution stems from the cosmological view of the Akan, the largest ethnic group in Ghana, which values harmony of the cosmic order within which a social system must operate. Maintaining order is instituted through accountability to elders, ancestors, and the spiritual world. She claims that elements of these older institutions still operate well even though colonial and postcolonial regimes have significantly undermined traditional authorities. For example, the market queen, who was historically chosen by consensus in an elaborate ceremony, is informally elected today. She has no legal standing and is subject to encroachment and retribution by municipal and government officials. Nevertheless, the queen continues to enjoy enough legitimacy to effectively arbitrate between traders in return for gifts and tribute.

The implications of all this for development begin to emerge from Chamlee-Wright's assertion that traditional religious beliefs in Ghana contain a "West African capitalist ethic" (ibid.: 113). According to her, the Akan believe that each person is assigned a unique destiny at birth (*nkrabea*), which may be fulfilled through good deeds and the search for higher truth. She interprets this belief as a concept of "personal progress" that one continually strives for through different choices, and suggests that *nkrabea* "constitutes the elements of a work ethic, providing a similar function as that which Weber described in relation to Protestant culture" (ibid.: 115). In practical terms, tending to one's kin and helping others could realize one's destiny. Entrepreneurship offers opportunities for reaching this spiritual end and, if wealth is seen as a reward for spiritual rectitude, she concludes, Akan religion promotes saving and capital accumulation. The logic is tenuous. Nonetheless, she proceeds to explain why women particularly represent this 'indigenous' capitalist ethic.

Ghanaian 'market women,' according to her, embody this philosophy, being an entrepreneur is constituent of the identity of "the West African woman" (ibid.: 121). The prominence of women traders in West Africa is well documented by historians and anthropologists, but Chamlee-Wright takes this phenomenon in an essentialist direction to claim it is a part of female identity. To demonstrate, she offers "interpretive" accounts of three urban businesswomen: a struggling street vendor, raising two children alone as she fights off frequent harassment by city officials; a mid-level seamstress, operating from a stall she could lock up at night; and a successful cloth trader, with her own shop. The three represent a continuum of incomes, marital status, education, and religious beliefs. The accounts were generated from a combination of interviews and direct observation.

Chamlee-Wright claims the entrepreneurial identity of Ghanaian women results from marital arrangements, which grant substantial autonomy between spouses. In addition, women find it necessary to enterprise because the husband's income is often too low to support an entire family. She also states that since most traditional rules of inheritance favor men, women strive to pass on their wealth to daughters. Training the next generation of female entrepreneurs is a communal process in which a girl's family, neighbors, and others participate. In consequence, relationships between women are often more important and enduring than matrimonial ties. This is instituted in "sororital alliances," that is, "female networks" (ibid.: 125) of kin, friends, and traders that expand women's access to finance, labor, and other resources. Chamlee-Wright argues these networks also build a shared culture and methods of conflict resolution that reduce transactions cost. Although interesting and informative, this ethnographic account does not explain why the same religious beliefs did not also motivate men to assume an entrepreneurial role. What is most pertinent is that her position departs from the WGAD view (e.g., World Bank 1990) that tradition constitutes an obstacle to development by lowering women's economic participation and productivity.

Putting these pieces together, Chamlee-Wright sees a similarity between Max Weber's (1958) "Protestant ethic" and the work ethic embodied in Ghanaian traditional religious beliefs. However, she cautions:

> [T]he capitalist ethic and the entrepreneurial mindset at work within the southern Ghanaian context is not the result of Western imperialism, but is rather an outgrowth of indigenous culture. Thus, economic development is not necessarily tied to becoming more Westernized, with a diminished reliance upon indigenous culture. Rather, the reverse might be the more promising solution, by taking advantage of the cultural resources inherent within an emerging economy.
>
> (ibid.: 131)

In other words, the existing cultural resources for conflict resolution, inheritance, credit, and mutual assistance contain the prerequisites for development. The notion of an 'indigenous' culture after the fact of colonialism and other major cultural encounters in Ghana's history is problematic, but this is not my concern at this moment. Here, I would like to situate Chamlee-Wright's argument within CAD literature (see Chapter 7). Although she avoids a crudely dualistic treatment of culture, her analysis falls in line with the idealist perspective, in which causality flows one way from culture to economy. This is consistent with CAD discussions of East Asia, where a notion of 'Confucian values' (Park 1997) has been theorized as a catalyst for economic growth. The parallel in Ghana is 'Akan religion.' On the other hand, despite her essentializing representation of Ghanaian women, and somewhat orientalist discussion of 'indigenous culture,' Chamlee-Wright did not purport to offer a general theory of women, culture, and development. Instead, she attempted to treat culture in a reasonably complex manner that—unlike the case of 'Confucian values'—does not produce a uniform result for an entire society.

Chamlee-Wright's monograph presents an interesting effort to theoretically locate women within the terrain of culture and development. The narrative is rich. However, it lacks critical discussion of development as a discursive construct imbued with cultural precepts. In other words, development is taken for granted. In this regard, her text displays the partial treatment of culture noted in the previous section. Moreover, she wishes to maintain the cultural specificity of the Ghanaian context, while also taking economic development and capitalism—with markets, private property rights, and freedom of international trade—to be universally valid and inevitable. Given her premise that "the basic logic of economics is applicable no matter what the cultural setting" (ibid.: 178), it is not clear what difference culture makes. The accounts of the three women entrepreneurs are analytically inconsequential since we never learn their own interpretations of development beyond the desire to acquire more credit or another sewing machine. Chamlee-Wright never takes them out of the construct of 'African market women.' As a result, one is left to wonder whether the whole exercise was simply a way to establish the suitability of 'indigenous' beliefs to capitalist modernity, and to claim women as its rightful vanguard.

Conclusion

The literature reviewed in this chapter shows that the majority of Feminist Economics critically draws on the three established schools of economics. But Feminist thought also defies easy profiling, as authors combine multiple theoretical traditions and a wide range of sources from within and outside the discipline to produce unique perspectives. In general, FE scholarship shows deeper more complex discussions of cultural problematics than the majority of work discussed in this book. Yet, the centrality of gender has led to *partial* treatments of culture that understate its role in framing economic discourse on women, gender, and development. Feminists have questioned the dualistic separation of culture and economy, and generally criticized dualisms, thereby contributing wide steps towards addressing a most profound issue in Economics. However, this critique has been confined to transparent gender-related dualisms, e.g., public/private and market/household, leaving such powerful binarisms as universal/particular and developed/under(less)developed insufficiently problematized.

One consequence of the partial treatment of culture is that Feminist Economic thought has yet to be 'integrated' into the general study of culture in Economics. In other words, the discipline shows little to no signs of gender 'mainstreaming.' This is demonstrated in two ways. First, discourses of culture and development, on one hand, and women/gender and development, on the other, run parallel to one another without any interaction. Second, Feminist contributions are hardly represented in current discussions of culture in Economics as reflected in prominent publications (see Appendix I for a chronological list). For example, Mark Casson's (1997) edited two-volume book *Culture, Social Norms and Economics*, which contains 54 articles on a wide range of topics, does not feature a single article by an FE author, or any work on women and gender issues, except Veblen's (1894) paper "The Economic Theory of Woman's Dress." This omission signals a lack of familiarity with or appreciation of the extensive body of contemporary Feminist economic thought. This is not one isolated case (see Ginsburgh and Throsby 2006, for a more recent example).[13] Some of the failure to include FE could be attributed to the disciplinary specialization that partitions the study of women and gender from other fields. I would argue, this effect is deepened by the partial treatment of culture, which may have hindered FE from having an even bigger impact on the discipline than it has already. If the goal is to effect more fundamental change in Economics, Feminists must undertake a broader, more direct, and bolder approach to culture.

Notes

1 The majority of texts discussed in this chapter are modernist in orientation. See Charusheela and Zein-Elabdin (2003) and Zein-Elabdin (2003) for a discussion of modernism and its presence in FE. See Zein-Elabdin (2009) on cultural modernism. Postmodernist contributions on development are generally few, as many have sought to distance themselves from the deterministic tendencies of modernization theory. See Barker (1998) for a literature review. Charusheela (2004) gives a critical comment on postmodern feminism in Economics.

2 For multidisciplinary anthologies of development feminism, see Visvanathan *et al.* (1997), Benería and Bisnath (2001), and Momsen (2008). See Mohanty (1991), Harcourt (1994), Nussbaum and Glover (1995), Jackson and Pearson (1998), and Perry and Schenck (2001) for critical discussions. Not all authors whose work is discussed in this chapter identify themselves as feminist. I have included significant work that deals with women or gender relations, regardless of political or ideological commitments (e.g., Boserup 1989 [1970]).

3 Most authors maintain the distinction between gender (social construction) and sex (biological characteristic) (e.g., Ferber and Nelson 1993, 2003). Although this conceptual framing has been disputed (Hewitson 1999), the dominant view remains tacitly rooted in a nature/culture dualism.

4 I have not included FE literatures on the history of economic thought, pedagogy, the economics of care, sexuality, globalization, economic history, and the vast empirical work on labor markets. For more, see Humphries (1995), Kuiper and Sap (1995), Barker and Kuiper (2009), Benería *et al.* (2011), Folbre (2001), and Ferber and Nelson (2003). For a concise history of FE, see Peterson and Lewis (1999).

5 For critiques of Becker's work, see Greenwood (1984), Folbre (1986), and Kabeer (1994). Examples of Neoclassical analyses of women and gender not discussed in this chapter can be found in Amsden (1980), Woolley (1993), and Humphries (1995).

6 For more examples of Institutionalist work, see Miller (1972), Peterson and Brown (1994), Zein-Elabdin (1996), and Waller (1999). Chapter 5 discusses the New Institutional Economics (NIE), which treats culture as a constraint on individual optimizing agency. Several Feminist Economists have critically adopted some NIE principles. For example, Harriss-White (1998) identifies commodity markets as a set of gendered institutional sites that is neglected in the NIE literature.

7 Among other things, Reimers found that "[d]ifferences in family size and age structure account for about a 0.05 gap in labor force participation rates between U.S.-born whites and Hispanics" (1985: 54). See Chapters 3, 5, 7 in this book for other examples and critiques of quantitative studies of culture.

8 The trust game is made of two randomly assigned participants interacting in a double-blind experiment. A "proposer" is given a certain sum of money that he/she could spend as they please: give some, all, or none to an anonymous "responder." This part of the experiment investigates trusting behavior. The sum that the proposer gives is then augmented (by the experimenter) and the responder chooses how much to return to the proposer. This part reveals the extent of reciprocating behavior.

9 Amott and Matthaei (1991) did not discuss culture itself, but made frequent references to cultural differences between women, e.g., African Americans vis-à-vis Latinas, in a very general manner.

10 See Zein-Elabdin and Charusheela (2004) for more on Postcolonial Theory and Economics. Wyss (1999) advocates an ethnographic method to study the complicated issue of child support; in particular, Gudeman's (1986) local models approach, which treats all economic practices and ideas as cultural constructions. Unfortunately, as Wyss realizes, the anthropological approach, despite its advantages, renders different cultures exotic and antithetical to modern market economies.

11 Tinker (1990) and Kabeer (1994) give concise histories of the emergence of women as a development constituency.

12 Another important text illustrating the shift away from WID is Agarwal's book *A Field of One's Own* (1994), which revealed silence or ambiguity on women's land rights in the development plans of India, Bangladesh, and Pakistan. Agarwal used the term "customary practices" rather than culture.

13 Casson's (1997) book discusses a wide range of topics, including preferences, altruism, status, norms, social order, the law, and religion. Ginsburgh and Throsby's (2006) volume on the economics of art and culture shows the same pattern, with no contributions on women or gender relations. The volume's 37 chapters cover history, value, culture and the economy, consumption and production, and labor markets, among other topics. The absence of gender is significant because Ginsburgh and Throsby adopt a broader, more anthropological meaning of culture rather than confine it to products and occupations of creativity.

References

Agarwal, Bina (1994) *A Field of One's Own: Gender and Land Rights in South Asia*, Cambridge: Cambridge University Press.

—— (1997) "'Bargaining' and Gender Relations: Within and Beyond the Household," *Feminist Economics*, 3 (1): 1–51.

Albelda, Randy (1997) *Economics and Feminism: Disturbances in the Field*, New York: Twayne Publishers.

Amott, Teresa and Julie Matthaei (1991) *Race, Gender, and Work: A Multicultural Economic History of Women in the United States*, Boston: South End Press.

Amsden, Alice H. (ed.) (1980) *The Economics of Women and Work*, New York: St. Martin's Press.

Barker, Drucilla K. (1998) "Dualisms, Discourse, and Development," *Hypatia*, 13 (3): 83–94.

—— and Edith Kuiper (eds.) (2003) *Toward a Feminist Philosophy of Economics*, London: Routledge.

—— and —— (eds.) (2009) *Feminist Economics: Critical Concepts in Economics*, vols. I–IV, London: Routledge.

Becker, Gary S. (1976) *The Economic Approach to Human Behavior*, Chicago: University of Chicago Press.

—— (1981) *A Treatise on the Family*, Cambridge, MA: Harvard University Press.

Benería, Lourdes (ed.) (1982) *Women and Development: The Sexual Division of Labor in Rural Societies*, New York: Praeger Publishers.

—— (1995) "Toward a Greater Integration of Gender in Economics," *World Development*, 23 (11): 1839–1850.

—— (2003) *Gender, Development, and Globalization: Economics as If All People Mattered*, London: Routledge.

—— and Savitri Bisnath (eds.) (2001) *Gender and Development: Theoretical, Empirical, and Practical Approaches*, vols. I–II, Cheltenham: Edward Elgar.

——, Ann Mari May, and Diana Strassmann (eds.) (2011) *Feminist Economics*, vols. I–III, Cheltenham: Edward Elgar.

—— and Gita Sen (1981) "Accumulation, Reproduction, and Women's Role in Economic Development: Boserup Revisited," *Signs: Journal of Women in Culture and Society*, 7 (2): 279–298.

Bergeron, Suzanne (2004) *Fragments of Development: Nation, Gender, and the Space of Modernity*, Ann Arbor, MI: University of Michigan Press.

Bergmann, Barbara R. (2005 [1987]) *The Economic Emergence of Women*, New York: Palgrave Macmillan.

Boettke, Peter J. (2001) "Why Culture Matters: Economics, Politics, and the Imprint of History," in *Calculation and Coordination: Essays on Socialism and Transitional Political Economy*, London: Routledge, 248–265, 334–337.

Boserup, Ester (1989 [1970]) *Woman's Role in Economic Development*, London: Earthscan Publications.

Brennan, David M. (2006) "Defending the Indefensible? Culture's Role in the Productive/ Unproductive Dichotomy," *Feminist Economics*, 12 (3): 403–425.

Brewer, Rose M., Cecilia A. Conrad, and Mary C. King (2002) "The Complexities and Potential of Theorizing Gender, Caste, Race, and Class," *Feminist Economics*, 8 (2): 3–17.

Casson, Mark (ed.) (1997) *Culture, Social Norms, and Economics*, vols. I, II, Cheltenham: Edward Elgar.

Chamlee-Wright, Emily (1997) *The Cultural Foundations of Economic Development: Urban Female Entrepreneurship in Ghana*, London: Routledge.

Charusheela, S. (2001) "Women's Choices and the Ethnocentrism/Relativism Dilemma," in S. Cullenberg, J. Amariglio, and D. Ruccio (eds.) *Postmodernism, Economics and Knowledge*, London: Routledge, 197–220.

—— (2004) "Postcolonial Thought, Postmodernism, and Economics: Questions of Ontology and Ethics," in E. Zein-Elabdin and S. Charusheela (eds.) *Postcolonialism Meets Economics*, London: Routledge, 40–58.

—— and Eiman Zein-Elabdin (2003) "Feminism, Postcolonial Thought, and Economics," in Marianne A. Ferber and Julie A. Nelson (eds.) *Feminist Economics Today: Beyond Economic Man*, Chicago: University of Chicago Press, 175–192.

Croson, Rachel and Nancy Buchan (1999) "Gender and Culture: International Experimental Evidence from Trust Games," *American Economic Review, Papers and Proceedings*, 89 (2): 386–391.

Drago, Robert (2001) "Time on the Job and Time with Their Kids: Cultures of Teaching and Parenthood in the US," *Feminist Economics*, 7 (3): 1–31.

Elson, Diane (ed.) (1991) *Male Bias in the Development Process*, Manchester: Manchester University Press.

—— and Ruth Pearson (1981) "Nimble Fingers Make Cheap Workers: An Analysis of Women's Employment in Third World Export Manufacturing," *Feminist Review*, Spring: 87–107.

Ensminger, Jean (1992) *Making a Market: The Institutional Transformation of an African Society*, Cambridge: Cambridge University Press.

Ferber, Marianne A. and Julie A. Nelson (eds.) (1993) *Beyond Economic Man: Feminist Theory and Economics*, Chicago: University of Chicago Press.

—— (eds.) (2003) *Feminist Economics Today: Beyond Economic Man*, Chicago: University of Chicago Press.

Fernández, Raquel (2008) "Culture and Economics," in Steven N. Durlauf and Lawrence E. Blume (eds.) *The New Palgrave Dictionary of Economics Online*, 2nd edn, Basingstoke: Palgrave Macmillan. Available at: www.dictionaryofeconomics.com/ article?id=pde2008_E000282, doi:10.1057/9780230226203.0346.

Folbre, Nancy (1982) "Exploitation Comes Home: A Critique of the Marxian Theory of Family Labour," *Cambridge Journal of Economics*, 6 (4): 317–329.

—— (1986) "Cleaning House: New Perspectives on Households and Economic Development," *Journal of Development Economics*, 22 (1): 5–40.

—— (1994) *Who Pays for the Kids? Gender and the Structures of Constraint*, London: Routledge.

—— (2001) *The Invisible Heart: Economics and Family Values*, New York: The New Press.

Ginsburgh, Victor A. and David Throsby (eds.) (2006) *Handbook of the Economics of Art and Culture*, Amsterdam: Elsevier North-Holland.

Grapard, Ulla (1995) "Robinson Crusoe: The Quintessential Economic Man?" *Feminist Economics* 1 (1): 33–52.

Greenwood, Daphne (1984) "The Economic Significance of 'Woman's Place' in Society: A New-Institutionalist View," *Journal of Economic Issues*, 18 (3): 663–680.

Gudeman, Stephen (1986) *Economics as Culture: Models and Metaphors of Livelihood*, London: Routledge & Kegan Paul.

Harcourt, Wendy (ed.) (1994) *Feminist Perspectives on Sustainable Development*, London: Zed Books.

—— (1995) "Gender and Culture," in *Our Creative Diversity*, The World Commission on Culture and Development Report, Paris: UNESCO, 129–149.

Harrison, Lawrence E. and Peter L. Berger (eds.) (2006) *Developing Cultures: Case Studies*, London: Routledge.

Harriss-White, Barbara (1998) "Female and Male Grain Marketing Systems: Analytical and Policy Issues for West Africa and India," in Cecile Jackson and Ruth Pearson (eds.) *Feminist Visions of Development: Gender, Analysis and Policy*, London: Routledge, 189–213.

Hartmann, Heidi I. (1979) "The Unhappy Marriage of Marxism and Feminism: Towards a More Progressive Union," *Capital and Class*, 3 (2): 1–33.

—— (1981) "The Family as the Locus of Gender, Class, and Political Struggle: The Example of Housework," *Signs: Journal of Women, Culture and Society*, 6 (3): 366–394.

Herz, Barbara (1989) "Bringing Women into the Economic Mainstream: Guidelines for Policymakers and Development Institutions," *Finance and Development*, 26 (4): 22–25.

Hewitson, Gillian J. (1999) *Feminist Economics: Interrogating the Masculinity of Rational Economic Man*, Northampton, MA: Edward Elgar Publishing.

Hopkins, Barbara E. (2007) "Western Cosmetics in the Gendered Development of Consumer Culture in China," *Feminist Economics*, 13 (3–4): 287–306.

Humphries, Jane (1977) "Class Struggle and the Persistence of the Working-Class Family," *Cambridge Journal of Economics*, 1 (3): 241–258.

—— (ed.) (1995) *Gender and Economics*, Brookfield, VT: Edward Elgar.

Jackson, Cecile and Ruth Pearson (eds.) (1998) *Feminist Visions of Development: Gender, Analysis and Policy*, London: Routledge.

Jennings, Ann L. (1993) "Public or Private? Institutional Economics and Feminism," in Marianne A. Ferber and Julie A. Nelson (eds.) *Beyond Economic Man: Feminist Theory and Economics*, Chicago: University of Chicago Press, 111–129.

—— (1999) "Dualisms," in Janice Peterson and Margaret Lewis (eds.) *The Elgar Companion to Feminist Economics*, Cheltenham: Edward Elgar, 142–153.

—— and Dell Champlin (1994) "Cultural Contours of Race, Gender, and Class Distinctions: A Critique of Moynihan and Other Functionalist Views," in Janice Peterson and Doug

Brown (eds.) *The Economic Status of Women Under Capitalism: Institutional Economics and Feminist Theory*, Aldershot: Edward Elgar, 95–110.

Kabeer, Naila (1991) "Cultural Dopes or Rational Fools? Women and Labour Supply in the Bangladesh Garment Industry," *The European Journal of Development Research*, 3 (November): 133–160.

—— (1994) *Reversed Realities: Gender Hierarchies in Development Thought*, London: Verso.

Koritz, Amy and Douglas Koritz (2001) "Checkmating the Consumer: Passive Consumption and the Economic Devaluation of Culture," *Feminist Economics*, 7 (1): 45–62.

Kuiper, Edith and Jolande Sap (eds.) (with Susan Feiner, Notburga Ott and Zafiris Tzannatos) (1995) *Out of the Margin: Feminist Perspectives on Economics*, London: Routledge.

Lewis, W. Arthur (1954) "Economic Development with Unlimited Supplies of Labour," *Manchester School*, 22: 139–191.

Matthaei, Julie (1996) "Why Feminist, Marxist, and Anti-Racist Economists Should Be Feminist-Marxist-Anti-Racist Economists," *Feminist Economics*, 2 (1): 22–42.

Meagher, Gabrielle (1997) "Recreating 'Domestic Service': Institutional Cultures and the Evolution of Paid Household Work," *Feminist Economics*, 3 (2): 1–27.

Miller, Edythe S. (1972) "Veblen and Women's Lib: A Parallel," *Journal of Economic Issues*, 6 (2/3): 75–86.

Mohanty, (1991 [1984]) "Under Western Eyes: Feminist Scholarship and Colonial Discourses Chandra Talpade" in Chandra Talpade Mohanty, Ann Russo, and Lourdes Torres (eds.) *Third World Women and the Politics of Feminism*, Bloomington, IN: Indiana University Press, 51–80.

Momsen, Janet D. (ed.) (2008) *Gender and Development: Critical Concepts in Development Studies*, vols. 1–4, London: Routledge.

Nelson, Julie A. (1992) "Gender, Metaphor, and the Definition of Economics," *Economics and Philosophy*, 8 (1): 103–125.

—— (1993) "The Study of Choice or the Study of Provisioning? Gender and the Definition of Economics," in Marianne A. Ferber and Julie A. Nelson (eds.) *Beyond Economic Man: Feminist Theory and Economics*, Chicago: University of Chicago, 23–36.

Nussbaum, Martha C. and Jonathan Glover (eds.) (1995) *Women, Culture, and Development: A Study of Human Capabilities*, Oxford: Clarendon Press.

Olmsted, Jennifer (2004) "Orientalism and Economic Methods: (Re)reading Feminist Economic Discussions of Islam," in E. Zein-Elabdin and S. Charusheela (eds.) *Postcolonialism Meets Economics*, London Routledge, 165–182.

Olson, Paulette (1994) "Feminism and Science Reconsidered: Insights from the Margins," in Janice Peterson and Doug Brown (eds.), *The Economic Status of Women Under Capitalism: Institutional Economics and Feminist Theory*, Aldershot: Edward Elgar, 77–94.

Park, Tae-Kyu (1997) "Confucian Values and Contemporary Economic Development in Korea," in Timothy Brook and Hy V. Luong (eds.) *Culture and Economy: The Shaping of Capitalism in Eastern Asia*, Ann Arbor, MI: Michigan University Press, 125–136.

Perry, Susan and Celeste Schenck (ed.) (2001) *Eye to Eye: Women Practising Development Across Cultures*, London: Zed Books.

Peterson, Janice and Doug Brown (eds.) (1994) *The Economic Status of Women Under Capitalism: Institutional Economics and Feminist Theory*, Aldershot: Edward Elgar.

Peterson, Janice, and Margaret Lewis (eds.) (1999) *The Elgar Companion to Feminist Economics*, Cheltenham: Edward Elgar.

Reimers, Cordelia W. (1985) "Cultural Differences in Labor Force Participation Among Married Women," *American Economic Review, Papers and Proceedings*, 75 (2): 251–255.

Sen, Amartya K. (1990) "Gender and Cooperative Conflict," in Irene Tinker (ed.) *Persistent Inequalities: Women and World Development*, Oxford: Oxford University Press, 123–149.

Sen, Gita and Caren Grown (1987) *Development, Crises, and Alternative Visions: Third World Women's Perspectives*, New York: Monthly Review Press.

Serageldin, Ismail and June Taboroff (eds.) (1994) *Culture and Development in Africa*, Washington, DC: The World Bank.

Strassmann, Diana (1993) "Not a Free Market: The Rhetoric of Disciplinary Authority in Economics," in Marianne Ferber and Julie Nelson (eds.) *Beyond Economic Man: Feminist Theory and Economics*, Chicago: University of Chicago Press, 54–68.

—— (1999) "Feminist Economics," in Janice Peterson and Margaret Lewis (eds.) *The Elgar Companion to Feminist Economics*, Cheltenham: Edward Elgar, 360–373.

Tinker, Irene (ed.) (1990) *Persistent Inequalities: Women and World Development*, Oxford: Oxford University Press.

United Nations Development Program (1995) *The Human Development Report 1995: Gender and Human Development*, New York: Oxford University Press.

Veblen, Thorstein (1894) "The Economic Theory of Woman's Dress," *The Popular Science Monthly*, 46: 198–205.

—— (1899) "The Barbarian Status of Women," *The American Journal of Sociology*, 4 (4): 503–514.

Visvanathan, Nalini, Lynn Duggan, Laurie Nisonoff, and Nan Wiegersma (eds.) (1997) *The Women, Gender and Development Reader*, London: Zed Books.

Waller, William T. (Jr.) (1999) "Institutional Economics, Feminism and Overdetermination," *Journal of Economic Issues*, 33 (4): 835–844.

—— and Ann Jennings (1990) "On the Possibility of a Feminist Economics: The Convergence of Institutional and Feminist Methodology," *Journal of Economic Issues*, 24 (2): 613–622.

Weber, Max (1958 [1930]) *The Protestant Ethic and the Spirit of Capitalism*, New York: Charles Scribner's Sons.

Wolfensohn, James D., Lamberto Dini, Gianfranco Facco Bonetti, Ian Johnson, and J. Martin-Brown (2000) *Culture Counts: Financing, Resources, and the Economics of Culture in Sustainable Development*, Washington, DC: The World Bank.

Wood, Cynthia A. (2003) "Economic Marginalia: Postcolonial Readings of Unpaid Domestic Labor and Development," in Drucilla K. Barker and Edith Kuiper (eds.) *Toward a Feminist Philosophy of Economics*, London: Routledge, 304–320.

Woolley, Frances R. (1993) "The Feminist Challenge to Neoclassical Economics," *Cambridge Journal of Economics*, 17 (4): 485–500.

World Bank (1990) *Women in Development: A Progress Report on the World Bank Initiative*, Washington, DC: World Bank.

—— (1999) *Culture and Sustainable Development: A Framework for Action*, Washington, DC: World Bank.

World Commission on Culture and Development (1995) *Our Creative Diversity*, Paris: UNESCO.

Wyss, Brenda (1999) "Culture and Gender in Household Economies: The Case of Jamaican Child Support Payments," *Feminist Economics*, 5 (2): 1–24.

Zein-Elabdin, Eiman O. (1996) "Development, Gender, and the Environment: Theoretical or Contextual Link? Toward an Institutional Analysis of Gender," *Journal of Economic Issues*, 30 (4): 929–947.

—— (2003) "The Difficulty of a Feminist Economics," in Drucilla K. Barker and Edith Kuiper (eds.), *Toward a Feminist Philosophy of Economics*, London: Routledge, 321–338.

—— (2009) "Economics, Postcolonial Theory, and the Problem of Culture: Institutional Analysis and Hybridity," *Cambridge Journal of Economics*, 33 (6): 1153–1167.

—— and S. Charusheela (eds.) (2004) *Postcolonialism Meets Economics*, London: Routledge.

9 Conclusion

The landscape of 'culture' in Economics is heterogeneous. Economists have spoken about culture in many different ways: as *one thing*—an industry or a constraint, capital, heritage, environment, equilibrium; as a *collection of things*—traits, habits, norms, values, endowments, resources, goods, and tastes; or as a *process* of learning, growth, change, lag, drift, evolution, and 'development.' Different cultures or *types* of cultures have been named: archaic, modern, Western, capitalist, national, collectivist, individualist, corporate, entrepreneurial, and economic. Culture has been described as the realm of meaning, a name for omitted variables, 'a nuisance variable,' and even a 'bubble.' This is a miniscule sample (see Appendix II for more interpretations). Most of these expressions are not clearly defined, and often when definitions are given, it is not clear what authors exactly have in mind, or whether each is speaking of the same thing.

In this book I have not attempted an analysis of culture (as a concept-phenomenon) or the process of economic development, but only offered an account of economic thought about culture, and its relationship to development from the viewpoints of four philosophical spheres—Neoclassical, Marxian, Institutionalist, and Feminist. In this exercise I have used the word culture to refer to broadly, though contestedly, shared, often taken-for-granted everyday sensibilities and practices of a society or a group, which sanction and censor its participants in multiple ways that may not always be coherent, and are never complete. Cultural dynamics and meanings are negotiated, maneuvered, and change in accord with individual idiosyncrasies, social gaps and fissures, and encounters with 'Other' cultural horizons.

In this final chapter I briefly recap and comparatively examine the material presented in the preceding chapters, and elucidate what I tentatively think are the main features of this complex terrain. Before doing so, however, it is essential to reiterate that my general review covers only Economics literature even though I am mindful of the inherent multidisciplinarity of all inquiry and discourse. I have done this only as a necessary first step toward a broader and deeper understanding of the issues.

The current landscape of culture in Economics

In the past four decades, the preoccupation with culture in Economics has expanded from the original Institutionalist tradition of Veblen, Commons, and Mitchell, where it had been largely confined through most of the twentieth century, to the general current of conversation in the discipline, with such new fields as Cultural and Feminist Economics being added to the lexicon of the profession (see Appendix I for a bibliographic history). Today, in the mainstream—that is, the theoretical framework of optimizing individual agency, and its various extensions—analyses of culture span three overlapping research programs: the Preferences Approach, in which culture theoretically resides within individual utility functions; Cultural Economics, which investigates 'the arts' and other components of the 'culture industry,' and grapples with the question of cultural vis-à-vis economic value; and the New Institutional Economics, where culture is theorized as a constraint on individual reason.

Critical branches of Economics have also responded to the culture imperative of the late twentieth century by addressing gaps in their own approaches to culture or by expanding their areas of culture analyses. In Marxism, multiple philosophical critiques and political upheavals in former socialist states brought about substantial "rethinking" and revision. Drawing on well-known interventions by Gramsci and Althusser, many in this tradition have renounced the much-criticized schema of base/superstructure. Instead, processes are now emphasized where fixed categories used to rule. In the postmodernist revision pioneered by Resnick and Wolff (1987), the social world consists of class and nonclass (also non-class) processes. Cultural processes, which refer to the production and distribution of meaning, reside in the nonclass category, and are considered to run "alongside," rather than being derived from, class processes. Meanwhile, the Institutionalist school has always been defined by its commitment to the idea of culture. For Veblen, economic action was so culturally embedded that one could not isolate certain phenomena to be named 'economic.' In his theoretical system, culture embodies both the habits of thought of a group as they are translated into institutions (ceremonial behavior) and the human proclivity to employ technology (instrumental behavior). Cultural change occurs in an evolutionary, path-dependent manner. Contemporary Institutionalists have maintained this vision while adding a few extensions.

The rise of Feminist economic thought has helped elevate the status of culture in the discipline. Feminists are primarily concerned with the role of cultural precepts in shaping economic action and knowledge. They critically draw on Neoclassical, Marxian, and Institutional Economics, as well as other disciplines, to expose the androcentric bias in economic models, methods, and pedagogies (see Ferber and Nelson 2003). However, the emphasis on gender as the central category of analysis has led to a partial treatment of culture. This may have limited the ability of Feminists to generate a bigger impact on the place of culture in the discipline. So far, scholarship on gender or the economic status of women (feminist or otherwise) has been conspicuously missing from general discussions of culture within Economics as represented in some prominent publications. For example, Mark Casson's (1997) edited two-volume set, *Culture, Social Norms, and Economics*, which contains 54 articles on a wide range of issues in economic behavior and performance, features only one gender-related paper—Veblen's

(1894) "Economic Theory of Woman's Dress." Casson's important book has completely by-passed contemporary economic thought on women and gender. A similar pattern is visible in Victor Ginsburgh and David Throsby's (2006) *Handbook of the Economics of Art and Culture.*[1]

The literature reviewed in this book is extremely diverse, and some might bristle at the level of generality with which I have approached it. Nonetheless, taken together, it does permit three tentative observations. First, there are two levels at which culture is discussed in Economics: a *shallow*, or minimal, level, and a *deep*, more thoughtful one. The shallow treatment entails no more than absorbing the concept into established models without much thought, and employing static and unproblematized notions of culture that have been abandoned in Anthropology or transcended by Cultural Studies. The deeper brand of scholarship struggles more earnestly with culture—as a concept, phenomenon, or both—and with how to meaningfully account for it, theoretically and empirically, in economic analysis. This shallow-deep division cuts across all four philosophical spheres examined in the book.

Second, with Economics being a thoroughly modernist discourse, most discussions of cultural problematics are entrenched in *dualistic ontology* that manifests itself in a series of dichotomies. The most foundational is culture/economy, broadly following the old dualism of ideal/material, and, ultimately, rooted in an existential problem of desire/limits (see Chapter 1). In either shallow or deep treatments, the majority of the literature, in different shades and intensities, projects culture as an external entity theoretically separate from what is conceived to be economic phenomena. In the various discussions, cultural dynamics take the form of a single force that exerts either a favorable or detrimental influence, and acts upon 'economy' in a uniform and predictable manner. The existential problem of desire/limits underlies how culture is conceptualized. Thus, debates about culture and development hinge on one of two interpretations: one sees culture as a constraining and limiting factor—barriers and obstacles that prohibit or retard development. The other interpretation perceives culture as an enabling, liberating force, or a catalyst that promotes economic growth.

Third, each of the three major schools of economic thought operates on the basis of a specific *paradigmatic dualism*—an overarching theoretical distinction between two non-negotiable categories—that directs its thinking about social phenomena, including what is perceived to be 'economic' or 'cultural.' Neoclassical theory maintains the preferences/constraints dichotomy, while in postmodern Marxism one finds the class/nonclass division. Institutional economics, though generally critical of "dualistic habits of thought" (Jennings 1999: 142), holds its own theoretical partition between the instrumental and the ceremonial. Let me elaborate on these three observations in turn.

Struggles with culture

Shallow treatment of culture is exhibited sharply in Neoclassical literature where the desire to maintain undisturbed individual agency allows no more than an inconsequential presence of culture. This is unabashedly expressed in the claim that it is not "necessary to modify the standard economic model in order to incorporate culture" (Fernández 2008: 10). Accordingly, 'religion' or 'trust'—approximated by some vaguely defined 'variable,' sometimes opportunistically obtained from aggregate data sources such as the World Values Survey—are simply inserted into an individual agent's decision function as a preference or a constraint. This strategy has been described as "the least ambitious" path to accounting for culture in Economics (Wyss 1999: 2). Whether seen in the Preferences or New Institutionalist literatures, this strategy has often produced very general or trivial conclusions. However, the minimal approach can also be found in heterodox scholarship whenever cultural themes are introduced without careful consideration or conceptual redress. This encompasses Marxian contributions that bracket cultural processes within the nonclass universe, then go on to apply age-old concepts such as surplus labor irrespective of context. Institutionalist writings in which different cultural traditions are routinely conceptualized as ceremonial relics, with no further scrutiny or elaboration, must also be included in this segment of the culture literature in Economics.

Deeper treatments explore culture in more courageous ways, and—regardless of whether they succeed or not—resist the urge to conveniently absorb it into preconceived models without much agonizing. As might be expected, this work typically crosses the borders between established schools of Economics, and borrows insights from other disciplines. Examples include Samuel Bowles' (1998) attempt to take up the issue of preference endogeneity, in which he draws on a wide range of literatures in Anthropology, Biology, and Sociology to conclude that "preference endogeneity gives rise to a kind of market failure" (ibid.: 104). In another example, Brenda Wyss (1999) draws on Postcolonial Studies to investigate the complexity of household approaches to child support in Jamaica. Roger McCain's (2006) effort to develop a consistent defensible approach to cultural and economic value should also be mentioned. Other examples of genuine, thoughtful efforts to articulate or struggle with concepts of culture in relation to economy, or generally deal with cultural problematics include Amariglio *et al.* (1988), Ruttan (1988), Klamer (1991, 1996), Nelson (1992), Jennings and Waller (1994), Kabeer (1994), Chamlee-Wright (1997), Rosenbaum (1999), Throsby (2001), Marini (2004), Sen (2004), Brennan (2006), and Jackson (2009).

The second observation concerns the ontological dualism of culture/economy, which I have argued is ultimately rooted in an existential problem of desire/limits. The culture/economy dualism is apparent in the attempt to find an 'effect' of culture on economic outcomes (e.g., Guiso *et al.* 2006). This assumes pre-existing patterns of behavior or organization, with culture acting upon them from an external location. In the field of Cultural Economics, this dualism takes the form of a perception that profound ontological and methodological differences exist between 'economics' or 'economy,' and 'the arts.' Arjo Klamer (1996: 20) argues the two belong to different "worlds." Economics—at least as it is constructed and practiced today—emphasizes objectivity, realism, and reason; it is ruled by modernism. In contrast, the world of art is characterized by 'non-modernist' values of subjectivity and romanticism. Throsby (2001) expands this view to argue that 'economics' and

'culture' (which, to him, means both creativity and a way of life) are two different "discourses" and "representations of human behavior." Economics reflects an
"individualistic impulse," while culture embodies a "collective" one (ibid.: 158).
The presumed ontological rift between economy and culture allows Throsby to
slide, almost imperceptibly, from a limited comparison between economics and art
to one between economics and culture at large.

Third, each of the three major economic philosophies is grounded in a particular paradigmatic dualism:

Neoclassicism	Preferences/Constraints
Postmodern Marxism	Class/Nonclass
Veblenian Institutionalism	Instrumental/Ceremonial

Each pair does not represent mutually exclusive entities, they are dualisms in the
sense of two poles that define and confine the analytical scope of each philosophy.
The specific role of each pair in the theoretical framework of each school of thought
is different, but they all exist at a deep axiomatic level. As I have argued in Chapter
1, these should not be looked at as mere analytical distinctions because analytical
decisions—most often rooted in ontological convictions—engender epistemological
consequences. I have already discussed the ramifications of Marx's tactical omission of culture (Chapter 6), and Veblen's dichotomy (Chapter 4) for the treatment
of culture in their respective schools of thought. Binary distinctions for analytical
purposes are sometimes necessary. The problem arises when these become deeply
entrenched into a general organizing principle in a way that leaves no theoretical
room for in-betweenness or alterity, and therefore does not allow adequate grasp of
cultural complexity.

Dualistic ontology in Economics is rooted in the existential problem of desire/
limits, namely, a perceived struggle between two aspects of existence—limits and
freedom. The first aspect refers to the problem of being hemmed in by limitations of the human body and the physical world. The second signifies the desire
to escape these limitations, to transcend 'nature' through will and imagination. In
economic thought, experiencing this freedom often conceptually takes the form
of acquiring *more*, of anything. This existential background crops up in economic
representations of culture. Thus, the economic problem is constructed as a contest
between scarce resources and unlimited wants, with culture residing either in the
scarcity, limits side (a constraint) or in the wants and desires side (preferences).
In the Institutionalist narrative, culture embodies both technological capabilities,
which are enabling, and ceremonial patterns of behavior, which are past-binding
and limiting. The postmodern Marxian view is more complicated. Nevertheless,
it is possible to read a parallel where class processes, dealing with surplus value
generation and distribution, signify material tangible (limiting) factors; whereas
cultural processes, located in the nonclass universe, define and regulate the realm
of meaning, the ideal, hence, more liberatory dimensions of existence.

The relatively young field of Feminist economics illustrates the depth of dualistic ontology in the discipline. Feminists have criticized methodological and

cultural dualisms. However, this critique has been mostly confined to those such as market/household and public/private that carry obvious gender associations. Insightful analyses took as a given the dichotomy between 'developed' and 'under' or 'less' developed countries, instead of recognizing it as a proper cultural dualism, with important policy implications for many women worldwide. Feminists simply mapped the global divide of developed/under(less)developed over the pre-existing binarism of male/female (Zein-Elabdin 2003). This rejection of the social devaluation of women, but inability to theoretically connect it to and systematically challenge the parallel devaluation of 'other' (subaltern) cultures constitutes what I have called the *Mill syndrome* (see Chapters 2 and 8). To the extent of their commitment to one or more of the three major economic philosophies discussed in this book, Feminist analyses have embodied these philosophies' dualistic modes of thought and cultural precepts of modernism. Confronting the limitations of these commitments remains an unfinished task for Feminist economics.

I am not suggesting that there is no validity to the three economic schools or their analytical strategies. Distinction between pairs of categories is not problematic *ipso facto*. It is an issue when these dichotomies restrict perceptions to a binary structure that is less capable of accommodating more complex phenomena. This is particularly important in the context of comparative analyses across cultures. The development discourse, in which dualism is replicated in many forms, illustrates the extent of the issue.

The question of development

Since the mid-twentieth century economic development has been predominantly understood as "wide and deep improvements in welfare for the masses of the population" (Higgins 1977: 98) to approach the levels of income and 'way of life' associated with affluent North Atlantic societies. Development constitutes the twentieth century's most important political mandate. Notwithstanding difficulties, failures and criticisms, the immense infrastructure of international development policy—most visibly enshrined in the World Bank—remains firmly in place, with the continuous addition of new initiatives and imperatives. In the preceding chapters I have discussed development thought in each of the four philosophical spheres examined in this book, with more review of Neoclassical development literature because of its greater economic and political influence. In the following paragraphs, I recap the general features of the development discourse, dwelling particularly on the currently fashionable culture and development (CAD) literature, which encompasses several overlapping strands: the New Institutional economics, the human development and capabilities approach, and East Asia discussions.[2]

Development economics (DE) began with general *hospitality* to the idea that a society's shared values and habits exert significant influence on individual behavior and, therefore, macroeconomic growth. However, the panoply of cultural values and habits found in low-income countries was thought to present an obstacle to economic development. This was a consensus among different schools of economics. Despite major philosophical differences, Neoclassical, Marxian, and Institutional economists converged on this general view of the development problem. Disagreements between them lay in the nature of the obstacle: lack of an economizing attitude (Lewis 1955), persistence of pre-capitalist modes of production (Baran 1973), or the prevalence of obsolete institutions and ceremonialism (Myrdal 1968). In the words of James Street (1967: 61), "[i]t is the culture that must be updated." Development has been a project of cultural erasure (see Zein-Elabdin 2004) from the beginning.

Since the late 1980s, Neoclassical development thought has taken two different stances with respect to culture. The first, represented by the New Development Economics, asserts that the only requirement for understanding the process of development is superior modeling techniques; there is no need to entertain cultural 'peculiarities' (Lucas 1988) or 'influences' (Krugman 1995). I described this as a *retreat* from culture. At the same time, a second stance emerged in writings that *return* to the idea that cultural 'variables' could help explain different patterns of economic growth. This is the CAD position, largely driven by the eagerness to account for the success of several East Asian economies. CAD's main departure from the early hospitable stance is that culture is no longer considered an obstacle. On the contrary, in the case of East Asia, culture—represented as 'Confucian values' (e.g., Gray 1996, Park 1997) or some such—is seen to have a largely positive influence on economic performance. CAD writers have been busy trying to quantitatively measure the economic 'effects' of culture.

Throughout this journey, from hospitality to return, DE has embodied the broad patterns of economic approaches to culture outlined in the previous section. First, there are both shallow and thoughtful discussions (e.g., Lian and Oneal 1997 vs. Kovács 2006). Second, analyses tend to be dualistic because of adherence to the theoretical split between economy and culture. This is found in both old (e.g., Hoselitz 1952) and current writings (e.g., Marini 2004). Third, discussions of development embody the three paradigmatic dualisms of economic thought. For example, in New Institutionalist discussions, culture—whether materializing in taboos or property rights regimes—is theorized as a constraint on individual maximizing impulses (e.g., North 1995). The existential problem of desire/limits is revealed in that cultural habits and rituals are constructed either as a facilitator, a force that could be harnessed to propel or accelerate economic development, or an obstacle that puts a curb on it.

Going further, the development discourse adds another set of dualisms, borrowed mostly from mid-twentieth-century Anthropology. In this book I have highlighted four:

Modern	Traditional
Individualist	Collective(Collectivist)
Developed	Under(less)developed
Universal	Particular

Chapter 7 explained the hierarchical, mutually reinforcing character of these four dualisms. What I would like to emphasize here is their persistence in CAD discourse. In early development texts, the most visible of these dualisms was the modern/traditional divide, explicitly adopted in classic "dualistic" development models (e.g., Lewis 1954). The distinction between so-called 'individualist' and 'collectivist' societies or cultures was also common then (e.g., Fei and Ranis 1969). It survives in CAD writings where some societies are thought to hold collectivist beliefs and modes of organization, which constitutes a major cause of their underdevelopment (see Greif, 1994, for this type of argument). The rapid growth of some East Asian economies has complicated this argument. Accordingly, some have argued that individualism may not be the universal source of superior economic performance it was thought to be (Gray 1996). Regardless of what one thinks of these two views about the significance of individualism vs. collectivism to economic performance, both perceive a fundamental opposition between two types of cultures that are often mapped geographically as West and East, a perception that carries a distinct flavor of orientalism.

The perceived division between universal transcendent truths, on one side, and particular, relative, or culturally specific practices, on the other, underlies human-ities and social science thinking generally. In DE, this division has been most palpable. The universal is identified with economic logic and modern European beliefs and ideals about such things as freedom or progress, and the particular with those of 'other' societies thought to be traditional, collectivist, and generally limited in physical and imaginative space. This division has been present within the field from Rostow (1971 [1960]) to Marini (2004). The human development and capabilities approach has not engaged in crude dualistic representations, but it is firmly grounded in a universalist perspective that struggles with how to accom-modate cultural difference. This struggle is discernible in Amartya Sen's writings (1998, 1999). From a different angle, Feminist economic authors also struggle with this tension; in this case, between a universalist agenda to end women's sub-ordination, and a wish to honor the global diversity of cultures. As Wendy Harcourt (1995:131) expressed it, development policy needs to avoid both "Western bias" and "unprincipled forms of cultural relativism." The issue, of course, lies in what exactly is thought to belong in each category. But, beyond that, the representation of the matter as an unavoidable 'choice' between two positions is another example of a limiting dualistic perception.

Overall, despite a genuine desire for understanding, with some interesting dis-cussions and occasional insights, much of the current discourse on culture and development is taking place at a shallow level. Many contributions present no more than simplified versions of Weber's (1958 [1930]) assessment of the role of religion in the rise of capitalism, and show little recognition that economic devel-opment is ultimately a philosophical, cultural question of ontology and purpose.[3] The predominant vision of development is part of a total interpretation of history and meaning, rooted in the historical context of European modernity. As such, development may be examined and critiqued as both a 'way of life' and a historical experience that has generated complex ecological and social impacts, and as a discourse, a normative construction that has devalued and alienated many cultures worldwide. The first critique is cultural in that a certain way of life engenders certain outcomes. The second is cross-cultural, that is, the perception that 'Other' ways of living are 'under' or 'less' developed has authorized the cultural hegemony of the twentieth-century international development mandate. Culture—whether interpreted as a certain way of living (e.g., industrial modernity), cultivation and elevation of being (distance from 'nature'), or as ideas, learning, and creativity—is at the heart of this twofold problematic of development. Most current exchanges about culture and development do not get to this more philosophical depth. In this sense, they may be considered shallow.

Future directions

The task of imagining something outside the dualistic framework of culture/economy is daunting. The most I can do in these final pages is pose some questions. In doing so, I return to the two themes introduced in Chapter 1: how is culture interpreted in Economics? and how are subaltern cultures perceived and represented? These two questions elicit larger inquiries: How are ideas embodied in modes of provisioning, which then become rooted in habits and institutions? How are cognitive and practical relationships with different aspects of life—such as community, conflict, consumption, corruption, wealth, and well being—translated and stylized into economic ideas? How do the peculiar vocabularies of Economics—scarcity, agent, choice, altruism, labor, class, exploitation, instrumental valuing, and waste, among others—take on different meanings across different cultures?

If culture is understood as a historical social frame of reference that imperfectly authorizes and or censors different sensibilities and lifeways, including economic ones, how could one speak of a relationship between culture *and* economy? Could there be a theoretical *third space* (Bhabha 1994; Gibson-Graham 1996) of *culture-economy*—an organic, not hierarchical, whole that ties together the meaning and the tangibility of action (see Zein-Elabdin 2011)?[4] How might an undoing of dualisms modify our framing and understanding of these and related questions? These types of questions have occupied anthropologists and other students of society, including many economists, for a long time. What new insights could come from those who study economies? And, what does all this mean for the discipline of Economics?

The issues raised in this book point in at least two future directions. The first is the need for a broad conversation among economists that struggles with the concept of culture and cultural problematics generally. Among other things, charting this complex terrain requires more in-depth scrutiny of the paradigmatic dualisms at the heart of each major economic tradition, and dualistic ontology in general. Many economists now profess that 'culture matters,' but, as others have pointed out (DiMaggio 1994; Sen 2004), this in itself means little. The question is how? Over many years, colleagues of different philosophical complexions have challenged the analytical separation and hierarchy between economy and culture, and dualistic thinking at large: Dixon (1970), Amariglio *et al.* (1988, 1996), Jennings (1993, 1999), Latouche (1993), Harcourt (1994), Kabeer (1994), Jackson (1999), Throsby (2001), Fine (2002), and Maseland (2008), to name some. They constitute a nucleus of common interest that could initiate a research project on culture-economy, which might succeed in giving form to what is typically omitted in current discussions and debates.

To be sure, it is naïve to think that economists would converge on such a project regardless of ideological and political commitments, or that this effort could move easily through the different modes of thought, methods, and discursive traditions. Nonetheless, the endeavor itself should be worthwhile. Nor do I believe that this type of rethinking could be successfully accomplished solely within the borders of Economics. The increasing interest in culture among economists has brought with it an unprecedented level of openness to interdisciplinary learning, exchange, and collaboration. My hope is that the map of culture discourses presented in this book would move more colleagues in other disciplines to engage in further conversations with those professionally dedicated to the study of economic phenomena.

The desired outcome of this broad conversation is not necessarily a unified concept of culture. Simply more clarity about current economic-cultural transformations, and about the many usages of the culture concept in relation to them, should be an improvement. Does culture simply signify the world of consumption? Is it a metaphor for freedom and desire, on one hand, and limits. on the other? Is it a word for difference? Inferiority? Or even race? Is it a convenient catch term for anything that might expedite more capitalist expansion worldwide—Confucian values or Akan religion? To what extent is the culture and development discourse implicated in reshaping current global and regional economic and political relations in East Asia, Africa, as well as Europe? The emerging literature on the development implications of different European cultures, North vs. South (Tabellini 2005) or East (Kovács 2006), is interesting, to say the least. Might there be a coextensive process of transformation in the meaning and role of 'culture,' and in social practices and institutions similar to that which Williams (1961) noticed over 50 years ago? (See Chapter 1 in this book.)

The second direction for future research, beside general exploration of the space of culture-economy, is to develop a concept of *economic hybridity* as a more complex framework that goes beyond the predominant dualistic representations of contemporary economies. As I have argued in this book, the binary apprehensions of reality derived from dualistic ontology do not allow adequate recognition and analysis of cultural complexity, as they leave no theoretical room for melding or alterity. Instead, they end up reducing tangled reality to the stale dichotomies of market/state, formal/informal, modern/traditional, and individual/collective, among many others. Any meaningful reflection on dualism, especially as it is displayed in the economic versus the cultural, and the developed against the under(less)developed, leads to a consideration of some idea of hybridity.

As suggested elsewhere (Zein-Elabdin 2009), an economic hybrid reflects a fusion of ideas, values, institutional set-ups, and practical uses that have emerged as a result of deep cultural mixing over time. The majority of economic action today takes place in *hybrid spaces*, that is, the intersections of multiple currents of cultural interaction whether at the level of very small local communities, or at a massive trans-continental scale. One might think of contemporary economies in Africa where processes of social provisioning and wealth accumulation embody a continuum of such currents, and thereby fuse different technologies, patterns of thinking, behaviors, and channels of interaction and organization. Colonialism, development programs, voluntary and forced migration, and dislocation, in addition to the continuous course of trade and travel, are all catalysts of hybridization, which takes place on at least four overlapping levels: structures, relations, sensibilities, and modes of expression. This is evident whether in business strategies or the character of political regimes. In the context of one country, like Tanzania, one finds the remains of a centrally planned national economy, active IMF financial stabilization programs, layered over villages, in which subsistence and market relations are imbricated with self-seeking and deep, unconditional social obligation. A well-defined concept of hybridity might offer a non-binary, and more accurately descriptive understanding of this feature of economic postcoloniality.[5] It might well capture that third space of culture-economy.

I will not try to give an extended explanation of this research direction here but only motivate it. As a phenomenon, economic hybridity is not new. Hybrid forms in actual economies were recognized in early development thought across the ideological spectrum. Indeed, dualism in development models represented an attempt to articulate a reality in which—as A. Hirschman (1958: 126) put it— "both airplane and mule" existed side by side. However, because they only thought in terms of the modern/traditional dichotomy, economists saw all unfamiliar patterns as a transient state rather than part of a contemporary coeval economy. Dualistic ontology prohibited an understanding of these economies and socialities as anything other than a prelude to a more 'real' system whether this is capitalism, socialism, or a 'formal' economy.

Current economic literature contains *de facto* as well as explicit references to hybrid spaces. Although the references are opaque and sporadic, they can be easily spotted in the language of 'transition economies,' 'market socialism,' or 'Confucian capitalism.' The premises of some of these characterizations are problematic, but the phenomena they describe indicate economic alloys of one kind or another. The word 'hybrid' is already in use. It has been suggested to describe institutional settings other than markets and hierarchies (Williamson 1996); the inter-weaving of incongruent modes of behavior in some households' approach to child support (Wyss 1999); and the combination of gift exchange, market transactions, and hierarchical structures in some African economies (Fafchamps 2004). Some of these phenomena are being discussed in the context of globalization. However, much of the globalization discourse rests on the theoretical foundation I have attempted to problematize in this book. A fresh, more systematic effort to understand and theorize contemporary hybrid spaces is needed.

Hybrid phenomena are the (as yet theoretically inaccessible) outcomes of appropriation, re-appropriation, synthesis, and implementation of economic theories, policies, and projects within different cultural contexts. Therefore, they problematize all dualistic representations (including, Western/non-Western) and the presumption of a predictable future path. Of course, the word 'hybrid' itself is flawed, in part because historically it has carried connotations of impurity and deformity (see Young 1995). I rely on it here as a working term, perhaps others will fashion a new, more descriptively capable term. In previous work (2009), I made a preliminary case for a concept of economic hybridity based on my tentative observation of contemporary economies in Africa and other postcolonial societies. It was an empirically inspired argument. In the course of writing this book, I have found that a strong epistemological case for it could also be made.

Endnote

This book leaves a great deal to be examined and contemplated in more depth. I hope my panoramic method—looking very broadly with minimal scrutiny of specific arguments, theories, and concepts—has not gotten in the way of presenting a useful general survey of culture in Economics, particularly in relation to the question of economic development. I hope this text is seen as a tentative account, a first trial at mapping the landscape of culture and development in Economics that highlights some commonalities between disparate philosophical traditions. I further hope the comparisons and connections will not be perceived as a case of false equivalence, lumping together things that do not belong together.

I have attempted to broach the issue of paradigmatic dualism, that is, when the entire philosophical structure of a school of thought is erected upon one binary theoretical framework that structures, defines, and binds it to a way of understanding the social world. The risk in this type of exercise is that the critique often ends up reinforcing the problem—in this case, dualistic ontology. It may well be that a dualistic mode of thought is insurmountable because dualism is one of the few cognitive representations we are capable of. I have not attempted to struggle with this question here, but only give an idea of the presence of dualistic thinking at a deep axiomatic level across the bulk of economic discourse.

In Chapter 1, I suggested that the idea of 'culture' is perhaps forever mired in archaic humanism and may have to be discarded, together with 'development.' A research project on 'culture-economy' across the different philosophical spheres of economic thought might go some distance toward answering the question of what to do about Economics.

Notes

1 Topics covered in Casson's book include preferences, altruism, status, cooperation, social order, and the law. Ginsburgh and Throsby's volume contains 37 chapters, ranging in subject area from consumption, production, and labor markets, to history, value, culture, and the economy. The omission of gender is telling since Ginsburgh and Throsby adopt a broader, anthropological meaning of culture rather than confine their scope to art and other products and occupations of creativity.
2 My observations do not equally apply to all three. See Chapter 5 for the New Institutionalism, and Chapter 7 for the other two literatures. See Appendix III for a chronological profile of development economics literature.
3 I have discussed some of the philosophical premises of the notion of economic development elsewhere (Zein-Elabdin 1998, 2001). J.B. Bury (1932) traces the roots of the idea of progress from the Greco-Roman tradition and early Christianity, to Enlightenment and post-Enlightenment philosophy. Also see Nisbet (1969) on the

intellectual roots of development. He covers the same ground as Bury, but with an added attention to economic literature.

4 Homi Bhabha described a Third Space (1994: 36) in the way culture is constituted and inflected over time, a space in the production of meaning that challenges dualistic—especially idealist/materialist—and static conceptions. It is not crucial to delve into the particulars of his usage of this expression in order to appreciate its potential. The mere idea of a 'third' space permits the imagination of something different and non-binary. Gibson-Graham (1996: 90) used the expression third space in reference to economic, but not necessarily capitalist, practices. This is a narrower usage than what I have in mind here.

5 See Zein-Elabdin and Charusheela (2004, Introduction) for an elaboration of a postcolonial economic perspective and analytical method.

References

Amariglio, Jack L., Antonio Callari, Stephen Resnick, David Ruccio, and Richard Wolff (1996) "Nondeterminist Marxism: The Birth of a Postmodern Tradition in Economics," in Fred Foldvary (ed.) *Beyond Neoclassical Economics: Heterodox Approaches to Economic Theory*, Cheltenham: Edward Elgar, 134–147.

——,Stephen A. Resnick, and Richard D. Wolff (1988) "Class, Power, and Culture," in Cary Nelson and Lawrence Grossberg (eds.) *Marxism and the Interpretation of Culture*, Urbana-Champaign, IL: University of Illinois Press, 487–501.

Baran, Paul A. (1973 [1957]) *The Political Economy of Growth*, Harmondsworth: Penguin Books.

Bhabha, Homi K. (1994) *The Location of Culture*, London: Routledge.

Bowles, Samuel (1998) "Endogenous Preferences: The Cultural Consequences of Markets and Other Economic Institutions," *Journal of Economic Literature*, 36 (1): 75–111.

Brennan, David M. (2006) "Defending the Indefensible? Culture's Role in the Productive/Unproductive Dichotomy," *Feminist Economics*, 12 (3): 403–425.

Bury, J.B. (1932) *The Idea of Progress: An Inquiry into its Origin and Growth*, New York: The Macmillan Company.

Casson, Mark (ed.) (1997) *Culture, Social Norms, and Economics*, vols. I, II, Cheltenham: Edward Elgar.

Chamlee-Wright, Emily (1997) *The Cultural Foundations of Economic Development: Urban Female Entrepreneurship in Ghana*, London: Routledge.

DiMaggio, Paul (1994) "Culture and Economy," in Neil J. Smelser and Richard Swedberg (eds.) *The Handbook of Economic Sociology*, Princeton, NJ: Princeton University Press, 27–57.

Dixon, Vernon, J. (1970) "The Di-Unital Approach to 'Black Economics,'" *American Economic Review, Papers and Proceedings*, 60 (2): 424–429.

Fafchamps, Marcel (2004) *Market Institutions in Sub-Saharan Africa: Theory and Evidence*, Cambridge, MA: MIT Press.

Fei, John C.H. and Gustav Ranis (1969) "Economic Development in Historical Perspective," *American Economic Review, Papers and* Proceedings, 59 (2): 386–400.

Ferber, Marianne A. and Julie A. Nelson (eds.) (2003) *Feminist Economics Today: Beyond Economic Man*, Chicago: University of Chicago Press.

Fernández, Raquel (2008) "Culture and Economics," in Steven N. Durlauf and Lawrence E. Blume (eds.) *The New Palgrave Dictionary of Economics Online*, Palgrave Macmillan., 2nd edition. Available at: www.dictionaryofeconomics.com/article?id=pde2008_E000282, doi:10.1057/9780230226203.0346.

Fine, Ben (2002) *The World of Consumption: The Material and Cultural Revisited*, London: Routledge.

Gibson-Graham, J. K. (1996) "How Do We Get Out of This Capitalist Place?" in *The End of Capitalism (As We Knew It): A Feminist Critique of Political Economy*, Minneapolis, MN: University of Minnesota Press, 72–91.

Ginsburgh, Victor A. and David Throsby (eds.) (2006) *Handbook of the Economics of Art and Culture*, Amsterdam: Elsevier North-Holland.

Gray, H. Peter (1996) "Culture and Economic Performance: Policy as an Intervening Variable," *Journal of Comparative Economics*, 23 (3): 278–291.

Greif, Avner (1994) "Cultural Beliefs and the Organization of Society: A Historical and Theoretical Reflection on Collectivist and Individualist Societies," *Journal of Political Economy*, 102 (5): 912–950.

Guiso, Luigi, Paola Sapienza, and Luigi Zingales (2006) "Does Culture Affect Economic Outcomes?" *Journal of Economic Perspectives*, 20 (2): 23–48.

Harcourt, Wendy (ed.) (1994) *Feminist Perspectives on Sustainable Development*, London: Zed Books.

—— (1995) "Gender and Culture," in *Our Creative Diversity*, The World Commission on Culture and Development Report, Paris: UNESCO, 129–149.

Higgins, Benjamin H. (1977) "Economic Development and Cultural Change: Seamless Web or Patchwork Quilt?" in Manning Nash (ed.) *Essays on Economic Development and Cultural Change, in Honor of Bert F. Hoselitz*, Chicago: University of Chicago Press, 99–120.

Hirschman, Albert O. (1958) *The Strategy of Economic Development*, New Haven, CT: Yale University Press.

Hoselitz, Bert F. (1952) "Non-Economic Barriers to Economic Development," *Economic Development and Cultural Change*, 1 (1): 8–21.

Jackson, William A. (1999) "Dualism, Duality and the Complexity of Economic Institutions," *International Journal of Social Economics*, 26 (4): 545–558.

—— (2009) *Economics, Culture and Social Theory*, Cheltenham: Edward Elgar.

Jennings, Ann L. (1993) "Public or Private? Institutional Economics and Feminism," in Marianne A. Ferber and Julie A. Nelson (eds.) *Beyond Economic Man: Feminist Theory and Economics*, Chicago: University of Chicago Press, 111–129.

—— (1999) "Dualisms," in Janice Peterson and Margaret Lewis (eds.) *The Elgar Companion to Feminist Economics*, Cheltenham: Edward Elgar, 142–153.

—— and William Waller (1994) "Evolutionary Economics and Cultural Hermeneutics: Veblen, Cultural Relativism, and Blind Drift," *Journal of Economic Issues*, 28 (4): 997–1030.

Kabeer, Naila (1994) *Reversed Realities: Gender Hierarchies in Development Thought*, London: Verso.

Klamer, Arjo (1991) "Towards the Native's Point of View: The Difficulty of Changing the Conversation," in Don Lavoie (ed.), *Economics and Hermeneutics*, London: Routledge, 19–33.

—— (ed.) (1996) *The Value of Culture: On the Relationship between Economics and Arts*, Amsterdam: Amsterdam University Press.

Kovács, János Mátyás (2006) "Which Past Matters? Culture and Economic Development in Eastern Europe After 1989," in Lawrence E. Harrison and Peter L. Berger (eds.) *Developing Cultures: Case Studies*, London: Routledge, 329–347.

Krugman, Paul (1995) *Development, Geography, and Economic Theory*, Cambridge, MA: MIT Press.

Latouche, Serge (1993) *In the Wake of the Affluent Society: An Exploration of Post-Development*, London: Zed Books.

Lewis, W. Arthur (1954) "Economic Development with Unlimited Supplies of Labour," *Manchester School*, (22): 139–191.

—— (1955) *The Theory of Economic Growth*, London: George Allen and Unwin.

Lian, Brad and John R. Oneal (1997) "Cultural Diversity and Economic Development: A Cross-National Study of 98 Countries, 1960–1985," *Economic Development and Cultural Change*, 46 (1): 61–77.

Lucas, Robert E. Jr. (1988) "On the Mechanics of Economic Development," *Journal of Monetary Economics*, 22: 3–42.

Marini, Matteo (2004) "Cultural Evolution and Economic Growth: A Theoretical Hypothesis with some Empirical Evidence," *The Journal of Socio-Economics*, 33: 765–784.

Maseland, Robbert (2008) "Taking Economics to Bed: About the Pitfalls and Possibilities of Cultural Economics," in Wolfram Elsner and Hardy Hanappi (eds.) *Varieties of Capitalism and New Institutional Deals: Regulation, Welfare and the New Economy*, Cheltenham: Edward Elgar, 299–321.

McCain, Roger (2006) "Defining Cultural and Artistic Goods," in Victor Ginsburgh and David Throsby (eds.) *The Handbook of the Economics of Art and Culture*, vol. 1, Amsterdam: Elsevier North-Holland, 148–167.

Myrdal, Gunnar (1968) *Asian Drama: An Inquiry into the Poverty of Nations*, vols. I, II. New York: Pantheon.

Nelson, Julie A. (1992) "Gender, Metaphor, and the Definition of Economics," *Economics and Philosophy*, 8 (1): 103–125.

Nisbet, Robert A. (1969) *Social Change and History: Aspects of the Western Theory of Development*, London: Oxford University Press.

North, Douglass C. (1995) "The New Institutional Economics and Third World Development," in John Harriss, Janet Hunter, and Colin M. Lewis (eds.) *The New Institutional Economics and Third World Development*, London: Routledge, 17–26.

Park, Tae-Kyu (1997) "Confucian Values and Contemporary Economic Development in Korea," in Timothy Brook and Hy V. Luong (eds.) *Culture and Economy: The Shaping of Capitalism in Eastern Asia*, Ann Arbor, MI: Michigan University Press, 125–136.

Resnick, Stephen A. and Richard D. Wolff (1987) *Knowledge and Class: A Marxian Critique of Political Economy*, Chicago: University of Chicago Press.

Rosenbaum, Eckehard F. (1999) "Against Naïve Materialism: Culture, Consumption and the Causes of Inequality," *Cambridge Journal of Economics*, 23 (3): 317–336.

Rostow, W. W. (1971 [1960]) *The Stages of Economic Growth: A Non-Communist Manifesto*, Cambridge: Cambridge University Press.

Ruttan, Vernon W. (1988) "Cultural Endowments and Economic Development: What Can We Learn from Anthropology?" *Economic Development and Cultural Change*, 36 (3) Supplement: 247–271.

Sen, Amartya K. (1998) "Culture, Freedom and Independence," *World Culture Report 1998*, Paris: UNESCO, 317–321.

—— (1999) *Development As Freedom*, New York: Alfred Knopf.

—— (2004) "How Does Culture Matter?" in Vijayendra Rao and Michael Walton (eds.) *Culture and Public Action*, Stanford, CA: Stanford University Press, 37–58.

Street, James H. (1967) "The Latin American 'Structuralists' and the Institutionalists: Convergence in Development Theory," *Journal of Economic Issues*, 1 (1): 44–64.

Tabellini, Guido (2005) "Culture and Institutions: Economic Development in the Regions of Europe," CESifo Working Paper No. 1492.

Throsby, David (2001) *Economics and Culture*, Cambridge: Cambridge University Press.

Veblen, Thorstein (1894) "The Economic Theory of Woman's Dress," *The Popular Science Monthly*, 46, 198–205.

Weber, Max (1958 [1930]) *The Protestant Ethic and the Spirit of Capitalism*, New York: Charles Scribner's Sons.

Williams, Raymond (1961) *Culture and Society, 1780–1950*, London: Penguin Books.

Williamson, E. Oliver (1996) *The Mechanisms of Governance*, New York: Oxford University Press.

Wyss, Brenda (1999) "Culture and Gender in Household Economies: The Case of Jamaican Child Support Payments," *Feminist Economics*, 5 (2): 1–24.

Young, Robert (1995) *Colonial Desire: Hybridity in Theory, Culture and Race*, London: Routledge.

Zein-Elabdin, Eiman O. (1998) "The Question of Development in Africa: A Conversation for Propitious Change," *African Philosophy*, 11 (2): 113–125.

—— (2001) "Contours of a Non-Modernist Discourse: The Contested Space of History and Development," *Review of Radical Political Economics*, 33 (3): 255–263.

—— (2003) "The Difficulty of a Feminist Economics," in Drucilla K. Barker and Edith Kuiper (eds.), *Toward a Feminist Philosophy of Economics*, London: Routledge. 321–338.

—— (2004) "Articulating the Postcolonial (with Economics in Mind)," in E. Zein-Elabdin and S. Charusheela (eds.) *Postcolonialism Meets Economics*, London: Routledge, 21–39.

—— (2009) "Economics, Postcolonial Theory, and the Problem of Culture: Institutional Analysis and Hybridity," *Cambridge Journal of Economics*, 33 (6): 1153–1167.

—— (2011) "Postcolonial Theory and Economics: Orthodox and Heterodox," in Jane Pollard, Cheryl McEwan, and Alex Hughes (eds.) *Postcolonial Economies*, London: Zed Books, 37–61.

—— and S. Charusheela (eds.) (2004) *Postcolonialism Meets Economics*, London: Routledge.

Appendix I Culture in Economics
A chronology

This is a list of published works containing the words 'culture' or 'cultural' in the title.

Prior to 1970

Ayres, Clarence E. (1962) *The Theory of Economic Progress: A Study of the Fundamentals of Economic Development and Cultural Change*, New York: Schocken Books.

Dixon, Russell A. (1941) *Economic Institutions and Cultural Change*, New York: McGraw-Hill.

Glade, W.P. (1952) "The Theory of Cultural Lag and the Veblenian Contribution," *American Journal of Economics and Sociology*, 11 (4): 427–437.

Hamilton, David (1957) "The Entrepreneur as a Cultural Hero," *Southwestern Social Science Quarterly*, 38 (3): 248–256.

—— (1962) "Drawing the Poverty Line at a Cultural Subsistence Level," *Southwestern Social Science Quarterly*, 42 (March): 337–345.

Kapp, K. William (1963) *Hindu Culture, Economic Development and Economic Planning in India*, Bombay: Asia Publishing House.

Watkins, Myron W. (1958) "Veblen's View of Cultural Evolution," in Douglas Dowd (ed.) *Thorstein Veblen: A Critical Reappraisal, Lectures and Essays Commemorating the Hundredth Anniversary of Veblen's Birth*, Ithaca, NY: Cornell University Press.

1970–1979

Boulding, Kenneth E. (1970) "Increasing the Supply of Black Economists: Is Economics Culture-Bound?" *American Economic Review*, 60 (2): S406–S411.

—— (1973) "Toward the Development of a Cultural Economics," in Louis Schneider and Charles Bonjean (eds.) *The Idea of Culture in the Social Sciences*, Cambridge, MA: Cambridge University Press.

—— (1977) "Notes on Goods, Services, and Cultural Economics," *Journal of Cultural Economics*, 1 (1): 1–12.

Higgins, Benjamin (1977) "Economic Development and Cultural Change: Seamless Web or Patchwork Quilt?" in Manning Nash (ed.) *Essays on Economic Development and Cultural Change, in Honor of Bert F. Hoselitz*, Chicago: University of Chicago Press.

Peacock, A.T. and G. Godfrey (1973) "Cultural Accounting," *Social Trends*, November: 61–65.

Strassmann, W. Paul (1974) "Technology: A Culture Trait, a Logical Category, or Virtue Itself?" *Journal of Economic Issues*, 8 (4): 671–687.

Vaughn, Roger J. (1977) "The Use of Subsidies in the Production of Cultural Services," *Journal of Cultural Economics*, 1 (1): 82–92.

1980–1989

Adams, John (1986) "Peasant Rationality: Individuals, Groups, Cultures," *World Development*, 14 (2): 273–282.

Alverson, Hoyt (1986) "Culture and Economy: Games That 'Play People,'" *Journal of Economic Issues*, 20 (3): 661–679.

Amariglio, J., S. Resnick, and R. Wolff (1988) "Class, Power, and Culture," in Cary Nelson and Lawrence Grossberg (eds.) *Marxism and the Interpretation of Culture*, Urbana-Champaign, IL: University of Illinois Press.

Benton, Raymond (1982) "Economics as a Cultural System," *Journal of Economic Issues*, 26 (2): 461–469.

Darity, William Jr. and Rhonda Williams (1985) "Peddlers Forever? Culture, Competition, and Discrimination," *American Economic Review*, 75 (2): 256–261.

Gapinski, James H. (1980) "The Production of Culture," *Review of Economics and Statistics*, 62 (4): 578–586.

Heap, S. and P. Hargreaves (1986) "Risk and Culture: A Missing Link in the Post Keynesian Tradition," *Journal of Post Keynesian Economics*, 9 (2): 267–279.

Hendon, William S. and James L. Shanahan (eds.) (1983) *Economics of Cultural Decisions*, Cambridge, MA: Abt Books.

Hendon, Williams, V. Shaw, and Nancy Grant (eds.) (1984) *The Economics of Cultural Industries*, Akron, OH: Association for Cultural Economics.

Hill, Lewis (1989) "Cultural Determinism or Emergent Evolution: An Analysis of the Controversy Between Clarence Ayres and David Miller," *Journal of Economic Issues*, 23 (2): 465–471.

Kolm, Serge Christophe (1985) "Must One Be Buddhist to Grow? An Analysis of the Cultural Basis of Japanese Productivity," in Peter Koslowski (ed.) *Economics and Philosophy*, (Series Civitas Resultate), Tübingen: Mohr Siebeck.

Mayhew, Anne (1980) "Atomistic and Cultural Analyses in Economic Anthropology: An Old Argument Repeated," in John Adams (ed.) *Institutional Economics Contributions to the Development of Holistic Economics: Essays in Honor of Allan Gruchy*, Boston: Martinus Nijhoff Publishing.

—— (1987) "Culture: Core Concept Under Attack," *Journal of Economic Issues*, 21 (2): 587–603.

Reimers, Cordelia (1985) "Cultural Differences in Labor Force Participation Among Married Women," *American Economic Review*, 75 (2): 251–255.

Ridley, F.F. (1983) "Cultural Economics and the Culture of Economists," *Journal of Cultural Economics*, 7 (1): 1–18.

Ruttan, Vernon W. (1988) "Cultural Endowments and Economic Development: What Can We Learn from Anthropology?" *Economic Development and Cultural Change*, 36 (3) Supplement: 247–271.

Schaniel, William (1988) "New Technology and Culture Change in Traditional Societies," *Journal of Economic Issues*, 22 (2): 493–498.

Scitovsky, T. (1989) "Culture Is a Good Thing: A Welfare Economic Judgment," *Journal of Cultural Economics*, 3 (1): 1–16.

Shaw, D.; William Hendon; and Virginia Owen (eds.) (1988) *Cultural Economics 88: An American Perspective*, Akron, OH: Association for Cultural Economics.

Throsby, D. and Glenn Withers (1985) "What Price Culture?" *Journal of Cultural Economics*, 9 (2): 1–34.

Vanberg, Viktor (1986) "Spontaneous Market Order and Social Rules: A Critical Examination of F.A. Hayek's Theory of Cultural Evolution," *Economics and Philosophy*, 2 (1): 75–100.

Waller, William T. (1987) "Ceremonial Encapsulation and Corporate Cultural Hegemony," *Journal of Economic Issues*, 21 (1): 321–328.

Wildavsky, Aaron (1985) "A Cultural Theory of Expenditure Growth and (Un)Balanced Budgets," *Journal of Public Economics*, 28 (3): 349–357.

Withers, Glenn (1983) "The Cultural Influence of Public Television," in J. Shanahan, W. Hendon, I. Hilhorst, and J. Van Straalen (eds.) *Markets for the Arts*, Akron, OH: Association for Cultural Economics.

1990–1999

Acheson, Keith and Christopher Maule (1994) "International Regimes for Trade, Investment, and Labor Mobility in the Cultural Industries," *Canadian Journal of Communication*, 19: 401–421.

—— (1999) *Much Ado About Culture: North American Trade Disputes*, Ann Arbor, MI: University of Michigan Press.

Amariglio, J. and David Ruccio (1999) "Literary/Cultural 'Economies,' Economic Discourse, and the Question of Marxism," in Martha Woodmansee and Mark Osteen (eds.) *The New Economic Criticism: Studies at the Intersection of Literature and Economics*, London: Routledge.

Amott, Teresa and Julie Matthaei (1991) *Race, Gender and Work: A Multicultural Economic History of Women in the United States*, Boston: South End Press.

Armour, Leslie (1995) "Economics and Social Reality: Professor O'Neil and the Problem of Culture," *International Journal of Social Economics*, 22 (9/10/11): 79–87.

Bendixen, Peter (1997) "Cultural Tourism: Economic Success at the Expense of Culture?" *International Journal of Cultural Policy*, 4 (1): 21–46.

Benton, Raymond (1999) "Culture," in Philip O'Hara (ed.) *Encyclopedia of Political Economy*, vol. I, London: Routledge.

Bikchandani, Sushil, D. Hirshleifer, and I. Welch (1992) "A Theory of Fads, Fashion, Custom, and Cultural Change as Informational Cascades," *Journal of Political Economy*, 100 (5): 992–1026.

Bille Hansen, Trine (1995) "Measuring the Value of Culture," *European Journal of Cultural Policy*, 1 (2): 309–322.

——, Henrik Christoffersen, and Stephen Wanhill (1998) "The Economic Evaluation of Cultural and Heritage Projects: Conflicting Methodologies," *Tourism, Culture and Communication*, 1 (1–2): 27–48.

Bowles, S. (1998) "Endogenous Preferences: The Cultural Consequences of Markets and Other Economic Institutions," *Journal of Economic Literature*, 36 (1): 75–111.

Brinkman, R.L. (1992) "Culture Evolution and the Process of Economic Evolution," *International Journal of Social Economics*, 19 (3/4/5): 248–259.

—— (1997) "Toward a Culture-Conception of Technology," *Journal of Economic Issues*, 31 (4): 1027–1038.

—— (1999) "The Dynamics of Corporate Culture: Conception and Theory," *International Journal of Social Economics*, 26 (5): 674–694.

—— and June E. Brinkman (1997) "Cultural Lag: Conception and Theory," *International Journal of Social Economics*, 24 (6): 609–627.

Buchanan, James M. (1995) "Economic Science and Cultural Diversity," *Kyklos*, 48 (2): 193–200.

Burt, G. (1997) "Cultural Convergence in Historical and Cultural Space-Time," *Journal of Cultural Economics*, 21 (4): 291–305.

Carroll, Christopher D., Byung Kum Rhee and C. Rhee (1994) "Are There Cultural Effects on Savings? Some Cross-Sectional Evidence," *Quarterly Journal of Economics*, 109 (3): 685–699.

—— (1999) "Does Cultural Origin Affect Saving Behavior? Evidence from Immigrants," *Economic Development and Cultural Change*, 48 (1): 33–50.

Casson, Mark (1991) *The Economics of Business Culture: Game Theory, Transaction Costs, and Economic Performance*, Oxford: Oxford University Press.

—— (1993a) "Entrepreneurship and Business Culture," in Jonathan Brown and Mary B. Rose (eds.) *Entrepreneurship, Networks and Modern Business*, Manchester: Manchester University Press.

—— (1993b) "Cultural Determinants of Economic Performance," *Journal of Comparative Economics*, 17: 418–442.

—— (ed.) (1997) *Culture, Social Norms, and Economics*, vols. I, II, Cheltenham: Edward Elgar.

Chamlee-Wright, Emily (1997) *The Cultural Foundations of Economic Development: Urban Female Entrepreneurship in Ghana*, London: Routledge.

Champlin, Dell (1997) "Culture, Natural Law, and the Restoration of Community," *Journal of Economic Issues*, 31 (2): 575–584.

Cipolla, Carlo M. (1991) *Between Two Cultures: An Introduction to Economic History*, New York: W.W. Norton & Co.

Cowen, Tyler (1998) *In Praise of Commercial Culture*, Cambridge, MA: Harvard University Press.

Cozzi, Guido (1998) "Culture as a Bubble," *Journal of Political Economy*, 106 (2): 376–394.

Croson, Rachel and Nancy Buchan (1999) "Gender and Culture: International Experimental Evidence from Trust Games," *American Economic Review Papers and Proceedings*, 89 (2): 386–391.

Dieckmann, O. (1996) "Cultural Determinants of Economic Growth: Theory and Evidence," *Journal of Cultural Economics*, 20 (4): 297–320.

Dos Anjos, M. (1999) "Money, Trust, and Culture: Elements for an Institutional Approach to Money," *Journal of Economic Issues*, 33 (3): 677–688.

Engerman, Stanley L. (1997) "Cultural Values, Ideological Beliefs, and Changing Labor Institutions: Notes on Their Interactions," in John N. Drobak and John V.C. Nye (eds.) *The Frontiers of the New Institutional Economics*, San Diego, CA: Academic Press.

Fershtman, C. and Y. Weiss (1993) "Social Status, Culture and Economic Performance," *Economic Journal*, 103 (419): 946–959.

Frederick, W.C. (1995) *Values, Nature, and Culture in the American Corporation*, New York: Oxford University Press.

Frey, Bruno (1994) "Cultural Economics and Museum Behavior," *Journal of Political Economy*, 41 (3): 325–335.

—— (1997) "Evaluating Cultural Property: The Economic Approach," *International Journal of Cultural Property*, 6 (2): 231–246.

Galbraith, J.K. (1992) *The Culture of Contentment*, Boston, MA: Houghton Mifflin.

Gray, H. Peter (1996) "Culture and Economic Performance: Policy as an Intervening Variable," *Journal of Comparative Economics*, 23 (3): 278–291.

Greif, Avner (1994) "Cultural Beliefs and the Organization of Society: A Historical and Theoretical Reflection on Collectivist and Individualist Societies," *Journal of Political Economy*, 102 (5): 912–950.

Harcourt, Wendy (1995) "Gender and Culture," in *Our Creative Diversity*, the World Commission on Culture and Development, Paris: UNESCO.

Heilbrun, James and Charles M. Gray (1993) *The Economics of Art and Culture: An American Perspective*, New York: Cambridge University Press.

Hodgson, G. (1991) "Hayek's Theory of Cultural Evolution: An Evaluation in the Light of Vanberg's Critique," *Economics and Philosophy*, 7 (1): 67–82.

—— (1994) "Cognition, Cultural and Institutional Influences," in G. Hodgson and W. Samuels (eds.) *The Elgar Companion to Institutional and Evolutionary Economics*, Cheltenham: Edward Elgar.

Huang, Peter and Ho-Mou Wu (1994) "More Order Without More Law: A Theory of Social Norms and Organizational Cultures," *Journal of Law, Economics, and Organization*, 10 (2): 390–406.

Hutter, Michael (1996) "The Impact of Cultural Economics on Economic Theory," *Journal of Cultural Economics*, 20 (4): 263–268.

—— and Ilde Rizzo (eds.) (1997) *Economic Perspectives on Cultural Heritage*, London: Macmillan.

Jackson, William A. (1993) "Culture, Society and Economic Theory," *Review of Political Economy*, 5 (4): 453–469.

—— (1996) "Cultural Materialism and Institutional Economics," *Review of Social Economy*, 54 (2): 221–244.

Jennings, Ann and Dell Champlin (1994) "Cultural Contours of Race, Gender, and Class Distinctions: A Critique of Moynihan and Other Functionalist Views," in Janice Peterson and Doug Brown (eds.) *The Economic Status of Women Under Capitalism: Institutional Economics and Feminist Theory*, Aldershot: Edward Elgar.

Jennings, Ann and William Waller (1994) "Evolutionary Economics and Cultural Hermeneutics: Veblen, Cultural Relativism, and Blind Drift," *Journal of Economic Issues*, 28 (4): 997–1030.

—— and —— (1994) "Cultural Hermeneutics and Evolutionary Economics," in G. Hodgson and W. Samuels (eds.) *The Elgar Companion to Institutional and Evolutionary Economics*, Cheltenham: Edward Elgar.

—— and —— (1995) "Culture: Core Concept Reaffirmed," *Journal of Economic Issues*, 29 (2): 407–418.

Kabeer, Naila (1991) "Cultural Dopes or Rational Fools?" Women and Labour Supply in the Bangladesh Garment Industry," *The European Journal of Development Research*, 3 (November): 133–160.

Klamer, Arjo (ed.) (1997) *The Value of Culture: On the Relationship Between Economics and Arts*, Amsterdam: Amsterdam University Press.

Kreps, David M. (1990) "Corporate Culture and Economic Theory," in James E. Alt and Kenneth A. Shepsle (eds.) *Perspectives on Positive Political Economy*, Cambridge: Cambridge University Press.

Lal, Deepak (1998) *Unintended Consequences: The Impact of Factor Endowments, Culture, and Politics on Long-Run Economic Performance*, Cambridge, MA: MIT Press.

Lazear, E.P. (1995) "Corporate Culture and the Diffusion of Values," in Horst Siebert (ed.) *Trends in Business Organization: Do Participation and Cooperation Increase Competitiveness?* Tübingen: JCB Mohr.

—— (1999) "Culture and Language," *Journal of Political Economy*, 107 (6): S95–S125.

Lian, Brad and John Oneal (1997) "Cultural Diversity and Economic Development: A Cross-National Study of 98 Countries, 1960–1985," *Economic Development and Cultural Change*, 46 (1): 61–77.

Lipset, S.M. (1993) "Culture and Economic Behavior: A Commentary," *Journal of Labor Economics*, 11(1) Part 2: S330–S347.

Marglin, Stephen A. (1990) "Losing Touch: The Cultural Conditions of Worker Accommodation and Resistance," in S. Marglin and F.A. Marglin (eds.) *Dominating Knowledge: Development, Culture, and Resistance*, Oxford: Clarendon Press.

—— and Frédérique Apffel Marglin (eds.) (1990) *Dominating Knowledge: Development, Culture, and Resistance*, Oxford: Clarendon Press.

Marvasti, A. (1994) "International Trade in Cultural Goods: A Cross-Sectional Analysis," *Journal of Cultural Economics*, 18 (2): 135–148.

Mason, Patrick (1996) "Race, Culture, and the Market," *Journal of Black Studies*, 26 (6): 782–808.

Mayhew, Anne (1994) "Culture," in G. Hodgson and W. Samuels (eds.) *The Elgar Companion to Institutional and Evolutionary Economics*, Cheltenham: Edward Elgar.

Meagher, Gabrielle (1997) "Recreating 'Domestic Service': Institutional Cultures and the Evolution of Paid Household Work," *Feminist Economics*, 3 (2): 1–27.

McKinley, Terry (1998) "Measuring the Contribution of Culture to Human Well-Being: Cultural Indicators of Development," in *The World Culture Report 1998*, Paris: UNESCO.

Neale, Walter C. (1990) "Absolute Cultural Relativism: Firm Foundation for Valuing and Policy," *Journal of Economic Issues*, 24 (2): 333–344.

Netzer, Dick (1992) "Arts and Culture," in Charles T. Clotfelter (ed.) *Who Benefits From the Nonprofit Sector?* Chicago: University of Chicago Press.

Nudler, Oscar and Mark A. Lutz (eds.) (1997) *Economics, Culture and Society: Alternative Approaches: Dissenting Views from Economic Orthodoxy*, New York: Apex Press, for the United Nations University.

O'Neil, Daniel J. (1995) "Culture Confronts Marx," *International Journal of Social Economics*, 22 (9–11): 43–54.

Ozawa, Terutomo (1994) "Exploring the Asian Economic Miracle: Politics, Economics, Society, Culture and History – A Review Article," *Journal of Asian Studies*, 53 (1): 124–131.

Peacock, A.T. (1994) *Paying the Piper: Culture, Music, and Money*, Edinburgh: Edinburgh University Press.

—— and Ilde Rizzo (eds.) (1994) *Cultural Economics and Cultural Policies*, Boston: Kluwer Publishers.

Pietrykowski, Bruce (1994) "Consuming Culture: Postmodernism, Post-Fordism and Economics," *Rethinking Marxism*, 7 (1): 62–80.

Rao, Mohan J. (1998) "Culture and Economic Development," in *The World Culture Report 1998*, Paris: UNESCO.

Reder, Melvin Warren (1999) *Economics: The Culture of a Controversial Subject*, Chicago: University of Chicago Press.

Rosenbaum, E.F. (1999) "Against Naïve Materialism: Culture, Consumption and the Causes of Inequality," *Cambridge Journal of Economics*, 23 (3): 317–336.

Rushton, M. (1999) "Methodological Individualism and Cultural Economics," *Journal of Cultural Economics*, 23 (3): 137–147.

Sen, Amartya K. (1998) "Culture, Freedom and Independence," in *The World Culture Report 1998*, Paris: UNESCO.

Sowell, Thomas (1994) *Race and Culture: A World View*, New York: Basic Books.

Stanfield, James Ronald (1995) *Economics, Power and Culture: Essays in the Development of Radical Individualism*, New York: St. Martin's Press.

Temin, Peter (1997) "Is It Kosher to Talk about Culture?" *Journal of Economic History*, 57: 267–287.

Throsby, David (1994) "The Production and Consumption of the Arts: A View of Cultural Economics," *Journal of Economic Literature*, 32 (1): 1–29.

—— (1995) "Culture, Economics, and Sustainability," *Journal of Cultural Economics*, 19 (3): 199–206.

—— (1999) "Cultural Capital," *Journal of Cultural Economics*, 23 (1–2): 3–12.

Tool, Marc (1990) "Culture Versus Social Value? A Response to Anne Mayhew," *Journal of Economic Issues*, 24 (4): 1122–1133.

Towse, Ruth (1997) (ed.) *Cultural Economics: The Arts, the Heritage and the Media Industries*, vols. I, II, Cheltenham: Edward Elgar.

—— and Abdul Khakee (eds.) (1992) *Cultural Economics*, Heidelberg: Springer-Verlag.

Wallerstein, Immanuel (1990a) "Culture as the Ideological Battleground of the Modern World-System," in Mike Featherstone (ed.) *Global Culture, Nationalism, Globalization and Modernity*, London: Sage Publications.

—— (1990b) "Culture Is the World-System: A Reply to Boyne," in Mike Featherstone (ed.) *Global Culture: Nationalism, Globalization and Modernity*, London: Sage Publications.

Woodbury, Stephen A. (1993) "Culture and Human Capital: Theory and Evidence or Theory Versus Evidence?" in William Darity Jr. (ed.) *Labor Economics: Problems in Analyzing Labor Markets*, Boston, MA: Kluwer.

World Bank (1999) *Culture and Sustainable Development: A Framework for Action*, Washington DC: World Bank.

Wyss, Brenda (1999) "Culture and Gender in Household Economies," *Feminist Economics*, 5 (2): 1–24.

2000–2009

Acheson, K. and C. Maule (2006) "Culture in International Trade," in Victor A. Ginsburgh and David Throsby (eds.) *Handbook of the Economics of Art and Culture*, Amsterdam: Elsevier North-Holland.

Amin, Samir (2006) *Eurocentrism: Modernity, Religion, and Democracy – A Critique of Eurocentrism and Culturalism*, New York: Monthly Review Press.

Austen, Siobahn (2000) "Culture and the Labor Market," *Review of Social Economy*, 58 (4): 505–521.

—— (2003) *Culture and the Labour Market*, Cheltenham: Edward Elgar.

Beugelsdijk, Sjoerd (2007) "Entrepreneurial Culture, Regional Innovativeness and Economic Growth," *Journal of Evolutionary Economics*, 17 (2): 187–210.

—— and Roger Smeets (2008) "Entrepreneurial Culture and Economic Growth: Revisiting McClelland's Thesis," *American Journal of Economics and Sociology*, 67 (5): 915–939.

Bille, T. and G. Schulze (2006) "Culture in Urban and Regional Development," in Victor A. Ginsburgh and David Throsby (eds.) *Handbook of the Economics of Art and Culture*, Amsterdam: Elsevier North-Holland.

Bisin, Alberto and Thierry Verdier (2000) "'Beyond the Melting Pot': Cultural Transmission, Marriage, and the Evolution of Ethnic and Religious Traits," *Quarterly Journal of Economics*, 115 (3): 955–988.

—— and —— (2001) "The Economics of Cultural Transmission and the Dynamics of Preferences," *Journal of Economic Theory*, 97: 298–319.

Blaug, Mark (2001) "Where Are We Now on Cultural Economics?" *Journal of Economic Surveys*, 15 (2): 123–143.

Boettke, P. (2001) "Why Culture Matters: Economics, Politics, and the Imprint of History," in *Calculation and Coordination: Essays on Socialism and Transitional Political Economy*, London: Routledge.

Brennan, David (2006) "Defending the Indefensible? Culture's Role in the Productive/Unproductive Dichotomy," *Feminist Economics*, 12 (3): 403–425.

Bush, Paul D. (2008) "Culture, Values and Institutions," in John B. Davis and Wilfred Dolfsma (eds.) *The Elgar Companion to Social Economics*, Cheltenham: Edward Elgar.

Casson, M. (2006) "Culture and Economic Performance," in Victor A. Ginsburgh and David Throsby (eds.) *Handbook of the Economics of Art and Culture*, Amsterdam: Elsevier North-Holland.

—— and A. Godley (eds.) (2000) *Cultural Factors in Economic Growth*, Heidelberg: Verlag-Springer.

Connell, Philip (2001) *Romanticism, Economics, and the Question of 'Culture,'* Oxford: Oxford University Press.

Cowen, T. (2002) *Creative Destruction: How Globalization Is Changing the World's Cultures*, Princeton, NJ: Princeton University Press.

—— and A. Tabarrok (2000) "An Economic Theory of Avant-Garde and Popular Art, or High and Low Culture," *Southern Economic Journal*, 67 (2): 232–253.

Cuesta, José (2004) "From Economicist to Culturalist Development Theories: How Strong Is the Relation Between Cultural Aspects and Economic Development?" *European Journal of Development Research*, 16 (4): 868–891.

Cullenberg, Stephen and Prasanta Pattanaik (eds.) (2004) *Globalization, Culture, and the Limits of the Market: Essays in Economics and Philosophy*, New York: Oxford University Press.

de Gregori, Thomas (2001) "Does Culture/Technology Still Matter to Institutionalists?" *Journal of Economic Issues*, 35 (4): 1009–1017.

de Jong, Eelke (2009) *Culture and Economics: On Values, Economics and International Business*, London: Routledge.

Drago, Robert (2001) "Time on the Job and Time with Their Kids: Cultures of Teaching and Parenthood in the US," *Feminist Economics*, 7 (3): 1–31.

Fernández, Raquel (2008) "Culture and Economics," in Steven N. Durlauf and Lawrence E. Blume (eds.)*The New Palgrave Dictionary of Economics Online*, 2nd edn, Basingstoke: Palgrave Macmillan. Available at: www.dictionaryofeconomics.com/article?id=pde2008_E000282 (accessed 17 September 2008). doi:10.1057/9780230226203.0346.

—— and Alessandra Fogli (2009) "Culture: An Empirical Investigation of Beliefs, Work, and Fertility," *American Economic Journal: Macroeconomics*, 1(1): 146–177.

Fine, Ben (2002) *The World of Consumption: The Material and Cultural Revisited*, London: Routledge.

Frey, Bruno (2000) *Arts and Economics: Analysis and Cultural Policy*, Heidelberg: Springer-Verlag.

Fukuda-Parr, Sakiko (2000) "In Search of Indicators of Culture and Development: Progress and Proposals," in *The World Culture Report 2000: Cultural Diversity, Conflict and Pluralism*, Paris: UNESCO.

Ginsburgh, Victor A. and David Throsby (eds.) (2006) *Handbook of the Economics of Art and Culture*, Amsterdam: Elsevier North-Holland.

Goldschmidt, Nils and Bernd Remmele (2005) "Anthropology as the Basic Science of Economic Theory: Towards a Cultural Theory of Economics," *Journal of Economic Methodology*, 12 (3): 455–469.

Goodwin, Craufurd (2006) "Art and Culture in the History of Economic Thought," in Victor A. Ginsburgh and David Throsby (eds.) *Handbook of the Economics of Art and Culture*, Amsterdam: Elsevier North-Holland.

Guiso, Luigi, Paola Sapienza, and Luigi Zingales (2006) "Does Culture Affect Economic Outcomes?" *Journal of Economic Perspectives*, 20 (2): 23–48.

—— (2009) "Cultural Biases in Economic Exchange?" *Quarterly Journal of Economics*, 124 (3): 1095–1131.

Henrich, J. (2000) "Does Culture Matter in Economic Behavior? Ultimatum Game Bargaining among the Machiguenga of the Peruvian Amazon," *American Economic Review*, 90 (4): 973–979.

Hojman, David E. (2006) "Economic Development and the Evolution of National Culture: The Case of Chile," in L. Harrison and P. Berger (eds.) *Developing Cultures: Case Studies*, London: Routledge.

Hopkins, Barbara E. (2007) "Western Cosmetics in the Gendered Development of Consumer Culture in China," *Feminist Economics*, 13 (3–4): 287–306.

Hutter, M. and D. Throsby (eds.) (2008) *Beyond Price: Value in Culture, Economics, and the Arts*, Cambridge: Cambridge University Press.

Jackson, W. (2005) "Capabilities, Culture and Social Structure," *Review of Social Economy*, 63 (1): 101–124.

—— (2009) *Economics, Culture and Social Theory*, Cheltenham: Edward Elgar.

Jones, Eric L. (2006) *Cultures Merging: A Historical and Economic Critique of Culture*, Princeton, NJ: Princeton University Press.

Katzner, Donald (2008) *Culture and Economic Explanation: Economics in the US and Japan*, London: Routledge.

Klamer, Arjo (2003) "Value of Culture," in Ruth Towse (ed.) *A Handbook of Cultural Economics*, Cheltenham: Edward Elgar.

—— and D. Throsby (2000) "Paying for the Past: The Economics of Cultural Heritage," in *The World Culture Report 2000: Cultural Diversity, Conflict and Pluralism*, Paris: UNESCO.

Koritz, Amy and Douglas Koritz (2001) "Checkmating the Consumer: Passive Consumption and the Economic Devaluation of Culture," *Feminist Economics*, 7 (1): 45–62.

Kovács, J. M. (2006) "Which Past Matters? Culture and Economic Development in Eastern Europe after 1989," in L.E. Harrison and P.L. Berger (eds.) *Developing Cultures: Case Studies*, London: Routledge.

Kunio, Y. (2006) "Japanese Culture and Postwar Economic Growth," in L.E. Harrison and P.L. Berger (eds.) *Developing Cultures: Case Studies*, London: Routledge.

Landes, David. S. (2000a) "Why Some Are So Rich and Others So Poor: The Role of Culture," in J. Wolfensohn *et al.* (eds) *Culture Counts: Financing, Resources, and the Economics of Culture in Sustainable Development*, Washington, DC: The World Bank.

—— (2000b) "Culture Makes Almost All the Difference," in L. Harrison and S. Huntington (eds.) *Culture Matters: How Values Shape Human Progress*, New York: Basic Books.

Lavoie, Don and Emily Chamlee-Wright (2000) *Culture and Enterprise: The Development, Representation and Morality of Business*, London: Routledge.

Licht, A.N., G. Chanan, and S.H. Schwartz (2007) "Culture Rules: The Foundations of the Rule of Law and Other Norms of Governance," *Journal of Comparative Economics*, 35 (4): 659–688.

Marini, M. (2004) "Cultural Evolution and Economic Growth: A Theoretical Hypothesis with Some Empirical Evidence," *The Journal of Socio-Economics*, 33: 765–784.

Maseland, Robbert (2008) "Taking Economics to Bed: About the Pitfalls and Possibilities of Cultural Economics," in Wolfram Elsner and Hardy Hanappi (eds.) *Varieties of Capitalism and New Institutional Deals: Regulation, Welfare and the New Economy*, Cheltenham: Edward Elgar.

Mayhew, Anne (2008) "Institutions, Culture and Values," in John B. Davis and Wilfred Dolfsma (eds.) *The Elgar Companion to Social Economics*, Cheltenham: Edward Elgar.

Mushinski, David and Kathleen Pickering (2000) "Inequality in Income Distributions: Does Culture Matter? An Analysis of Western Native American Tribes," *Journal of Economic Issues*, 34 (2): 403–412.

Navrud, Stale, and Richard C. Ready (2002) *Valuing Cultural Heritage: Applying Environmental Valuation Techniques to Historic Buildings, Monuments and Artifacts*, Northampton, MA: Edward Elgar.

Netzer, D. (2006) "Cultural Policy: An American View," in Victor A. Ginsburgh and David Throsby (eds.) *Handbook of the Economics of Art and Culture*, Amsterdam: Elsevier North-Holland.

Noonan, Douglas (2003) "Contingent Valuation and Cultural Resources: A Meta-Analytic Review of the Literature," *Journal of Cultural Economics*, 27 (3–4): 159–176.

—— (2004) "Valuing Arts and Culture: A Research Agenda for Contingent Valuation," *Journal of Arts Management, Law, and Society*, 34 (3): 205–221.

Park, Hoon, Clifford Russell and Junsoo Lee (2007) "National Culture and Environmental Sustainability: A Cross-National Analysis," *Journal of Economics and Finance*, 31 (1): 104–121.

Ploeg, F. van der (2006) "The Making of Cultural Policy: A European Perspective," in Victor A. Ginsburgh and David Throsby (eds.) *Handbook of the Economics of Art and Culture*, Amsterdam: Elsevier North-Holland.

Rao, Vijayendra and Michael Walton (eds.) (2004) *Culture and Public Action*, Stanford, CA: Stanford University Press.

Rizzo, I. and D. Throsby (2006) "Cultural Heritage: Economic Analysis And Public Policy," in Victor A. Ginsburgh and David Throsby (eds.) *Handbook of the Economics of Art and Culture*, Amsterdam: Elsevier North-Holland.

Santagata, W. (2006) Cultural Districts and Their Role in Developed and Developing Countries," in Victor A. Ginsburgh and David Throsby (eds.) *Handbook of the Economics of Art and Culture*, Amsterdam: Elsevier North-Holland.

—— and Giovanni Signorello (2000) "Contingent Valuation of a Cultural Public Good and Policy Design: The Case of 'Napoli Musei Aperti,'" *Journal of Cultural Economics*, 24 (3): 181–204.

Schuster, J.M. (2006) "Tax Incentives in Cultural Policy," in Victor A. Ginsburgh and David Throsby (eds.) *Handbook of the Economics of Art and Culture*, Amsterdam: Elsevier North-Holland.

Starr, Martha A. (2004) "Consumption, Identity, and the Sociocultural Constitution of 'Preferences:' Reading Women's Magazines," *Review of Social Economy*, 62 (3): 291–305.

—— (2007) "Saving, Spending, and Self-Control: Cognition Versus Consumer Culture," *Review of Radical Political Economics*, 39 (2): 214–229.

Stulz, R.M. and R. Williamson (2003) "Culture, Openness, and Finance," *Journal of Financial Economics*, 70 (3): 313–349.

Tabellini, Guido (2005) "Culture and Institutions: Economic Development in the Regions of Europe," CESifo Working Paper No. 1492.

—— (2008) "Institutions and Culture," *Journal of the European Economic Association*, 6 (2–3): 255–294.

Tadesse, Bedassa and Roger White (2008) "Do Immigrants Counter the Effect of Cultural Distance on Trade? Evidence from US State-level Exports," *Journal of Socio-Economics*, 37 (6): 2304–2318.

Throsby, David (2001) *Economics and Culture*, Cambridge: Cambridge University Press.

—— (2003) "Determining the Value of Cultural Goods: How Much (Or How Little) Does Contingent Valuation Tell Us?" *Journal of Cultural Economics*, 27 (3/4): 275–285.

Towse, R. (ed.) (2003) *A Handbook of Cultural Economics*, Cheltenham: Edward Elgar.

—— (ed.) (2007) *Recent Developments in Cultural Economics*, Aldershot: Edward Elgar.

Waller, William (2003) "It's Culture All the Way Down," *Journal of Economic Issues*, 37 (1): 35–45.

White, Roger and Bedassa Tadesse (2007) "Immigration Policy, Cultural Pluralism and Trade: Evidence from the White Australia Policy," *Pacific Economic Review*, 12 (4): 489–509.

—— and —— (2008a) "Immigrants, Cultural Distance and US State-Level Exports of Cultural Products," *North American Journal of Economics and Finance*, 19 (3): 331–348.

—— and —— (2008b) "Cultural Distance and the US Immigrant-Trade Link," *The World Economy*, 31 (8): 1078–1096.

—— and —— (2009) "Cultural Diversity, Immigrants and International Trade: Some Empirical Examination of the Relationship in Nine OECD Nations," in Lydia B. Kerwin (ed.) *Cultural Diversity: Issues, Challenges and Perspectives*, Hauppauge: Nova Science Publishers.

Wolfensohn, James, L. Dini, G. F. Bonetti, I. Johnson, and J. Martin-Brown (2000) *Culture Counts: Financing, Resources, and the Economics of Culture in Sustainable Development*, Washington, DC: The World Bank.

Zein-Elabdin, Eiman (2009) "Economics, Postcolonial Theory, and the Problem of Culture: Institutional Analysis and Hybridity," *Cambridge Journal of Economics*, 33 (6): 1153–1167.

2010–

Adkisson, Richard (2014) "Quantifying Culture: Problems and Promises," *Journal of Economic Issues*, 48 (1): 89–107.

Aigrain, Philippe (2012) *Sharing: Culture and the Economy in the Internet Age*, Amsterdam: Amsterdam University Press.

Beugelsdijk, Sjoerd and R. Maseland (2011) *Culture in Economics: History, Methodological Reflections, and Contemporary Applications*, Cambridge: Cambridge University Press.

Bokros, Lajos (2013) *Accidental Occidental: Economics and Culture of Transition in Mitteleuropa, the Baltic and the Balkan Area*, Budapest: Central European University.

Chamlee-Wright, Emily (2010) *The Cultural and Political Economy of Recovery: Social Learning in a Post-Disaster Environment*, London: Routledge.

De Jong, Eelke (2011) "Culture, Institutions and Economic Growth," *Journal of Institutional Economics*, 7 (4): 523–527.

Felbermayr, Gabriel J. and Farid Toubal (2010) "Cultural Proximity and Trade," *European Economic Review*, 54 (2): 279–293.

Greif, Avner and Guido Tabellini (2010) "Cultural and Institutional Bifurcation: China and Europe Compared," *American Economic Association Papers and Proceedings*, 100 (2): 1–10.

Hamilton, David (2010) *Cultural Economics and Theory: The Evolutionary Economics of David Hamilton* (with G. Atkinson, W. Dugger, and W. Waller), London: Routledge.

Kovács, J.M. and Violetta Zentai (eds.) (2012) *Capitalism from Outside? Economic Cultures in Eastern Europe After 1989*, Budapest: Central European University Press.

Mathers, Rachel L. and Claudia R. Williamson (2011) "Cultural Context: Explaining the Productivity of Capitalism," *Kyklos*, 64 (2): 231–252.

Ossome, Lyn (2014) "Can the Law Secure Women's Rights to Land in Africa? Revisiting Tensions between Culture and Land Commercialization," *Feminist Economics*, 20 (1): 155–177.

Ranjith, Sri and Anil Rupasingha (2012) "Social and Cultural Determinants of Child Poverty in the United States," *Journal of Economic Issues*, 46 (1): 119–141.

Spolaore, Enrico (ed.) (2014) *Culture and Economic Growth*, Aldershot: Edward Elgar.

Tabellini, Guido (2010) "Culture and Institutions: Economic Development in the Regions of Europe," *Journal of the European Economic Association*, 8 (4): 677–716.

Throsby, David (2010) *Economics of Cultural Policy*, Cambridge: Cambridge University Press.

White, Roger and Bedassa Tadesse (2010) "Does Cultural Distance Hinder Trade in Goods? A Comparative Study of Nine OECD Member Nations," *Open Economies Review*, 21 (2): 237–261.

—— and —— (2010) "Cultural Distance as a Determinant of Bilateral Trade Flows: Do Immigrants Counter the Effect of Cultural Differences?" *Applied Economics Letters*, 17 (2): 147–152.

Williamson, C.R. and R.L. Mathers (2011) "Economic Freedom, Culture, and Growth," *Public Choice*, 148 (3–4): 313–335.

Appendix II Some interpretations of culture in Economics

Listed in alphabetical order by author's last name. See Appendix I and III for full citations of the entries not indicated here.

> an aggregation of past decisions made by people in something like the same circumstances.
>
> (John Adams 1986: 279)

> cultural processes are processes of the production and circulation of meaning.
>
> (Jack Amariglio *et al.* 1988: 487)

> an integrative hermeneutic system that encompasses language, custom, norms, moral, laws, values and beliefs.
>
> (Siobhan Austen 2000: 517)

> culture, the organized corpus of behavior of which economic activity is but a part, is a phenomenon *sui generis*.
>
> (Clarence Ayres 1962: 95)

> the body of lore which pervades and sustains that system of relationships and which has been (in varying amounts) learned by all the members of the community.
>
> (Clarence Ayres 1952: 11. See Chapter 4 in this book)

> shared values and preferences handed down from one generation to another through families, peer groups, ethnic groups, classes, and other groups.
>
> (Gary Becker 1996: 16. See Chapter 3 in this book)

> those beliefs and ritual practices which legitimate institutions.
>
> (Peter Boettke 2001: 254)

> that complexity.
>
> (Richard Brinkman and June Brinkman 1997: 623)

> collective subjectivity.
>
> (Mark Casson 1993: 420)

shared values and beliefs relating to fundamental issues, together with the forms in which they are expressed.

(Mark Casson 2006: 363)

a context rather than an independent force ... not just a list of rules constraining behavior that would otherwise maximize profit or utility. Culture is the context in which meaning is negotiated and renegotiated.

(Emily Chamlee-Wright 1997: 24)

a system of values, beliefs and behaviours present in a society.

(José Cuesta 2004: 869)

total way of life of a people, their interpersonal relations, as well as their attitudes.

(Oliver Dieckmann 1996: 297)

a set of values common to a group.

(Vernon Dixon 1970: 424. See Chapter 1 in this book)

differences in beliefs and preferences that vary systematically across groups of individuals separated by space (either geographic or social) or time.

(Raquel Fernández 2008: 2)

culture is a service industry.

(James Gapinski 1980: 578)

a set of attitudes, beliefs or values common to a group that somehow identifies and binds the group together. Thus it is possible to speak of a national culture, a religious culture, a corporate culture and so on.

(Victor Ginsburgh and David Throsby 2006: 6)

a flexible form of social organization that makes possible adaptations to different environments and inner structural development.

(Nils Goldschmidt and Bernd Remmele 2005: 457)

Cultural beliefs: the ideas and thoughts common to several individuals that govern interaction—between these people, and between them, their gods, and other groups.

(Avner Greif 1994: 915)

an ongoing complex of ideas, attitudes, and beliefs that is absorbed by individuals in a habitual manner through institutional arrangements as they mature in their cultural milieu. All cultures are ongoing processes whose structure and functioning change under the impact of many factors such as scientific advance, technological change, population movements, and political developments.

(Allan Gruchy 1987: 4. See Chapter 4 in this book)

those customary beliefs and values that ethnic, religious, and social groups transmit fairly unchanged from generation to generation.

(Luigi Guiso *et al.* 2006: 23)

a synthesis—or at least an aggregation—of institutions.

(Walton Hamilton 1932: 84. See Chapter 4 in this book)

a collective systemic mental construct which contains a group's abstract ideas, ideals, and values from the superorganic and supernatural world and is found in legends, mythology, supernatural visions, folklore, literature, elaborated superstitions, and sagas.

(Gregory Hayden 1993: 308. See Chapter 4 in this book)

a process, ... the cultivation of individuals over time.

(William Jackson 1993: 454)

a process, a way of life, and the arts.

(William Jackson 2009: 15)

a system of symbolic interpretation that unites human thought and action.

(Ann Jennings 1993: 113. See Chapter 8 in this book)

an unfolding hermeneutic process ... an interpretive integration of material objects, behavior, and their meanings.

(Ann Jennings and William Waller 1994: 997, 1000)

unconsciously assimilated beliefs with consequences that are more dimly perceived.

(Eric Jones 2006: x)

the basic rules and patterns of human behaviour. As such it has reference to the patterns of thought, emotions, values, ideas and categories often expressed in symbols which shape human awareness and human experience ... Culture conditions our conscious and unconscious desires and feelings, gives meaning to behaviour and provides the rationale for living.

(William Kapp 1963: 7)

a complex of ideas, thought-forms, behavior patterns, and judgmental criteria that determine a community's way of life.

(Donald Katzner 2008: 1)

shared values.

· (Arjo Klamer 1996: 11)

values, habits, lifestyles, knowledge, skills, etc. and the institutions in which they are embedded.

(János Mátyás Kovács 2006: 331)

the sum and the interaction of the values and attitudes of a group—thus the aspirations and ambitions of the members of the group, the relations between the members, between old and young people, between the genders, between rich and poor, the religious beliefs and relations between different faiths, the attitudes toward work and play, the value placed on different kinds of activities.

(David Landes 2000: 27)

the whole of a people's patterns of regular and recurring behaviour.

(Anne Mayhew 1994: 115)

everything that people derive from their tradition and heritage, including folklore and kinship patterns, 'material culture', religion, and so on.

(Roger McCain 2006: 150)

the way that people live together, interact and co-operate – together with how they justify such interactions through a system of beliefs, values and norms.

(Terry McKinley 1998: 322)

a primary and therefore undefined rubric for all the rules and folkviews to which its members subscribe.

(Walter C. Neale 1990: 335)

the transmission from one generation to the next, via teaching and imitation, of knowledge, values, and other factors that influence behavior.

(Douglas North 1990: 37. See Chapter 5 in this book)

people's shared beliefs and attitudes, lifestyles and values.

(J. Mohan Rao 1998: 25)

Cultural processes are the diverse ways in which human beings produce meanings for their existence.

(Stephen Resnick and Richard Wolff 1987: 20.
See Chapter 6 in this book)

a device through which one sees but which is seldom perceived itself and which, therefore, remains essentially tacit and unquestioned ... also a blueprint of human activity in terms of rules and language games which govern how we can and should act in that world.

(Eckehard Rosenbaum 1999: 321)

the preliminary information we must have to enjoy the processing of further information.

(Tibor Scitovsky 1976: 226. See Chapter 3 in this book)

patterns of skills and behavior.

(Thomas Sowell 1983: 1)

a set of significant meanings that emanate from and structure interpersonal relationships. Any society carries on a culture by means of the stories told and models of, and for, reality that are displayed within it.

(Ronald Stanfield 1995: 137)

culture goes far beyond the field traditionally assigned to Ministries of Culture. Culture is indeed concerned with artistic creation and with ethnic and indigenous issues, but culture has also social and political dimensions.

(Paul Streeten 2006: 411)

the social norms and the individual beliefs that sustain Nash equilibria as focal points in repeated social interactions.

(Guido Tabellini 2005: 2)

the distinctive attitudes and actions that differentiate groups of people. Culture in this sense is the result of and expressed through religion, language, institutions, and history. The attributes that make up culture change slowly, but they can and do change over time.

(Peter Temin 1997: 268)

all those activities undertaken within 'the arts' and more broadly within the so-called 'cultural industries,' the latter term embracing areas such as publishing and the media as well as the core artistic fields. In short, culture in this functional sense can be thought of as being represented by the 'cultural sector' of the economy.

attitudes, practices and beliefs that are fundamental to the functioning of different societies. Culture in this sense is expressed in a particular society's values and customs, which evolve over time as they are transmitted from one generation to another.

(David Throsby 1995: 202)

a set of attitudes, beliefs, mores, customs, values and practices which are common to or shared by any group ... certain activities that are undertaken by people, and the products of those activities, which have to do with the intellectual, moral and artistic aspects of human life.

(David Throsby 2001: 4)

complex, interconnected, multidimensional symbolic systems that structure meaning and social behavior.

(William Waller 1999: 838. See Chapter 8 in this book)

the 'culture', that is the idea-system, of this capitalist world-economy is the outcome of our collective historical attempts to come to terms with the contradictions, the ambiguities, the complexities of the socio-political realities of this particular system. We have done it in part by creating the concept of 'culture' (usage I) as the assertion of unchanging realities amidst a world that is in fact ceaselessly changing. And we have done it in part by creating the concept of 'culture' (usage II) as the justification of the inequities of the system, as the attempt to keep them unchanging in a world which is ceaselessly threatened by change ... Culture is the ideological battleground of the modern world-system.

(Immanuel Wallerstein 1990a: 38–39, 31)

a word that describes what constrains us (in the most effective way possible, by shaping our 'will' that seeks to assert its 'freedom'), and is not a word that describes our ability to escape these constraints ... Culture is the world-system.

(Immanuel Wallerstein 1990b: 63–64)

culture applies to very large groups, sometimes an entire society, and involves very low levels of intentionality.

(Oliver Williamson 1996: 268. See Chapter 5 in this book)

socially constructed meaning systems made up of ideas and processes that represent the world, that create cultural entities (like 'family,' or 'marriage,' or 'church'), that direct individuals to do certain things, and that evoke certain feelings.

(Brenda Wyss 1999: 1)

an incomplete, unpredictable, historically specific social frame of reference that gives rise to different practices and ideas, including economy and economics.

(Eiman Zein-Elabdin 2004: 28. See Chapter 1 in this book)

Appendix III Development in Economics

A select chronology

This is a partial list intended to give an indication of the evolution of literature on development in different schools of economic thought. Textbooks are not included.

Prior to 1950

Ayres, C.E. (1944) *The Theory of Economic Progress*, New York: Schocken Books.

Benson, W. (1942) "The Economic Advancement of Under-developed Areas," in E.F.M. Durbin (ed.) *The Economic Basis of Peace*, London: National Peace Council.

Clark, Colin (1940) *The Conditions of Economic Progress*, London: Macmillan & Co.

Knowles, L.C.A. (1924) *The Economic Development of the British Overseas Empire*, London: George Routledge & Sons.

Mandelbaum, K. (1945) *The Industrialization of Backward Areas*, Oxford: Basil Blackwell.

Rosenstein-Rodan, P.N. (1944) "The International Development of Economically Backward Areas," *International Affairs*, 20 (April): 157–165.

Schumpeter, J. (1934) *The Theory of Economic Development: An Inquiry into Profits, Capital, Credit, Interest, and the Business Cycle*, Cambridge, MA: Harvard University Press.

Singer, H. W. (1949) "Economic Progress in Underdeveloped Countries," *Social Research*, 16 (March): 1–11.

Sweezy, Paul (1942) *The Theory of Capitalist Development*, New York: Monthly Review Press.

1950–1959

Baran, P. (1952) "On the Political Economy of Backwardness," *The Manchester School of Economic and Social Studies*, 56: 66–84.

—— (1957) *The Political Economy of Growth*, New York: Monthly Review Press.

Dobb, M. H. (1951) *Some Aspects of Economic Development*, Delhi: Delhi School of Economics.

Higgins, Benjamin H. (1956) "The 'Dualistic Theory' of Underdeveloped Areas," *Economic Development and Cultural Change*, 4 (2): 99–115.

Hirschman, Albert O. (1958) *The Strategy of Economic Development*, New Haven, CT: Yale University Press.

Hoselitz, B.F. (1952) "Non-Economic Barriers to Economic Development," *Economic Development and Cultural Change*, 1 (1): 8–21.

Leibenstein, Harvey (1957) *Economic Backwardness and Economic Growth*, New York: John Wiley & Sons.

Lewis, W. Arthur (1954) "Economic Development with Unlimited Supplies of Labor," *The Manchester School*, (22): 139–191.

—— (1955) *The Theory of Economic Growth*, London: Allen and Unwin.

Myint, Hla (1954) "An Interpretation of Economic Backwardness," *Oxford Economic Papers*, 6 (2): 132–163.

Myrdal, Gunnar (1957) *Economic Theory and Underdeveloped Regions*, London: G. Duckworth.

Nurkse, R. (1953) *Problems of Capital Formation in Underdeveloped Countries*, New York: Oxford University Press.

Prebisch, R. (1950) *The Economic Development of Latin America and its Principal Problems*, New York: UN Department of Economic Affairs, Economic Commission for Latin America.

Singer, Hans (1952) "The Mechanics of Economic Development," *Indian Economic Review*, 1 (2) August: 1–18.

Solow, R. (1956) "A Contribution to the Theory of Economic Growth," *Quarterly Journal of Economics*, 70 (1): 65–94.

Tinbergen, Jan (1958) *The Design of Development*, Baltimore, MD: Johns Hopkins University Press (for IBRD).

1960–1969

Adelman, Irma and Cynthia Taft Morris (1965) "A Factor Analysis of the Interrelationship between Social and Political Variables and Per Capita Gross National Product," *The Quarterly Journal of Economics*, 79 (4): 555–578.

Ayres, Clarence E. (1960) "Institutionalism and Economic Development," *The Southwestern Social Science Quarterly*, 41: 45–62.

—— (1962) *The Theory of Economic Progress: A Study of the Fundamentals of Economic Development and Cultural Change*, New York: Schocken Books.

Dowd, D. (1967) "Some Issues of Economic Development and of Development Economics," *Journal of Economic Issues*, 1 (3): 149–160.

Easterlin, R.I. (1965) "Is There Need for Historical Research on Underdevelopment?" *American Economic Review Proceedings*, 55 (2): 104–108.

Fei, John and Gustav Ranis (1969) "Economic Development in Historical Perspective" *American Economic Review*, 59 (2): 386–400.

Frank, André Gunder (1966) "The Development of Underdevelopment," *Monthly Review*, 18 (4): 17–31.

—— (1967) *Capitalism and Underdevelopment in Latin America: Historical Studies of Chile and Brazil*, New York: Monthly Review Press.

Furtado, C. (1964) *Development and Underdevelopment*, Berkeley, CA: University of California Press.

Galbraith, John K. (1964) *Economic Development*, Cambridge, MA: Harvard University Press.

Gerschenkron, A. (1965) *Economic Backwardness in Historical Perspective*, Cambridge, MA: Belknap Press.

Hirschman, A.O. (1965) "Obstacles to Development: A Classification and a Quasi-vanishing Act," *Economic Development and Cultural Change*, 13 (4): 385–393.

Ishikawa, Shigeru (1967) *Economic Development in Asian Perspective*, Tokyo: Kinokuniya Bookstore Co.

Junker, L. (1967) "Capital Accumulation, Savings-Centered Theory, and Economic Development," *Journal of Economic Issues*, 1 (1): 25–43.

Kapp, K. William (1963) *Hindu Culture, Economic Development and Economic Planning in India*, Bombay: Asia Publishing House.

—— (1965) "Economic Development in a New Perspective: Existential Minima and Substantive Rationality," *Kyklos* 17 (1): 49–79.

Myrdal, Gunnar (1968) *Asian Drama: An Inquiry into the Poverty of Nations*, vols. I–III, New York: Pantheon.

Randall, Laura (ed.) (1964) *Economic Development, Evolution or Revolution*, Boston, MA: D.C. Heath.

Ranis, G. and John Fei (1961) "A Theory of Economic Development," *American Economic Review*, 51 (4): 533–565.

Robbins, L. (1968) *The Theory of Economic Development in the History of Economic Thought*, London: Macmillan.

Rostow, W. W. (1960) *The Stages of Economic Growth: A Non-Communist Manifesto*, Cambridge: Cambridge University Press.

Schultz, Theodore (1964) *Transforming Traditional Agriculture*, New Haven, CT: Yale University Press.

Sen, Amartya K. (1962) *Choice of Techniques: An Aspect of the Theory of Planned Economic Development*, Oxford: Blackwell.

Streeten, Paul (1967) "The Frontiers of Development Studies: Some Issues of Development Policy," *Journal of Development Studies*, 4 (1): 2–24.

1970–1979

Amin, Samir (1974) "Accumulation and Development: A Theoretical Model," *Review of African Political Economy*, 1 (1): 9–26.

—— (1976) *Unequal Development: An Essay on the Social Formations of Peripheral Capitalism*, New York: Monthly Review Press.

Bauer, Peter T. (1972) *Dissent on Development*, Cambridge, MA: Harvard University Press.

Boserup, Ester (1970) *Woman's Role in Economic Development*, New York: St. Martin's Press.

Cardoso, Fernando Henrique and Enzo Faletto (1979) *Dependency and Development in Latin America*, Berkeley, CA: University of California Press.

Chenery, H. (1974) *Redistribution with Growth: Policies to Improve Income Distribution in Developing Countries in the Context of Economic Growth*, London: Oxford University Press.

Dos Santos, T. (1970) "The Structure of Dependence," *American Economic Review*, 60 (2): 231–236.

Ghai, D.P. (1977) *The Basic-Needs Approach to Development: Some Issues Regarding Concepts and Methodology*, Geneva: International Labour Office.

Gordon, Wendell (1973) "Institutionalized Consumption Patterns in Underdeveloped Countries," *Journal of Economic Issues*, 7 (2): 267–287.

Gurley, John G. (1979) "Economic Development: A Marxist View," in Kenneth P. Jameson and Charles K. Wilber (eds.) *Directions in Economic Development*, Notre Dame, IN: University of Notre Dame Press.

Harris, J.R. and Michael Todaro (1970) "Migration, Unemployment and Development: A Two-Sector Model," *American Economic Review*, 60 (1): 126–142.

Higgins, B. (1977) "Economic Development and Cultural Change: Seamless Web or Patchwork Quilt?" in Manning Nash (ed.) *Essays on Economic Development and Cultural Change, in Honor of Bert F. Hoselitz*, Chicago: University of Chicago Press.

Little, I.M.D. and J.A. Mirrlees (1974) *Project Appraisal and Planning for Developing Countries*, New York: Basic Books.

Myrdal, G. (1970) *The Challenge of World Poverty*, New York: Pantheon Books.

Robinson, Joan (1979) *Aspects of Development and Underdevelopment*, Cambridge: Cambridge University Press.

Wallerstein, Immanuel (1974) *The Modern World System*, New York: Academic Press.

1980–1989

Balassa, B. (1988) "Lessons of East Asian Development: An Overview," *Economic Development and Cultural Change*, 36 (3): S273–S290.

Bardhan, Pranab (1985) "Marxist Ideas in Development Economics: A Brief Evaluation," *Economic and Political Weekly*, 20 (13): 550–555.

Bauer, P. (1984) *Reality and Rhetoric: Studies in the Economics of Development*, Cambridge, MA: Harvard University Press.

Bener´ıa, Lourdes (ed.) (1982) *Women and Development: The Sexual Division of Labor in Rural Societies*, New York: Praeger.

——and Gita Sen (1981) "Accumulation, Reproduction, and Women's Role in Economic Development: Boserup Revisited," *Signs*, 7 (2): 141–157.

Bhagwati, Jagdish (1984) "Development Economics: What Have We Learned?" *Asian Development Review*, 2 (1): 23–38.

Bolin, Meb (1984) "An Institutionalist Perspective on Economic Development," *Journal of Economic Issues*, 18 (2): 643–650.

De Gregori, T. (1985) *A Theory of Technology: Continuity and Change in Human Development*, Ames, IA: Iowa State University Press.

Easterlin, R. A. (1981) "Why Isn't The Whole World Developed?" *Journal of Economic History*, 41 (1): 1–19.

Folbre, Nancy (1986) "Cleaning House: New Perspectives on Households and Economic Development," *Journal of Development Economics*, 22 (1): 5–40.

Herz, Barbara (1989) "Bringing Women into the Economic Mainstream: Guidelines for Policymakers and Development Institutions," *Finance and Development*, 26 (4): 22–25.

Hirschman, Albert O. (1981) "The Rise and Decline of Development Economics," in *Essays in Trespassing: Economics to Politics and Beyond*, Cambridge: Cambridge University Press.

Hunt, Diana (1989) *Economic Theories of Development: An Analysis of Competing Paradigms*, Savage, MD: Barnes and Nobles.

Lal, D. (1983) *The Poverty of Development Economics*, Cambridge, MA: MIT Press.

Lewis, W.A. (1984) "The State of Development Theory," *American Economic Review*, 74 (1): 1–10.

Little, I.M.D. (1982) *Economic Development: Theory, Policy, and International Relations*, New York: Basic Books.

Lucas, Robert (1988) "On the Mechanics of Economic Development," *Journal of Monetary Economics*, 22: 3–42.

Meier, G.M., D. Seers, and P. Bauer (eds.) (1984) *Pioneers in Development*, vol. 1, New York: The World Bank.

Murphy, K.M., A. Shleifer, and R.W. Vishny (1989) "Industrialization and the Big Bush," *Journal of Political Economy*, 97 (5): 1003–1026.

Ruttan, Vernon W. (1988) "Cultural Endowments and Economic Development: What Can We Learn from Anthropology?" *Economic Development and Cultural Change*, 36 (3): Supplement, 247–271.

Schultz, T. (ed.) (1987) *Pioneers in Development*, vol. 2, New York: The World Bank.

Sen, A. K. (1983) "Development: Which Way Now?" *Economic Journal*, 93 (372): 745–762.

—— (1984) *Resources, Values, and Development*, Cambridge, MA: Harvard University Press.

Sen, Gita and Caren Grown (1987) *Development, Crises, and Alternative Visions: Third World Women's Perspectives*, New York: Monthly Review Press.

Stiglitz, Joseph (1986) "The New Development Economics," *World Development*, 14 (2): 257–265.

Street, James H. (1987) "The Institutionalist Theory of Economic Development," *Journal of Economic Issues*, 21 (4): 1861–1887.

Streeten, Paul (1985) "A Problem to Every Solution: Development Economics Has Not Failed," *Finance and Development*, 22 (2): 14–16.

—— (with S.J. Burki, M. ul Haq, and F. Stewart) (1981) *First Things First: Meeting Basic Needs in Developing Countries*, London: Oxford University Press.

Toye, John (1987) *Dilemmas of Development: Reflections on the Counter-Revolution in Development Theory and Policy*, Oxford: Blackwell.

1990–1999

Adams, John (1993) "Institutions and Economic Development: Structure, Process, and Incentives," in Marc Tool (ed.) *Institutional Economics: Theory, Method, Policy*, Boston: Kluwer.

Amin, Samir (1990) *Maldevelopment: Anatomy of a Global Failure*, Tokyo: United Nations University Press.

Amsden, Alice (1991) "Diffusion of Development: The Late-Industrializing Model and Greater East Asia," *American Economic Association Papers and Proceedings*, 81 (2): 282–286.

Banuri, Tariq (1990) "Modernization and its Discontents: A Cultural Perspective on the Theories of Development," in Stephen Marglin and Frédérique Marglin (eds.) *Dominating Knowledge: Development, Culture, and Resistance*, Oxford: Clarendon Press.

Bardhan, Pranab (1993) "Economics of Development and the Development of Economics," *Journal of Economic Perspectives*, 7 (2): 129–142.

Barker, Drucilla K. (1998) "Dualisms, Discourse, and Development," *Hypatia*, 13 (3): 83–94.

Brinkman, Richard (1995) "Economic Growth Versus Economic Development: Toward a Conceptual Clarification," *Journal of Economic Issues*, 29 (4): 1171–1188.

Casson, Mark (1993) "Cultural Determinants of Economic Performance," *Journal of Comparative Economics*, 17: 418–442.

Chamlee-Wright, Emily (1997) *The Cultural Foundations of Economic Development: Urban Female Entrepreneurship in Ghana*, London: Routledge.

Dieckmann, O. (1996) "Cultural Determinants of Economic Growth: Theory and Evidence," *Journal of Cultural Economics*, 20 (4): 297–320.

Elson, Diane (1991) *Male Bias in the Development Process*, Manchester: Manchester University Press.

Esteva, G. (1991) "Preventing Green Redevelopment," *Development: Journal of the Society for International Development*, 2: 74–78.

Harcourt, Wendy (ed.) (1994) *Feminist Perspectives on Sustainable Development*, London: Zed Books.

—— (1995) "Gender and Culture," in *Our Creative Diversity*, The World Commission on Culture and Development Report, Paris: UNESCO.

Harriss, John, Janet Hunter, and Colin M. Lewis (eds.) (1995) *The New Institutional Economics and Third World Development*, London: Routledge.

Hayami, Yujiro and Masahiko Akoi (eds.) (1998) *The Institutional Foundations of East Asian Economic Development*, London: Macmillan.

Kabeer, Naila (1994) *Reversed Realities: Gender Hierarchies in Development Thought*, London: Verso.

Krueger, Anne (1990) "Government Failures in Development," *Journal of Economic Perspectives*, 4 (3): 9–23.

Krugman, P. (1995) *Development, Geography and Economic Theory*, Cambridge, MA: MIT Press.

Latouche, Serge (1993) *In the Wake of the Affluent Society: An Exploration of Post-Development*, London: Zed Books.

Lian, Brad and John Oneal (1997) "Cultural Diversity and Economic Development: A Cross-National Study of 98 Countries, 1960–1985," *Economic Development and Cultural Change*, 46 (1): 61–77.

Marglin, Stephen and Frédérique Apffel (1990) *Dominating Knowledge: Development, Culture, and Resistance*, Oxford: Oxford University Press.

—— and —— (1996) *Decolonizing Knowledge: From Development to Dialogue*, Oxford: Oxford University Press.

McIntyre, R. (1992) "Theories of Uneven Development and Social Change," *Rethinking Marxism*, 5 (3): 75–105.

North, Douglass (1995) "The New Institutional Economics and Third World Development," in John Harriss, Janet Hunter, and Colin M. Lewis (eds.) *The New Institutional Economics and Third World Development*, London: Routledge.

Rahnema, Majid (ed.) (1997) *The Post-Development Reader,* London: Zed Books.

Rao, M. (1998) "Culture and Economic Development," in *The World Culture Report 1998*, Paris: UNESCO.

Romer, P. (1993) "Idea Gaps and Object Gaps in Economic Development," *Journal of Monetary Economics*, 32: 543–573.

Sachs, Wolfgang (ed.) (1992) *The Development Dictionary: A Guide to Knowledge As Power*, London: Zed Books.

Sen, A.K. (1990) "Gender and Cooperative Conflict," in Irene Tinker (ed.) *Persistent Inequalities: Women and World Development*, Oxford: Oxford University Press.

—— (1999) *Development as Freedom*, New York: Knopf.

Srinivasan, T.N. (1994) "Human Development: A New Paradigm or Reinvention of the Wheel?" *American Economics Association Papers and Proceedings*, 84 (2): 238–243.

Strassmann, W. Paul (1993) "Development Economics from a Chicago Perspective," in Warren Samuels (ed.) *The Chicago School of Political Economy*, London: Transaction Publishers.

Streeten, P. (1994) "Human Development: Means and Ends" *American Economics Association Papers and Proceedings*, 84 (2): 232–237.

—— (1995) *Thinking about Development*, Cambridge: Cambridge University Press.

Tinker, Irene (ed.) (1990) *Persistent Inequalities: Women and World Development*, Oxford: Oxford University Press.

Williamson, O. (1996) "The Institutions and Governance of Economic Development and Reform," in *The Mechanisms of Governance*, New York: Oxford University Press.

World Bank (1999) *Culture and Sustainable Development: A Framework for Action*, Washington, DC: World Bank.

Zein-Elabdin, Eiman (1996) "Development, Gender, and the Environment: Theoretical or Contextual Link? Toward an Institutional Analysis of Gender," *Journal of Economic Issues*, 30 (4): 929–947.

2000–

Acemoglu, D., S. Johnson and J.A. Robinson (2001) "The Colonial Origins of Comparative Development: An Empirical Investigation," *American Economic Review*, 91 (5): 1369–1401.

Bardhan, B. (2005) *Scarcity, Conflicts, and Cooperation: Essays in the Political and Institutional Economics of Development*, Cambridge, MA: MIT Press.

Benería, Lourdes (2003) *Gender, Development, and Globalization: Economics As If All People Mattered*, London: Routledge.

Bergeron, Suzanne (2004) *Fragments of Development: Nation, Gender and the Space of Modernity*, Ann Arbor, MI: University of Michigan Press.

Chakrabarti, Anjan and Stephen Cullenberg (2001) "Development and Class Transition in India: A New Perspective," in J.K. Gibson-Graham, S. Resnick, and R. Wolff (eds.) *Re/Presenting Class: Essays in Postmodern Marxism*, Durham, NC: Duke University Press.

Chang, Ha-Joon (ed.) (2003) *Rethinking Development Economics*, London: Anthem Press.

—— (2011) "Institutions and Economic Development: Theory, Policy and History," *Journal of Institutional Economics*, 7 (4): 473–498.

Cuesta, José (2004) "From Economicist to Culturalist Development Theories: How Strong Is the Relation Between Cultural Aspects and Economic Development?" *European Journal of Development Research*, 16 (4): 868–891.

Fukuda-Parr, Sakiko and A.K. Shiva Kumar (eds.) (2003) *Readings in Human Development: Concepts, Measures and Policies for a Development Paradigm*, New Delhi: Oxford University Press.

Jomo, K.S. and B. Fine (eds.) (2006) *The New Development Economics: After the Washington Consensus,* London: Zed Books.

Kanbur, Ravi (ed.) (2005) "New Directions in Development Economics: Theory or Empirics?" A symposium in *Economic and Political Weekly*, Mumbai.

Kovács, J. M. (2006) "Which Past Matters? Culture and Economic Development in Eastern Europe After 1989," in Lawrence E. Harrison and Peter L. Berger (eds.) *Developing Cultures: Case Studies*, London: Routledge, 329–347.

Meier, G. M. and Joseph Stiglitz (2000) *Frontiers of Development Economics: The Future in Perspective*, Oxford: Oxford University Press.

Stein, H. (2008) *Beyond the World Bank Agenda: An Institutional Approach to Development*, Chicago: University of Chicago Press.

Streeten, P. (2006) "Culture and Economic Development," in V.A. Ginsburgh and D. Throsby (eds.) *The Handbook of the Economics of Art and Culture*, Amsterdam: Elsevier North-Holland.

Tabellini, Guido (2010) "Culture and Institutions: Economic Development in the Regions of Europe," *Journal of the European Economic Association*, 8 (4): 677–716.

Wolfensohn, James D. *et al.* (2000) *Culture Counts: Financing, Resources, and the Economics of Culture in Sustainable Development*, Washington, DC: World Bank.

Wood, Cynthia (2003) "Economic Marginalia: Postcolonial Readings of Unpaid Domestic Labor and Development," in Drucilla Barker and Edith Kuiper (eds.) *Toward a Feminist Philosophy of Economics*, London: Routledge.

Zein-Elabdin, Eiman (2001) "Contours of a Non-Modernist Discourse: The Contested Space of History and Development," *Review of Radical Political Economics*, 31 (3): 255–263.

Index